PRENTICE HALL MATHEMATICS

COURSE 2

ALL-IN-ONE Teaching Resources

CHAPTERS 5–8

Boston, Massachusetts
Upper Saddle River, New Jersey

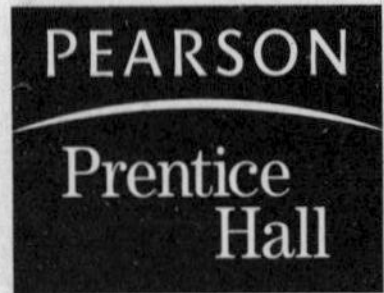

ISBN 0-13-201455-6

3 4 5 6 7 8 9 10 10 09 08 07

All-In-One Teaching Resources

Chapters 1–4

Chapters 5–8

Chapters 9–12

To the Teacher:

During the school year, you use several sources to help create your daily lesson plans. In Prentice Hall's *All-In-One Teaching Resources*, these lesson and chapter based sources are organized for you so that you can plan easily and effectively.

The *All-In-One Teaching Resources* are split into 3 volumes — Chapters 1–4, Chapters 5–8, and Chapters 9–12 — in the same order as the student edition chapters. Inside, you'll find several resources to support and extend every lesson:

- Practice (regular and adapted)
- Guided Problem Solving
- Reteaching
- Enrichment
- Activity Labs
- Daily Puzzles

Additional resources have been designed to support and assess every chapter:

- Vocabulary and Study Skills support
- Checkpoint Quizzes
- Chapter Projects
- Chapter Tests (regular and below level)
- Alternative Assessment
- Cumulative Review

To assist you in effective lesson planning, a special 2-page detail showing each resource page is included in each volume. All resources have been aligned either to a particular lesson, as review, or as assessment material.

At the end of each book, you will also find all of the answers for the chapters in that volume.

How To Read

Chapter

Lessons

Chapter 1: Whole Numbers and Decimals

Lesson	1-1	1-2	1-3	1-4	1-5	1-6	1-7	1-8	1-9		Review	Assess
For Each Lesson												
Practice (regular)	1	9	17	25	35	43	51	59	67			
Practice (adapted)	3	11	19	27	37	45	53	61	69			
Reteaching	5	13	21	29	39	47	55	63	71			
Guided Problem Solving	2	10	18	26	36	44	52	60	68			
Enrichment	6	14	22	30	40	48	56	64	72			
Activity Lab	4	12	20	28	38	46	54	62	70			
Daily Puzzle	8	16	23	33	42	50	57	65	74			
For Each Chapter												
Vocabulary and Study Skills												
Graphic Organizer	7											
Reading Comprehension		15										
Math Symbols					41							
Visual Vocabulary Practice						49						
Vocabulary Check				31								
Vocabulary Review/Puzzle											73	
Chapter Project											75	
Checkpoint Quizzes												79
Chapter Test (regular)												81
Chapter Test (below level)												83
Alternative Assessment												85
Cumulative Review											87	

Resource Types

Page References

Contents Chart

Contents Chart (continued)

Chapter 7: Geometry

Chapter 8: Measurement

Name ______________________ Class ______________ Date ______________

Practice 5-1

Write a ratio for each situation in three ways.

1. Ten years ago in Louisiana, schools averaged 182 pupils for every 10 teachers.

____

2. Between 1899 and 1900, 284 out of 1,000 people in the United States were 5–17 years old.

____

Use the chart below for Exercises 3–4.

Three seventh-grade classes were asked whether they wanted chicken or pasta served at their awards banquet.

Room Number	Chicken	Pasta
201	10	12
202	8	17
203	16	10

3. In room 201, what is the ratio of students who prefer chicken to students who prefer pasta?

____

4. Combine the totals for all three rooms. What is the ratio of the number of students who prefer pasta to the number of students who prefer chicken?

____

Write each ratio as a fraction in simplest form.

5. 12 to 18 ________ 6. 81 : 27 ________ 7. $\frac{6}{28}$ ________

Tell whether the ratios are *equivalent* or *not equivalent*.

8. 12 : 24, 50 : 100 ______________

9. $\frac{22}{1}, \frac{1}{22}$ ______________

10. 2 to 3, 24 to 36 ______________

11. A bag contains green, yellow, and orange marbles. The ratio of green marbles to yellow marbles is 2 : 5. The ratio of yellow marbles to orange marbles is 3 : 4. What is the ratio of green marbles to orange marbles?

____

Name ______________________ Class ______________________ Date ______________

5-1 • Guided Problem Solving

GPS Student Page 230, Exercise 27:

Cooking To make pancakes, you need 2 cups of water for every 3 cups of flour. Write an equivalent ratio to find how much water you will need with 9 cups of flour.

Understand

1. Circle the information you will need to solve.
2. What are you being asked to do?

   ____

   ____

3. Why will a ratio help you to solve the problem?

   ____

   ____

Plan and Carry Out

4. What is the ratio of the cups of water to the cups of flour? ____________
5. How many cups of flour are you using? ____________
6. Write an equivalent ratio to use 9 cups of flour. ____________
7. How many cups of water are needed for 9 cups of flour? ____________

Check

8. Why is the number of cups of water triple the number of cups needed for 3 cups of flour?

   ____

   ____

Solve Another Problem

9. Rebecca is laying tile in her bathroom. She needs 4 black tiles for every 16 white tiles. How many black tiles are needed if she uses 128 white tiles?

   ____

Name ______________________ Class ______________ Date ______________

Practice 5-1

Ratios

Write a ratio for each situation in three ways.

1. Ten years ago in Louisiana, schools averaged 182 pupils for every 10 teachers.

____

2. Between 1899 and 1900, 284 out of 1,000 people in the United States were 5–17 years old.

____

Use the chart below for Exercise 3.

Three seventh-grade classes were asked whether they wanted chicken or pasta served at their awards banquet.

Room Number	Chicken	Pasta
201	10	12
202	8	17
203	16	10

3. Combine the totals for all three rooms. What is the ratio of the number of students who prefer pasta to the number of students who prefer chicken?

____

Write each ratio as a fraction in simplest form.

4. 12 to 18 ____________ 5. 81 : 27 ____________ 6. $\frac{6}{28}$ ____________

Tell whether the ratios are *equivalent* or *not equivalent*.

7. 12 : 24, 50 : 100

____

8. $\frac{22}{1}, \frac{1}{22}$

____

Solve.

9. A bag contains green, yellow, and orange marbles. The ratio of green marbles to yellow marbles is 2 : 5. The ratio of yellow marbles to orange marbles is 3 : 4. What is the ratio of green marbles to orange marbles?

____

Name ______________________ Class ______________ Date ____________

Activity Lab 5-1

Ratios

Whenever you compare two quantities by division, you create a ratio. Fill in the table below by comparing the quantities of various things in your classroom. You may need to survey your classmates to find some of the answers. Write all of your ratios as fractions.

Quantity A	Quantity B	Ratio $\left(\frac{A}{B}\right)$	Ratio in simplest form
Number of girls	Number of boys		
Number of right-handed students	Number of left-handed students		
Number of students who ride the bus to school	Number of students who do not ride the bus to school		
Number of students who have laces on their shoes	Number of students who do not have laces on their shoes		
Number of students who have brothers or sisters	Number of students who do not have brothers or sisters		
Number of desks	Number of students		
Number of doors	Number of windows		

Were any of your ratios equivalent to any of the other ratios? If so, which ones?

____

Which of your ratios is closest in value to $\frac{1}{1}$?

____

Which ratio showed the greatest difference between the two quantities?

____

Name ______________________ Class ______________ Date ______________

Reteaching 5-1

Ratios

A ratio is a comparison of two numbers by division. You can write a ratio three ways.

Compare the number of red tulips to the number of yellow tulips.

red tulips	yellow tulips	orange mums	white mums

6 to 2, 6 : 2, or $\frac{6}{2}$

To find equal ratios, multiply or divide each part of the ratio by the same nonzero number.

$\frac{6}{2} = \frac{6 \times 2}{2 \times 2} = \frac{12}{4}$ ← **Multiply by 2.**

The ratio $\frac{3}{1}$ is in **simplest form.**

$\frac{6}{2} = \frac{6 \div 2}{2 \div 2} = \frac{3}{1}$ ← **Divide by 2.**

Use the drawings at the top of the page. Write each ratio in three ways.

1. yellow tulips to red tulips ______________________

2. white mums to orange mums ______________________

3. red tulips to orange mums ______________________

4. yellow tulips to white mums ______________________

5. red tulips to all flowers ______________________

6. orange mums to all flowers ______________________

7. tulips to mums ______________________

8. white mums to tulips ______________________

9. yellow tulips to all flowers ______________________

10. yellow tulips to orange mums ______________________

Write two ratios equal to the given ratio.

11. 2 : 5 ______________________

12. 18 to 30 ______________________

Write each ratio in simplest form.

13. 10 : 15 ______________________

14. $\frac{48}{24}$ ______________________

15. $\frac{6}{100}$ ______________________

16. 8 : 18 ______________________

Name ______________________ Class ______________ Date ____________

Enrichment 5-1

Ratios

Patterns in Geometry

The Parthenon is an ancient, very famous temple built in Athens, Greece, to honor Athena, the goddess of wisdom. It has the proportions of the *Golden Ratio,* which is often considered to be the most visually pleasing shape for a rectangle. Such a rectangle is called a *Golden Rectangle.*

1. Find the dimensions of the Golden Rectangle around the Parthenon.

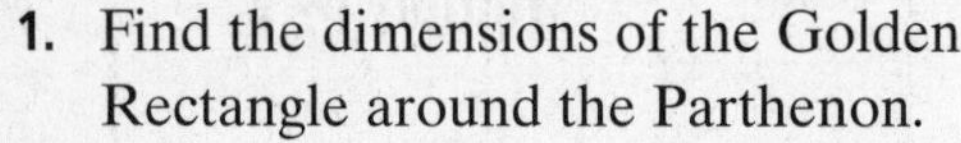

   Length: ______ mm   Width: ______ mm

2. Use your answer to Question 1 to find the Golden Ratio. Then write the ratio as a decimal.

   ____

3. Without measuring, which of the rectangles below do you think is a Golden Rectangle?

   ____

3 cm A

3 cm B

4. Measure the length of each rectangle above. Find the ratio of the length to the width and write it as a decimal. Circle the letter of the Golden Rectangle.

   a. Length: ______ cm Ratio: ______ cm to 3 cm = ______

   b. Length: ______ cm Ratio: ______ cm to 3 cm = ______

   c. Length: ______ cm Ratio: ______ cm to 3 cm = ______

5. Design a small picture frame in the shape of a Golden Rectangle. Label the dimensions.

Name ______________________ Class ______________ Date ______________

5A: Graphic Organizer

For use before Lesson 5-1

Study Skill As you read over the material in the chapter, keep a paper and pencil handy to write down notes and questions in your math notebook. Review notes taken in class as soon as possible.

Write your answers.

1. What is the chapter title? ______________________
2. How many lessons are there in this chapter? ______________________
3. What is the topic of the Test-Taking Strategies page? ______________________
4. Complete the graphic organizer below as you work through the chapter.
   - In the center, write the title of the chapter.
   - When you begin a lesson, write the lesson name in a rectangle.
   - When you complete a lesson, write a skill or key concept in a circle linked to that lesson block.
   - When you complete the chapter, use this graphic organizer to help you review.

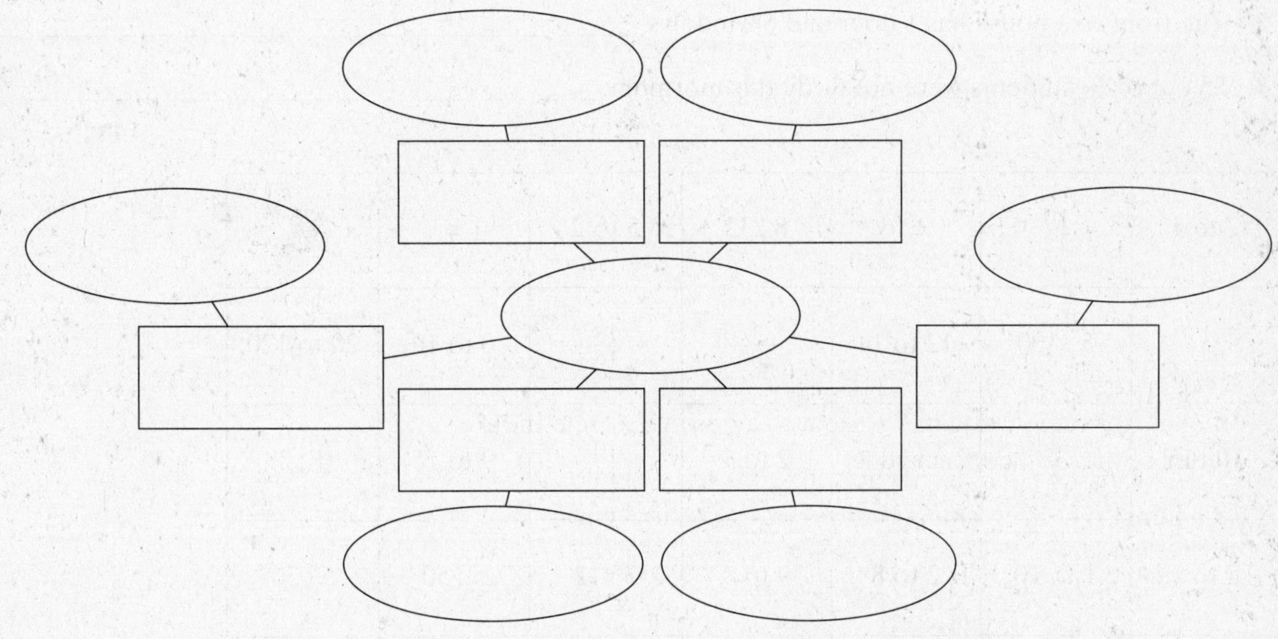

Name ______________________ Class ______________ Date ____________

Puzzle 5-1

Ratios

For each exercise, write a ratio comparing the first quantity to the second. Then, look in the chart to find two ratios that are equivalent to your answer. Mark the equivalent ratios by drawing an "X" through each box.

Example: A ranch has 14 horses and 28 cows.
Ratio: 14 to 28 *Equivalent Ratios in Chart:* 1 : 2 ; 2 to 4

Exercises:

1. John received an A on three of the last four math quizzes. ____________
2. The fishpond is 10 feet wide, and 4 feet deep. ____________
3. The Sherman family has 1 dog and 3 cats. ____________
4. Our front yard has 4 trees and 6 bushes. ____________
5. A company employs 30 men and 35 women. ____________
6. 10 out of 16 cookies contained chocolate chips. ____________
7. The front of a house has 1 door and 6 windows. ____________
8. 25 out of 30 students were not tardy this morning. ____________

2 to 4	$\frac{10}{12}$	2 : 6	8 : 32	5 to 2	$\frac{2}{3}$	$\frac{20}{32}$
$\frac{1}{4}$	5 : 100	12 to 14	$\frac{20}{200}$	$\frac{18}{16}$	6 to 10	20 to 120
10 : 15	$\frac{6}{8}$	5 : 8	2 to 5	$\frac{10}{14}$	9 to 15	1 : 2
3 to 9	1 to 10	2 to 8	9 to 8	3 : 12	5 : 50	5 : 30
$\frac{100}{40}$	5 to 6	15 : 20	5 : 7	$\frac{3}{5}$	$\frac{1}{20}$	$\frac{6}{7}$

Name ______________________ Class ______________ Date ______________

Practice 5-2

Unit Rates and Proportional Reasoning

Write the unit rate for each situation.

1. travel 250 mi in 5 h

2. earn $75.20 in 8 h

3. read 80 pages in 2 h

4. type 8,580 words in 2 h 45 min

5. manufacture 2,488 parts in 8 h

6. 50 copies of a book on 2 shelves

Find each unit price. Then determine the better buy.

7. paper: 100 sheets for $.99
   500 sheets for $4.29

8. peanuts: 1 lb for $1.29
   12 oz for $.95

9. crackers: 15 oz for $1.79
   12 oz for $1.49

10. apples: 3 lb for $1.89
    5 lb for $2.49

11. mechanical pencils: 4 for $1.25
    25 for $5.69

12. bagels: 4 for $.89
    6 for $1.39

13. a. Yolanda and Yoko ran in a 100-yd dash. When Yolanda crossed the finish line, Yoko was 10 yd behind her. The girls then repeated the race, with Yolanda starting 10 yd behind the starting line. If each girl ran at the same rate as before, who won the race? By how many yards?

    b. Assuming the girls run at the same rate as before, how far behind the starting line should Yolanda be in order for the two to finish in a tie?

Name ______________________ Class ______________ Date ______________

5-2 • Guided Problem Solving

GPS Student Page 235, Exercise 27a:

Geography Population density is the number of people per unit of area. Alaska has the lowest population density of any state in the United States. It has 626,932 people in 570,374 mi^2. What is its population density? Round to the nearest person per square mile.

Understand

1. What is *population density*?

____

____

2. What are you being asked to do?

____

3. What does the phrase *people per unit of area* imply?

____

____

____

Plan and Carry Out

4. What is the population of Alaska? ______________
5. What is the area of Alaska? ______________
6. Write a division expression for the population density. ______________
7. What is its population density? ______________
8. Round to the nearest person per square mile. ______________

Check

9. Why is the population density only about 1 person/mi^2?

____

____

Solve Another Problem

10. Mr. Boyle is buying pizza for the percussion band. The bill is $56.82 for 5 pizzas. If there are 12 members of the band, how much does the pizza cost per member? Round to the nearest cent.

____

Name ______________________ Class ______________ Date ____________

Practice 5-2

Unit Rates and Proportional Reasoning

Write the unit rate for each situation.

1. travel 250 mi in 5 h

2. earn $75.20 in 8 h

3. read 80 pages in 2 h

4. type 8,580 words in 2 h 45 min

Find each unit price. Then determine the better buy.

5. paper: 100 sheets for $.99
   500 sheets for $4.29

6. peanuts: 1 lb for $1.29
   12 oz for $.95

7. crackers: 15 oz for $1.79
   12 oz for $1.49

8. apples: 3 lb for $1.89
   5 lb for $2.49

9. mechanical pencils: 4 for $1.25
   25 for $5.69

10. bagels: 4 for $.89
    6 for $1.39

Solve.

11. Yolanda and Yoko ran in a 100-yd dash. When Yolanda crossed the finish line, Yoko was 10 yd behind her. The girls then repeated the race, with Yolanda starting 10 yd behind the starting line. If each girl ran at the same rate as before, who won the race? By how many yards?

Name ______________________ Class ______________ Date ____________

Activity Lab 5-2

Unit Rates and Proportional Reasoning

Decision Making

Glynnis wants to take dance lessons during her summer break. School ends May 29. She has called three dance schools to see when classes start, the days and times they are offered, how much they cost, and whether the school charges by class or by session.

	Clodagh's Dance	New Steps	Stepping High
Start Date	No specific time, can start at any time	June 15	May 17
Class Times	Mon., Wed., or Fri. 3:00–4:00 P.M.	Tues. 4:00–5:30 P.M.	Sat. 9:00–10:15 A.M.
Minimum Number of Classes	One class	Ten classes	Eight classes
Cost	$6 per class	$75 for ten classes	$52 for eight classes

1. What is the unit rate for each class?

a. Clodagh's Dance ______________

b. New Steps ______________

c. Stepping High ______________

2. How would your answers to Question 1 change if you were to write the unit rate in cost per *hour*?

	Total hours for each payment	Cost per hour
a. Clodagh's Dance	______	______
b. New Steps	______	______
c. Stepping High	______	______

3. What other things should Glynnis consider when making her choice?

____

____

____

4. Which dance school would you advise Glynnis to attend? Explain the advantage of taking these classes.

____

____

____

Name ______________________ Class ______________ Date ______________

Reteaching 5-2

Unit Rates and Proportional Reasoning

A **rate** is a ratio that compares two quantities measured in different units.

The cost for 10 copies is $1.50.

The rate is $1.50/10 copies ($1.50 per 10 copies).

A **unit rate** is a rate that has a denominator of 1. You can compare using unit rates.

To find the unit rate for 10 copies:

$$\$1.50/10 \text{ copies} = \frac{\$1.50}{10} = \frac{\$1.50 \div 10}{10 \div 10} = \frac{\$.15}{1}$$

The unit rate is $.15 per copy. This is also the *unit price.*

COPY CENTER	
Color Copies	
1 copy	$.25
10 copies	$1.50
25 copies	$2.50
50 copies	$4.50
100 copies	$6.00

For the better buy, compare unit rates.

The unit price for 10 copies is $.15/copy.

The unit price for 1 copy is $.25/copy.

Since $.15 < $.25, the 10-copy price is the better buy.

Use the Copy Center chart. Find the unit rate.

1. 25 copies
$\frac{\$2.50}{25} = \frac{\$2.50 \div \square}{25 \div \square} =$ ______

2. 100 copies
$\frac{\$6.00}{100} = \frac{\$6.00 \div \square}{100 \div \square} =$ ______

3. 50 copies
$\frac{\$4.50}{50} = \frac{\$4.50 \div \square}{50 \div \square} =$ ______

Write the unit rate for each situation.

4. drive 1,800 mi in 30 h ______

5. 390 mi on 15 gal of gasoline ______

6. jog 4,000 m in 12 min ______

7. $25.50 for 17 tickets ______

Find each unit price. Then determine the better buy.

8. juice: 18 oz for $1.26
8 oz for $.70
______

9. cloth: 2 yd for $3.15
6 yd for $7.78
______

10. socks: 2 pairs for $3.50
6 pairs for $9.00
______

11. pecans: 1 lb for $4.80
2 oz for $1.00
______

Name ______________________ Class ______________ Date ____________

Enrichment 5-2

Unit Rates and Proportional Reasoning

Critical Thinking

The table on the right shows exchange rates for several foreign currencies.

Country	Currency	Rate Per Dollar
Mexico	Peso	10.77
Britain	Pound	0.58
Germany	Euro	0.84
Croatia	Kuna	6.24

1. For each country, give the exchange rate as a unit rate in foreign currency per dollar. Then find an equivalent rate to show how much foreign currency you would receive for the given amount of U. S. dollars. The first one is done for you.

	Unit rate	Foreign currency
a. Mexican pesos, 10 dollars	$\frac{10.77 \text{ pesos}}{1 \text{ dollar}}$ ________	________ ________
b. British pounds, 5 dollars	________ ________	________ ________
c. German euros, 7 dollars	________ ________	________ ________
d. Croatia kunas, 3 dollars	________ ________	________ ________

2. Suppose your company wants to sell a software package in Mexico and in Germany. It sells for $250 in the United States. What will you charge in each country?

   a. Write an equivalent ratio to show how many pesos are in $250.

   ________ ________

   ____

   b. Write an equivalent ratio to show how many euros are in $250.

   ________ ________

   ____

3. Suppose your marketing manager travels from Great Britain to Germany to meet you.

   a. Write a rate comparing German euros to British pounds. Then give the unit rate per pound. Round your answer to the nearest hundredth.

   ____

   ____

   b. Write an equivalent ratio to show the cost in German euros of a software package that costs 48 British pounds.

   ________ ________

   ____

Name ______________________ Class ______________ Date ______________

Puzzle 5-2

Unit Rates and Proportional Reasoning

Which item should you buy? Circle the item with the lowest unit cost. Match the letter of each answer with the exercise number in the spaces below.

1. **A.** 2 nutrition bars cost $2.60.
   B. A box of 12 nutrition bars costs $16.00.

2. **C.** An 8 oz box of pecans costs $3.60
   D. In bulk, pecans cost $0.54 per oz.

3. **K.** A 12-ounce package of rice costs $1.56.
   L. A 16-ounce package of rice costs $2.04.

4. **E.** 5 gallons of gasoline for $13.30
   F. 7 gallons of gasoline for $18.90

5. **V.** Bulk raisins cost $1.32 per pound.
   W. An eight-ounce box of raisins costs $0.76.

6. **R.** A 2-pound can of pumpkin costs $3.76.
   S. A 5-pound can of pumpkin costs $10.06.

7. **S.** The 60 fl oz bottle of detergent costs $7.53.
   T. Two 24 fl oz bottles cost $6.23.

8. **G.** 56 kg of gravel costs $525.65.
   H. 22 kg of gravel costs $198.78.

9. **N.** An eight-ounce box of cereal costs $2.88.
   O. A twelve-ounce box of the same cereal is on sale for $3.96.

10. **P.** The 16 fl oz bottle of conditioner is on sale for $5.80.
    Q. The 12 fl oz bottle of conditioner costs $4.45.

To save the most, you must learn to be:

___	___	___	___	___	___	___		___	___	___	___	___	___	___
1	2	3	4	5	4	6		7	8	9	10	10	4	6

Name ____________ Class ____________ Date ____________

Practice 5-3

Proportions

Determine if the ratios in each pair are proportional.

1. $\frac{12}{16}, \frac{30}{40}$ ____________
2. $\frac{8}{12}, \frac{15}{21}$ ____________
3. $\frac{27}{21}, \frac{81}{56}$ ____________
4. $\frac{45}{24}, \frac{75}{40}$ ____________
5. $\frac{5}{9}, \frac{80}{117}$ ____________
6. $\frac{15}{25}, \frac{75}{125}$ ____________
7. $\frac{2}{14}, \frac{20}{35}$ ____________
8. $\frac{9}{6}, \frac{21}{14}$ ____________
9. $\frac{24}{15}, \frac{16}{10}$ ____________
10. $\frac{3}{4}, \frac{8}{10}$ ____________
11. $\frac{20}{4}, \frac{17}{3}$ ____________
12. $\frac{25}{6}, \frac{9}{8}$ ____________

Decide if each pair of ratios is proportional.

13. $\frac{14}{10} \stackrel{?}{=} \frac{9}{7}$ ____________
14. $\frac{18}{8} \stackrel{?}{=} \frac{36}{16}$ ____________
15. $\frac{6}{10} \stackrel{?}{=} \frac{15}{25}$ ____________
16. $\frac{7}{16} \stackrel{?}{=} \frac{4}{9}$ ____________
17. $\frac{6}{4} \stackrel{?}{=} \frac{12}{8}$ ____________
18. $\frac{19}{3} \stackrel{?}{=} \frac{114}{8}$ ____________
19. $\frac{5}{14} \stackrel{?}{=} \frac{6}{15}$ ____________
20. $\frac{6}{27} \stackrel{?}{=} \frac{8}{36}$ ____________
21. $\frac{27}{15} \stackrel{?}{=} \frac{45}{25}$ ____________
22. $\frac{3}{18} \stackrel{?}{=} \frac{4}{20}$ ____________
23. $\frac{5}{2} \stackrel{?}{=} \frac{15}{6}$ ____________
24. $\frac{20}{15} \stackrel{?}{=} \frac{4}{3}$ ____________

Solve.

25. During the breaststroke competitions of the 1992 Olympics, Nelson Diebel swam 100 meters in 62 seconds, and Mike Bowerman swam 200 meters in 130 seconds. Are the rates proportional?

____

26. During a vacation, the Vasquez family traveled 174 miles in 3 hours on Monday, and 290 miles in 5 hours on Tuesday. Are the rates proportional?

____

Name _________________________ Class _______________ Date _______________

5-3 • Guided Problem Solving

GPS Student Page 240, Exercise 29:

Decorating A certain shade of green paint requires 4 parts blue to 5 parts yellow. If you mix 16 quarts of blue paint with 25 quarts of yellow paint, will you get the desired shade of green? Explain.

Understand

1. Circle the information you will need to solve.
2. What are you being asked to do?

____

____

3. Will a ratio help you to solve the problem? Explain.

____

____

Plan and Carry Out

4. What is the ratio of blue parts to yellow parts? ___________
5. What is the ratio of blue quarts to yellow quarts? ___________
6. Check to see if the cross products of the two ratios are equal.

____

7. Are the ratios the same? ___________________
8. Will you get the desired shade of green? Explain.

____

Check

9. How do you know that the ratios are not the same?

____

Solve Another Problem

10. There are 15 boys and 12 girls in your math class. There are 5 boys and 3 girls in your study group. Determine if the boy to girl ratio is the same in study group as it is in your math class. Explain.

____

____

Name ______________________ Class ______________ Date ______________

Practice 5-3

Proportions

Determine if the ratios in each pair are proportional.

1. $\frac{12}{16}, \frac{30}{40}$ ______
2. $\frac{8}{12}, \frac{15}{21}$ ______
3. $\frac{27}{21}, \frac{81}{56}$ ______
4. $\frac{45}{24}, \frac{75}{40}$ ______
5. $\frac{5}{9}, \frac{80}{117}$ ______
6. $\frac{15}{25}, \frac{75}{125}$ ______
7. $\frac{2}{14}, \frac{20}{35}$ ______
8. $\frac{9}{6}, \frac{21}{14}$ ______
9. $\frac{24}{15}, \frac{16}{10}$ ______

Decide if each pair of ratios is proportional.

10. $\frac{14}{10} \stackrel{?}{=} \frac{9}{7}$ ______
11. $\frac{18}{8} \stackrel{?}{=} \frac{36}{16}$ ______
12. $\frac{6}{10} \stackrel{?}{=} \frac{15}{25}$ ______
13. $\frac{7}{16} \stackrel{?}{=} \frac{4}{9}$ ______
14. $\frac{6}{4} \stackrel{?}{=} \frac{12}{8}$ ______
15. $\frac{19}{3} \stackrel{?}{=} \frac{114}{8}$ ______
16. $\frac{5}{14} \stackrel{?}{=} \frac{6}{15}$ ______
17. $\frac{6}{27} \stackrel{?}{=} \frac{8}{36}$ ______

Solve.

18. During the breaststroke competitions of the 1992 Olympics, Nelson Diebel swam 100 meters in 62 seconds, and Mike Bowerman swam 200 meters in 130 seconds. Are the rates proportional?

______

19. During a vacation, the Vasquez family traveled 174 miles in 3 hours on Monday, and 290 miles in 5 hours on Tuesday. Are the rates proportional?

______

Name ______________________ Class ______________ Date ____________

Activity Lab 5-3

Proportions

Decision Making

Alfonso, Bryan, and four of their friends are going to the lake. They want to rent a canoe and have a picnic lunch on the island.

1. Alfonso wants to make potato salad. His recipe will serve 8 people. Use unit ratios to rewrite the recipe to serve 6 people.

$\frac{1}{3}$ cup Italian dressing	5 medium potatoes
1 cup chopped celery	4 hard boiled eggs
1 teaspoon salt	$\frac{1}{2}$ cup salad dressing or mayonnaise

____

____

____

2. They stop at the deli to buy ham for their sandwiches. One package of ham sells for 0.5 pound for $2.50. There are about 8 slices in each package. How much ham should they buy? How much will it cost?

____

____

3. Each canoe can hold 4 people. It will cost them $16 to rent one canoe for 4 hours or $25 for the day. It takes 15 minutes to row to the island. How can they rent only one canoe?

____

____

4. How many canoes should they rent and for how long? Explain.

____

____

5. They need to tell their families about when they should be home. It takes about 10 minutes to get to the park. About how long will they be on the outing? Explain.

____

____

____

Name ______________________ Class ______________ Date ______________

Reteaching 5-3

Proportions

A **proportion** is an equation stating that two ratios are equal.

Consider $\frac{2}{10}$ and $\frac{5}{25}$.

$\frac{2}{10} = \frac{2 \div 2}{10 \div 2} = \frac{1}{5}$

$\frac{5}{25} = \frac{5 \div 5}{25 \div 5} = \frac{1}{5}$

Both ratios are equal to $\frac{1}{5}$, the ratios are proportional.

If two ratios form a proportion, the **cross products** are equal.

$\frac{100}{2} = \frac{200}{4}$

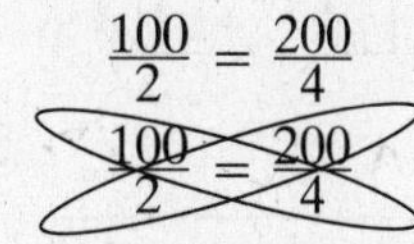

$100 \cdot 4 = 200 \cdot 2$

$400 = 400$

Complete the cross products to determine which pairs of ratios could form a proportion. Then write *yes* or *no*.

1. $\frac{3}{10} \stackrel{?}{=} \frac{6}{20}$

   $3 \cdot 20 =$ ______

   $10 \cdot 6 =$ ______

   ______

2. $\frac{12}{24} \stackrel{?}{=} \frac{2}{4}$

   $12 \cdot 4 =$ ______

   $24 \cdot \square =$ ______

   ______

3. $\frac{8}{5} \stackrel{?}{=} \frac{16}{8}$

   $8 \cdot \square =$ ______

   $5 \cdot \square =$ ______

   ______

Determine if the ratios in each pair are proportional.

4. $\frac{25}{35}, \frac{5}{7}$

5. $\frac{15}{3}, \frac{10}{2}$

6. $\frac{9}{3}, \frac{12}{4}$

7. $\frac{2}{5}, \frac{6}{15}$

8. $\frac{3.6}{200}, \frac{1.8}{100}$

9. $\frac{6}{12}, \frac{4}{8}$

10. $\frac{16}{11}, \frac{96}{24}$

11. $\frac{3}{7}, \frac{2}{5}$

12. $\frac{2}{22}, \frac{1}{11}$

Name ______________________ Class ______________ Date ____________

Enrichment 5-3

Proportions

Thinking Critically

Complete each table. The numbers in each column should form equal ratios. Then write four proportions involving ratios in the table.

1.

3	6	9	12
5			

2.

4	8	20	32
11			

Copy each ratio into the table. Then create three equal ratios. Use your ratios to write three proportions.

3. $\frac{11}{15}$

4. $\frac{16}{20}$

Use each proportion to write two other proportions.

5. $\frac{5}{8} = \frac{15}{24}$

6. $\frac{4}{18} = \frac{6}{27}$

7. $\frac{\$2}{\text{7 apples}} = \frac{\$6}{\text{21 apples}}$

8. $\frac{\text{80 miles}}{\text{15 hours}} = \frac{\text{32 miles}}{\text{6 hours}}$

9. An electronics kit contains 7 resistors, 3 capacitors, and 2 transistors. Tell how many of each part would be in 3 and 4 kits.

3 kits: ______________________

4 kits: ______________________

Name ______________________ Class ______________ Date ______________

5B: Reading Comprehension

For use after Lesson 5-3

Study Skill When you read mathematics, look for words like "more than," "less than," "above," "times as many," "divided by." These clues will help you decide what operation you need to solve a problem.

Read the paragraph and answer the questions that follow.

> A tropical storm is classified as a hurricane when it has wind speeds in excess of 74 mi/h. The winds of Hurricane Gordon (1994) reached 12.4 mi/h above the minimum. How fast were the winds of Hurricane Gordon?

1. What numbers are in the paragraph? ______________
2. What question are you asked to answer?
   ____
   ____
3. What units will you use in your answer? ______________
4. Does a storm with winds of 74 mi/h qualify as a hurricane? Explain.
   ____
   ____
   ____
5. When did Hurricane Gordon occur? ______________
6. How much above the minimum were Hurricane Gordon's winds?
   ____
7. Let *x* represent Hurricane Gordon's wind speed. Write an equation to help you solve the problem.
   ____
8. What is the answer to the question asked in the paragraph?
   ____
9. **High-Use Academic Words** In Exercise 7, what does it mean to *solve*?

   a. to find an answer for   b. to keep something going

Name ______________________ Class ____________ Date ____________

Puzzle 5-3

Proportions

Fact 1: These two ratios form a proportion:

△/□ and ○/⬡

Fact 2: These two ratios also form a proportion:

○/🦴 and ☆/△

Using the two facts above, determine which of the following pairs of ratios must also form a proportion.

A. △/☆ and 🦴/○

B. ○/△ and □/⬡

C. ⬡/○ and △/□

D. □/⬡ and △/○

E. △/🦴 and ⬡/☆

F. ○/☆ and 🦴/△

G. ○/△ and ☆/🦴

H. △/☆ and ○/⬡

Name ______________________ Class ______________ Date ____________

Practice 5-4

Solving Proportions

Use mental math to solve for each value of *n*.

1. $\frac{n}{14} = \frac{20}{35}$ ______________
2. $\frac{9}{6} = \frac{21}{n}$ ______________
3. $\frac{24}{n} = \frac{16}{10}$ ______________
4. $\frac{3}{4} = \frac{n}{10}$ ______________

Solve each proportion using cross products.

5. $\frac{k}{8} = \frac{14}{4}$ $k =$ ________
6. $\frac{u}{3} = \frac{10}{5}$ $u =$ ________
7. $\frac{14}{6} = \frac{d}{15}$ $d =$ ________
8. $\frac{5}{1} = \frac{m}{4}$ $m =$ ________
9. $\frac{36}{32} = \frac{n}{8}$ $n =$ ________
10. $\frac{5}{30} = \frac{1}{x}$ $x =$ ________
11. $\frac{t}{4} = \frac{5}{10}$ $t =$ ________
12. $\frac{9}{2} = \frac{v}{4}$ $v =$ ________

Solve.

13. A contractor estimates it will cost $2,400 to build a deck to a customer's specifications. How much would it cost to build five similar decks?

    ____

14. A recipe requires 3 c of flour to make 27 dinner rolls. How much flour is needed to make 9 rolls?

    ____

Solve using a calculator, paper and pencil, or mental math.

15. Mandy runs 4 km in 18 min. She plans to run in a 15 km race. How long will it take her to complete the race?

    ____

16. Ken's new car can go 26 miles per gallon of gasoline. The car's gasoline tank holds 14 gal. How far will he be able to go on a full tank?

    ____

17. Eleanor can complete two skirts in 15 days. How long will it take her to complete eight skirts?

    ____

18. Three eggs are required to make two dozen muffins. How many eggs are needed to make 12 dozen muffins?

    ____

Name ______________________ Class ______________ Date ______________

5-4 • Guided Problem Solving

GPS Student Page 247, Exercise 28:

There are 450 students and 15 teachers in a school. The school hires 2 new teachers. To keep the student-to-teacher ratio the same, how many students in all should attend the school?

Understand

1. What are you being asked to do?

____

____

2. Will a proportion help you to solve the problem? Explain.

____

____

____

Plan and Carry Out

3. Write a ratio for the current student-to-teacher ratio. ________

4. Write a ratio for the new student-to-teacher ratio. ________

5. Write a proportion using the ratios in Steps 3 and 4. ________

6. How many total students should attend the school?

____

Check

7. Are the two ratios equivalent? Explain.

____

____

Solve Another Problem

8. There are 6 black marbles and 4 red marbles in a jar. If you add 4 red marbles to the jar, how many black marbles do you need to add to keep the ratio of black marbles to red marbles the same?

____

Name ______________________ Class ______________ Date ______________

Practice 5-4

Solving Proportions

Use mental math to solve for each value of *n*.

1. $\frac{n}{14} = \frac{20}{35}$ ______________

2. $\frac{9}{6} = \frac{21}{n}$ ______________

3. $\frac{24}{n} = \frac{16}{10}$ ______________

4. $\frac{3}{4} = \frac{n}{10}$ ______________

Solve each proportion using cross products.

5. $\frac{k}{8} = \frac{14}{4}$

   $k =$ ______________

6. $\frac{u}{3} = \frac{10}{5}$

   $u =$ ______________

7. $\frac{14}{6} = \frac{d}{15}$

   $d =$ ______________

8. $\frac{36}{32} = \frac{n}{8}$

   $n =$ ______________

9. $\frac{5}{30} = \frac{1}{x}$

   $x =$ ______________

10. $\frac{t}{4} = \frac{5}{10}$

    $t =$ ______________

Solve.

11. A contractor estimates it will cost \$2,400 to build a deck to a customer's specifications. How much would it cost to build five similar decks?

    ____

12. A recipe requires 3 c of flour to make 27 dinner rolls. How much flour is needed to make 9 rolls?

    ____

Solve using a calculator, paper and pencil, or mental math.

13. Mandy runs 4 km in 18 min. She plans to run in a 15 km race. How long will it take her to complete the race?

    ____

14. Ken's new car can go 26 miles per gallon of gasoline. The car's gasoline tank holds 14 gal. How far will he be able to go on a full tank?

    ____

15. Eleanor can complete two skirts in 15 days. How long will it take her to complete eight skirts?

    ____

Name ______________________ Class ______________ Date ______________

Activity Lab 5-4

Solving Proportions

Suppose you are asked to plan a poster that will be enlarged for a mural in the science lab and reduced for flyers that advertise the school science fair. The wall mural will be 15 ft long and 10 ft high. The flyers will be on $8\frac{1}{2}$ by 11 inch paper. Plan the size of the poster so that the enlargement and reduction will be as easy as possible to make.

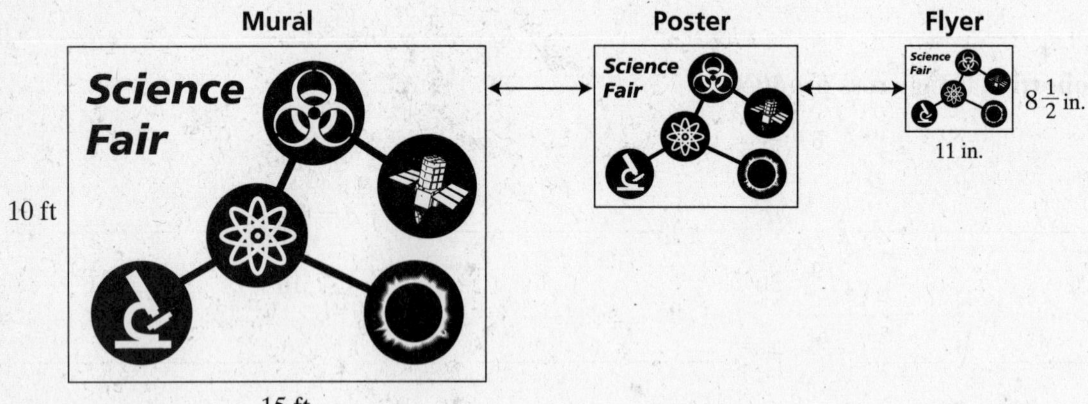

1. What is the length : width ratio for the wall mural? ______________

2. What is the length : width ratio for the flyer? ______________

3. Are the ratios for the mural and flyer the same? ______________

4. Suppose you decide to use $\frac{3}{2}$ as the ratio for the poster. What are some possible dimensions for your poster using this ratio?

____

5. Will your poster completely fill the wall space when it is enlarged for the mural? Explain.

____

____

6. Will your poster completely fill the paper when it is reduced for the flyer? Explain.

____

____

____

____

7. Will you be able to write the name of the school on the flyer? If so, where will it go?

____

Name ______________________ Class ______________ Date ______________

Reteaching 5-4

Solving Proportions

Solving a proportion means finding a missing part of the proportion. You can use unit rates to solve a proportion. First find the unit rate. Then multiply to solve the proportion.

Shawn filled 8 bags of leaves in 2 hours. At this rate, how many bags would he fill in 6 hours?

① Find a unit rate for the number of bags per hour. Divide by the denominator.

$$\frac{8 \text{ bags}}{2 \text{ hours}} = \frac{8 \text{ bags} \boxed{\div 2}}{2 \text{ hours} \boxed{\div 2}} = \frac{4 \text{ bags}}{1 \text{ hour}}$$ The unit rate is 4 bags per hour.

② Multiply the unit rate by 6 to find the number of bags he will fill in 6 hours.

Unit rate		Number of hours		Total
↓		↓		↓
4	×	6	=	24

At this rate, Shawn can fill 24 bags in 6 hours.

If two ratios form a proportion, the **cross products** are equal.

Solve. $\frac{5}{15} = \frac{n}{3}$

① Write the cross products. $5 \cdot 3 = 15 \cdot n$

② Simplify. $15 = 15n$

③ Solve the equation. $n = 1$

Solve.

1. The bookstore advertises 5 notebooks for $7.75. At this rate, how much will 7 notebooks cost?

   ____

2. Leroy can lay 144 bricks in 3 hours. At this rate, how many bricks can he lay in 7 hours?

   ____

Solve each proportion using cross products.

3. $\frac{4}{24} = \frac{n}{6}$

   $4 \cdot$ ______ $= 24 \cdot$ ______

   $n =$ ______

4. $\frac{30}{5} = \frac{6}{n}$

   ______ = ______

   $n =$ ______

5. $\frac{n}{6} = \frac{27}{9}$

   ______ = ______

   $n =$ ______

Solve each proportion.

6. $\frac{4}{10} = \frac{n}{15}$ ______________

7. $\frac{4}{200} = \frac{n}{100}$ ______________

8. $\frac{6}{n} = \frac{5}{10}$ ______________

9. $\frac{32}{22} = \frac{96}{n}$ ______________

10. $\frac{6}{3} = \frac{n}{5}$ ______________

11. $\frac{2}{n} = \frac{4}{10}$ ______________

Name ______________________ Class ______________ Date ______________

Enrichment 5-4

Solving Proportions

Decision Making

Suppose your family needs to buy the following grocery items: 8 pounds of chicken, 2 packages of frozen broccoli, 2 pints of strawberries, and 12 dinner rolls. Read these advertisements to find the cost of each item at Best Supermarket and at Top Value Supermarket.

Best Supermarket		Top Value Supermarket	
Chicken	\$3.89 per pound	Chicken	\$3.96 per pound
Broccoli	1 package for \$0.99	Broccoli	3 packages for \$2.89
Strawberries	2 pints for \$1.98	Strawberries	4 pints for \$3.87
Dinner rolls	6 rolls for \$0.90	Dinner rolls	15 rolls for \$1.50

1. Find the unit price for each item at each store. Round answers to nearest cent.

	Best Supermarket	Top Value Supermarket
Chicken		
Broccoli		
Strawberries		
Dinner rolls		

2. Determine the cost of purchasing all the items on your list for each market.

____

3. Which market offers the better buy? ______________

4. It is 20 miles to Best Supermarket and 5 miles to Top Value Supermarket. Your car uses 1 gallon of gas for each 20 miles it travels. If a gallon of gas costs \$2.59, how much will you spend to get to and from each supermarket?

____

5. Explain how this might affect your choice of supermarkets.

____

____

Name ____________ Class ____________ Date ____________

5C: Reading/Writing Math Symbols

For use after Lesson 5-4

Study Skill When you take notes in any subject, use abbreviations and symbols whenever possible.

Write each statement or expression using the appropriate mathematical symbols.

1. the ratio of a to b ____________
2. x to 4 is less than 5 to 2 ____________
3. 4 more than 5 times n ____________
4. $5:24$ is not equal to $1:5$ ____________

Write each mathematical statement in words.

5. $x \leq 25$ ____________

6. $|-20| > |15|$ ____________

7. $1 \text{ oz} \approx 28 \text{ g}$ ____________

8. $\frac{1}{3} = \frac{4}{12}$ ____________

Match the symbolic statement or expression in Column A with its written form in Column B.

Column A	Column B
9. $k < 12$	A. 12 times x
10. $\lvert -5 \rvert$	B. negative 2 plus negative 4 is p
11. $n \geq 15$	C. the ratio of 4 to 8
12. $x = -4 + 5$	D. k is less than 12
13. $4:8$	E. the quotient of x and 9
14. $12x$	F. x equals negative 4 plus 5
15. $-2 + (-4) = p$	G. the absolute value of negative 5
16. $x \div 9$	H. n is greater than or equal to 15

Name ______________________ Class ______________ Date ______________

Puzzle 5-4

Solving Proportions

Two teams are competing in a math competition. The teams are given a set of solutions and are asked to write proportion problems to match each solution. The problems created by each team are listed below, but have not been checked for errors. On a separate sheet of paper, solve the proportions and check that the given answer satisfies the problem created by each team.

Given Solution	Problems created by Team A	Problems created by Team B
1. $x = 6$	$\frac{3}{7} = \frac{x}{14}$	$\frac{3}{12} = \frac{x}{36}$
2. $x = \frac{1}{4}$	$\frac{5}{160} = \frac{x}{8}$	$\frac{1}{12} = \frac{x}{3}$
3. $x = 2$	$\frac{8}{20} = \frac{x}{5}$	$\frac{1}{x} = \frac{21}{42}$
4. $x = 12$	$\frac{2}{4} = \frac{x}{18}$	$\frac{3}{x} = \frac{8}{32}$
5. $x = 7$	$\frac{5}{x} = \frac{25}{35}$	$\frac{x}{3} = \frac{28}{12}$
6. $x = \frac{1}{2}$	$\frac{x}{4} = \frac{6}{46}$	$\frac{7}{x} = \frac{84}{6}$
7. $x = 4$	$\frac{x}{12} = \frac{2}{6}$	$\frac{75}{100} = \frac{3}{x}$

Which team should win the competition?

Name ____________________ Class ____________ Date ____________

Practice 5-5

Using Similar Figures

$\triangle MNO \sim \triangle JKL$. Complete each statement.

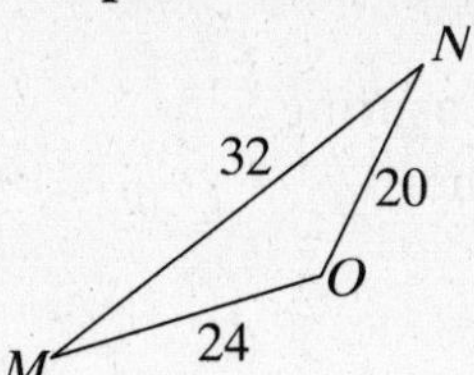

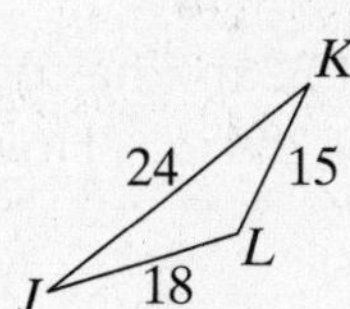

1. $\angle M$ corresponds to ____________.
2. $\angle L$ corresponds to ____________.
3. $\overline{JL}$ corresponds to ____________.
4. $\overline{MN}$ corresponds to ____________.
5. What is the ratio of the lengths of the corresponding sides? ____________

The pairs of figures below are similar. Find the value of each variable.

6. 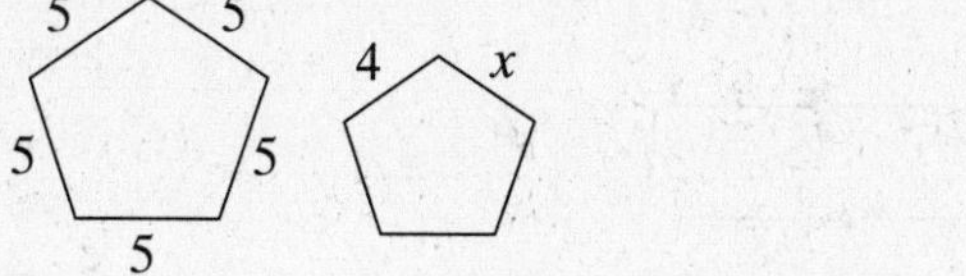

____

7. 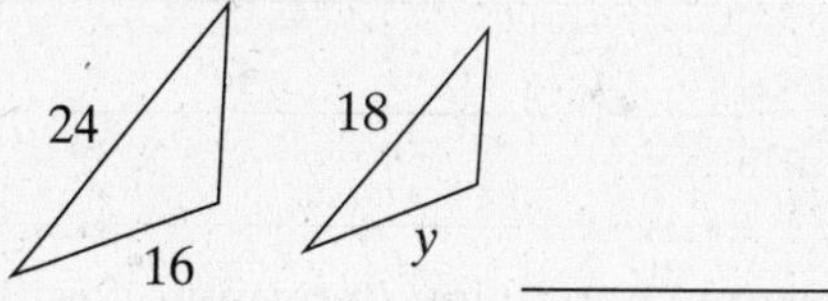

____

8. 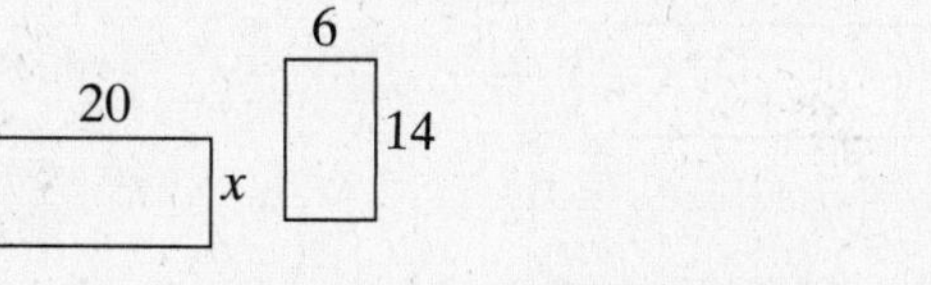

____

9. 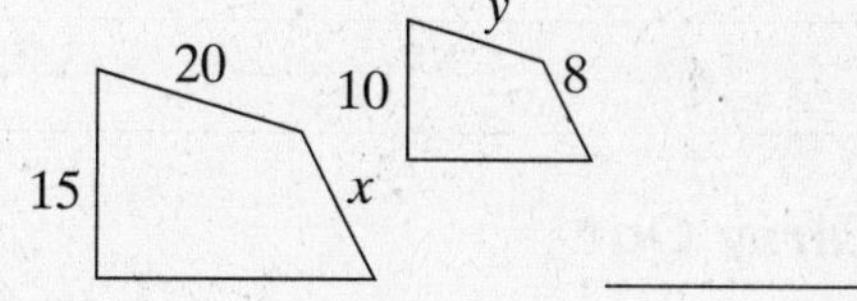

____

10. 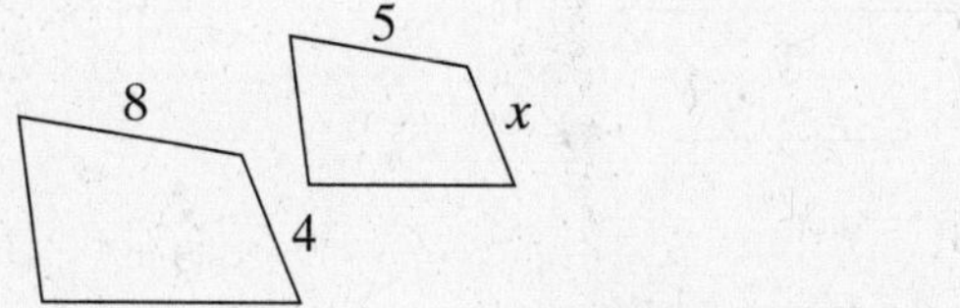

____

11. 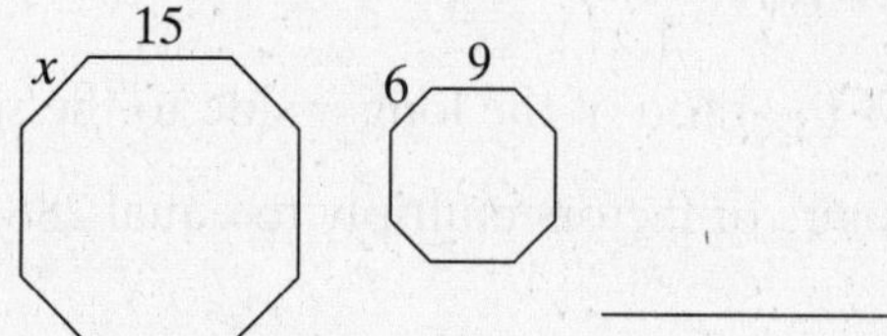

____

12. On a sunny day, if a 36-inch yardstick casts a 21-inch shadow, how tall is a building whose shadow is 168 ft?

____

13. Oregon is about 400 miles from west to east, and 300 miles from north to south. If a map of Oregon is 15 inches tall (from north to south), about how wide is the map?

____

Name ______________________ Class ______________ Date ______________

5-5 • Guided Problem Solving

GPS Student Page 254, Exercise 13:

Geometry A rectangle with an area of 32 in.^{2} has one side measuring 4 in. A similar rectangle has an area of 288 in.^{2}. How long is the longer side in the larger rectangle?

Understand

1. What are you being asked to do?

____

____

2. Will a proportion that equates the ratio of the areas to the ratio of the shorter sides result in the desired answer? Explain.

____

____

____

3. What measure should you determine first?

____

____

Plan and Carry Out

4. What is the length of the longer side of the rectangle whose area is 32 in.^{2} and whose shorter side is 4 in.? __________
5. What is the ratio of the longer side to the shorter side? __________
6. What pairs of factors multiply to equal 288?

____

7. Which pair of factors has a ratio of $\frac{2}{1}$? __________
8. What is the length of the longer side? __________

Check

9. Why must the ratio between the factors be $\frac{2}{1}$?

____

____

Solve Another Problem

10. A triangle with perimeter 26 in. has two sides that are 8 in. long. What is the length of the third side of a similar triangle which has two sides that are 12 in. long? __________

Name ______________________ Class ______________ Date ______________

Practice 5-5

Using Similar Figures

$\triangle MNO \sim \triangle JKL$. Complete each statement.

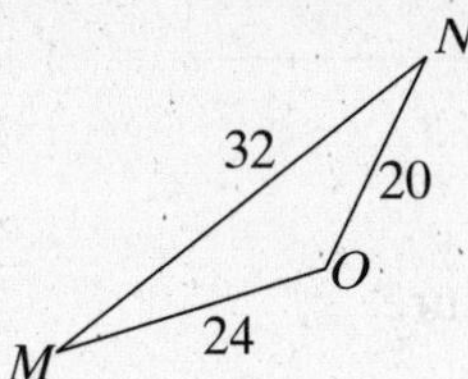

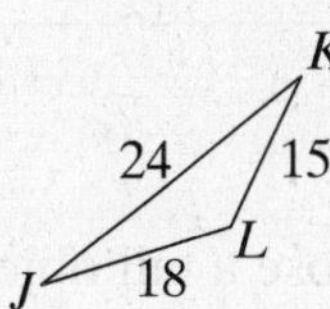

1. $\angle M$ corresponds to ______________.

2. $\overline{JL}$ corresponds to ______________.

3. What is the ratio of the lengths of the corresponding sides?

____

The pairs of figures below are similar. Find the value of each variable.

4.

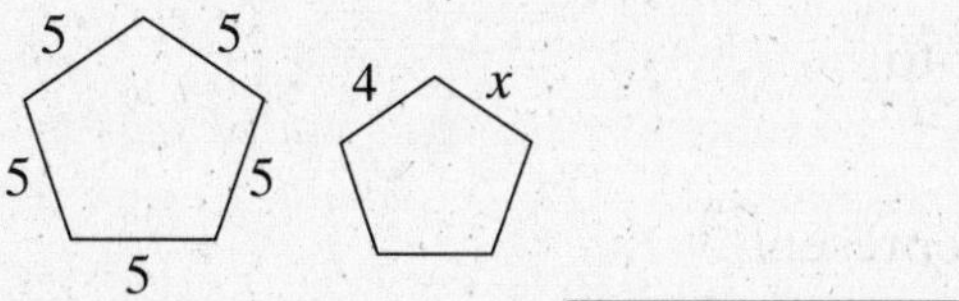

____

5.

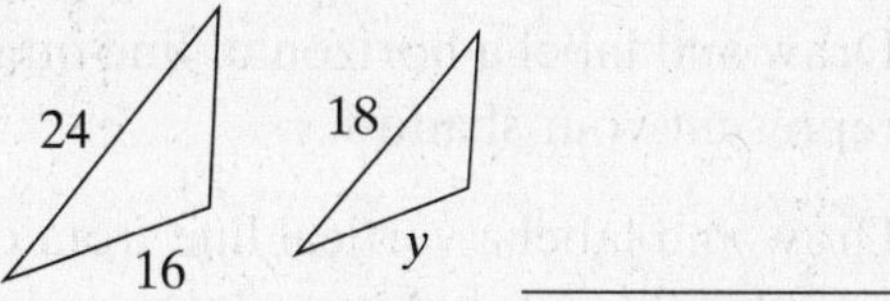

____

6.

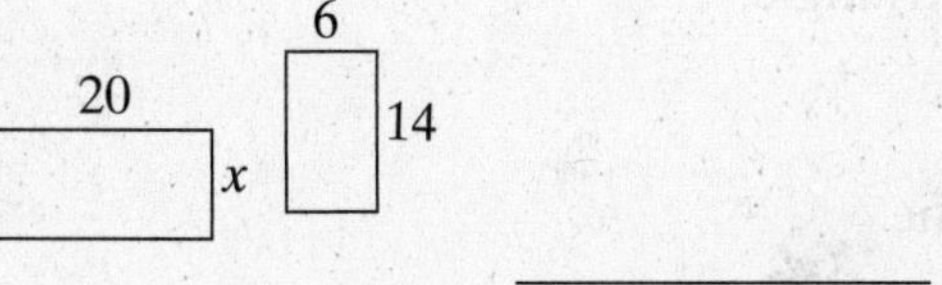

____

7.

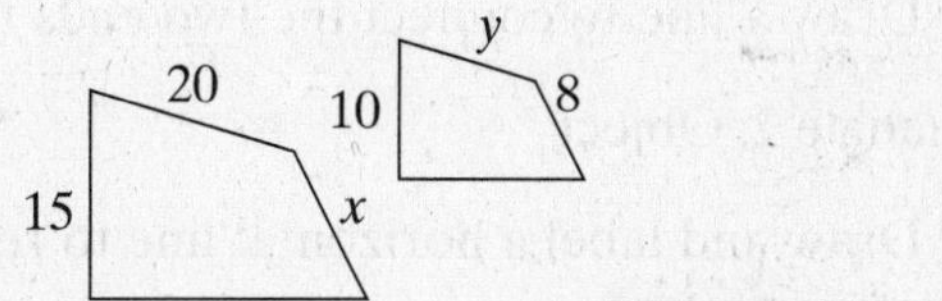

____

8.

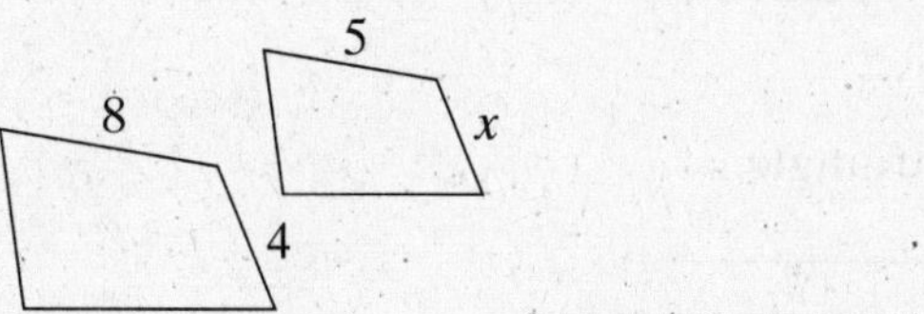

____

9.

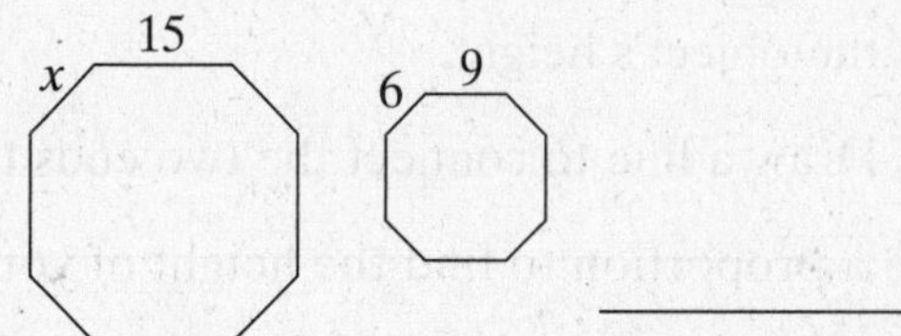

____

Solve.

10. Oregon is about 400 miles from west to east, and 300 miles from north to south. If a map of Oregon is 15 inches tall (from north to south), about how wide is the map?

____

Name ______________________ Class ______________ Date ______________

Activity Lab 5-5

Using Similar Figures

Materials needed: ruler, protractor, graph paper

Work with a partner.

Do this on a sunny day outdoors. Choose a tall object to measure, such as a tree or flagpole. Record the data on a piece of paper.

1. a. Measure your partner's height.

   b. Measure the length of your partner's shadow.

2. Measure the shadow of the tall object for which you would like to know its height.

3. Draw two triangles to scale on graph paper to show these relationships. Let each square on the graph paper equal one inch.

   - Triangle 1: You

     a. Draw and label a horizontal line on graph paper to represent your shadow.

     b. Draw and label a vertical line from one end to represent your height.

     c. Draw a line to connect the two ends to form a triangle.

   - Triangle 2: Object

     a. Draw and label a horizontal line to represent the object's shadow.

     b. Draw and label a vertical line from one end to represent the object's height.

     c. Draw a line to connect the two ends to form a triangle.

4. Write a proportion to find the height of your object.

Name ____________________ Class ____________ Date ____________

Reteaching 5-5

Using Similar Figures

Two polygons are **similar** if

- corresponding angles have the same measure, and
- the lengths of corresponding sides are proportional.

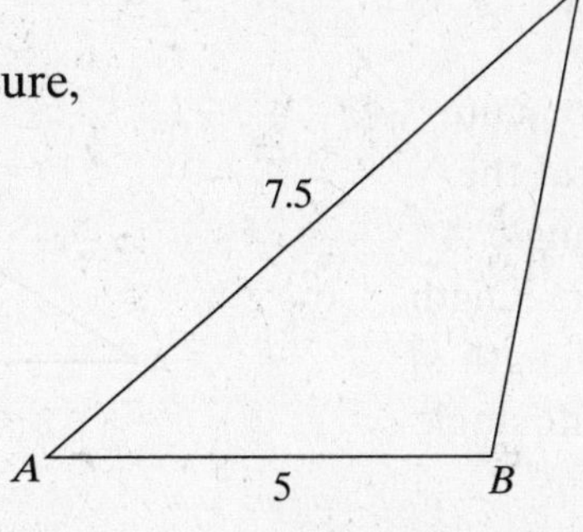

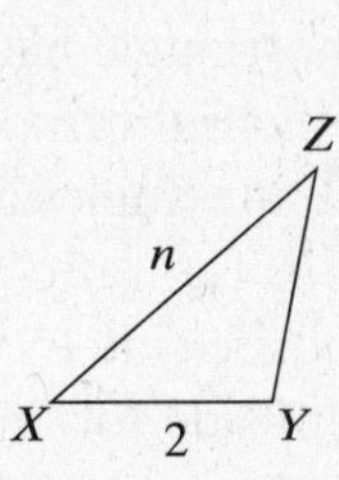

$\triangle ABC \sim \triangle XYZ$

You can use proportions to find missing lengths in similar (~) figures.

① Find corresponding sides.

$\overline{AB}$ corresponds to $\overline{XY}$.
$\overline{AC}$ corresponds to $\overline{XZ}$.
$\overline{BC}$ corresponds to $\overline{YZ}$.

② Write ratios of their lengths in a proportion.

$$\frac{AB}{XY} = \frac{AC}{XZ}$$

③ Substitute the information you know.

$$\frac{5}{2} = \frac{7.5}{n}$$

④ Write cross products. Solve for n.

$$5n = 2 \cdot 7.5$$
$$n = 3$$

The length of $\overline{XZ}$ is 3 units.

The figures are similar. Find the corresponding sides. Then complete the proportion and solve for *n*.

1. $\overline{AB}$ corresponds to ________.

$\overline{BC}$ corresponds to ________.

$\overline{CA}$ corresponds to ________.

2. $\frac{CA}{SQ} = \frac{\square}{RS}$

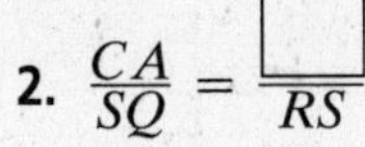

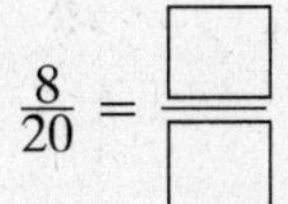

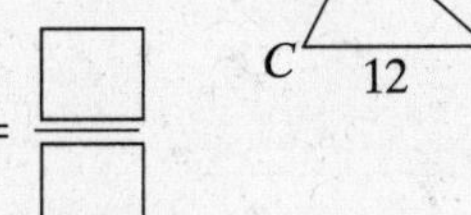

$\frac{8}{20} = \frac{\square}{\square}$

$n =$ ________

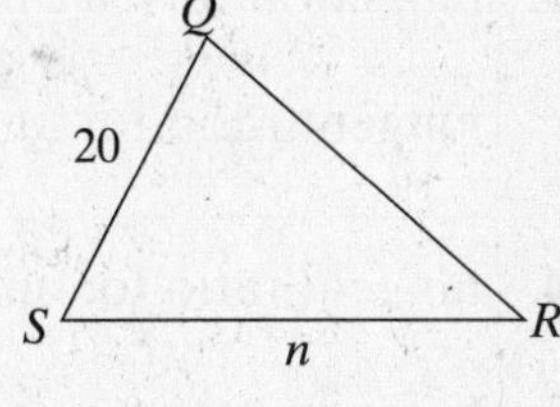

The pairs of figures below are similar. Find the value of each variable.

3. ________

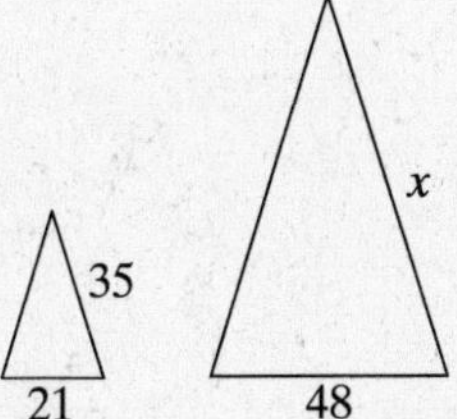

4. ________

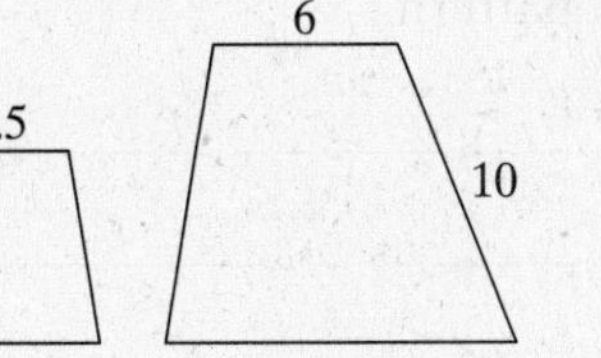

Enrichment 5-5

Using Similar Figures

Patterns in Geometry

Every right triangle has two acute angles. In the right triangle at the right, the acute angles are angle A and angle B. The ratio of the length of the opposite side to the length of the adjacent side for an acute angle is called the *tangent* ratio.

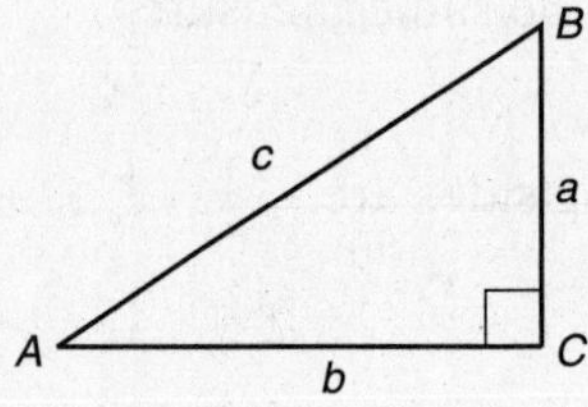

In triangle ABC, the tangent ratio for angle A is $\frac{a}{b}$, and the tangent ratio for angle B is $\frac{b}{a}$. In the table below, each right triangle has one acute angle that measures 57° and another that measures 33°. Find the tangent ratio for the acute angles in each triangle. Round each answer to the nearest hundredth.

1. tangent ratio for angle A ______ tangent ratio for angle B ______	B, c, 57°, $a = 6$, 33°, A, C, $b = 9.24$
2. tangent ratio for angle A ______ tangent ratio for angle B ______	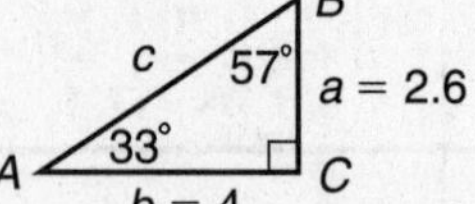
3. tangent ratio for angle A ______ tangent ratio for angle B ______	B, c, 57°, $a = 7.79$, 33°, A, C, $b = 12$
4. tangent ratio for angle A ______ tangent ratio for angle B ______	B, c, 57°, $a = 3$, 33°, A, C, $b = 4.62$
5. tangent ratio for angle A ______ tangent ratio for angle B ______	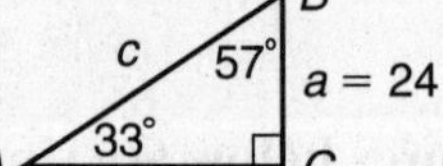

6. Describe the pattern.

____

____

Name ______________________ Class ______________ Date ______________

Puzzle 5-5

Using Similar Figures

You are creating a diagram of interlocking polygons, and it is almost complete. Use the hints below to see if "the missing piece" will complete your diagram.

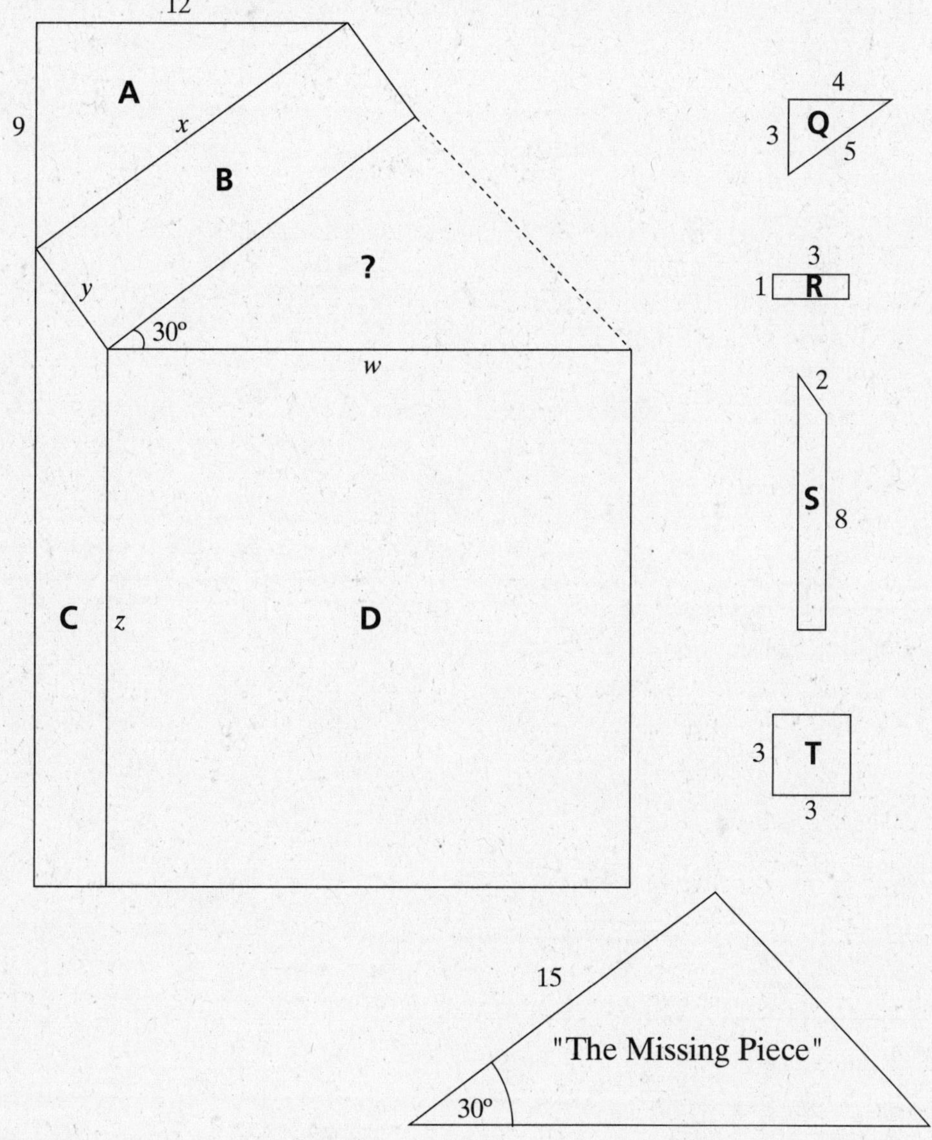

Hints:

1. Triangle A in your diagram is similar to Triangle Q.
2. Rectangle B is similar to Rectangle R.
3. Trapezoid C is similar to Trapezoid S.
4. Rectangle D in your diagram is similar to Rectangle T.

Does the missing piece fit in your diagram?

Name ______________________ Class ______________ Date ______________

Practice 5-6

Maps and Scale Drawings

The scale of a map is 2 cm : 21 km. Find the actual distances for the following map distances.

1. 9 cm ______________
2. 12.5 cm ______________
3. 14 mm ______________
4. 3.6 m ______________
5. 4.5 cm ______________
6. 7.1 cm ______________

A scale drawing has a scale of $\frac{1}{4}$ in. : 12 ft. Find the length on the drawing for each actual length.

7. 8 ft ______________
8. 30 ft ______________
9. 15 ft ______________
10. 18 ft ______________
11. 20 ft ______________
12. 40 ft ______________

Use a metric ruler to find the approximate distance between the towns.

13. Hickokburg to Kidville ______________
14. Dodgetown to Earp City ______________
15. Dodgetown to Kidville ______________
16. Kidville to Earp City ______________
17. Dodgetown to Hickokburg ______________
18. Earp City to Hickokburg ______________

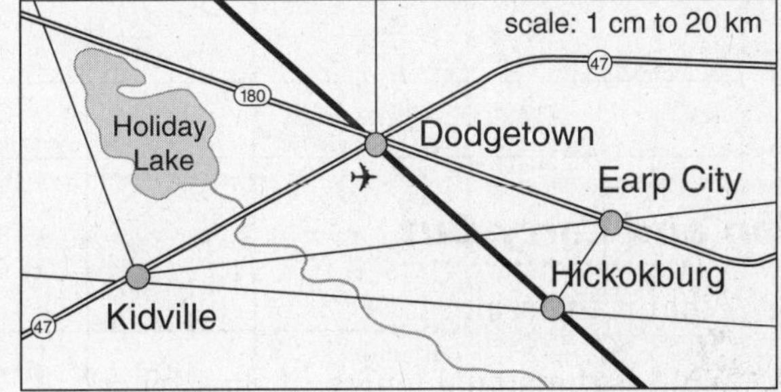

Solve.

19. The scale drawing shows a two-bedroom apartment. The master bedroom is 9 ft × 12 ft. Use an inch ruler to measure the drawing.

    a. The scale is ______________.

    b. Write the actual dimensions in place of the scale dimensions.

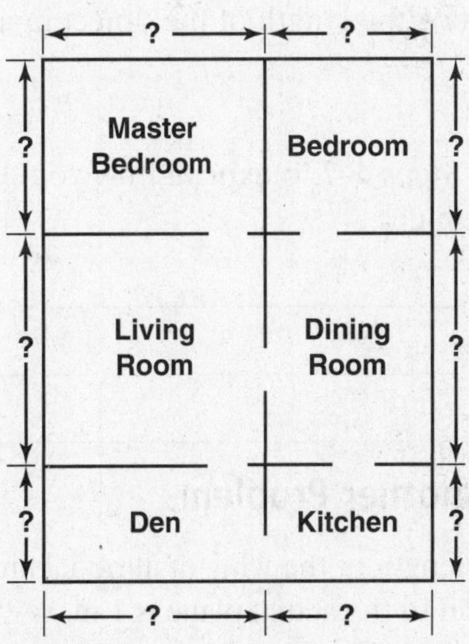

Name ______________________ Class ______________ Date ____________

5-6 • Guided Problem Solving

GPS Student Page 263, Exercise 24:

Writing in Math You are making a scale drawing with a scale of 2 in. = 17 ft. Explain how you find the length of the drawing of an object that has an actual length of 51 ft.

Understand

1. What are you being asked to do?

____

____

2. What points should you include in your explanation?

____

____

3. What is a scale?

____

____

Plan and Carry Out

4. What is the scale? ____________________

5. What is the actual length of the object? ____________

6. Write a proportion using the scale, the actual length, and the unknown length of the drawing. __________

7. What is the length of the object in a drawing? __________

Check

8. Use Steps 4–7 to explain how you decided how long to draw the object.

____

____

____

Solve Another Problem

9. The length of the wing of a model airplane is 3 in. If the scale of the model to the actual plane is 1 in. = 25 ft, what is the length of the actual wing?

____

Name ______ Class ______ Date ______

Practice 5-6

Maps and Scale Drawings

The scale of a map is 2 cm : 21 km. Find the actual distances for the following map distances.

1. 9 cm ______

2. 12.5 cm ______

3. 3.6 m ______

4. 4.5 cm ______

A scale drawing has a scale of $\frac{1}{4}$ in. : 12 ft. Find the length on the drawing for each actual length.

5. 8 ft ______

6. 30 ft ______

7. 18 ft ______

8. 20 ft ______

Use a metric ruler to find the approximate distance between the towns.

9. Hickokburg to Kidville

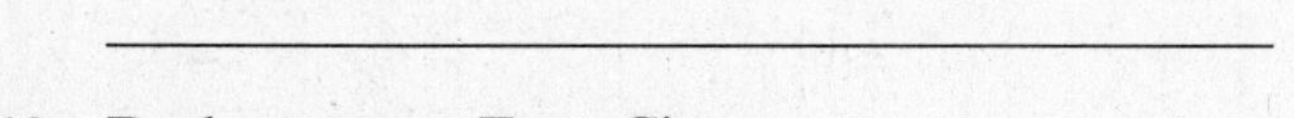

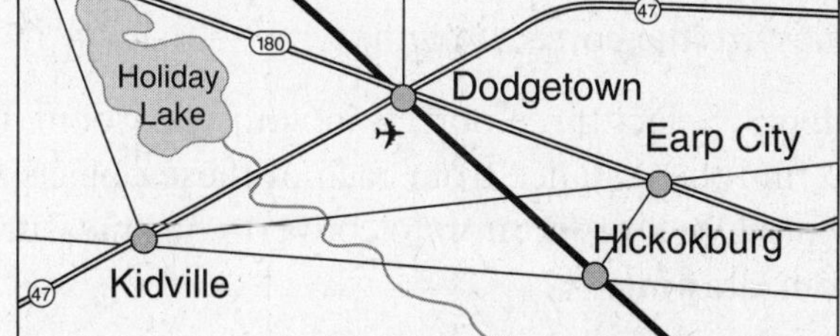

10. Dodgetown to Earp City ______

11. Dodgetown to Kidville ______

12. Kidville to Earp City ______

Solve.

13. The scale drawing shows a two-bedroom apartment. The master bedroom is 9 ft × 12 ft. Use an inch ruler to measure the drawing.

a. The scale is ______.

b. Write the actual dimensions for each room alongside the scale drawing.

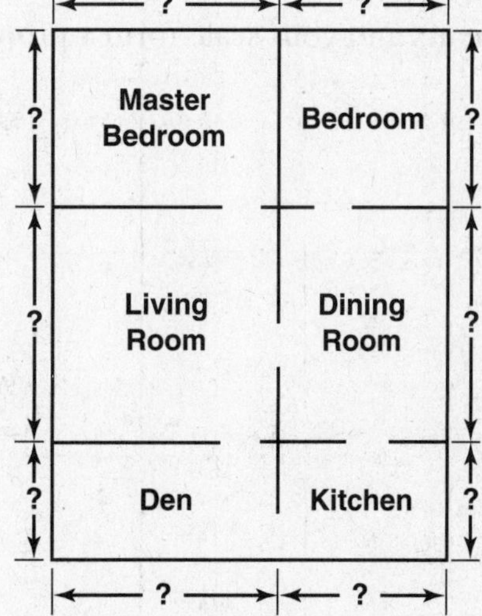

Activity Lab 5-6

Maps and Scale Drawings

Materials needed: tape measure, ruler, paper, pencil

In this activity, you will create a scale drawing of your classroom.

Step 1: Use the tape measure to measure the length and width of your classroom. Record the measurements.

Step 2: Decide on a scale for your drawing. Since you will be drawing on a sheet of paper, select a scale that is appropriate for a sheet of paper. For example, if your classroom is 20 feet long, an appropriate scale might be 1 inch = 2 feet.

Step 3: Use a proportion and the measurements of your classroom to determine how long and how wide the outline of your classroom will be on your scale drawing.

Step 4: Using the values you found in Step 3, draw the outline of your classroom on a separate sheet of paper. Use a ruler to make sure the lines are the correct length.

Step 5: Select three objects in your classroom. Use the tape measurc to find the distance from each of these objects to the front and side walls. Use a proportion to convert your measurements to the scale of your drawing.

Step 6: Using the scale measurements from Step 5, sketch the three objects onto your drawing. Make sure each one is the correct scaled distance from the front and side walls in your drawing.

Step 7: Label all of the objects in your drawing.

Step 8: Test the accuracy of your drawing by measuring the distance between the objects in real life and on your scale drawing. Do the measurements and your scale form a proportion?

Name ______________________ Class ______________ Date ______________

Reteaching 5-6

Maps and Scale Drawings

A **scale drawing** is an enlarged or reduced drawing of an object. A map is a scale drawing. On this map, the pool is 3 cm from the horse corral. What is the actual distance from the corral to the pool?

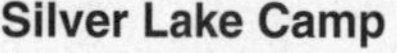

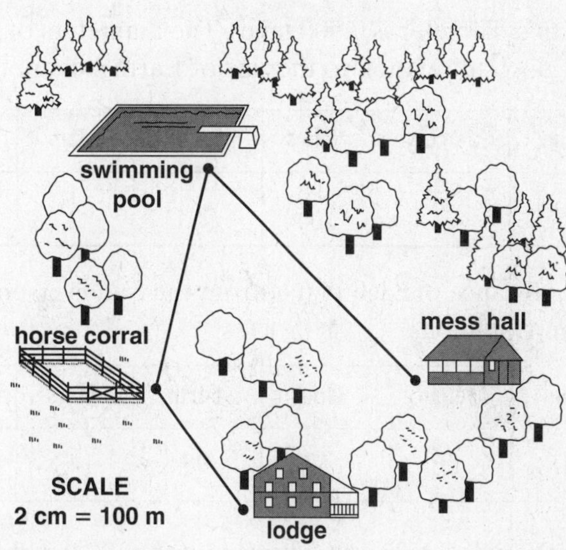

① Use the scale. Write a ratio of distance on the map to actual distance.

$$\frac{\text{map (cm)}}{\text{actual (m)}} = \frac{2}{100}$$

② Write a proportion using the scale.

$$\frac{\text{map (cm)}}{\text{actual (m)}} = \frac{2}{100} = \frac{3}{n}$$

③ Use cross products. Solve for *n*.

$$2n = 100 \cdot 3$$
$$n = 150 \text{ m}$$

The pool is 150 m from the corral.

Use the information on the map. Write and solve a proportion to find the distance.

1. On the map, the mess hall is 4 cm from the pool. What is the actual distance from the pool to the mess hall?

$$\frac{\text{map}}{\text{actual}} = \frac{\square}{100} = \frac{\square}{n}$$

$n =$ ________

2. The lodge is 2 cm from the horse corral on the map. What is the actual distance from the corral to the lodge?

$$\frac{\text{map}}{\text{actual}} = \frac{\square}{100} = \frac{\square}{n}$$

$n =$ ________

3. The pool is actually 225 m from the lodge. How far would the pool be from the lodge on the map?

$$\frac{\text{map}}{\text{actual}} = \frac{\square}{100} = \frac{n}{\square}$$

$n =$ ________

4. The mess hall is 150 m from the lodge. How far would the mess hall be from the lodge on the map?

$$\frac{\text{map}}{\text{actual}} = \frac{\square}{100} = \frac{n}{\square}$$

$n =$ ________

5. A volleyball court will be built 175 m from the lodge. How far would the volleyball court be from the lodge on the map?

____

Name ______________________ Class ______________ Date ______________

Enrichment 5-6

Maps and Scale Drawings

Decision Making

Suppose you want to make a model of the solar system to place in your classroom. Here is some data about the solar system you may need.

Earth's diameter is 7,900 miles. The diameters of the Sun and planets are given in relation to the size of Earth's diameter.

Sun	Mercury	Venus	Earth	Mars	Jupiter	Saturn	Uranus	Neptune	Pluto
100	$\frac{1}{3}$	$\frac{95}{100}$	1	$\frac{1}{2}$	11	$9\frac{1}{2}$	4	4	$\frac{1}{5}$

The distance of each planet from the Sun is given in miles rounded to nearest million.

Sun	Mercury	Venus	Earth	Mars	Jupiter	Saturn	Uranus	Neptune	Pluto
0	36	67	93	142	484	887	1,782	2,794	3,666

1. You decide to use a baseball (about 2.9 inches in diameter) to represent Earth.

a. To the nearest whole number, what will 1 inch on the scale represent if you use the baseball to represent Earth?

____

b. Write the scale distance of the diameter for the Sun.

____

c. About how many inches from the Sun must you place Earth? Is this reasonable? Explain.

____

____

____

2. Choose other objects to represent Earth. Can you devise a model that is true to scale that can be contained in your classroom? Explain.

____

____

____

5E: Vocabulary Check

For use after Lesson 5-6

Study Skill Strengthen your vocabulary. Use these pages and add cues and summaries by applying the Cornell Notetaking style.

Write the definition for each word or term at the right. To check your work, fold the paper back along the dotted line to see the correct answers.

Definition	Term
______________________	polygon
______________________	proportion
______________________	unit rate
______________________	ratio
______________________	scale drawing

Name ______________________ Class ______________ Date ______________

5E: Vocabulary Check (continued)

For use after Lesson 5-6

Write the vocabulary word or term for each definition. To check your work, fold the paper forward along the dotted line to see the correct answers.

a closed figure formed by three or more line segments that do not cross ______________________

an equation stating that two ratios are equal ______________________

the rate for one unit of a given quantity ______________________

a comparison of two quantities by division ______________________

an enlarged or reduced drawing of an object that is similar to the actual object ______________________

Name ______________________ Class ______________ Date ______________

5D: Visual Vocabulary Practice

For use after Lesson 5-6

Study Skill When you come across something you don't understand, view it as an opportunity to increase your brain power.

Concept List

cross products	equivalent ratios	indirect measurement
proportion	rate	scale
similar polygons	unit cost	unit rate

Write the concept that best describes each exercise. Choose from the concept list above.

1. $\frac{18}{16}$ and 4.5 : 4 ______________	**2.** A 6-ft-tall person standing near a building has a shadow that is 60 ft long. This can be used to determine the height of the building. ______________	**3.** A bakery sells a dozen donuts for \$3.15. This can also be represented as $\frac{\$3.15}{12\text{ donuts}}$. ______________
4. The expression "45 words per minute" represents this. ______________	**5.** $\frac{30}{75} = \frac{2}{5}$ ______________	**6.** For the equation $\frac{15}{16} = \frac{3z}{4}$, these are represented by 15×4 and $3z \times 16$. ______________
7. The equation $\frac{1}{2}$ in. = 50 mi represents this on a map. ______________	**8.** $\frac{\$4.25}{5\text{ lb}} = \$.85/\text{lb}$ ______________	**9.** 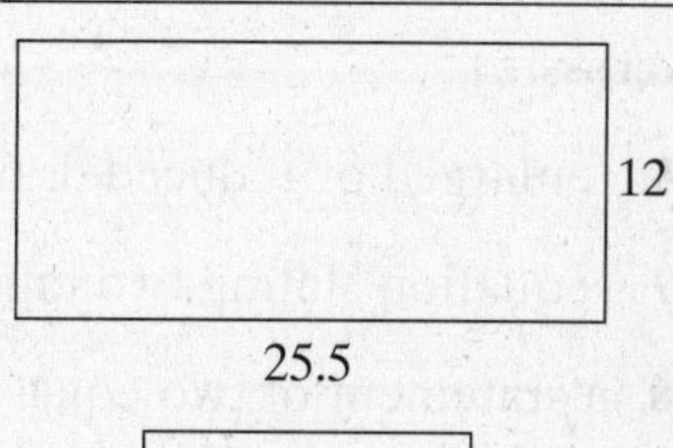 ______________

Name ______________________ Class ______________ Date ____________

5F: Vocabulary Review Puzzle

For use with the Chapter Review

Study Skill Use a special notebook or section of a loose-leaf binder for math.

Complete the crossword puzzle. For help, use the Glossary in your textbook.

Here are the words you will use to complete this crossword puzzle:

equation	factor	figures	fraction
inequality	mixed number	prime	proportion
ratio	scale drawing		

Across

5. enlarged or reduced drawing of an object
7. equation stating two ratios are equal
8. a statement of two equal expressions
10. a whole number that divides another whole number evenly

Down

1. Similar ______________ have the same shape but not necessarily the same size.
2. a statement that two expressions are not equal
3. a number made up of a nonzero whole number and a fraction
4. a number with only two factors, one and itself
6. a number in the form $\frac{a}{b}$
9. a comparison of two numbers by division

Name ______________________ Class ______________ Date ______________

Puzzle 5-6

Maps and Scale Drawings

Rick and Sven are trying to chart the shortest route through a section of the forest. They each began and ended at the same points, but took different trails along the way. Use the provided scales to compare the maps and complete the charts below. Who created the shorter route?

Sven's Map—Scale: 1 in. = 50 yards

Section	Measured Distance	Actual Distance
a		
b		
c		
d		
e		
f		

Rick's Map—Scale: 1 in. = 70 yards

Section	Measured Distance	Actual Distance
w		
x		
y		
d		

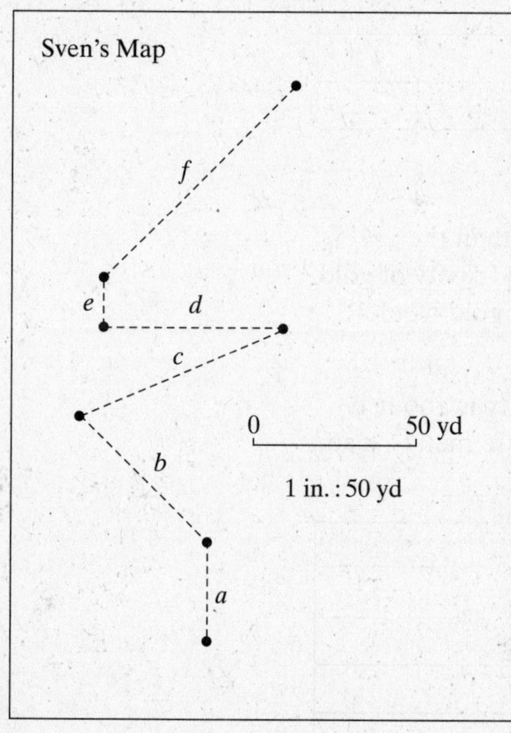

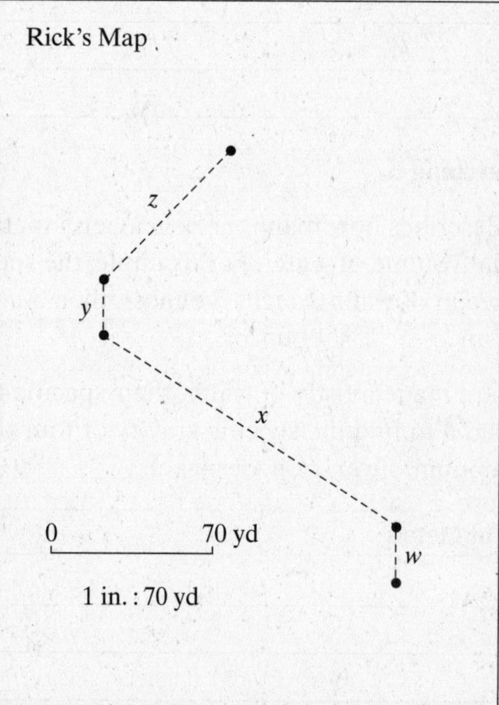

Name ______________________ Class ______________ Date ____________

Chapter 5 Project: Weighty Matters

Using Specific Gravity

Beginning the Chapter Project

Have you ever loved a pet so much that you wanted a statue made of it? Imagine a statue of your pet on the front steps of your home. "Gee, what a wise way to spend hard-earned money," your admiring neighbors would say. Or maybe not. In addition to being expensive, these statues would also be heavy. For instance, a 35-lb dog cast in gold would weigh about 670 lb.

For the chapter project, you will find the weight of different animals and the weight of different metals. Your final project will be a table of animals with their weights, the weight of their statues in different materials, and the cost of the statues.

Activities

Activity 1: Measuring

Find the weights of five animals. You can include the weight of a pet on your list, if you have one.

Weights of Animals
1.
2.
3.
4.
5.

Activity 2: Researching

Specific gravity describes how many times heavier a metal is than the weight of an equal volume of water. For example, the specific gravity of gold is about 19.3. If a cup of water weighs 8 ounces, then a cup of gold would weigh 8×19.3 ounces or 154.4 ounces.

Since mammals are made mostly of water, their specific gravity is about 1. Use an encyclopedia to find the specific gravity of four of these metals: lead, copper, zinc, aluminum, silver, iron, or nickel.

Specific Gravity of Metals
1.
2.
3.
4.

Name ______________________ Class ______________ Date ______________

Chapter 5 Project: Weighty Matters (continued)

Activity 3: Calculating

Use the weights of the different animals and the specific gravities of the different metals. Find the weight of a statue of each animal in metal.

Activity 4: Calculating

Find the price of the different metals you used. Include the source of your information. Use this data to calculate how much each statue would cost.

Finishing the Project

Choose your favorite statue. Pretend that you are going to present this statue as a gift to a city, museum, or park. Explain why you chose that statue. How much would it weigh? How much would it cost?

Be sure your work is neat and clear. Show your data and calculations. Write any explanations you think are necessary.

Reflect and Revise

Review your project with a friend or someone at home. Are your calculations accurate? Are your numbers realistic? If necessary, make changes to improve your project.

Visit PHSchool.com for information and links you might find helpful as you complete your project.

Name ______________________ Class ______________ Date ____________

Chapter Project Manager

Getting Started

Read about the project. As you work on it, you will need several sheets of paper. If available, a spreadsheet program also can be used. Keep all your work for the project in a folder, along with this Project Manager.

Checklist	Suggestions
❑ Activity 1: measuring	❑ If you do not have a pet, think of some animals that are in one of your favorite books.
❑ Activity 2: researching	❑ Find objects in your home made of these metals, such as a soda can, a coin, a necklace, to help you visualize the material.
❑ Activity 3: calculating	❑ Round your calculations to the nearest thousandth.
❑ Activity 4: calculating	❑ Be sure your units are the same before calculating.
❑ Recommendations	❑ To better present your calculations, display the data in a table.

Scoring Rubric

3 You collected all the data required for the statues, and you displayed the data in an organized list or table. You accurately estimated the weight and cost of each statue. You offered an explanation for why your chose one statue to offer as a gift to a city, museum, park, or other organization.

2 Your collected five animal weights, five specific gravity values, and at least two of the costs of the metals used. Most of your estimations of statue weights and costs were accurate, and you displayed the data in an organized manner.

1 You omitted some of the data, some of your calculations were inaccurate, or your presentation was not organized properly.

0 You neglected to collect a significant portion of the data, or you failed to complete and display all of the required calculations.

Your Evaluation of Project Evaluate your work, based on the Scoring Rubric.

Teacher's Evaluation of Project

Name ______________________ Class ______________ Date ____________

Chapter Project Teacher Notes

About the Project

Students will have an opportunity to apply their knowledge of unit rates, proportional reasoning, and decimals by making a table that shows the weights and costs of various statues.

Introducing the Project

Ask students:

- *Have you ever used decimal numbers? Describe a situation in which you have used decimals.*
- *How can you calculate the cost of a certain amount of a material if you know the price per pound and the weight?*
- *How can two objects the same size have different weights?*

Activity 1: Measuring

Tell students that one method for weighing small animals is to hold the animal while standing on a scale. Then subtract your weight from the total weight shown of the scale.

Activity 2: Researching

You may want to bring chemistry books to class so that students have another type of source in which to find the specific gravities.

Activity 3: Calculating

You may wish to show students samples of metallic statues of different animals. These can be found in art books.

Activity 4: Calculating

One source for the current prices of the metals is in the business section of newspapers that contain futures.

Finishing the Project

You may wish to plan a project day on which students share their completed projects. Encourage students to explain their process as well as their products. Have them explain how calculating with decimals helped them select the statue.

Visit PHSchool.com for information and links you might find helpful as you complete your project.

Name ______________________ Class ______________ Date ____________

✔ Checkpoint Quiz 1

Use with Lessons 5-1 through 5-2.

Write each ratio in two other ways.

1. 4 : 60 ______________ 2. $\frac{5}{2}$ ______________ 3. 3 to 15 ______________

Write each ratio in simplest form.

4. 6 to 10 ______________ 5. $\frac{25}{45}$ ______________ 6. 12 : 48 ______________

7. Calculate each unit price. Determine which is the better buy.
6 oz for $1.25; 8 oz for $1.33; 12 oz for $1.50; 16 oz for $2.05 ______________

8. Use any strategy to solve this problem. Show your work. Sam and Ralph were paid $234 to pressure wash a deck. Sam worked 4 hours and Ralph worked 2.5 hours. If they get paid the same rate, what is Sam's share of the money?

____

____

____

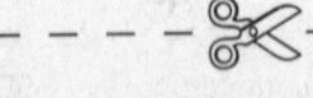

✔ Checkpoint Quiz 2

Use with Lessons 5-3 through 5-5.

Determine whether the ratios in each pair are proportional.

1. $\frac{2.2}{16}, \frac{8.8}{64}$ ______________ 2. $\frac{95}{42}, \frac{19}{7}$ ______________ 3. $\frac{3}{14}, \frac{1.5}{7}$ ______________

Solve each proportion.

4. $\frac{6}{9} = \frac{x}{108}$ ______________ 5. $\frac{x}{5} = \frac{81}{45}$ ______________ 6. $\frac{15}{24} = \frac{5}{x}$ ______________

7. A jet airplane takes 45 min to fly 495 mi from Dallas to Kansas City. Suppose another jet travels at the same rate from New York to Los Angeles, a distance of 2,786 mi. How long will the flight take? Round to the nearest minute.

____

8. The triangles on the right are similar. Find the value of x.

24 · x · 13 · 12 · 5

____

9. A man is 6 ft tall, and his shadow is 4 ft long. A nearby tree has a shadow 20 ft long. How tall is the tree?

____

Name ______ Class ______ Date ______

Chapter Test — Form A

Chapter 5

1. There are 14 boys and 16 girls in a class. Write the ratio of boys to girls in simplest form.

______

Determine whether the ratios in each pair are proportional.

2. 1 : 10; 2 : 5

3. 4 to 7; 28 to 49

4. $\frac{6}{19}; \frac{2}{5}$

______ ______ ______

5. Which is a better buy, 6 apples for \$1.74 or 5 apples for \$1.20? Why?

______

Write the unit rate for each situation.

6. bike 21 km in 50 min ______

7. earn \$18 for 1 hr 15 min work ______

8. sew 9 curtain panels in 15 days ______

9. Wyatt spent $\frac{1}{4}$ of his money on a train set and $\frac{1}{2}$ on tickets to a play. He now has \$18. How much money did Wyatt start with? Explain why you chose the method you did.

______

Write each ratio in two other ways.

10. $\frac{5}{9}$

11. 8 to 3

12. 12 : 15

______ ______ ______

Solve each proportion.

13. $\frac{n}{6} = \frac{25}{30}$

14. $\frac{6.1}{x} = \frac{2}{3}$

15. $\frac{100}{25} = \frac{t}{4}$

______ ______ ______

16. Alonso can jog 2 miles in 16 minutes. Is it reasonable to assume that it will take him 24 minutes to jog 3 miles? Explain.

______

______

Name ______________________ Class ______________ Date ______________

Chapter Test (continued) Form A

Chapter 5

17. Find the unit price of a 16 oz can of juice that costs $1.59.

____

18. These triangles are similar. Find the values of x and y.

____

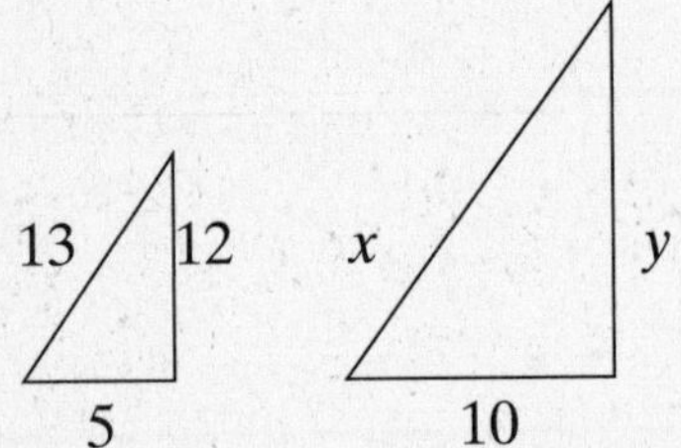

19. Taylor wants to enlarge this photograph so that the longest side measures 15 in. How wide will she need to make the photograph?

____

4 in.

6 in.

The scale of a map is 2.5 cm : 40 km. Find the actual distance for each map distance. Round your answer to the nearest tenth if necessary.

20. 15 cm ______________ **21.** 4 cm ______________ **22.** 21 cm ______________

23. Find three consecutive even numbers that have a sum of 36.

____

24. Can you make two similar triangles using exactly 9 toothpicks? If so, explain how.

____

____

____

Name ______________________ Class ______________ Date ______________

Chapter Test

Form B

Chapter 5

1. There are 14 boys and 16 girls in a class. Write the ratio of boys to girls in simplest form.

____

Determine whether the ratios in each pair are proportional.

2. 1 : 10; 2 : 5

____

3. 4 to 7; 28 to 49

____

4. Which is a better buy, 6 apples for \$1.74 or 5 apples for \$1.20? Why?

____

Write the unit rate for each situation.

5. bike 21 km in 50 min

____

6. earn \$18 for 1 hr 15 min work

____

Write each ratio in two other ways.

7. $\frac{5}{9}$

____

8. 8 to 3

____

Solve each proportion.

9. $\frac{n}{6} = \frac{25}{30}$

____

10. $\frac{6.1}{x} = \frac{2}{3}$

____

11. Alonso can jog 2 miles in 16 minutes. Is it reasonable to assume that it will take him 24 minutes to jog 3 miles? Explain.

____

____

Chapter Test (continued) Form B

Chapter 5

12. Find the unit price of a 16 oz can of juice that costs $1.59.

______

13. These triangles are similar.

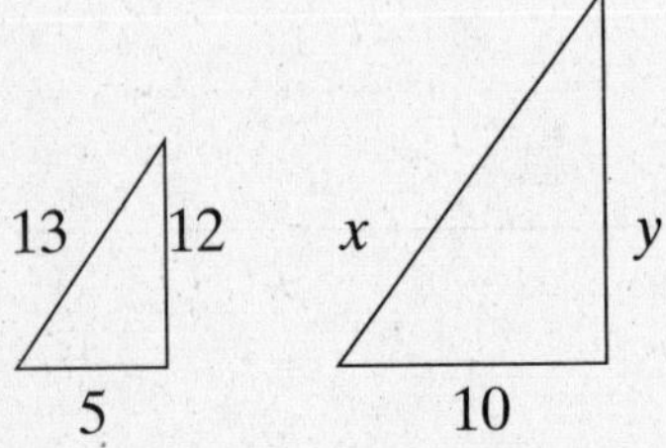

Find the values of x and y.

______

14. Taylor wants to enlarge this picture so that the length measures 15 in. How wide will she need to make the picture?

4 in.

6 in.

______

The scale of a map is 2.5 cm : 40 km. Find the actual distance for each map distance. Round your answer to the nearest tenth if necessary.

15. 15 cm

______

16. 4 cm

______

17. Find three consecutive even numbers that have a sum of 36.

______

______

______

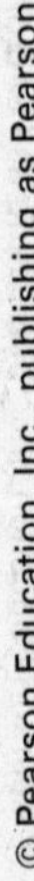

Name ________________ Class ________________ Date ________________

Alternative Assessment Form C

Chapter 5

SUPER COOPER ATHLETES

Each year thousands of student athletes take the Cooper test. Its purpose is to measure an athlete's physical condition. Test results can be used to plan an exercise program.

The Cooper test is very simple. It measures how far a person can run in 12 min. An athlete who is in good physical condition can run farther than an athlete whose physical condition is not as good. Since it is easier to measure laps than to measure miles, athletes usually take the test on a school track. One lap equals $\frac{1}{4}$ mi on a standard track.

This chart shows how to use the Cooper test results to determine an individual's physical condition.

Condition	Number of Laps Run in 12 min	Miles
Excellent	7–8	1.75–2.00
Good	6–7	1.50–1.75
Fair	5–6	1.25–1.50
Poor	4–5	1.00–1.25

Solve.

1. Martina ran $6\frac{1}{2}$ laps in 12 min. Approximately how many miles did she run? According to the Cooper test results, what is Martina's physical condition?

2. Jeb is getting in shape to play baseball this summer. He can't run on the school track. However, there is a measured mile on a road near his house. He can run that mile in 10 min. What kind of shape is Jeb in? Explain your thinking.

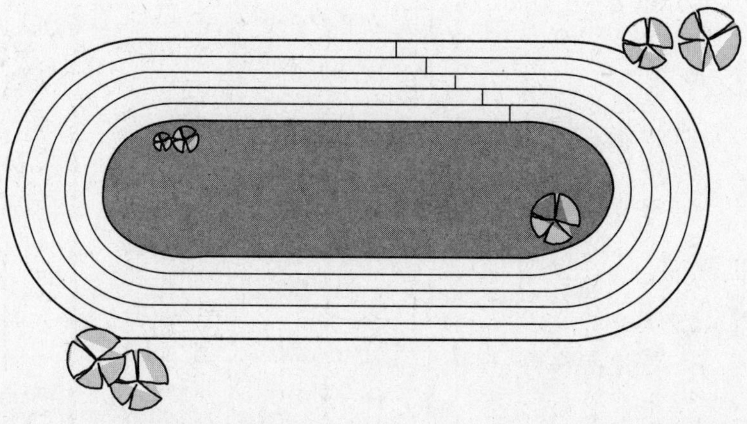

Alternative Assessment (continued) Form C

3. Emilio and Ron both took the Cooper test. Emilio ran just over 6 laps; his distance was equivalent to 1.53 mi. Ron ran just under 6 laps; his distance was equivalent to 1.48 mi. What conclusion might their coach draw about their level of conditioning? Explain.
4. Brittany is in excellent condition, as measured by her Cooper test results. She ran 8 laps in 12 min. How would you determine how many feet she could run in 1 min? Explain the method you would use. Then do the calculations.
5. Coach DiMare wants to put the Cooper test information in a graph. She thinks that a graph will be easier for students to understand. She hopes that a graph might help motivate them to get in better shape. Design a graph that presents the information in the chart.

Excursion

Roger knows he is in poor shape. When he tried to do the Cooper test on his own, he could complete only 4 laps in 12 min. Roger really wants to make the soccer team. He knows he must be in good to excellent shape to be considered for the team.

Soccer tryouts are in 4 weeks. Roger wants to use those 4 weeks to improve his conditioning. He can spend up to one hour a day, 4 days each week, to improve.

Develop a plan for Roger. Be sure to include his goal and how he can measure his progress.

Name ______________________ Class ______________ Date ______________

Cumulative Review

Chapters 1–5

Multiple Choice. Choose the letter of the best answer.

1. Which point on the number line shows the product $(-5) \times 2$?

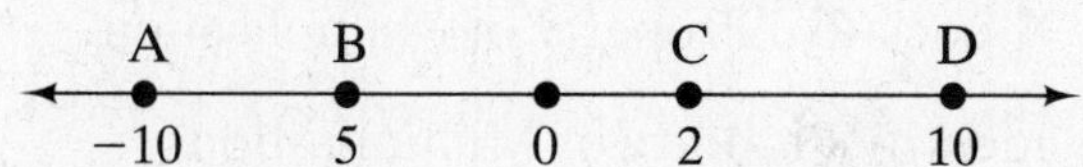

2. Which equation is *not* equivalent to $2x - 4 = 9$?

F. $-4 + 2x = 9$

G. $2x - 9 = 4$

H. $-9 + 2x = 4$

J. $4 - 2x = 9$

3. Solve $\frac{x}{6} = -8$.

A. $x = -2$

B. $x = -48$

C. $x = 14$

D. $x = -8$

4. Solve $-9m = -63$.

F. $m = -72$

G. $m = -54$

H. $m = 567$

J. $m = 7$

5. Which decimal is equal to $\frac{3}{8}$?

A. 0.125 **B.** 0.375

C. 0.38 **D.** 0.83

6. What is the LCD for $\frac{2}{9}$ and $\frac{5}{6}$?

F. 9 **G.** 18

H. 27 **J.** 54

7. Solve $6d > -36$.

A. $d > 216$ **B.** $d < -6$

C. $d < \frac{1}{6}$ **D.** $d > -6$

8. Estimate how many $\frac{1}{3}$-lb boxes can be filled from a $5\frac{3}{4}$-lb bag of rice.

F. about 10 **G.** about 12

H. about 15 **J.** about 18

9. $\triangle ABC$ is similar to $\triangle DEF$. What is the value of x?

A. 1.5 **B.** 2

C. 2.5 **D.** 5

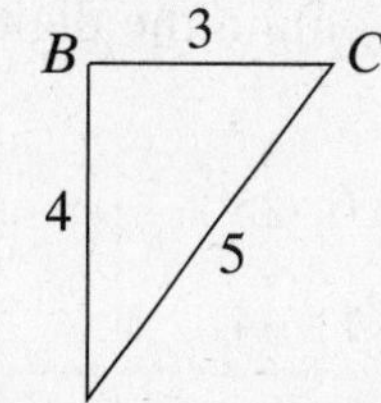

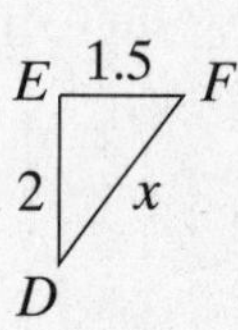

10. What is the ratio $\frac{45}{90}$ in simplest form?

F. $\frac{9}{18}$ **G.** $\frac{15}{30}$

H. $\frac{3}{6}$ **J.** $\frac{1}{2}$

11. Jason bought $4\frac{2}{3}$ yd of rope to make a swing. What is this number as an improper fraction?

A. $\frac{6}{3}$ **B.** $\frac{14}{3}$

C. $\frac{7}{2}$ **D.** $\frac{12}{3}$

12. Solve $\frac{m}{-6} > 2$.

Which number line correctly represents the solution?

F.
−14 −13 −12 −11 −10

G.
10 11 12 13 14

H.
−14 −13 −12 −11 −10

J.
10 11 12 13 14

Name ______________________ Class ______________ Date ______________

Cumulative Review (continued)

Chapters 1–5

13. Bob spent $\frac{5}{6}$ h doing his homework. His brother Gene spent $\frac{3}{4}$ h, his sister Shirley spent $\frac{4}{5}$ h, and his sister Mary Jane spent $\frac{2}{3}$ h doing homework. Who spent the most time doing homework?

A. Bob

B. Gene

C. Shirley

D. Mary Jane

14. The pages in a book are numbered from 1 to 250. How many pages contain the digit 5 at least once?

F. 20 **G.** 25

H. 45 **J.** 44

15. The ratio of boys to girls in Austin Middle School is 9 to 10. There are 189 boys in the school. How many girls are there?

A. 1,890 **B.** 189

C. 210 **D.** 21

16. At one store, the same socks are packaged four different ways. Which is the best buy?

F. 1 for $1.29

G. 2 for $2.49

H. 4 for $4.79

J. 6 for $7.39

17. Suzanne needed material for her school project. She bought 2.75 yards of material selling for $3.82 a yard. What was the total cost of the material? Round to the nearest cent.

A. $105.50

B. $11.53

C. $10.51

D. $9.50

18. What property is illustrated by the fact that $71.7 \times 1 = 71.7$?

F. Zero Property of Multiplication

G. Associative Property of Multiplication

H. Identity Property of Multiplication

J. Commutative Property of Multiplication

Gridded Response

19. If a map scale is 0.5 cm : 15 km, then 4.0 cm = __________ km.

Short Response

20. How would you show that $\frac{16}{19} = \frac{32}{39}$ is not a proportion? Which number in these ratios would you change to form a proportion?

____

____

____

____

Extended Response

21. Find the decimal equivalents for the following fractions: $\frac{1}{11}$; $\frac{2}{11}$; $\frac{3}{11}$; $\frac{4}{11}$. Predict from the pattern found what the decimal equivalents would be for $\frac{5}{11}$, $\frac{6}{11}$. Show your work.

____

____

Name ______________________ Class ______________ Date ______________

Practice 6-1

Understanding Percents

Shade each grid to represent each of the following percents.

1. 53%

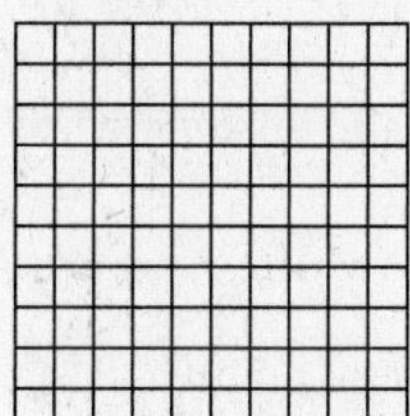

2. 23%

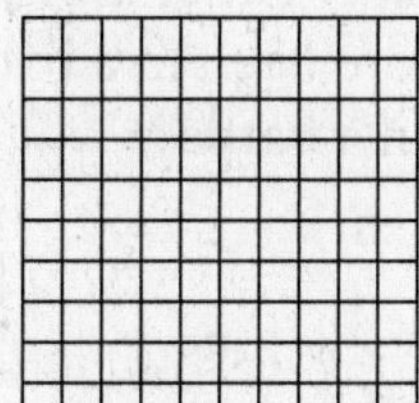

3. 71%

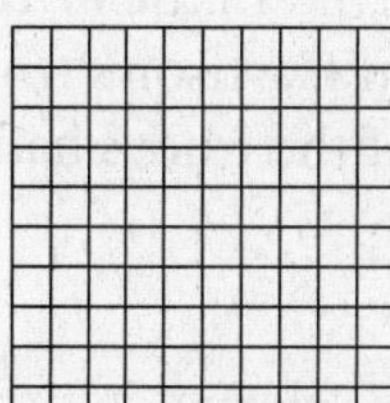

Write each ratio as a percent.

4. $\frac{4}{5}$ __________
5. $\frac{3}{5}$ __________
6. $\frac{9}{10}$ __________
7. $\frac{3}{10}$ __________
8. $\frac{6}{25}$ __________
9. $\frac{7}{100}$ __________
10. $\frac{9}{50}$ __________
11. $\frac{9}{25}$ __________
12. $\frac{2}{5}$ __________
13. $\frac{7}{10}$ __________
14. $\frac{4}{25}$ __________
15. $\frac{16}{25}$ __________
16. $\frac{11}{20}$ __________
17. $\frac{19}{20}$ __________
18. $\frac{27}{50}$ __________
19. 41 : 50 __________

Write a percent for each shaded figure.

20. 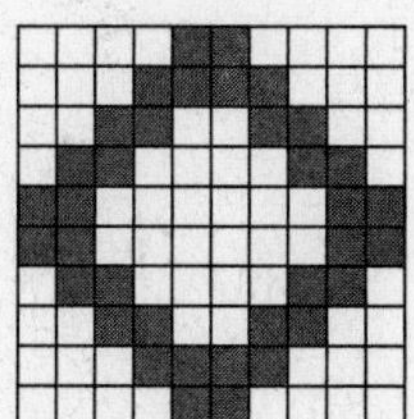 ______

21.  ______

22. 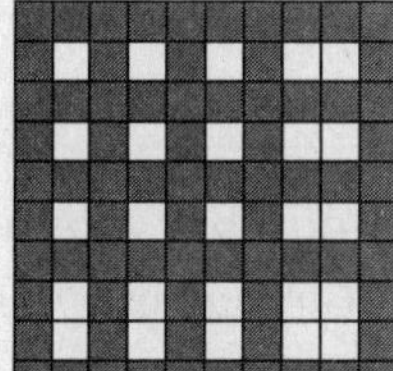 ______

Complete the following.

Ancient Egyptians did not write the fraction $\frac{4}{5}$ as "$\frac{4}{5}$". Instead, they used *unit fractions.* The numerator of a unit fraction is always 1. No denominator used to represent a given fraction can be repeated. For this reason, Egyptians would have written $\frac{4}{5}$ as $\frac{1}{2} + \frac{1}{5} + \frac{1}{10}$ and not as $\frac{1}{2} + \frac{1}{10} + \frac{1}{10} + \frac{1}{10}$. Write each of the following as a sum of unit fractions.

23. $\frac{3}{4}$ ______________________
24. $\frac{5}{8}$ ______________________
25. $\frac{9}{10}$ ______________________
26. $\frac{7}{12}$ ______________________

Name ______________________ Class ______________ Date ______________

6-1 • Guided Problem Solving

GPS Student Page 277, Exercise 30:

History Before the Battle of Tippecanoe, nineteen twentieths of General William Harrison's troops had never before been in a battle. What percent of the troops had previously been in a battle?

Understand

1. What is the relevant information?

____

____

2. What are you being asked to do?

____

Plan and Carry Out

3. What fraction of the troops had never before been in a battle?

____

4. What fraction of the troops had previously been in a battle?

____

5. To write a number as a percent, first write an equivalent ratio with a denominator of what number?

____

6. Write an equivalent ratio of $\frac{1}{20}$. ______________________

7. Convert the fraction to a percent. ______________________

Check

8. What percent is nineteen twentieths? Does the sum of the percent you found in Step 7 and the equivalent percent of nineteen twentieths equal 100%?

____

____

Solve Another Problem

9. A marathon runner has run two fifths of the race. What percent of the race is left to run?

____

Name ________________ Class ________________ Date ________________

Practice 6-1

Understanding Percents

Shade each grid to represent each of the following percents.

1. 53%

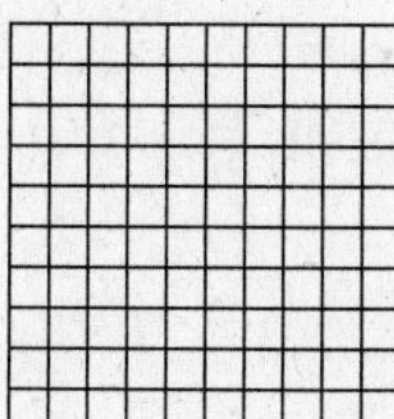

2. 23%

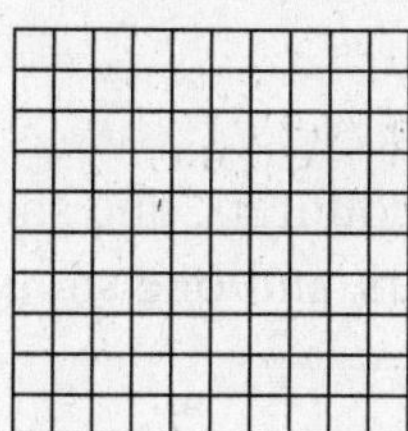

3. 71%

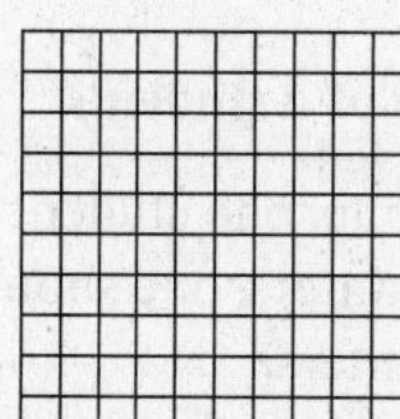

Write each ratio as a percent.

4. $\frac{4}{5}$ ________________
5. $\frac{3}{5}$ ________________
6. $\frac{9}{10}$ ________________
7. $\frac{6}{25}$ ________________
8. $\frac{7}{100}$ ________________
9. $\frac{9}{50}$ ________________
10. $\frac{2}{5}$ ________________
11. $\frac{7}{10}$ ________________
12. $\frac{4}{25}$ ________________

Write a percent for each shaded figure.

13.

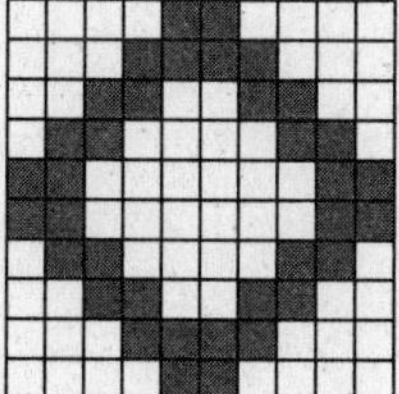

____

14.

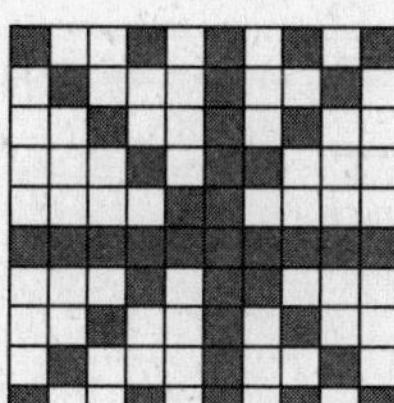

____

15.

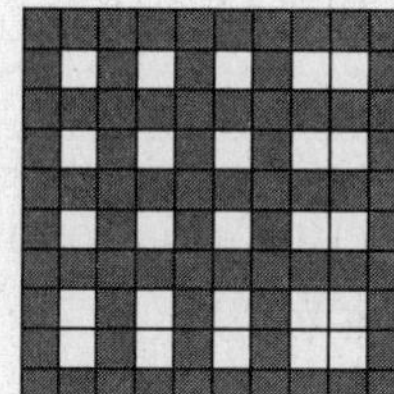

____

Complete the following.

Ancient Egyptians did not write the fraction $\frac{4}{5}$ as "$\frac{4}{5}$". Instead, they used *unit fractions.* The numerator of a unit fraction is always 1. No denominator used to represent a given fraction can be repeated. For this reason, Egyptians would have written $\frac{4}{5}$ as $\frac{1}{2} + \frac{1}{5} + \frac{1}{10}$ and not as $\frac{1}{2} + \frac{1}{10} + \frac{1}{10} + \frac{1}{10}$. Write each of the following as a sum of unit fractions.

16. $\frac{3}{4}$ ________________
17. $\frac{5}{8}$ ________________
18. $\frac{7}{12}$ ________________

Name ______________________ Class ______________ Date ______________

Activity Lab 6-1

Understanding Percents

Materials needed: counters, paper

Work in groups of 4 students.

1. In each group, one student should have 100 counters, one should have 50 counters, one should have 20 counters, and one should have 5 counters.

2. Each group member should remove the number of counters necessary to model $\frac{1}{5}$ of his or her counters.

3. a. How many counters did each group member remove?

   b. Copy and complete the table below.

Number of Counters	To model $\frac{1}{5}$, remove ___ counters.
1. 100 counters	
2. 50 counters	
3. 20 counters	
4. 5 counters	

   c. Use the information in the table to write the fractions equivalent to $\frac{1}{5}$.

4. The term *percent* means "per hundred." How can you use the models above to determine the percent equivalent to $\frac{1}{5}$? Write the percent.

5. Have the group member with 100 counters count out 20 counters. This represents 0.20 of the counters. How does the model compare or differ from the model of 20% or $\frac{1}{5}$? Explain.

6. Have each group member use their counters to model the following fraction, decimal, and percent. Copy and complete the table.

Number of Counters	To model 60%, remove ___ counters.	To model $\frac{4}{5}$, remove ___ counters.	To model 0.40, remove ___ counters.
1. 100 counters			
2. 50 counters			
3. 20 counters			
4. 5 counters			

7. Use your counters and the table to help you to write the equivalent fractions, decimals, and percents that correspond to 60%, to $\frac{4}{5}$, and to 0.40.

Name ______________________ Class ______________ Date ______________

Reteaching 6-1

Understanding Percents

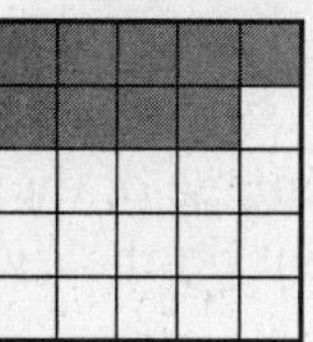

A **percent** is a ratio that compares a number to 100. The figure at the right contains 25 squares.

$\frac{9}{25}$ of the squares are shaded.

To write $\frac{9}{25}$ as a percent, follow these steps.

① Write a ratio with a denominator of 100 that is equal to $\frac{9}{25}$.

$$\frac{9}{25} = \frac{9 \cdot 4}{25 \cdot 4} = \frac{36}{100}$$

② Write the ratio as a percent.

$$\frac{36}{100} = 36\%$$

36% of the squares are shaded.

Write a percent for each shaded figure.

1. 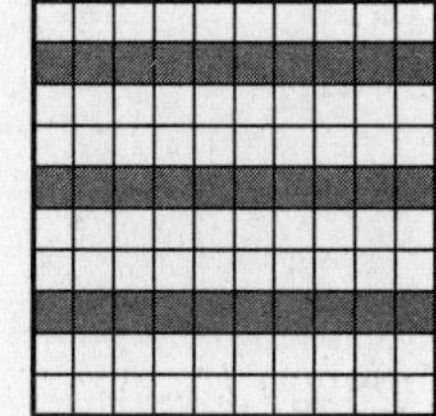 ______________

2. 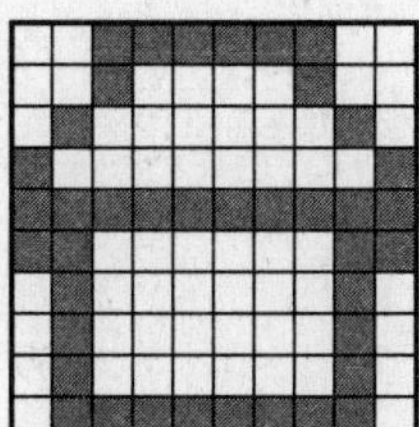 ______________

3. 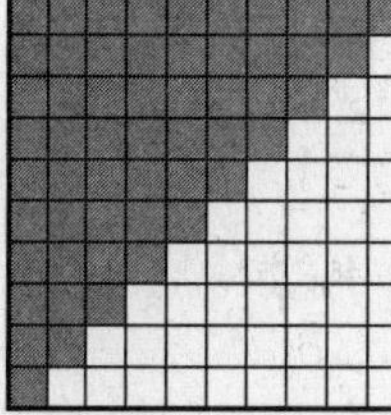 ______________

4.  ______________

5. 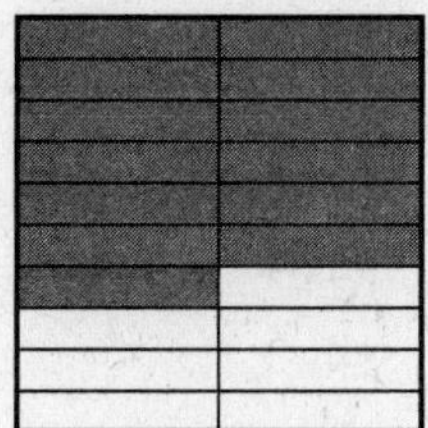 ______________

6. 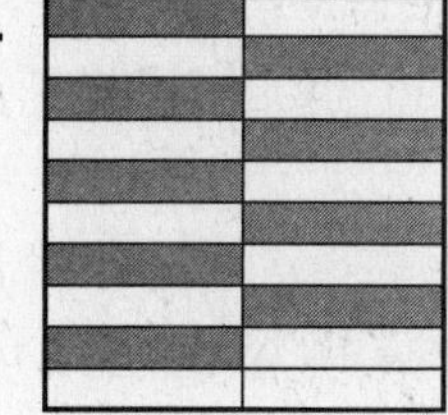 ______________

Write each ratio as a percent.

7. $\frac{3}{5}$ ______________
8. $\frac{17}{100}$ ______________
9. $\frac{18}{25}$ ______________
10. $\frac{8}{10}$ ______________
11. $\frac{1}{4}$ ______________
12. $\frac{17}{50}$ ______________
13. $\frac{7}{20}$ ______________
14. $\frac{21}{25}$ ______________
15. $\frac{3}{10}$ ______________
16. $\frac{2}{5}$ ______________
17. $\frac{99}{100}$ ______________
18. $\frac{11}{20}$ ______________
19. $\frac{1}{10}$ ______________
20. $\frac{39}{50}$ ______________
21. $\frac{19}{20}$ ______________

Name ______________________ Class ______________ Date ______________

Enrichment 6-1

Understanding Percents

Visual Thinking

Estimate the percentage of the figure that is shaded. Then circle the approximate percent on the right. Explain your answers.

1. 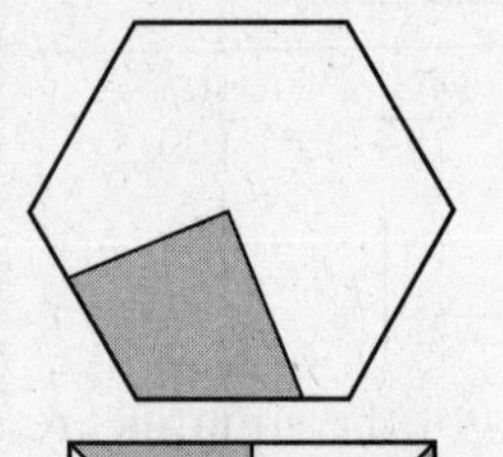

25%	33%	75%	90%
a.	**b.**	**c.**	**d.**

2. 

60%	25%	50%	37.5%
a.	**b.**	**c.**	**d.**

3. 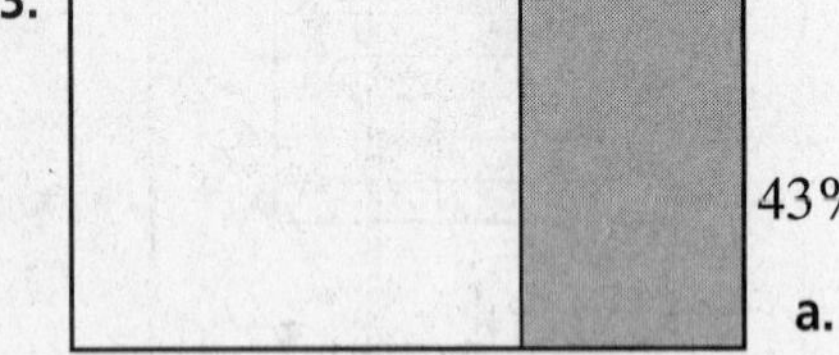

43%	50%	$33\frac{1}{3}\%$	25%
a.	**b.**	**c.**	**d.**

4. 

25%	40%	55%	70%
a.	**b.**	**c.**	**d.**

5. 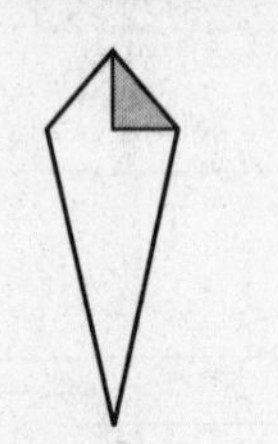

40%	$33\frac{1}{3}\%$	25%	14%
a.	**b.**	**c.**	**d.**

6. 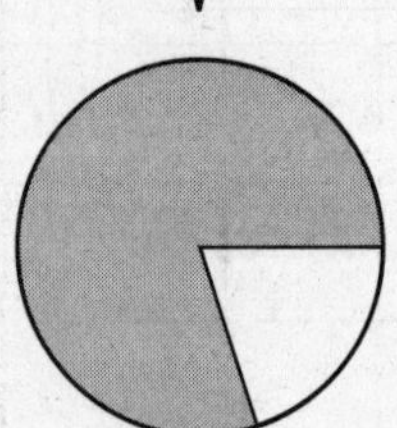

90%	80%	70%	60%
a.	**b.**	**c.**	**d.**

6A: Graphic Organizer

For use before Lesson 6-1

Study Skill As you read over the material in the chapter, keep a paper and pencil handy to write down notes and questions that you have.

Write your answers.

1. What is the chapter title? ____________________
2. How many lessons are there in this chapter? ____________________
3. What is the topic of the Test-Taking Strategies page? ____________________
4. Complete the graphic organizer below as you work through the chapter.
   - In the center, write the title of the chapter.
   - When you begin a lesson, write the lesson name in a rectangle.
   - When you complete a lesson, write a skill or key concept in a circle linked to that lesson block.
   - When you complete the chapter, use this graphic organizer to help you review.

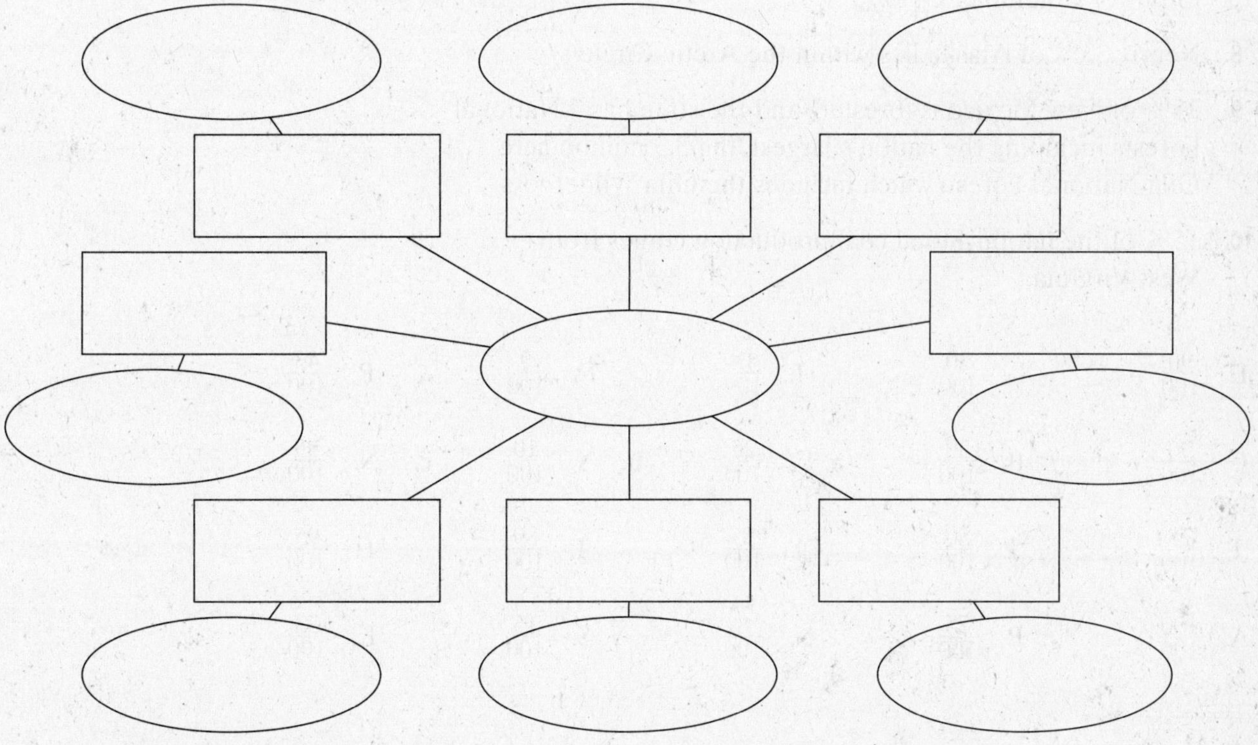

Name ____________________ Class ____________ Date ____________

Puzzle 6-1

Understanding Percents

Match the ratio to the percent fact. Use the letter of each ratio to decode the secret word.

1. Forests cover nearly 75% of West Virginia.
2. New Jersey has the highest percent urban population in the U.S. with about 89% of the people living in an urban area.
3. Nevada is the seventh largest state with an area of 110,540 square miles, 85% of them federally owned including the secret Area 51 near the little town of Rachel.
4. Maine produces 90% of the toothpick supply in the United States.
5. The only state whose eastern and western borders are 100% formed by water is Iowa.
6. Maryland's forests cover approximately 2.7 million acres, which is 43% of the state's land surface.
7. 50% of the United States population lives within a 500-mile radius of Columbus, Ohio.
8. Nearly 33% of Alaska lies within the Arctic Circle.
9. 25% of New Mexico is forested, and the state has 7 National Forests including the nation's largest, the 3.3 million acre Gila National Forest, which includes the Gila Wilderness.
10. 15% of the nation's total coal production comes from West Virginia.

E. $\frac{90}{100}$	L. $\frac{30}{100}$	I. $\frac{1}{10}$	R. $\frac{9}{100}$	P. $\frac{43}{100}$
C. $\frac{30}{100}$	P. $\frac{50}{100}$	E. $\frac{25}{100}$	A. $\frac{10}{100}$	N. $\frac{85}{100}$
T. $\frac{28}{100}$	I. $\frac{80}{100}$	O. $\frac{55}{100}$	I. $\frac{89}{100}$	F. $\frac{95}{100}$
A. $\frac{100}{100}$	P. $\frac{75}{100}$	N. $\frac{8}{100}$	S. $\frac{15}{100}$	L. $\frac{33}{100}$

More than 33% of the world's commercial supply of this crop comes from Hawaii.

___ ___ ___ ___ ___ ___ ___ ___ ___ ___

1 2 3 4 5 6 7 8 9 10

Name ______________________ Class ______________ Date ____________

Practice 6-2

Percents, Fractions, and Decimals

Write each percent as a fraction in simplest form and as a decimal.

1. 65% ________ **2.** 37.5% ________ **3.** 80% ________ **4.** 25% ________

5. 18% ________ **6.** 46% ________ **7.** 87% ________ **8.** 8% ________

9. 43% ________ **10.** 55% ________ **11.** 94% ________ **12.** 36% ________

Write each number as a percent. Round to the nearest tenth of a percent where necessary.

13. $\frac{8}{15}$ ________ **14.** $\frac{7}{50}$ ________ **15.** 0.56 ________

16. 0.0413 ________ **17.** $\frac{3}{8}$ ________ **18.** $\frac{7}{12}$ ________

19. 0.387 ________ **20.** 0.283 ________ **21.** $\frac{2}{9}$ ________

Write each number as a percent. Place the number into the puzzle without using the percent sign or decimal point.

22.

Across

1. 0.134
3. $\frac{53}{100}$
5. 0.565
7. $1\frac{7}{50}$
9. 0.456
10. 0.63
11. $\frac{11}{200}$
13. 0.58
14. $\frac{191}{200}$
16. 0.605

Down

2. 0.346
4. 0.324
5. $\frac{1}{2}$
6. 0.515
8. $\frac{33}{200}$
9. 0.4385
10. $\frac{659}{1,000}$
12. $\frac{1,087}{20,000}$
15. $\frac{14}{25}$

1.	2.			
			3.	4.
5.		6.		
		7.	8.	
	9.			
10.			11.	12.
13.				
14.		15.		
		16.		

Name ______________________ Class ______________ Date ____________

6-2 • Guided Problem Solving

GPS Student Page 283, Exercise 35:

Your teacher uses different methods of grading quizzes. Your quiz grades are 85%, $\frac{9}{10}$, $\frac{16}{20}$, 92%, $\frac{21}{25}$, and 79%.

a. Write your quiz grades in order from least to greatest.

b. Find the average percent grade of your quizzes.

Understand

1. What are you being asked to do in part (a)?

____

____

2. In order to compare the grades, what should you do first?

____

____

3. Besides knowing the grades of the quizzes, explain what else is needed to find the average.

____

Plan and Carry Out

4. What are all your grades in percent form?

____

5. Order the grades from smallest to largest.

____

6. What is the total of all your grades? ____________

7. Find the average percent grade of your six quizzes. ____________

Check

8. Does the average grade fall between the smallest and largest grade?

____

Solve Another Problem

9. Your classmate had quiz grades of 75%, $\frac{13}{20}$, $\frac{15}{25}$, 89%, $\frac{8}{10}$, and 81%. Order the grades from least to greatest and find the average.

____

Name ______________________ Class ______________ Date ______________

Practice 6-2

Percents, Fractions, and Decimals

Write each percent as a fraction in simplest form and as a decimal.

1. 65% ______________ **2.** 37.5% ______________ **3.** 80% ______________

4. 18% ______________ **5.** 46% ______________ **6.** 87% ______________

7. 43% ______________ **8.** 55% ______________ **9.** 94% ______________

Write each number as a percent. Round to the nearest tenth of a percent where necessary.

10. $\frac{8}{15}$ ______________ **11.** $\frac{7}{50}$ ______________

12. 0.0413 ______________ **13.** $\frac{3}{8}$ ______________

14. 0.387 ______________ **15.** 0.283 ______________

Write each number as a percent. Place the number into the puzzle without using the percent sign or decimal point.

16.

Across

1. 0.134
3. $\frac{53}{100}$
5. 0.565
7. $1\frac{7}{50}$
9. 0.456
10. 0.63
11. $\frac{11}{200}$

Down

2. 0.346
4. 0.324
5. $\frac{1}{2}$
6. 0.515
8. $\frac{33}{200}$
9. 0.43

1.	2.			
			3.	4.
5.		6.		
		7.	8.	
	9.			
10.			11.	

Name ______________________ Class ______________ Date ______________

Activity Lab 6-2

Percents, Fractions, and Decimals

Francisca started a stock portfolio. She bought 20 shares of Stock 1 for $62.50 and 20 shares of Stock 2 for $75.00. In the first week after she bought the stock, she recorded these daily closing prices. You may want to change the stock prices to decimals to solve.

Stock	Date of Purchase	Mon.	Tues.	Wed.	Thurs.	Fri.
Stock 1		$3\frac{1}{2}$	$3\frac{1}{8}$	$3\frac{7}{8}$	$2\frac{3}{4}$	$3\frac{7}{8}$
Stock 2		$3\frac{1}{8}$	$2\frac{3}{4}$	$3\frac{1}{4}$	$3\frac{1}{8}$	$2\frac{5}{8}$

1. Find the cost Francisca paid for one share of each stock. Record the price in the table.

2. What was the percent change in the price of Stock 1 from date of purchase to the Friday's closing price? Was it an increase or a decrease?

   ____

3. What was the percent change in the price of Stock 2 from date of purchase to the Friday's closing price? Was it an increase or a decrease?

   ____

4. Which stock had the greatest one-day change? Was it an increase or a decrease?

   ____

5. Francisca would like to see the price of Stock 1 increase at least 12% in one year. What will the price of one share be if it has that percent increase?

   ____

6. Francisca would like to see the price of Stock 2 increase at least 16% in one year. What will the price of one share be if it has that percent increase?

   ____

7. If both of Francisca's stocks achieve the minimum price increase, what will be the average percent increase in her portfolio? Show how you determined your answer.

   ____

   ____

8. Select a stock. Record the stock price from the daily newspaper. Determine the daily and weekly percent change. Remember that one week may not adequately reflect the true value of the stock.

Name ______________________ Class ______________ Date ______________

Reteaching 6-2

Percents, Fractions, and Decimals

To write a percent as a fraction, write a fraction with 100 as the denominator.

$45\% = \frac{45}{100}$ ← **Denominator 100**

$= \frac{45 \div 5}{100 \div 5} = \frac{9}{20}$ ← **Simplify.**

$45\% = \frac{9}{20}$

To write a decimal as a percent, multiply by 100.

Write 0.85 as a percent.

$0.85 \cdot 100 = 85$

$0.85 = 85\%$

To write a percent as a decimal, divide by 100.

Write 46% as a decimal.

$46 \div 100 = 0.46$

$46\% = 0.46$

Write each fraction as a percent.

1. $\frac{3}{4}$ ______
2. $\frac{12}{25}$ ______
3. $\frac{4}{5}$ ______
4. $\frac{23}{4}$ ______

Write each percent as a fraction in simplest form.

5. 45% ______
6. 60% ______
7. 16% ______
8. 25% ______
9. 37.5% ______
10. 99% ______
11. 40% ______
12. 86% ______

Write each percent as a decimal or each decimal as a percent.

13. 35% ______
14. 48% ______
15. 8% ______
16. 12% ______
17. 5.5% ______
18. 0.6% ______
19. 0.39 ______
20. 0.735 ______
21. 0.34 ______
22. 0.4 ______
23. 0.6 ______
24. 6 ______

Name ______________________ Class ______________ Date ______________

Enrichment 6-2

Percents, Fractions, and Decimals

Critical Thinking

Use the clues below to complete the Venn Diagram. Write a percent for each clue. Then, write the number that appears in each section below. The total of the numbers in all of the sections is 100.

1. 0.5 of the total is in the entire area of Circle A. ______
2. 45% of the total is in the entire area of Circle B. ______
3. $\frac{13}{20}$ of the total is in the entire area of Circle C. ______
4. 0.15 of the total is in Circles A and B. ______
5. 27% of the total is in Circles A and C. ______
6. $\frac{6}{25}$ of the total is in Circles B and C. ______
7. 0.09 of the total is in Circles A and B, but *not* in Circle C. ______
8. 21% of the total is in Circles A and C, but *not* in Circle B. ______
9. 0.18 of the total is in Circles B and C, but *not* in Circle A. ______
10. $\frac{3}{50}$ of the total is in Circles A, B, and C. ______
11. Write the numbers in each section of the Venn Diagram.

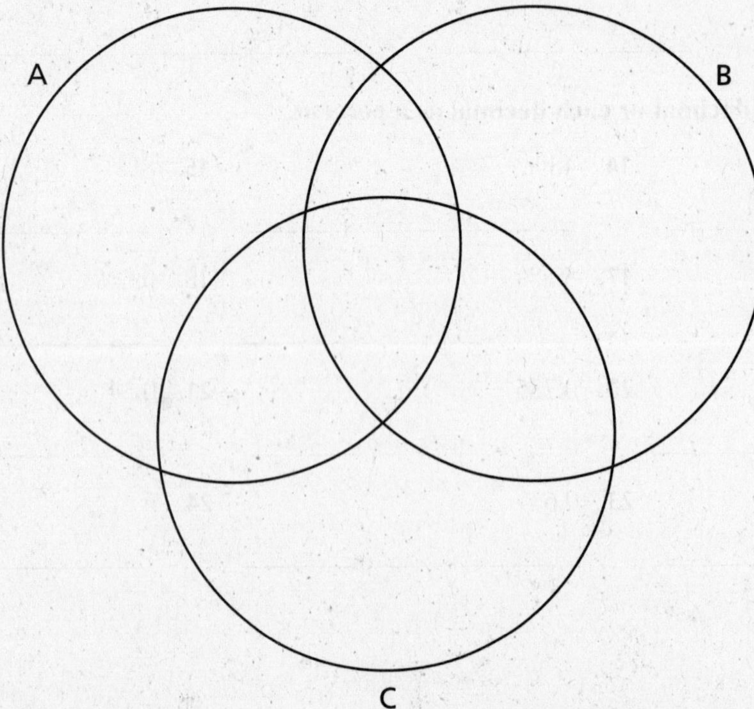

6B: Reading Comprehension

For use after Lesson 6-2

Study Skill Use a special notebook (or section of a loose-leaf binder) for your math handouts and homework. Keep your notebook neat and organized by reviewing its contents often.

Use the graphs shown below to answer the questions that follow.

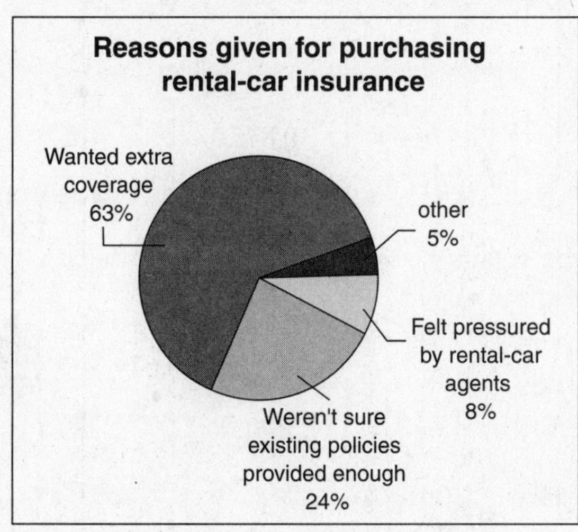

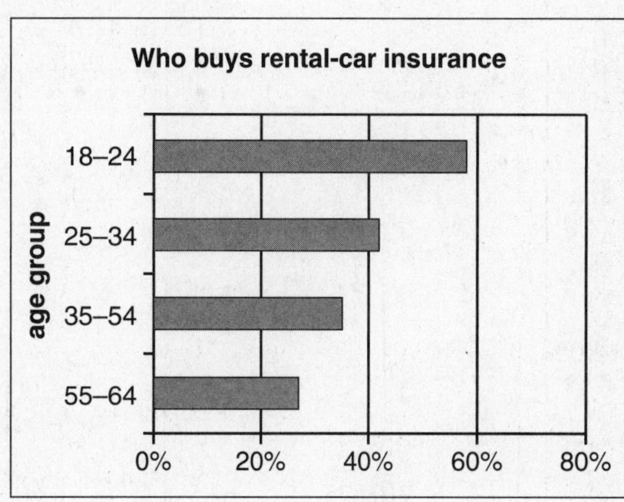

1. What information do the graphs show?

 ____

 ____

2. What is the top reason people purchase rental-car insurance?

 ____

3. What is the total of the percents for reasons people purchase rental-car insurance?

 ____

4. Which age group is most likely to purchase rental-car insurance?

 ____

5. Approximately $\frac{1}{3}$ of the renters in which age group purchase rental-car insurance?

 ____

6. Approximately $\frac{1}{4}$ of the renters purchase rental-car insurance for what reason?

 ____

7. **High-Use Academic Words** In Exercise 1, what does the word *show* mean?

 a. to display b. to put in a sequence

Name ______________________ Class ______________ Date ____________

Puzzle 6-2

Percents, Fractions, and Decimals

Some of the percents, decimals, and fractions in the diagram are equivalent. Decimals are rounded to the nearest hundredth. To find the hidden pattern in the diagram, use a ruler to draw straight lines between equivalent values.

50% • $\frac{1}{3}$ • 0.78 • $\frac{3}{12}$ •

75% • 0.875 •

$\frac{5}{8}$ • $\frac{20}{25}$ •

90% • 0.67 •

0.625 • 62.5% • 0.80 • 80% •

0.75 • $\frac{3}{4}$ • $\frac{7}{8}$ • 87.5% •

$\frac{1}{2}$ • 0.5 • 25% • 0.25 •

Name ______________________ Class ______________ Date ______________

Practice 6-3

Percents Greater Than 100% or Less Than 1%

Classify each of the following as: (A) less than 1%, (B) greater than 100%, or (C) between 1% and 100%.

1. $\frac{1}{2}$ ______
2. $\frac{4}{3}$ ______
3. $\frac{2}{300}$ ______
4. $\frac{3}{10}$ ______
5. 1.03 ______
6. 0.009 ______
7. 0.635 ______
8. 0.0053 ______

Use >, <, or = to compare the numbers in each pair.

9. $\frac{1}{4}$ ☐ 20%
10. $\frac{1}{2}$% ☐ 50
11. 0.008 ☐ 8%
12. 150% ☐ $\frac{5}{4}$
13. 3 ☐ 300%
14. $\frac{7}{250}$ ☐ 0.3%

Write each fraction as a percent. Round to the nearest tenth of a percent if necessary.

15. $\frac{7}{5}$ ______
16. $\frac{137}{100}$ ______
17. $\frac{0.8}{100}$ ______
18. $\frac{21}{4}$ ______
19. $\frac{17}{10}$ ______
20. $\frac{65}{40}$ ______
21. $\frac{37}{20}$ ______
22. $\frac{7}{500}$ ______
23. $\frac{9}{8}$ ______

Write each decimal as a percent.

24. 0.003 ______
25. 1.8 ______
26. 0.0025 ______
27. 5.3 ______
28. 0.0041 ______
29. 0.083 ______
30. 0.0009 ______
31. 0.83 ______
32. 20 ______

Write each percent as a decimal and as a fraction in simplest form.

33. 175% ______ ______
34. 120% ______ ______
35. $\frac{2}{5}$% ______ ______
36. $\frac{5}{8}$% ______ ______
37. 750% ______ ______
38. $8\frac{1}{4}$% ______ ______

39. In 1990, the population of Kansas was 2,477,574, which included 21,965 Native Americans. What percent of the people living in Kansas were Native Americans?

____

40. The mass of Earth is $\frac{1}{318}$ of the mass of Jupiter. What percent is this?

____

6-3 • Guided Problem Solving

GPS Student Page 287, Exercise 40:

Write the percent as a decimal and as a fraction in simplest form.

Weather On March 1, the snowpack in the Northern Great Basin of Nevada was 126% of the average snowpack.

Understand

1. What is the relevant information?

____

____

2. What are you being asked to do?

____

3. How do you convert a percent to a decimal?

____

Plan and Carry Out

4. When changing 126% to a fraction, what will be your numerator and denominator?

____

5. Write this fraction as a mixed number in simplest form.

____

6. Convert 126% to a decimal. ______________________

Check

7. Multiply the answer to Step 6 by 100. Does it equal the percent?

____

Solve Another Problem

Write the percent as a decimal and as a fraction in simplest form.

8. Of the students in a class, 66% are female.

____

Name ______________________ Class ______________ Date ____________

Practice 6-3

Percents Greater Than 100% or Less Than 1%

Classify each of the following as: (A) less than 1%, (B) greater than 100%, or (C) between 1% and 100%.

1. $\frac{1}{2}$ ____________
2. $\frac{4}{3}$ ____________
3. $\frac{2}{300}$ ____________
4. 1.03 ____________
5. 0.009 ____________
6. 0.635 ____________

Use >, <, or = to compare the numbers in each pair.

7. $\frac{1}{4}$ ☐ 20%
8. $\frac{1}{2}$% ☐ 50
9. 0.008 ☐ 8%
10. 150% ☐ $\frac{5}{4}$
11. 3 ☐ 300%
12. $\frac{7}{250}$ ☐ 0.3%

Write each fraction as a percent. Round to the nearest tenth of a percent if necessary.

13. $\frac{7}{5}$ ____________
14. $\frac{137}{100}$ ____________
15. $\frac{21}{4}$ ____________
16. $\frac{17}{10}$ ____________
17. $\frac{37}{20}$ ____________
18. $\frac{7}{500}$ ____________

Write each decimal as a percent.

19. 0.003 ____________
20. 1.8 ____________
21. 5.3 ____________
22. 0.0041 ____________
23. 0.0009 ____________
24. 0.83 ____________

Write each percent as a decimal and as a fraction in simplest form.

25. 175% ____________ ____________
26. 120% ____________ ____________
27. $\frac{2}{5}$% ____________ ____________

Solve.

28. In 1990, the population of Kansas was 2,477,574, which included 21,965 Native Americans. What percent of the people living in Kansas were Native Americans?

____

Name ______________________ Class ______________ Date ____________

Activity Lab 6-3 **Percents Greater than 100% or Less than 1%**

Materials needed: graphing calculator

Example 1: Write 120% as a decimal and fraction in simplest form.

① Enter 120 [%] [ENTER]. The calculator displays 1.2, which is the decimal equivalent of 120%.

② Press [F↔D] [ENTER]. This converts the previous answer, 1.2, to a fraction. The calculator displays $1\frac{1}{5}$. You can also just enter 1.2, and then press [F↔D] [ENTER].

Example 2: Write $5\frac{4}{7}$ as a percent rounded to the nearest whole percent.

① Enter 5 [UNIT] 4 [b/c] 7 [▶] [F↔D] [ENTER].

The calculator displays 5.571428571, which is a decimal approximation of $5\frac{4}{7}$. This is actually a non-terminating decimal that repeats the digits 571428 over and over without stopping.

② Press [×] 100 [ENTER]. This multiplies the previous answer (ans) by 100, which is what you must do to convert a decimal to a percent. The calculator displays 557.1428571.

③ Rounded to the nearest whole percent, $5\frac{4}{7}$ is 557%.

Exercises

Write each percent as a decimal and fraction in simplest form.

1. 130%

2. 0.6%

3. 421%

4. 6,172%

Write each fraction as a percent rounded to the nearest whole percent.

5. $1\frac{1}{4}$

6. $2\frac{5}{16}$

7. $8\frac{19}{32}$

8. $12\frac{27}{28}$

Name ______________________ Class ______________ Date ______________

Reteaching 6-3

Percents Greater Than 100% or Less Than 1%

You can express a percent that is less than 1% or greater than 100% as a decimal and as a fraction. A percent that is less than 1% is a quantity that is less than $\frac{1}{100}$. A percent that is greater than 100% is a quantity that is greater than 1.

- Write 0.5% as a decimal and as a fraction.

Move the decimal point two places to the left to write a percent as a decimal. Add zeros as needed. $00.5\% = 0.005$

Since percent means per 100, you can write the percent as a fraction with a denominator of 100. $0.5\% = \frac{0.5}{100}$

Then rewrite the numerator as a whole number. Since $10 \times 0.5 = 5$, multiply the numerator and the denominator by 10. Then simplify. $\frac{0.5}{100} = \frac{0.5 \times 10}{100 \times 10} = \frac{5}{1{,}000} = \frac{1}{200}$

So, $0.5\% = 0.005 = \frac{1}{200}$.

- Write 125% as a decimal and as a fraction.

Move the decimal point two places to the left to write a percent as a decimal. Add zeros as needed. $125\% = 1.25.$

Since percent means per 100, you can write the percent as a fraction with a denominator of 100. $125\% = \frac{125}{100}$

Then simplify. $\frac{125}{100} = \frac{125 \div 25}{100 \div 25} = \frac{5}{4} = 1\frac{1}{4}$

So, $125\% = 1.25 = 1\frac{1}{4}$.

Write each percent as a fraction in simplest form and as a decimal.

1. 0.01% ______________

2. 0.45% ______________

3. 0.2% ______________

4. 0.67% ______________

5. 150% ______________

6. 225% ______________

7. 186% ______________

8. 201% ______________

Name ______________________ Class ____________ Date ____________

Enrichment 6-3

Percents Greater Than 100% or Less Than 1%

Critical Thinking

Answer the questions with the information given.

A small percent of bats carries rabies—generally, about $\frac{1}{2}$%. In how large a group of bats would you expect to find exactly one bat carrying rabies? Explain how you found your answer.

1. What percent of bats carries rabies? ____________

2. Write $\frac{1}{2}$% as a fraction. ____________

3. Write your fraction from Exercise 2 with a whole number in the numerator.

   ____

4. Explain what your fraction means by giving the number of bats that may have rabies and the group size.

   ____

   ____

5. Write a fraction with a numerator of 1 equivalent to the fraction you wrote in Exercise 3.

   ____

6. About how large would you expect a group of bats to be if one bat carries rabies?

   ____

7. Explain how you found your answer.

   ____

   ____

   ____

8. Does your answer mean that every group of bats this size will have exactly one bat with rabies? Explain.

   ____

   ____

   ____

Name ______________________ Class ______________ Date ______________

Puzzle 6-3

Percents Greater Than 100% or Less Than 1%

Match each fraction with a percent. The extra answer is the solution to the puzzle at the bottom of the page. Values are rounded to the nearest hundredth where necessary.

Fraction	Percent
$\frac{67}{20} =$	0.61%
$\frac{129}{50} =$	258%
$\frac{19}{8} =$	178.79%
$\frac{23}{200} =$	43.75%
$\frac{75}{20} =$	237.5%
$\frac{2}{329} =$	0.24%
$\frac{6}{767} =$	11.5%
$\frac{35}{80} =$	335%
$\frac{45}{13} =$	346.15%
$\frac{59}{33} =$	375%
	0.78%

Puzzle: The area of Rhode Island is _____ of the area of Alaska.

Name _______________ Class _______________ Date _______________

Practice 6-4

Finding a Percent of a Number

Find each answer.

1. 20% of 560 ______
2. 42% of 200 ______
3. 9% of 50 ______
4. 40% of 70 ______
5. 25% of 80 ______
6. 50% of 80 ______
7. 40% of 200 ______
8. 5% of 80 ______
9. 75% of 200 ______

Find each answer using mental math.

10. 14% of 120 ______
11. 30% of 180 ______
12. 62.5% of 24 ______
13. 34% of 50 ______
14. 25% of 240 ______
15. 85.5% of 23 ______
16. 120% of 56 ______
17. 80% of 90 ______
18. 42% of 120 ______

Solve.

19. A farmer grew a watermelon that weighed 20 lb. From his experience with growing watermelons, he estimated that 95% of the watermelon's weight is water.

    a. How much of the watermelon is water?

    ______

    b. How much of the watermelon is not water?

    ______

    c. The watermelon was shipped off to market, where it sat until it had dehydrated (lost water). If the watermelon is still 90% water, what percent of it is not water?

    ______

    d. The solid part of the watermelon still weighs the same. What was the weight of the watermelon at this point?

    ______

20. A bicycle goes on sale at 75% of its original price of $160. What is its sale price?

    ______

6-4 • Guided Problem Solving

GPS Student Page 293, Exercise 41:

Forestry Russia had 17,000 forest fires in 2001. Aircraft put out 40% of the fires. How many of the fires were put out by aircraft?

Understand

1. What is the relevant information in the problem?

____

2. What are you being asked to do?

____

____

3. How will changing 40% to an equivalent decimal help you solve the problem?

____

Plan and Carry Out

4. What is the percent of fires in Russian forests that were put out by aircraft?

____

____

5. Write 40% as a decimal. ____________
6. What is the total number of Russian forest fires? ____________
7. Multiply your decimal answer from Step 5 by 17,000.

____

8. How many of the fires were put out by aircraft? ____________

Check

9. What is 50% of 17,000? Is the number of fires put out by aircraft less than this?

____

Solve Another Problem

10. Your mother says that 80% of your shirts are dirty. If you have 30 shirts, how many are dirty?

____

Name ______________________ Class ______________ Date ______________

Practice 6-4

Finding a Percent of a Number

Find each answer.

1. 20% of 560 ______
2. 42% of 200 ______
3. 9% of 50 ______
4. 40% of 70 ______
5. 25% of 80 ______
6. 50% of 80 ______

Find each answer using mental math.

7. 14% of 120 ______
8. 30% of 180 ______
9. 34% of 50 ______
10. 25% of 240 ______

Solve.

11. A farmer grew a watermelon that weighed 20 lb. From his experience with growing watermelons, he estimated that 95% of the watermelon's weight is water.
    a. How much of the watermelon is water?

    ______

    b. How much of the watermelon is not water?

    ______

    c. The watermelon was shipped off to market, where it sat until it had dehydrated (lost water). If the watermelon is still 90% water, what percent of it is not water?

    ______

12. A bicycle goes on sale at 75% of its original price of $160. What is its sale price?

______

Name ______________________ Class ______________ Date ______________

Activity Lab 6-4

Finding a Percent of a Number

What's the Question?

Each expression below shows how to find a percent of a number. For each exercise, write the percent question that the expression was created to answer, and then solve the expression. Round your answers to the nearest tenth. The first one is done for you.

1. 0.35×47

Question: What is 35% of 47?

Answer: 16.5

2. 0.75×4

Question: ______________________

Answer: ______________________

3. $\frac{1}{4} \times 80$

Question: ______________________

Answer: ______________________

4. $40 \times \frac{6}{25}$

Question: ______________________

Answer: ______________________

5. $\frac{3}{100} \times 90$

Question: ______________________

Answer: ______________________

6. 0.2×55

Question: ______________________

Answer: ______________________

7. 74×0.08

Question: ______________________

Answer: ______________________

8. $\frac{1}{10} \times 15$

Question: ______________________

Answer: ______________________

9. $\frac{8}{50} \times 36$

Question: ______________________

Answer: ______________________

10. 0.01×100

Question: ______________________

Answer: ______________________

Name ______________________ Class ______________ Date ______________

Reteaching 6-4

Finding a Percent of a Number

	Find 12% of 50.	Find 150% of 90.
① Write the percent as a decimal.	0.12	1.5
② Multiply.	$0.12 \cdot 50 = 6$	$1.5 \cdot 90 = 135$
	12% of 50 is 6.	150% of 90 is 135.

Complete to find each answer.

1. 15% of 80

15% = ________

________ $\cdot$ 80 = ________

2. 4% of 70

4% = ________

________ $\cdot$ 70 = ________

3. 70% of 20

70% = ________

________ $\cdot$ 20 = ________

Find each answer.

4. 10% of 80 ________

5. 20% of 80 ________

6. 50% of 80 ________

7. 9% of 70 ________

8. 2% of 66 ________

9. 28% of 50 ________

10. 16% of 35 ________

11. 94% of 22 ________

12. 33% of 50 ________

13. 120% of 30 ________

14. 110% of 70 ________

15. 160% of 200 ________

16. 145% of 78 ________

17. 187% of 40 ________

18. 164% of 350 ________

Solve.

19. Pablo's weekly salary is $105. Each week he saves 60% of his salary. How much does he save each week?

____

20. The sixth-grade class is selling magazine subscriptions to raise money for charity. They will give 55% of the money they raise to the homeless. If they raise $2,670, how much do they give to the homeless?

____

Name _______________ Class _______________ Date _______________

Enrichment 6-4

Finding a Percent of a Number

Patterns in Data

You can graph some percents and use the graph to estimate other values. Use these interest rates and principal amounts to find the annual amount of interest due on each loan. Then graph your results.

1. You borrow money and pay 15% interest. Solve to find the interest due for each loan amount.

a. 15% of 100 _______

b. 15% of 80 _______

c. 15% of 40 _______

d. 15% of 60 _______

2. Graph each of your solutions from Exercise 1. Connect the points. Label the line 15%.

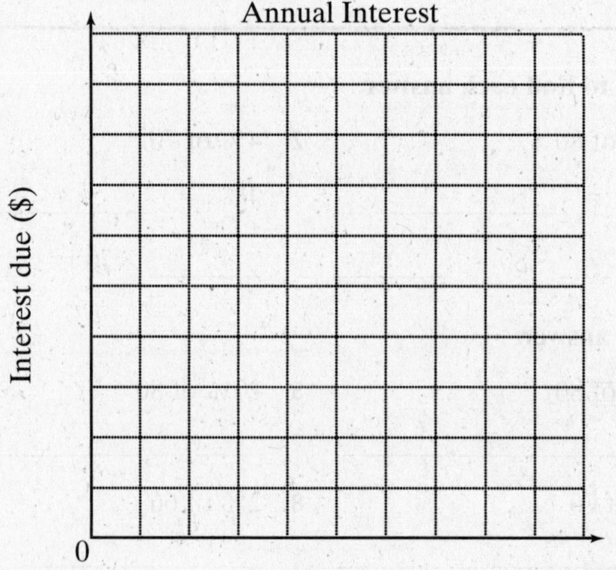

3. Describe the graph. _______________

____

4. How can you use the graph to estimate 15% of 65.2? _______________

____

____

5. Why might it be helpful to graph this information? _______________

____

6. Choose another interest rate and find the interest for these principal amounts. Then graph your solutions.

a. _______ of 100 _______ **b.** _______ of 80 _______

c. _______ of 40 _______ **d.** _______ of 60 _______

7. Use the graph for the interest rate you chose to predict the annual interest due for a loan of $25.

____

Name ______________________ Class ______________ Date ______________

6C: Reading/Writing Math Symbols

For use after Lesson 6-4

Study Skill When working on your math homework, use a pencil and have an eraser nearby.

Write each of the following using appropriate mathematical symbols and abbreviations.

1. 3 feet to 1 yard ______________________
2. 47 and 6 tenths percent ______________________
3. 37 percent is greater than $\frac{1}{3}$ ______________________
4. 1 meter to 100 centimeters ______________________
5. 106 percent ______________________
6. $\frac{1}{4}$ is less than 26% ______________________
7. 8 quarts to 2 gallons ______________________
8. 93 and 32 hundredths percent ______________________
9. the absolute value of negative 16 ______________________
10. 78 out of 100 ______________________

Write each of the following in words.

11. $|-7.3| = 7.3$

    ____

12. 30.08%

    ____

13. $50\% > \frac{2}{5}$

    ____

14. 2 h : 120 min

    ____

15. $\frac{55}{100}$

    ____

16. $\frac{1}{10} < 12\%$

    ____

Name ______________________ Class ______________ Date ____________

Puzzle 6-4

Finding a Percent of a Number

The rectangle below is divided into six sections. The area of each section has been labeled. On the blanks, write the letter that describes the area of each section as either a percent, a decimal, or a fraction of the total area of the rectangle.

A. 30%	N. 39%	I. $\frac{3}{100}$
E. 0.4	A. 2.5	G. $\frac{1}{4}$
O. $\frac{1}{25}$	S. 5%	D. 3.9
E. $\frac{1}{50}$	O. $\frac{1}{10}$	R. 0.2
I. 35%	L. $\frac{4}{10}$	T. 0.36

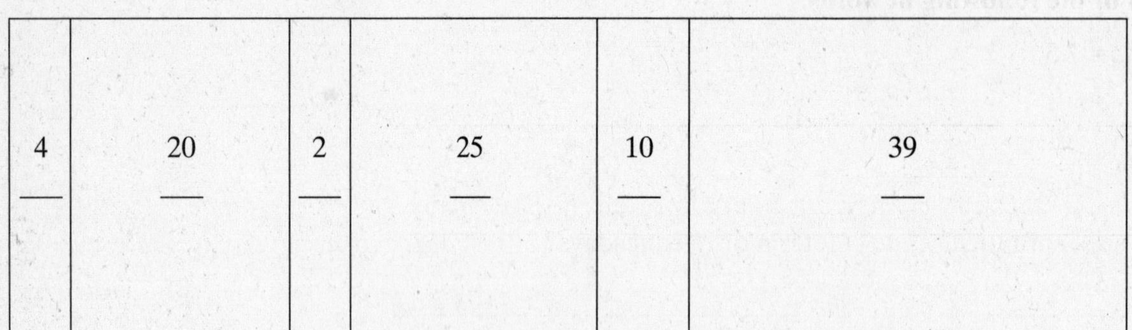

_____ _____ _____ _____ _____ _____ is the only state that has an official state nut, the hazelnut.

Name ______________ Class ______________ Date ______________

Practice 6-5

Solving Percent Problems Using Proportions

Use a proportion to solve.

1. 48 is 60% of what number? ______________

2. What is 175% of 85? ______________

3. What percent of 90 is 50? ______________

4. 76 is 80% of what number? ______________

5. What is 50% of 42.88? ______________

6. 96 is 160% of what number? ______________

7. What percent of 24 is 72? ______________

8. What is 85% of 120? ______________

9. What is 80% of 12? ______________

10. 56 is 75% of what number? ______________

Solve.

11. The sale price of a bicycle is $120. This is 75% of the original price. Find the original price.

____

12. The attendance at a family reunion was 160 people. This was 125% of last year's attendance. How many people attended the reunion last year?

____

13. A company has 875 employees. On "Half-Price Wednesday," 64% of the employees eat lunch at the company cafeteria. How many employees eat lunch at the cafeteria on Wednesdays?

____

14. There are 1,295 students attending a small university. There are 714 women enrolled. What percentage of students are women?

____

Name ______________________ Class ______________ Date ______________

6-5 • Guided Problem Solving

GPS Student Page 297, Exercise 34:

At the library, you find 9 books on a certain topic. The librarian tells you that 55% of the books on this topic have been signed out. How many books does the library have on the topic?

Understand

1. Circle the information you will need to solve.
2. What are you being asked to do?

____

____

3. If 55% of the books have been signed out, what percent of the books have *not* been signed out?

____

Plan and Carry Out

4. Choose a variable to represent the total number of books the library has on the topic.

____

5. How many books did you find on the topic? ______________
6. Write a proportion comparing the percent of books in the library to the number of books in the library.

____

7. Solve the proportion. ______________________
8. How many books does the library have on the topic? ______________

Check

9. Is 55% of your answer plus 9 equal to your answer?

____

Solve Another Problem

10. There are 12,000 people attending a concert. You learn that 20% of the people who bought tickets to the concert did not attend. How many people bought tickets to the concert?

____

____

Name ______________________ Class ______________ Date ______________

Practice 6-5

Solving Percent Problems Using Proportions

Use a proportion to solve.

1. 48 is 60% of what number?

2. What is 175% of 85?

3. What percent of 90 is 50?

4. 76 is 80% of what number?

5. What is 50% of 42.88?

6. 96 is 160% of what number?

7. What percent of 24 is 72?

8. What is 85% of 120?

Solve.

9. The sale price of a bicycle is $120. This is 75% of the original price. Find the original price.

10. The attendance at a family reunion was 160 people. This was 125% of last year's attendance. How many people attended the reunion last year?

11. A company has 875 employees. On "Half-Price Wednesday," 64% of the employees eat lunch at the company cafeteria. How many employees eat lunch at the cafeteria on Wednesdays?

12. There are 1,295 students attending a small university. There are 714 women enrolled. What percentage of students are women?

Name ______________________ Class ______________ Date ______________

Activity Lab 6-5

Solving Percent Problems Using Proportions

Write proportions to find multiple percents of a number.

1. What is 25% of 40% of 45?

   a. Write a proportion to find 40% of 45. ____________

   b. What is 25% of your answer to Exercise 1a? ____________

2. a. Write a proportion to find 25% of 45. ____________

   b. What is 40% of your answer to Exercise 2a? ____________

3. a. What is 25% of 40%? ____________

   b. What is 45 multiplied by your answer to Exercise 3a? ____________

4. Compare how you found the answers to Exercises 1, 2, and 3. What are the similarities? What are the differences?

   ____

   ____

5. How can you use this observation to solve percent problems, such as 50% of 140% of 200 mentally?

   ____

   ____

6. If 50% of 120% of 30% of a number is 108, what is the number? Show how you found your answer.

   ____

   ____

   ____

7. If 40% of 60% of 25% is 54, what is the number? Show how you found your answer.

   ____

   ____

   ____

Name ______________ Class ______________ Date ______________

Reteaching 6-5

Solving Percent Problems Using Proportions

You can use proportions to solve percent problems. Remember, the percent is compared to 100.

Finding the part:

10% of 40 is _?_.

$\frac{10}{100} = \frac{n}{40}$

$100 \cdot n = 10 \cdot 40$

$n = 4$

10% of 40 is 4.

Finding the whole:

20% of _?_ is 8.

$\frac{20}{100} = \frac{8}{n}$

$20 \cdot n = 100 \cdot 8$

$n = 40$

20% of 40 is 8.

Finding the percent:

_?_ % of 25 is 20.

$\frac{n}{100} = \frac{20}{25}$

$25 \cdot n = 100 \cdot 20$

$n = 80$

80% of 25 is 20.

Complete to solve for *n*.

1. 75% of _?_ is 12.

   $\frac{75}{100} = \frac{12}{n}$

   $75 \cdot$ ______ $= 100 \cdot$ ______

   $n =$ ______

2. 20% of _?_ is 82.

   $\frac{20}{100} = \frac{82}{\square}$

   $20 \cdot$ ______ $= 100 \cdot$ ______

   $n =$ ______

3. 5% of _?_ is 9.

   $\frac{5}{100} = \frac{\square}{n}$

   ______ $=$ ______

   $n =$ ______

4. 60 is 5% of *n*.

   $\frac{5}{100} = \frac{\square}{n}$

   $5n = 100 \cdot$ ______

   $n =$ ______

5. 6% of *n* is 4.8.

   $\frac{6}{\square} = \frac{\square}{n}$

   $6n =$ ______ $\cdot\ 4.8$

   $n =$ ______

6. 51 is 170% of *n*.

   $\frac{\square}{100} = \frac{\square}{n}$

   ______ $=$ ______

   $n =$ ______

Use a proportion to solve.

7. 12% of *n* is 9.

   ____

8. 49% of *n* is 26.95.

   ____

9. 18% of *n* is 27.

   ____

10. What is 210% of 44?

    ____

11. What is 30% of 200?

    ____

12. 64 is what percent of 80?

    ____

Name ______________________ Class ______________ Date ______________

Enrichment 6-5

Solving Percent Problems Using Proportions

Decision Making

A library conducted a survey of the community about the kind of novels they read most often. A total of 40,000 people were surveyed. The results are shown in the circle graph at the right.

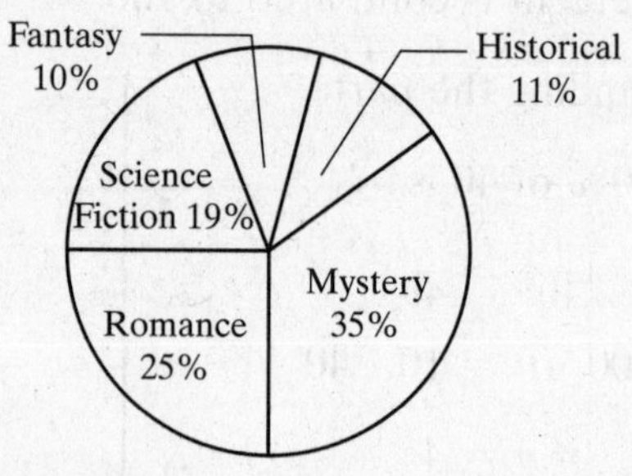

1. Use the information in the circle graph to find the number of people preferring each kind of book. Use a proportion to solve.

Kind of Novel	Percent of Community	Number of People in Community	Budget
Fantasy			
Historical			
Science Fiction			
Romance			
Mystery			

2. Why is a circle graph a good way to show percent information?

____

____

3. You can spend $250,000 on new library books. Write the amount you would spend for each kind of book in the table. Explain.

____

____

4. A patron gave the library $50,000 to expand the children's fiction section. How would you decide which kinds of books to buy? Would you use the survey results above?

____

____

____

____

Name ______________________ Class ______________ Date ______________

Puzzle 6-5

Solving Percent Problems Using Proportions

The middle school basketball coach was preparing awards for the upcoming sports banquet. During the season, he kept track of the number of freethrows each of his players attempted. He also recorded how many of the attempts were successful baskets. Help the coach determine which player should win the award for Highest Percent Freethrow Scorer by using the attempts and baskets to calculate the percent. Round each answer to the nearest tenth of a percent.

H. Player 3 : 64 attempts
51 baskets

G. Player 22 : 48 attempts
40 baskets

T. Player 7 : 36 attempts
28 baskets

E. Player 8 : 75 attempts
72 baskets

I. Player 55 : 82 attempts
77 baskets

Order your answers from greatest to least. Using the same order, write the exercise letter in the spaces below to complete the sentence.

Player number _____ _____ _____ _____ _____ should win the award.

Name ______________________ Class ______________ Date ______________

Practice 6-6

Solving Percent Problems Using Equations

Write and solve an equation. Round answers to the nearest tenth.

1. What percent of 64 is 48?

2. 16% of 130 is what number?

3. 25% of what number is 24?

4. What percent of 18 is 12?

5. 48% of 83 is what number?

6. 40% of what number is 136?

7. What percent of 530 is 107?

8. 74% of 643 is what number?

9. 62% of what number is 84?

10. What percent of 84 is 50?

11. 37% of 245 is what number?

12. 12% of what number is 105?

Solve.

13. A cafe offers senior citizens a 15% discount off its regular price of $8.95 for the dinner buffet.

    a. What percent of the regular price is the price for senior citizens?

    b. What is the price for senior citizens?

14. In 1990, 12.5% of the people in Oregon did not have health insurance. If the population of Oregon was 2,880,000, how many people were uninsured?

Name ______________________ Class ______________ Date ______________

6-6 • Guided Problem Solving

GPS Student Page 301, Exercise 28:

Food You make 72 cookies for a bake sale. This is 20% of the cookies at the bake sale. How many cookies are at the bake sale?

Understand

1. Circle the information you will need to solve.
2. What are you being asked to do?

   ____
3. What word indicates an equal sign?

   ____

Plan and Carry Out

4. Choose a variable to represent the number of cookies at the bake sale.

   ____
5. What number is 20% of the cookies at the bake sale? __________
6. Write an expression for the phrase, *20% of the cookies at the bake sale.*

   ____
7. Write an equation using what you wrote in Steps 5 and 6 to find the number of cookies at the bake sale.

   ____
8. Solve the equation. ______________________
9. How many cookies are at the bake sale? __________

Check

10. Find 20% of your answer. Does it equal 72?

    ____

Solve Another Problem

11. You collect trading cards and so far you have 12 different cards. If this is 30% of the possible cards, how many cards are there to collect?

    ____

Name ______________________ Class ______________ Date ______________

Practice 6-6

Solving Percent Problems Using Equations

Write and solve an equation. Round answers to the nearest tenth.

1. What percent of 64 is 48?

2. 16% of 130 is what number?

3. 25% of what number is 24?

4. What percent of 18 is 12?

5. 48% of 83 is what number?

6. 40% of what number is 136?

7. What percent of 530 is 107?

8. 74% of 643 is what number?

Solve.

9. A cafe offers senior citizens a 15% discount off its regular price of $8.95 for the dinner buffet.

a. What percent of the regular price is the price for senior citizens?

b. What is the price for senior citizens?

10. In 1990, 12.5% of the people in Oregon did not have health insurance. If the population of Oregon was 2,880,000, how many people were uninsured?

Name ____________________ Class ____________ Date ____________

Activity Lab 6-6

Solving Percent Problems Using Equations

You can graph some percents and use the graph to estimate other values. Use these interest rates and principal amounts to find the annual amount of interest due on each loan. Then graph your results.

1. You borrow money and pay 15% interest. Write an equation for each percent problem, and solve to find the interest due for each loan amount.

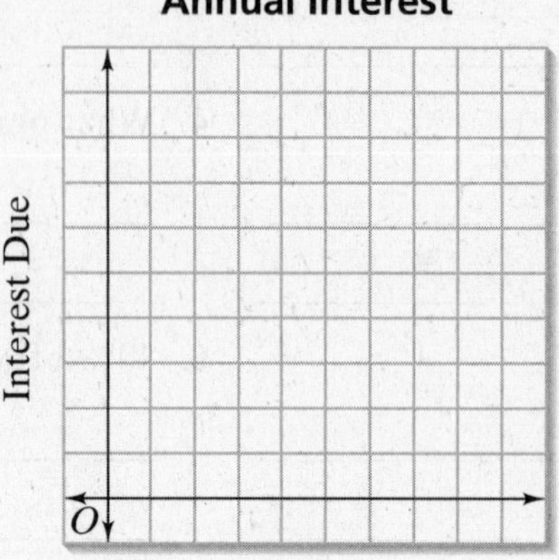

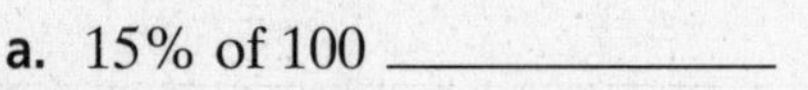

a. 15% of 100 ____________

b. 15% of 80 ____________

c. 15% of 40 ____________

d. 15% of 60 ____________

2. Graph each of your solutions from Exercise 1. Connect the points. Label the line 15%.

3. Describe the graph.

____

____

4. How can you use the graph to estimate 15% of 65.2?

____

____

5. Why might it be helpful to graph this information?

____

6. Choose another interest rate and find the interest for these principal amounts. Then graph your solutions.

a. ______ of 100 ______

b. ______ of 80 ______

c. ______ of 40 ______

d. ______ of 60 ______

7. Use the graph for the interest rate you chose to predict the annual interest due for a loan of $25.

____

Name ______________________ Class ______________ Date ______________

Reteaching 6-6

Solving Percent Problems Using Equations

You can write equations to solve percent problems by substituting amounts into the statement: "______ % of ______ is ______?"

- 64% of 50 is what number?

① Choose a variable for the unknown amount.	Let n = unknown number.
② Reword the statement, ______ % of ______ is ______.	64% of 50 is n
③ Write an equation.	$64\% \cdot 50 = n$
④ Write the percent as a decimal.	$0.64 \cdot 50 = n$
⑤ Multiply to solve for n.	$32 = n$
⑥ So, 64% of 50 is 32.	

- What percent of 36 is 18?

① Choose a variable for the unknown amount.	Let p = unknown percent.
② Reword the statement, ______ % of ______ is ______.	p% of 36 is 18.
③ Write an equation.	$36 \cdot p = 18$
④ Divide each side by 36.	$36 \cdot \frac{p}{36} = \frac{18}{36}$
⑤ Simplify and write the decimal as a percent.	$p = 0.5 = 50\%$
⑥ So, 18 is 50% of 36.	

Answer each question.

1. Write an equation for: 9% of 150 is what number. ______ · ______ = n
2. Solve the equation to find 9% of 150 is what number? ______
3. 48% of 250 is what number? ______
4. 82% of 75 is what number? ______
5. 32% of 800 is what number? ______
6. Reword the statement: What percent of 75 is 12? ______ % of ______ is ______
7. Use the statement to find what percent of 75 is 12. ______
8. What percent of 60 is 18? ______
9. What percent of 50 is 35? ______

Name ______________________ Class ______________ Date ____________

Enrichment 6-6

Solving Percent Problems Using Equations

Critical Thinking

A bin contains 120 ears of white corn and yellow corn. Of these, 78 ears are yellow. What percent of the ears of corn are yellow? What percent are white?

1. How many ears of corn are in the bin?

   ____

2. How many of the ears of corn in the bin are yellow?

   ____

3. What are you asked to find?

   ____

4. What percent of the corn is made up of both the yellow and the white ears?

   ____

5. Write an equation to find the percent of yellow ears.

   ____

6. Which operation can you use to find the percent of white corn once you know what percent is yellow and the total percent?

   ____

7. Solve your equation to find the percent of yellow corn.

   ____

8. What is the percent of white corn in the bin?

   ____

9. Check your answer by writing, then solving, an equation to find the percent of *white* corn in the bin.

   ____

10. Suppose corn with white and yellow kernels is added to the bin so that the percentage of the white corn becomes 28%. How many ears of white-and-yellow corn were added to the bin? Explain.

   ____

Name ______________________ Class ______________ Date ______________

Puzzle 6-6

Solving Percent Problems Using Equations

Read the clues below. Write an equation to solve for the unknown number, then solve each equation.

CLUE	**EQUATION**
1. What number is 35% of 900?	______________
2. 1,554 is 25% of what number?	______________
3. What number is 20% of 4,985?	______________
4. 35,012 is 80% of what number?	______________
5. What number is 2% of 404,750?	______________
6. 567 is 63% of what number?	______________

Check your answers by entering them in the puzzle.

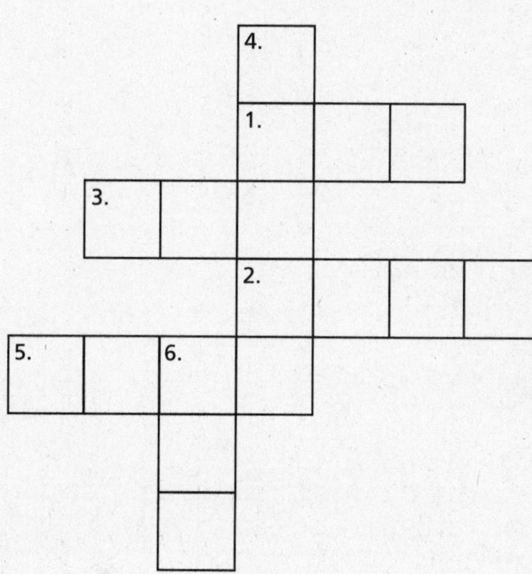

Name ______________________ Class ______________ Date ______________

Practice 6-7

Applications of Percent

Find the total cost.

1. $17.50 with a 7% sales tax

2. $21.95 with a 4.25% sales tax

3. $52.25 with an 8% sales tax

4. $206.88 with a 5.75% sales tax

5. The price of a pair of shoes is $85.99 before sales tax.The sales tax is 7.5%. Find the total cost of the shoes.

Estimate a 15% tip for each amount.

6. $12.68

7. $18.25

8. $15.00

Find each commission.

9. 2% on $1,500 in sales

10. 8% on $80,000 in sales

11. 5% on $600 in sales

12. 12% on $3,200 in sales

Find the total earnings when given the salary, commission rate, and sales.

13. $1,000 plus 6% on sales of $2,000

14. $500 plus 10% on sales of $1,400

15. $850 plus 8% on sales of $8,000

16. $1,200 plus 4.5% on sales of $6,500

17. To recover a large chair in your home, you purchase $9\frac{1}{2}$ yards of upholstery fabric at $11.00 per yard. If there is a 7% sales tax, what is the total cost of the fabric?

18. You and your sister rake and pick up leaves from your grandmother's yard. She says she'll pay you $35.00 for the job. Upon completion of your work, she also decides to add a separate 20% tip for each of you. You and your sister each keep your individual tips, and you decide to split your other earnings in half. How much will each of you earn from the job?

Name ______________________ Class ______________ Date ____________

6-7 • Guided Problem Solving

GPS Student Page 307, Exercise 26:

Sales A store pays a 6% commision on the first \$500 in sales and 8% on sales over \$500. Find the commission on an \$800 sale.

Understand

1. Circle the information you will need to solve.
2. Define commission.

 ____

 ____

3. Which operations do you need to use to solve this problem?

 ____

Plan and Carry Out

4. \$800 = \$500 + ? ______________
5. What is 6% of \$500? ______________
6. What is 8% of \$300? ______________
7. What is the commission on a \$800 sale? ______________

Check

8. Find 10% of \$500 and 10% of \$300. Since 6% is a little more than half of 10%, what is half of 10% of 500? Add this with 10% of 30, since 8% is close to 10%. Does your answer make sense?

 ____

Solve Another Problem

9. Dan's uncle asks him to come work for him at his men's clothing store. He will pay him 5% on his first \$1,000 in sales and 8% on sales above \$1,000. How much will Dan earn if he sells \$2,500 in merchandise?

 ____

 ____

Name ______________________ Class ______________ Date ______________

Practice 6-7

Applications of Percent

Find the total cost.

1. $17.50 with a 7% sales tax

2. $21.95 with a 4.25% sales tax

3. $52.25 with an 8% sales tax

4. $206.88 with a 5.75% sales tax

Estimate a 15% tip for each amount.

5. $18.25

6. $15.00

Find each commission.

7. 2% on $1,500 in sales

8. 8% on $80,000 in sales

9. 5% on $600 in sales

10. 12% on $3,200 in sales

Find the total earnings when given the salary, commission rate, and sales.

11. $1,000 plus 6% on sales of $2,000

12. $500 plus 10% on sales of $1,400

Solve

13. To recover a large chair in your home, you purchase $9\frac{1}{2}$ yards of upholstery fabric at $11.00 per yard. If there is a 7% sales tax, what is the total cost of the fabric?

14. The price of a pair of shoes is $85.99 before sales tax. The sales tax is 7.5%. Find the total cost of the shoes.

Name ____________________ Class ____________ Date ____________

Activity Lab 6-7

Applications of Percent

Daniela is considering buying a bicycle. She is comparing the price of the bicycle from several different stores, some of which are outside of the state in which she lives.

There are three conditions that Daniela needs to consider in addition to the price tag on each bicycle.

A. Most states have a sales tax that is added to the price of the bicycle, but the amount of the tax differs from state to state.

B. At some of the stores, there is a discount on the bicycle's price that will be subtracted before the tax is added.

C. Some stores charge a shipping fee that is a percentage of the total cost of the bike after taxes are added.

In the table below, Daniela gathered information about each store. Complete the table by finding the total cost of purchasing the bicycle from each store listed. Round answers to the nearest cent.

Store	Price	Discount	Tax	Shipping	Total Cost
1	$199.99	15%	4%	5%	
2	$250.00	20%	10%	No Cost	
3	$229.00	10%	5%	2%	
4	$179.00	5%	7%	15%	
5	$150.00	None	12%	20%	

1. Where should Daniela purchase her bicycle? Explain.

____

____

____

2. Store #5 offered the lowest price on the bicycle. Was the total cost also the lowest in Store #5?

____

Explain.

____

____

____

Name ______________________ Class ______________ Date ______________

Reteaching 6-7

Applications of Percent

Finding Sales Tax

sales tax = percent of tax · purchase price

Find the amount of sales tax on a television that costs $350 with an 8% sales tax.

sales tax = 8% · $350
sales tax = 0.08 · 350
sales tax = 28

The sales tax is $28.

How much does the television cost with sales tax?

$350 + $28 = $378

Finding a Commission

commission = commission rate · sales

Find the commission earned with a 3% commission rate on $3,000 in sales.

commission = 3% · $3,000
commission = 0.03 · 3,000
commission = 90

The commission earned is $90.

How much do you earn if you have a base salary of $500 plus 3% commission on sales of $3,000?

$90 + $500 = $590

Find the total cost.

1. $10.00 with a 4% sales tax ______________
2. $8.75 with a 5.25% sales tax ______________
3. $61.00 with an 7% sales tax ______________
4. $320.00 with a 6.5% sales tax ______________
5. $6.30 with a 8% sales tax ______________
6. $26.75 with a 7.5% sales tax ______________

Find each commission.

7. 6% on $3,000 in sales ______________
8. 1.5% on $400,000 in sales ______________
9. 8% on $1,200 in sales ______________
10. 5.5% on $2,400 in sales ______________

Name ______________________ Class ______________________ Date ______________________

Enrichment 6-7

Applications of Percent

Decision Making

Some sales positions pay a salary plus commission. A commission is an additional payment based on the amount sold. To find a 5% commission on a sale of $10,000, find 5% of 10,000.

The Supply House has offered you a position with a starting salary of $12,000 plus a commission of 4% on sales up to $5,000 and 8% on sales over $5,000. An experienced salesperson can sell $500,000 in supplies each year.

1. What is the minimum annual salary for Supply House employees?

____

2. What is the commission on the first $5,000 in sales?

____

3. What is the additional amount of sales that is needed to earn another $10,000 in income? ______________________

4. What is the total commission on sales of $500,000? Show your calculations. Remember to use the two different rates.

____

____

5. If you sell $500,000 in supplies, how much will you earn in all?

____

You are also offered a position at Office Stores, Inc. with a salary of $25,000, but no commission.

6. What is the advantage of accepting this position instead of the one at The Supply House?

____

____

7. What is the disadvantage of accepting the position at Office Stores, Inc. instead of the one at The Supply House?

____

____

8. Which position would you accept? Explain.

____

____

Name ______________________ Class ______________ Date ______________

6D: Visual Vocabulary Practice

For use after Lesson 6-7

High-Use Academic Words

Study Skill When making a sketch, make it simple but make it complete.

Concept List

represent	graph	solve
model	explain	pattern
substitute	calculate	verify

Write the concept that best describes each exercise. Choose from the concept list above

1.

35% of 70 is
$0.35 \times 70 = 24.5$

____

2.

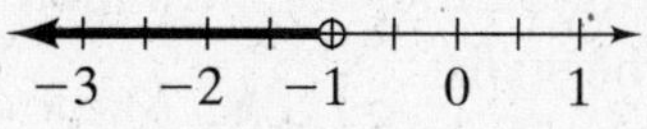

____

3.

5 : 7
5 to 7
$\frac{5}{7}$

____

4.

$n + 76 \geq 64$
$n + 76 - 76 \geq 64 - 76$
$n \geq -12$

____

5.

Sales tax is a percent of a purchase price you must pay when buying certain items. The formula for sales tax is sales tax = tax rate × purchase price.

____

6.

If $\frac{t}{18} = \frac{7}{126}$, then $t = 1$.
Check: $1 \times 126 = 7 \times 18$

____

7.

A	B
3	15
6	30
9	45
12	60
15	75

____

8.

$7a = 161$; a is either 23 or 26

$7(21) \stackrel{?}{=} 147$ False
$7(23) \stackrel{?}{=} 161$ True

____

9.

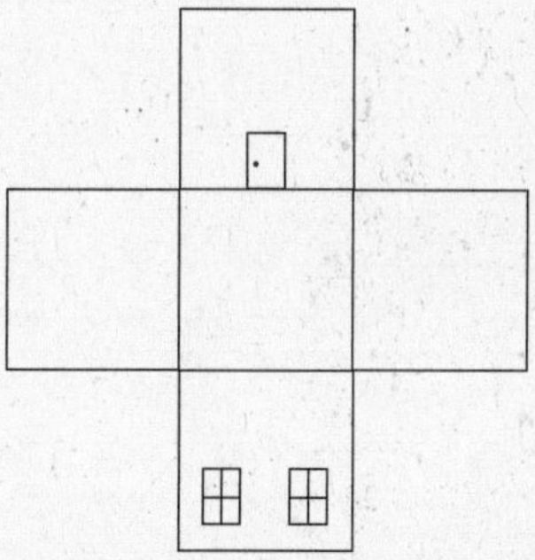

____

Name ______________________ Class ______________ Date ______________

Puzzle 6-7

Applications of Percent

Answer each of the clues to solve the crossword puzzle below. Round each answer to the nearest hundredth. Remember that each decimal point is entered in its own box. The solution to 1 across is done for you.

Across

1. A bike is on sale for $265.00. What is the total cost of the bike including a 5% sales tax? *278.25*
3. Find the commission on a $4,500.00 sale with a 10.5% commission rate.
5. Nancy has her hair cut at a salon for $35.00. She always leaves a 15% tip for the stylist. How much is the tip?
7. Find the 7.2% sales tax on a $9.78 book.

Down

1. Find the total cost: $19.99 with a 4% sales tax
2. You have lunch at a restaurant. Your bill is $6.70 and you decide to leave a 20% tip. How much should you pay in total?
4. Including a 6% sales tax, what is the cost of a motorcycle priced at $2,002.00?
6. Mario earns a weekly salary of $440.00 plus a 12% commission on any sales. This week he sold $525.00 worth of merchandise. How much did Randy earn?

1. 2	7	2. 8	.	4. 2	5

3.

6.

7.

5.

Name ______________________ Class ______________ Date ______________

Practice 6-8

Finding Percent of Change

Find each percent of change. State whether the change is an increase or a decrease.

1. A $50 coat is put on sale for $35.

2. Mayelle earns $18,000 a year. After a raise, she earns $19,500.

3. Last year Anthony earned $24,000. After a brief lay-off this year, Anthony's income is $18,500.

4. In 1981, about $1.1 million was lost due to fires. In 1988, the loss was about $9.6 million.

5. In a recent year, certain colleges and universities received about $268 million in aid. Ten years later, they received about $94 million.

6. A coat regularly costing $125 is put on sale for $75.

7. Complete the table.

Enrollment in Center City Schools From 1995 to 2000

Year	Enrollment	Change from Last Year (number of students)	Change from Last Year (%)	Increase or Decrease
1995	18,500	—	—	—
1996	19,300			
1997	19,700			
1998	19,500			
1999	19,870			
2000	19,200			

Name ______________ Class ______________ Date ______________

6-8 • Guided Problem Solving

GPS Student Page 313, Exercise 29:

Sports A football player gained 1,200 yd last season and 900 yd this season. Find the percent of change. State whether the change is an increase or a decrease.

Understand

1. What two numbers will you be comparing?

____

2. Did the football player gain more yards last season or this season?

____

3. What are you being asked to do?

____

Plan and Carry Out

4. What is the difference in the number of yards gained last season and this season? ______________

5. Write a proportion comparing the difference and the percent of change. ______________

6. What are the cross products? ______________

7. What number do you divide each side by? ______________

8. What is the percent of change? ______________

9. Is it a decrease or increase? ______________

Check

10. Explain your answer to Step 9.

____

____

____

Solve Another Problem

11. In a previous game the school's star basketball player scored 25 points. In today's game he scored 40 points. What was the percent of change in the player's scoring? Is the change an increase or decrease?

____

Name ______________________ Class ______________ Date ______________

Practice 6-8

Finding Percent of Change

Find each percent of change. State whether the change is an increase or a decrease.

1. A $50 coat is put on sale for $35.

____

____

2. Mayelle earns $18,000 a year. After a raise, she earns $19,500.

____

____

3. Last year Anthony earned $24,000. After a brief lay-off this year, Anthony's income is $18,500.

____

____

4. In 1981, about $1.1 million was lost due to fires. In 1988, the loss was about $9.6 million.

____

____

5. In a recent year, certain colleges and universities received about $268 million in aid. Ten years later, they received about $94 million.

____

____

6. The table below shows enrollment in Center City Schools from 1995 to 2000. Complete the table.

Enrollment in Center City Schools From 1995 to 2000

Year	Enrollment	Change from Last Year (number of students)	Change from Last Year (%)	Increase or Decrease
1995	18,500	—	—	—
1996	19,300	800	4%	increase
1997	19,700	400		
1998	19,500			
1999	19,870			
2000	19,200			

Name ______________________ Class ______________ Date ____________

Activity Lab 6-8

Finding Percent of Change

You are conducting an experiment about rainfall and evaporation for your Earth science class. You collected your data by placing a container outside to collect rainwater. Each day, you measured the depth of the water to determine how much rain had fallen or how much water had evaporated. To begin, the container was filled to a depth of 2 cm.

Day of Week	Depth of Water
Sunday	2.00 cm
Monday	1.42 cm
Tuesday	1.02 cm
Wednesday	3.46 cm

Day of Week	Depth of Water
Thursday	4.24 cm
Friday	4.09 cm
Saturday	1.45 cm

Analyze the data collected by finding the percent increase or decrease of the water level. Round answers to the nearest percent.

1. a. What was the change in water level between Sunday and Monday?

   ____

   b. Did the water level increase or decrease?

   ____

   c. Find the percent change in water level between Sunday and Monday.

   ____

2. Find the percent change in water level between Sunday and Tuesday.

   ____

3. Find the percent change in water level between Wednesday and Thursday.

   ____

4. Find the percent change over the entire week (from Sunday to Saturday).

   ____

5. Between which two consecutive days did the largest percent increase occur? The largest percent decrease?

   ____

6. In this case, how did finding percent increase and decrease help you analyze and understand the collected data? What other methods might you use to compare the collected values?

   ____

   ____

   ____

Name ______________________ Class ______________ Date ______________

Reteaching 6-8

Finding Percent of Change

Percent of change is the percent something increases or decreases from its original amount.

	Find the percent of increase from 12 to 18.	Find the percent of decrease from 20 to 12.
① Subtract to find the amount of change.	$18 - 12 = 6$	$20 - 12 = 8$
② Write a proportion. $\frac{\text{change}}{\text{original}} = \frac{\text{percent}}{100}$	$\frac{6}{12} = \frac{n}{100}$ $6 \cdot 100 = 12n$	$\frac{8}{20} = \frac{n}{100}$ $8 \cdot 100 = 20n$
③ Solve for n.	$n = 50$	$n = 40$
	The percent of increase is 50%.	The percent of decrease is 40%.

State whether the change is an *increase* or *decrease.* Complete to find the percent of change.

1. 40 to 60

$60 - 40 =$ ______

$\frac{\square}{40} = \frac{n}{100}$

______ $\cdot 100 = 40n$

$n =$ ______

______

2. 15 to 9

$15 - 9 =$ ______

$\frac{\square}{15} = \frac{n}{100}$

______ $\cdot 100 = 15n$

$n =$ ______

______

3. 0.4 to 0.9

$0.9 - 0.4 =$ ______

$\frac{\square}{0.4} = \frac{n}{\square}$

______ $= 0.4n$

$n =$ ______

______

Find the percent of *increase.*

4. 16 to 40 ______

5. 20 to 22 ______

6. 9 to 18 ______

7. 28 to 35 ______

8. 80 to 112 ______

9. 150 to 165 ______

Find the percent of *decrease.*

10. 20 to 15 ______

11. 100 to 57 ______

12. 52 to 26 ______

13. 140 to 126 ______

14. 75 to 72 ______

15. 1,000 to 990 ______

Name ______________________ Class ______________ Date ____________

Enrichment 6-8

Finding Percent of Change

Decision Making

Answer the questions given the information.

A softball diamond is a 60 ft by 60 ft square. The sides of a baseball diamond are 50% longer than this. What is the percent increase in the area from the softball diamond to the baseball diamond?

1. Will you find the percent increase or decrease? ______________

2. What are the dimensions of a softball diamond? ______________

3. How much longer is the side of a baseball diamond than the side of a softball diamond? ______________

4. Draw a diagram to show the areas of the two fields. Use another piece of paper if you need more space.

5. Which expression gives you the length of one side of the baseball diamond?

   ____

   a. $60 + 0.5(60)$ **b.** $60 - (60 \cdot 0.5)$ **c.** $(60 \cdot 0.5) \div 60$

6. What is the length of the side of the baseball diamond?

   ____

7. What is the formula for the area of a square?

   ____

8. What is the area of the softball diamond?

   ____

9. What is the area of the baseball diamond?

   ____

10. How much larger is the area of the baseball diamond?

    ____

11. What is the percent increase?

    ____

12. What other strategies could you use to find the answer?

    ____

    ____

Name ______________________ Class ______________ Date ____________

6E: Vocabulary Check

For use after Lesson 6-8

Study Skill Strengthen your vocabulary. Use these pages and add cues and summaries by applying the Cornell Notetaking style.

Write the definition for each word or term at the right. To check your work, fold the paper back along the dotted line to see the correct answers.

______________________	commission
______________________	discount
______________________	markup
______________________	percent
______________________	percent of change

Name ______________________ Class ______________ Date ______________

6E: Vocabulary Check (continued)

For use after Lesson 6-8

Write the vocabulary word or term for each definition. To check your work, fold the paper forward along the dotted line to see the correct answers.

pay that is equal to a percent of sales ______________________

the difference between the original price and the sale price of an item ______________________

the difference between the selling price and the original cost ______________________

a ratio that compares a number to 100 ______________________

the percent a quantity increases or decreases from its original amount ______________________

Name ______________________ Class ______________ Date ______________

6F: Vocabulary Review

For use with the Chapter Review

Study Skill When you have to match words and descriptions from two columns, read the list of words and the definitions carefully and completely so you can quickly find the obvious matches. Then do the rest, one at a time. Cross out words and definitions as you use them.

Match the word in Column A with its definition in Column B.

Column A	Column B
1. percent	A. difference between the original price and the sale price
2. factor	B. equation stating two ratios are equal
3. discount	C. whole number that divides into another whole number evenly
4. ratio	D. difference between the selling price and the original cost of an item
5. proportion	E. comparison of two numbers by division
6. markup	F. ratio comparing a number to 100

Match the word in Column A with its definition in Column B.

Column A	Column B
7. mode	G. percent a quantity increases or decreases from its original amount
8. equation	H. enlarged or reduced drawing of an object
9. commission	J. statement that two expressions are equal
10. tip	K. number that occurs most often in a data set
11. scale drawing	L. percent of sales
12. percent of change	M. percent of a bill that you give to a person for providing a service

Name ______________________ Class ______________ Date ______________

Puzzle 6-8

Finding Percent of Change

The high temperature on Sunday was 71° F. Look at the thermometers below. Use the Percent of Change table to match each thermometer to a day of the week.

Percent of Change

Sunday – Monday	20% increase
Monday – Tuesday	15% decrease
Tuesday – Wednesday	6% decrease
Wednesday – Thursday	18% increase
Thursday – Friday	3% decrease
Friday – Saturday	17% decrease

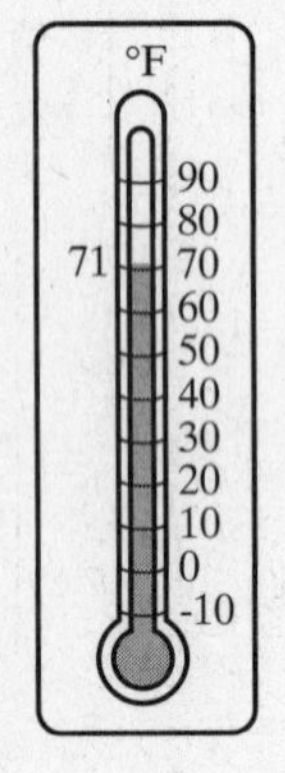

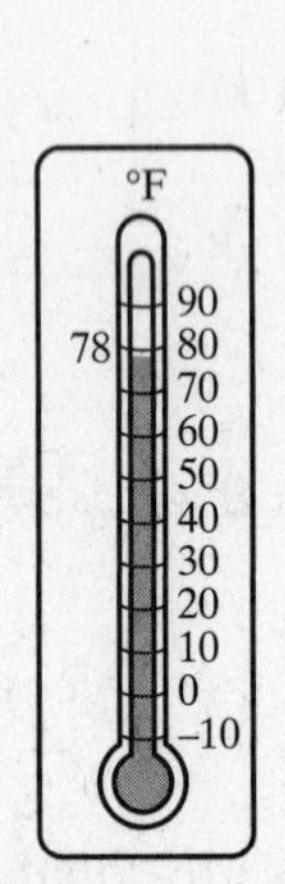

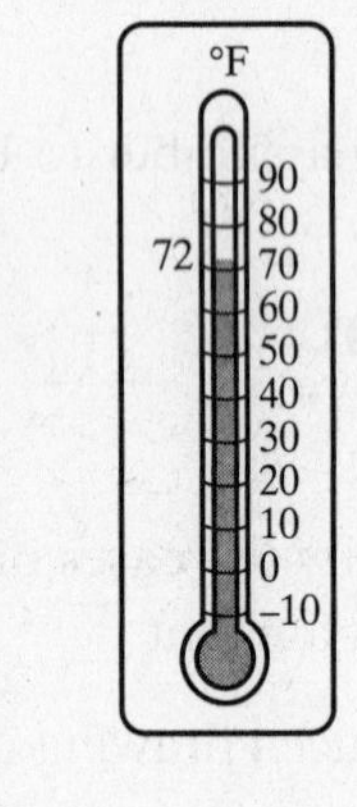

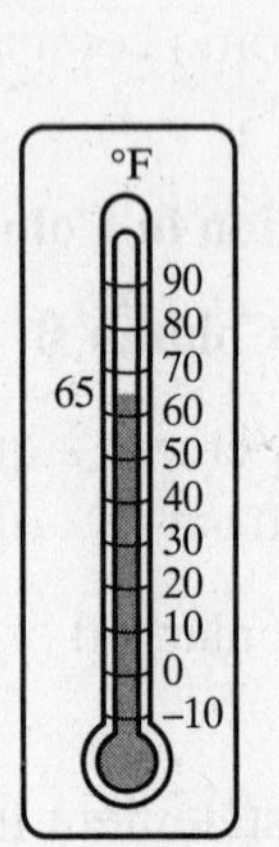

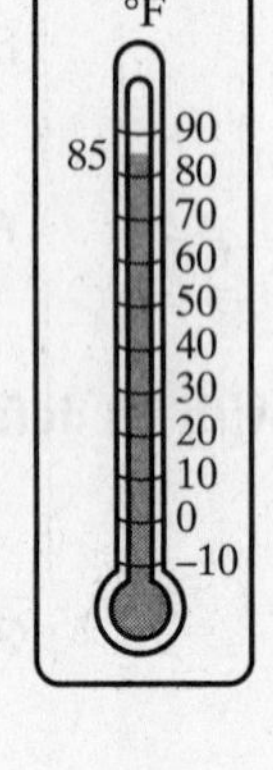

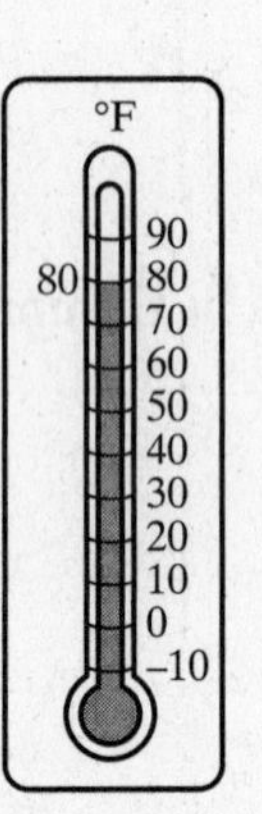

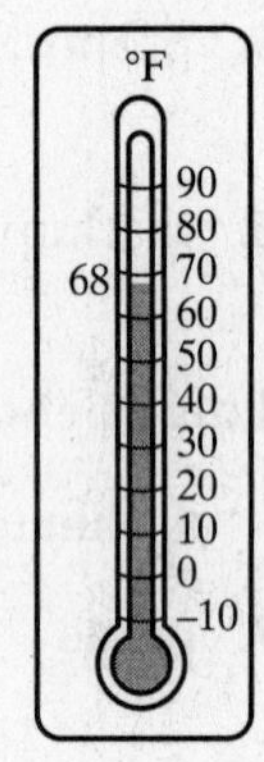

Sunday **Monday** **Tuesday** **Wednesday**

Thursday **Friday** **Saturday**

Name _______________ Class _______________ Date _______________

Chapter 6 Project: Chills and Thrills

Take a Survey

Beginning the Chapter Project

Your world is spinning. You are screaming. And you love every minute of it! Even though you are scared, you know that you will come to a safe stop at the end of the ride.

Clearly a successful amusement park attraction must be both fun and safe. Planners of amusement parks use a lot of math to create thrills but avoid any spills.

In this chapter project, you will decide which rides are likely to be most popular. Your final product will be a recommendation about which rides to include in a proposed amusement park for your town.

Activities

Activity 1: Surveying

Design and conduct a survey to find out which amusement park rides are most popular. Make certain that the survey is fair so that the results are accurate and useful. Keep track of the results and the number of people you survey.

Activity 2: Organizing

Create a chart to display the results from the survey in Activity 1. Organizing your data will help you to analyze your results.

Your chart should include a column for the type of ride and the number of people who choose it as their favorite. Include as many rows as types of rides mentioned in the survey. Label the last row "Total." For example:

Type of Ride	Number of People
Roller Coaster	12
Merry-Go-Round	22
Total	34

Chapter 6 Project: Chills and Thrills (continued)

Activity 3: Calculating

Use the results of your survey and your chart from Activity 2 to determine the ratios and percents of people who prefer each ride to the total number of people surveyed. Add another column to your chart to display each ratio and percent.

Type of Ride	Number of People	Ratio and Percent
Roller Coaster	12	12 : 34 or 35%
Merry-Go-Round	22	22 : 34 or 65%
Total	**34**	

Activity 4: Researching

Use the data from your chart and order the percents, in order from least to greatest.

Which ride is the most popular?

Find the number of students in your school. Assuming that all the students in your school visit the park, predict, using proportions, how many students would choose each ride as their favorite.

Finishing the Project

Pretend that your town has a limited amount of space for rides in a proposed amusement park. Which rides would you recommend they include? Explain your reasoning and present your findings in an organized display.

Reflect and Revise

Ask a classmate to review your project with you. Together, check that the survey questions, chart, and explanations are clear and accurate. Revise your work as needed. Consider doing more research.

Visit PHSchool.com for information and links you might find helpful as you complete your project.

Name ______________________ Class ______________ Date ______________

Chapter Project Manager

Getting Started

Read about the project. As you work on it, you will need several sheets of paper. If available, a spreadsheet program can also be used. Keep all your work for the project in a folder, along with this Project Manager.

Checklist	Suggestions
❑ Activity 1: surveying	❑ Verify that your survey questions are not biased.
❑ Activity 2: organizing	❑ Count the number of rides in the survey to find the number of rows needed for the chart.
❑ Activity 3: calculating	❑ Use a proportion to find the percent.
❑ Activity 4: researching	❑ Ask a school official for the total number of students enrolled in the school.
❑ Recommendations	❑ Use sketches of the recommended amusement park rides to add interest to your display.

Scoring Rubric

3 Your data is accurate and complete. You conduct a survey and complete a chart showing the amusement park preferences of a reasonable sample of people. You describe these preferences using ratios and percents, and you correctly use these values to estimate the projected number of people in a larger population who would prefer each ride.

2 Your data may be missing some key elements. You provide a chart of your survey data and the ratios of people who prefer each ride. You attempt to use the survey data to estimate the preferences of a larger population.

1 Much of the data is incorrect or incomplete. You don't gather adequate data from your survey, you incorrectly calculate ratios, or you do not make any projections for a larger population.

0 Major elements of the project are incomplete or missing. You fail to complete a survey, chart the results, or make any calculations based on these results.

Your Evaluation of Project Evaluate your work, based on the Scoring Rubric.

Teacher's Evaluation of Project

Name ________________ Class ________________ Date ________________

Chapter Project Teacher Notes

About the Project

Students will apply their knowledge of ratios and percents to conduct a survey and write a recommendation as to which rides to include in a proposed amusement park.

Introducing the Project

- Have students discuss and make a list as to what makes an amusement park ride a favorite.
- Discuss with students how to make a survey accurate and useful.

Activity 1: Surveying

Have students research amusement park advertisements, brochures, etc. to make a list of choices for the survey. Make sure students allow for additional rides to be included by those being surveyed.

Activity 2: Organizing

Have students make and label a chart to display the results of their survey.

Activity 3: Calculating

Encourage students to use their charts to write the ratio of the number of people who prefer each ride to the total number of people. Have students also display the ratio as a percent.

Activity 4: Researching

Explain how to use the survey results to make predictions. Show students how to apply the survey ratios to the larger school population.

Finishing the Project

You may wish to plan a project day on which students share their completed projects. Encourage students to explain their process as well as their products.

- Have students review their methods for conducting their surveys, making their charts, and making predictions for the project.
- Ask students to share any insight they gained when completing the project, such as what their ride recommendation is based on.

Visit PHSchool.com for information and links you might find helpful as you complete your project.

Name ____________ Class ____________ Date ____________

✔ Checkpoint Quiz 1

Use with Lessons 6-1 through 6-3.

Write each percent as a decimal and as a fraction in simplest terms.

1. 60% ____________ **2.** 125% ____________ **3.** 0.8% ____________

Write each fraction as a percent.

4. $\frac{18}{20}$ ____________ **5.** $\frac{9}{8}$ ____________ **6.** $\frac{1}{125}$ ____________

Order the numbers from least to greatest.

7. 33%, $1\frac{1}{3}$, 0.36, $\frac{2}{3}$

____

8. 5%, 0.5, 0.052, $\frac{1}{5}$

____

9. $1\frac{2}{3}$, 0.13, 0.013, 113%

____

10. 75%, 0.075, $\frac{1}{2}$, 0.00759

____

Name ____________ Class ____________ Date ____________

✔ Checkpoint Quiz 2

Use with Lessons 6-4 through 6-7.

Find each answer using a proportion.

1. What percent of 84 is 21? ____________ **2.** What percent of 120 is 72? ____________

3. What is 20% of 30? ____________ **4.** 80 is what percent of 640? ____________

Find each answer using an equation.

5. 50 is what percent of 80? ____________ **6.** 32 is 20% of what number? ____________

7. What percent of 260 is 52? ____________ **8.** What is 45% of 90? ____________

9. Find the commission for a rate of 2.5% and $800 in sales.

____

10. Find the total for items costing $149.99 with a sales tax of 5.75%.

____

Name ______________________ Class ______________ Date ______________

Chapter Test — Form A

Chapter 6

Write each decimal as a percent and write each percent as a decimal.

1. 4% ______________ **2.** 0.6 ______________ **3.** 225% ______________

4. 0.0032 ______________ **5.** 0.72% ______________ **6.** 5.2 ______________

Write each fraction as a percent and each percent as a fraction.

7. 85% ______________ **8.** $\frac{3}{5}$ ______________ **9.** 6% ______________

10. $\frac{3}{8}$ ______________ **11.** 350% ______________ **12.** $\frac{8}{5}$ ______________

Model each percent on these 10 × 10 grids.

13. 60%

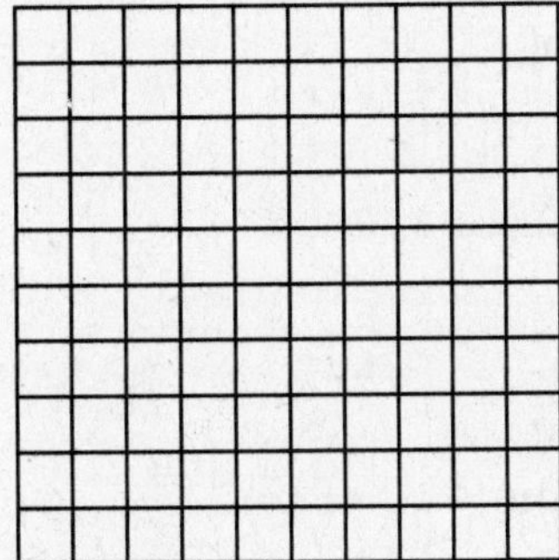

14. 15%

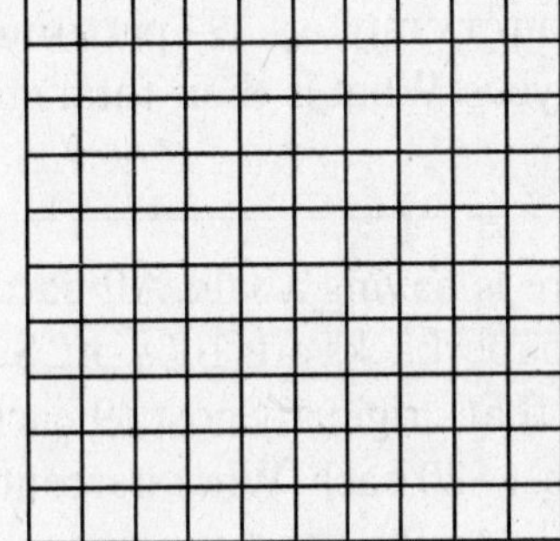

Write a proportion and solve.

15. What percent of 80 is 42? ______________

16. 80% of 70 is what number? ______________

Write an equation for each question. Then solve the equation.

17. 63 is 25% of what number? ______________

18. 20% of what number is 80? ______________

19. What percent of 72 is 12? ______________

20. 12% of 600 is what number? ______________

Chapter Test (continued) Form A

Chapter 6

Find each percent of change. Round to the nearest tenth. State whether the change is an increase or decrease.

21. 758 to 604

____

22. 8.3 to 9.10

____

Solve.

23. A big-screen TV that previously sold for $2,400 has been marked down to $2,040. What is the percent of decrease?

____

24. Since Todd received a 3% salary increase, his new yearly salary is $25,750. What was his yearly salary before the increase?

____

25. A manufacturer employs 294 part-time workers. This is 30% of their employees. What is their total employee count?

____

26. A book store is having a sale. All hardback books are 20% off, and all paperbacks are 10% off. Suppose you buy four paperbacks that originally cost $9 each and two hardbacks that originally cost $20 each. What percent of the total cost have you saved? Round to the nearest percent.

____

27. While visiting your cousin, who lives in another state, you buy a souvenir for $12.00. Upon entering the purchase price into the cash register, the sales clerk advises you that the total amount due, including tax, is $12.72. What is the sales tax in this state?

____

28. Six-sevenths of the tickets to a local community's group's annual performance were sold. If 82 tickets were left over, how many tickets were sold?

____

Name ______________________ Class ____________ Date ____________

Chapter Test — Form B

Chapter 6

Write each decimal as a percent and write each percent as a decimal.

1. 4% ______________________

2. 0.6 ______________________

3. 0.0032 ______________________

4. 0.72% ______________________

Write each fraction as a percent and each percent as a fraction.

5. 85% ______________________

6. $\frac{3}{5}$ ______________________

7. $\frac{3}{8}$ ______________________

8. 350% ______________________

Model each percent on these 10 × 10 grids.

9. 60%

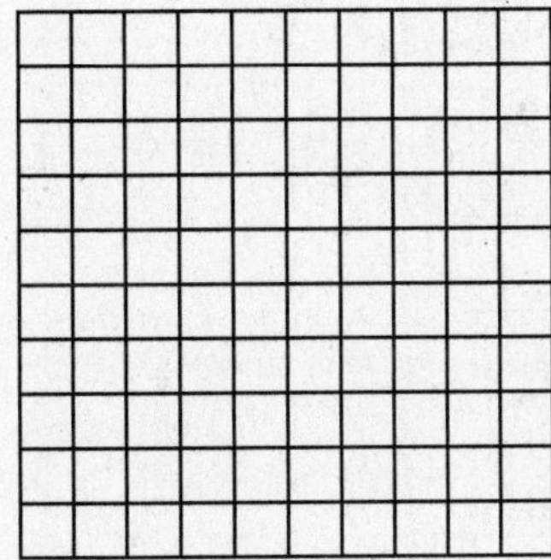

10. 15%

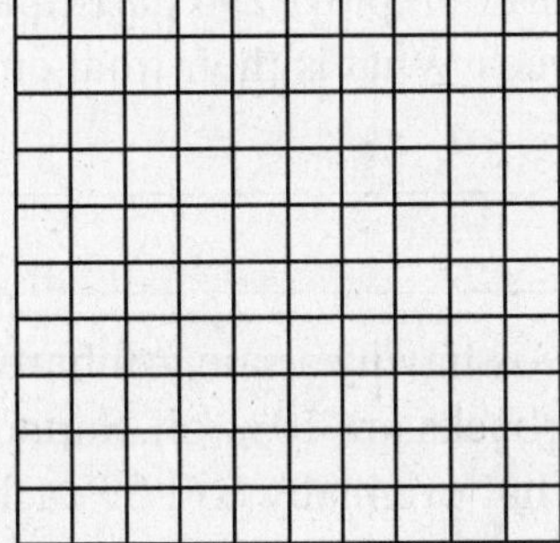

Write a proportion and solve.

11. What percent of 80 is 42?

____

12. 80% of 70 is what number?

____

Write an equation for each question. Then solve the equation.

13. 63 is 25% of what number?

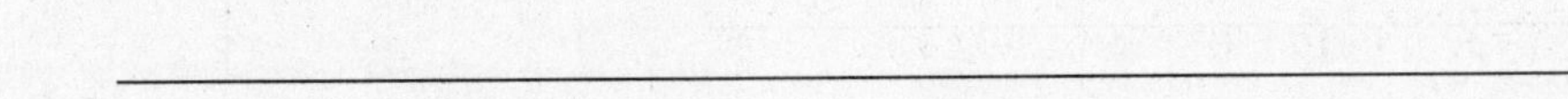

14. 20% of what number is 80?

____

15. What percent of 72 is 12?

____

Chapter Test (continued) Form B

Chapter 6

Find each percent of change. Round to the nearest tenth. State whether the change is an increase or decrease.

16. 758 to 604

____

17. 8.3 to 9.10

____

Solve.

18. A big-screen TV that previously sold for $2,400 has been marked down to $2,040. What is the percent of decrease?

____

19. A manufacturer employs 294 part-time workers. This is 30% of their employees. What is their total employee count?

____

20. A book store is having a sale. All hardback books are 20% off, and all paperbacks are 10% off. Suppose you buy four paperbacks that originally cost $9 each and two hardbacks that originally cost $20 each. What percent of the total cost have you saved? Round to the nearest percent.

____

21. Six-sevenths of the tickets to a local community's group's annual performance were sold. If 82 tickets were left over, how many tickets were sold?

____

Alternative Assessment

Form C

Chapter 6

SAVING FOR COLLEGE

Michelle has to make a presentation to parents, advocating savings accounts to help pay for their children's college. She knows that interest rates change all the time. Michelle created this table to give parents an idea of how much different amounts of money would be worth after a year at different simple interest rates.

1. Copy and complete the table.

	1%	2%	3%	4%	5%	6%	7%	8%	9%
$1,000	$1,010	$1,020	$1,030						
$2,000	$2,020	$2,040							
$3,000	$3,030								
$4,000									
$5,000									
$6,000									
$7,000									
$8,000									
$9,000									

2. Suppose Michelle had written the interest rates in the table as decimals rather than percents. What decimals would appear?

3. How can you use the table to find the amount after one year if $1,000 is invested at $1\frac{1}{2}$%? If $5,000 is invested at $8\frac{1}{2}$%?

4. How can you use the table to find the amount after one year if $1,500 is invested at 1%? If $6,500 is invested at 6%?

5. How can you use the table to find the amount after one year if $1,000 is invested at 10%? If $5,000 is invested at 12%?

6. Use the information in the table to write a general formula for calculating the amount saved (S) after 1 year in terms of the interest rate (R) and the initial amount invested (I).

Name ______________________ Class ______________ Date ______________

Alternative Assessment (continued) Form C

Chapter 6

Excursion

Jocelyn decided that she is going to college. For her birthday her grandparents told her they would give her some money for her to save for college. Jocelyn knows that the current interest rates at local banks are between 2% and 6%.

Estimate how much Jocelyn needs to go to college. Include tuition, room and board, and books for 1 year. Then, create a table that shows how much Jocelyn's grandparents will have to give her in order for her to have enough to go to college.

Name ______________________ Class ______________ Date ______________

Cumulative Review

Chapter 1–6

Multiple choice. Circle the letter of the best answer.

1. Which number is 1.92509 rounded to the nearest ten-thousandth?

   A. 1.9251 B. 1.9250
   C. 1.93000 D. 1.90000

2. Find the value of (3.1 + 9.8) + 0.9.

   F. 138 G. 13.8
   H. 12.9 J. 12

3. Find the product. 2.4 × 0.06

   A. 0.0144 B. 0.144
   C. 1.44 D. 14.4

4. Find the quotient. 0.45 ÷ 9

   F. 5 G. 0.5
   H. 0.05 J. 0.005

5. Which variable expression could you use to find the number of pencils in *b* boxes if there are 12 pencils in a box?

   A. $b + 12$ B. $b - 12$
   C. $\frac{b}{12}$ D. $12b$

6. Which of the following is in order from least to greatest?

   F. $-9, -5, 0, |-2|$
   G. $|-5|, -4, 2, 6.7$
   H. $1.5, 0.9, -4, -6$
   J. $-1, 0, -0.3, 7$

7. Evaluate $-3 - (-9) + 4$.

   A. −10 B. −8
   C. 10 D. 8

8. Solve the equation $-9x = -72$.

   F. −9 G. −8
   H. 8 J. 9

9. Solve $\frac{x}{5} + 8 = 3$.

   A. 1 B. 0
   C. −1 D. −25

10. Find the LCM of 16 and 20.

    F. 20 G. 40
    H. 60 J. 80

11. Order these fractions from least to greatest. $\frac{2}{5}, \frac{1}{3}$, and $\frac{3}{8}$

    A. $\frac{3}{8}, \frac{2}{5}, \frac{1}{3}$ B. $\frac{1}{3}, \frac{3}{8}, \frac{2}{5}$
    C. $\frac{3}{8}, \frac{1}{3}, \frac{2}{5}$ D. $\frac{2}{5}, \frac{3}{8}, \frac{1}{3}$

12. Evaluate $2^4 \times 3^2$.

    F. 144 G. 96
    H. 72 J. 48

13. Find the GCF of 48 and 60.

    A. 20 B. 40
    C. 60 D. 12

14. Write $\frac{8}{15}$ as a decimal.

    F. 1.875 G. 0.5
    H. 0.53 J. $0.5\overline{3}$

15. Find the sum. $\frac{5}{6} + \frac{1}{3}$

    A. $\frac{4}{9}$ B. $\frac{2}{3}$
    C. $1\frac{1}{6}$ D. $\frac{6}{7}$

16. Find the difference. $8\frac{1}{4} - 5\frac{3}{5}$

    F. $3\frac{13}{20}$ G. $3\frac{2}{9}$
    H. $2\frac{13}{20}$ J. $2\frac{2}{9}$

17. Solve $x - \frac{5}{6} = 2\frac{1}{3}$.

    A. $1\frac{1}{2}$ B. $2\frac{2}{3}$
    C. 3 D. $3\frac{1}{6}$

Cumulative Review (continued)

Chapters 1–6

18. Find the product. $3 \cdot 4\frac{3}{4}$

F. $\frac{12}{19}$ **G.** $8\frac{1}{4}$

H. $12\frac{3}{4}$ **J.** $14\frac{1}{4}$

19. Find the quotient. $2\frac{2}{3} \div 2\frac{2}{5}$

A. $1\frac{1}{9}$ **B.** $1\frac{13}{27}$

C. $4\frac{1}{5}$ **D.** $6\frac{2}{5}$

20. Complete. $4\frac{1}{3}$ yd = __?__ in.

F. 13 **G.** 52

H. 144 **J.** 156

21. Solve $\frac{w}{1.5} \geq -6$.

Which number line correctly represents the solution?

A.
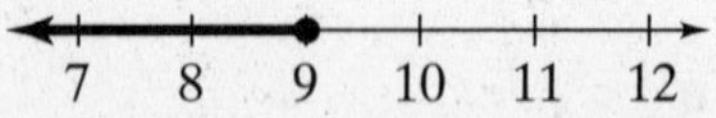

B.
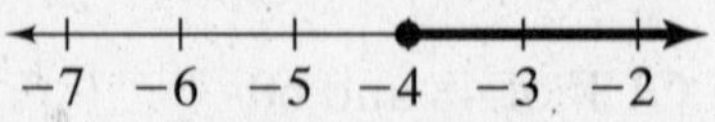

C.
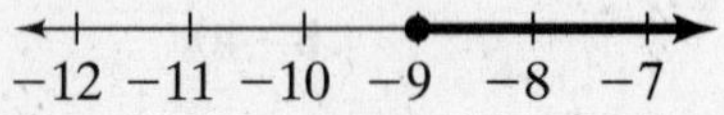

D.
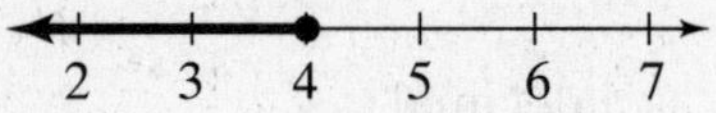

22. A radio is on sale for 15% off the regular price of \$29.99. About how much is the sale price of the radio?

F. \$15.00 **G.** \$18.00

H. \$25.00 **J.** \$30.00

23. Which number is *not* the same as $2\frac{4}{5}$?

A. $2\frac{8}{10}$ **B.** 28%

C. 2.8 **D.** $\frac{14}{5}$

24 Solve: $-4n < -20$

F. $n < 80$ **G.** $n < -24$

H. $n > 5$ **J.** $n > 16$

25. Solve $\frac{2}{3}x + 9 = -3$.

A. −18 **B.** −9

C. −8 **D.** −4

Gridded Response

26. What percent of 300 is 126?

____

Short Response

27. If you spend eight hours of your day asleep, which form, fraction, decimal, or percent, would be most exact in relating this activity? Explain.

____

____

____

____

____

Extended Response

28. Of fractions, decimals, and percents, which two forms are the most alike? Explain your answer.

____

____

____

____

Name ______________________ Class ______________ Date ______________

Practice 7-1

Lines and Planes

Describe the lines or line segments as *parallel* or *intersecting*.

1. the rows on a spreadsheet ______________________
2. the marks left by a skidding car ______________________
3. sidewalks on opposite sides of a street ______________________
4. the cut sides of a wedge of apple pie ______________________
5. the wires suspended between telephone poles ______________________
6. the hands of a clock at 7:00 P.M. ______________________
7. the trunks of grown trees in a forest ______________________

Use the diagram below for Exercises 8–12.

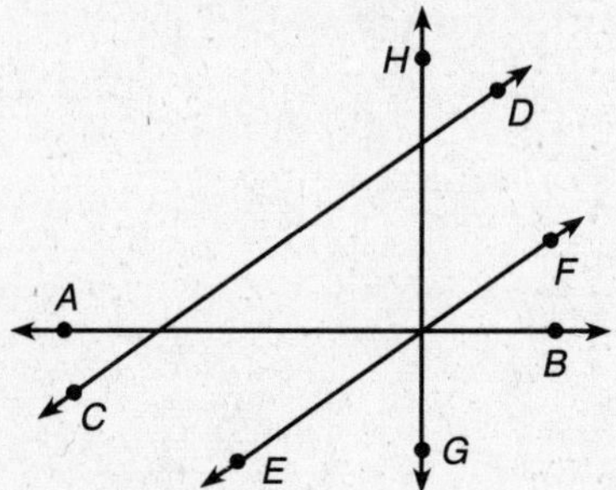

8. Name a pair of parallel lines. ______________________
9. Name a segment. ______________________
10. Name three points. ______________________
11. Name two rays. ______________________
12. Name a pair of intersecting lines. ______________________

Use a straightedge to draw each figure.

13. a line parallel to $\overline{UV}$

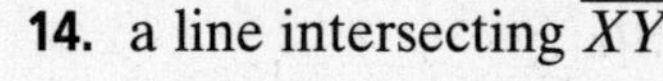

14. a line intersecting $\overline{XY}$

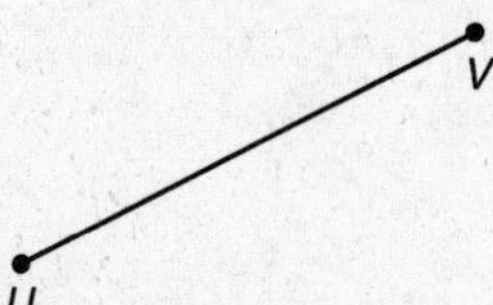

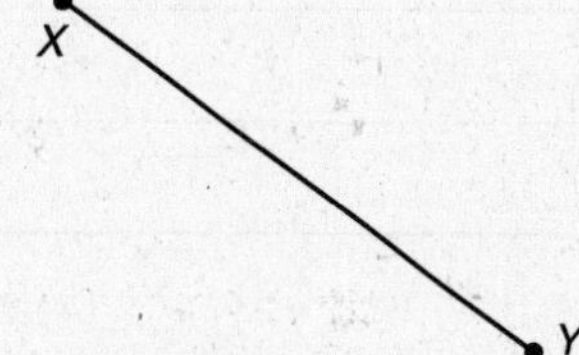

Name ________________ Class ________________ Date ________________

7-1 • Guided Problem Solving

GPS Student Page 327, Exercise 23:

Are the rungs on a ladder parallel, intersecting, or skew?

Understand

1. What is a ladder? Draw a sketch of one.

____

____

2. What are the rungs of a ladder? Circle the rungs on your sketch.

____

____

3. What are you being asked to do?

____

____

Plan and Carry Out

4. Do the rungs have any points in common? ________________
5. Are the rungs in the same plane? ________________
6. Are the rungs intersecting? ________________
7. Are the rungs skew? ________________
8. Are the rungs parallel? ________________

Check

9. Define *parallel*. Does this describe the rungs?

____

____

Solve Another Problem

10. Are the lines on your palm parallel, intersecting, or skew?

____

____

____

Name ______________________ Class ______________ Date ______________

Practice 7-1

Lines and Planes

Describe the lines or line segments as *parallel* or *intersecting*.

1. the rows on a spreadsheet

____

2. the marks left by a skidding car

____

3. sidewalks on opposite sides of a street

____

4. the cut sides of a wedge of apple pie

____

Use the diagram below for Exercises 5–8.

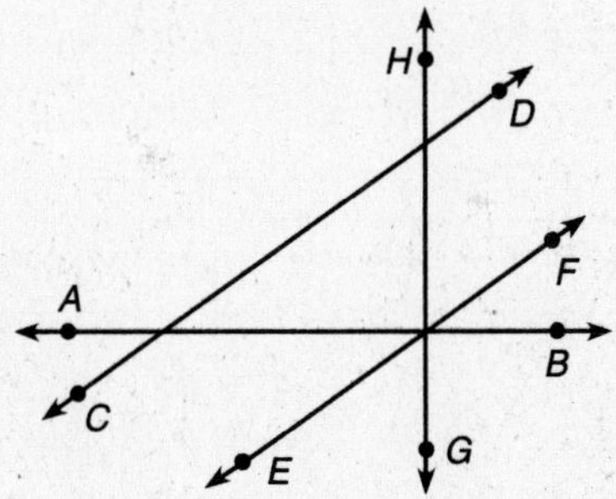

5. Name a pair of parallel lines. ______________

6. Name a segment. ______________

7. Name three points. ______________

8. Name two rays. ______________

Use a straightedge to draw each figure.

9. a line parallel to $\overline{UV}$

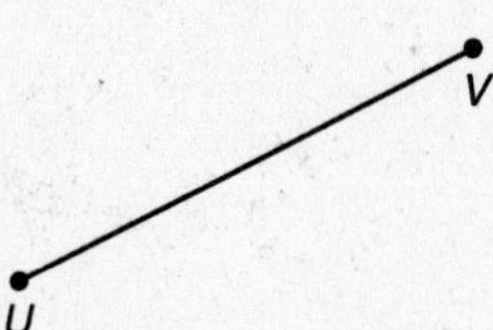

10. a line intersecting $\overline{XY}$

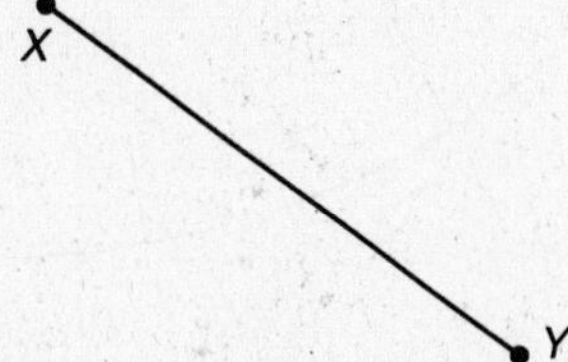

Name ______________________ Class ______________ Date ______________

Activity Lab 7-1

Lines and Planes

Patterns in Geometry

You can use a corner or a ruler to draw perpendicular lines.

1. Draw a line perpendicular to radius 1 at point *A*. Label its intersection with radius 2, *B*.
2. Draw a line perpendicular to radius 2 at point *B*. Label its intersection with radius 3, *C*.
3. Draw a line perpendicular to radius 3 at point *C*. Label its intersection with radius 4, *D*.
4. Describe the pattern in the drawing. ______________________

   ____
5. Continue this pattern until you reach the outer edge of the circle.

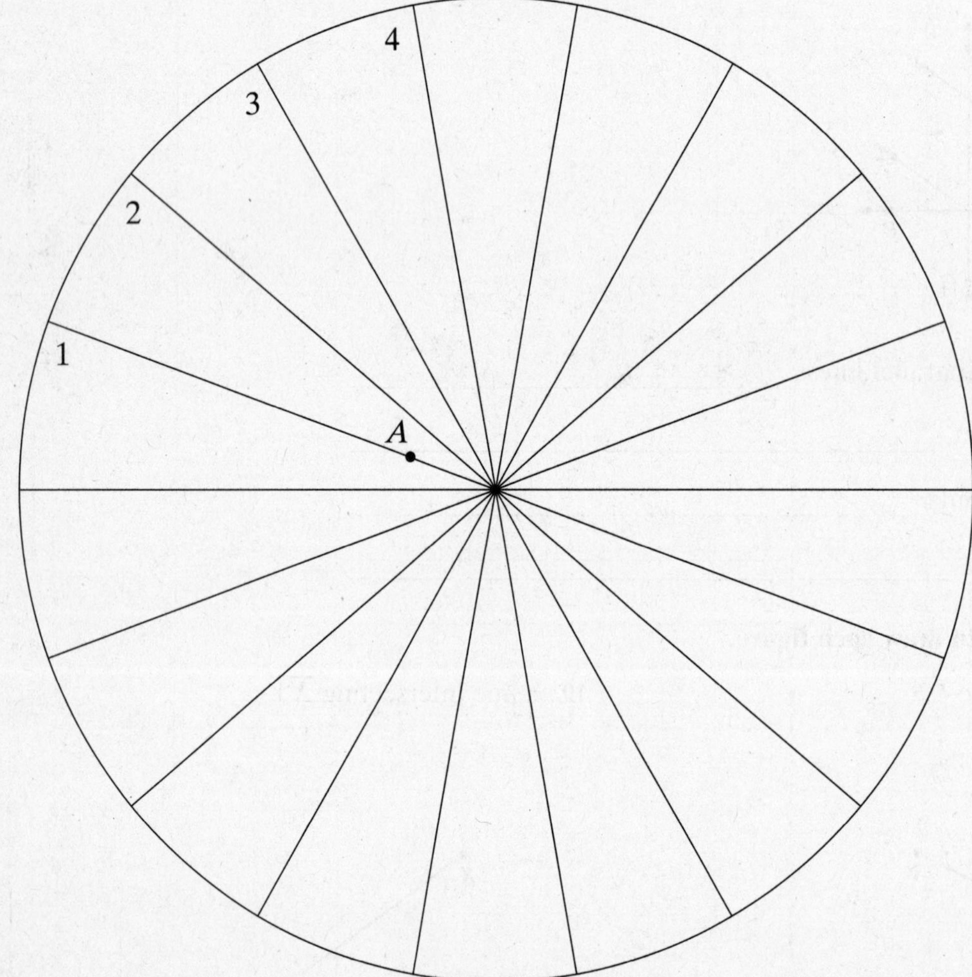

Name ______________________ Class ______________ Date ______________

Reteaching 7-1

Lines and Planes

A plane is an infinite flat surface. A line is a set of points that extends in two opposite directions without end. Lines in a plane that never meet are called **parallel** lines. Lines that cross each other are called **intersecting** lines. Intersecting lines have exactly one common point. **Skew** lines are in different planes and are neither intersecting nor parallel.

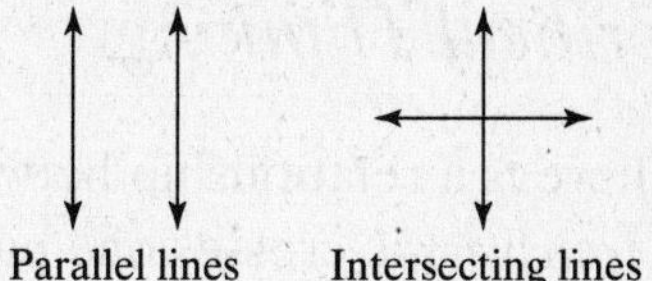

A line segment is formed by two endpoints and all the points between them.

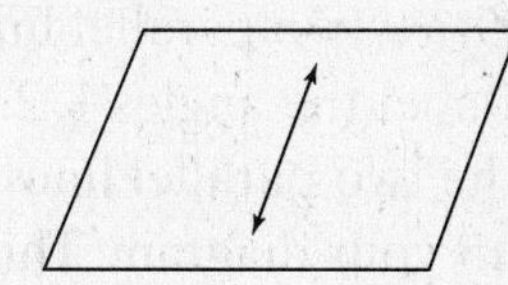

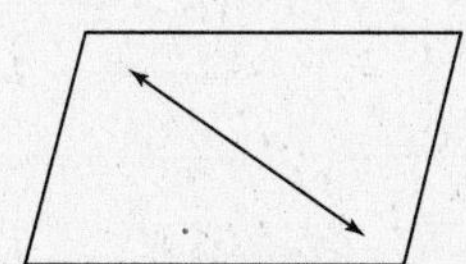
Skew lines

- Use the figure to name a line segment, a point, two intersecting lines, and a pair of parallel lines.

Two endpoints are S and U, so they form a line segment, $\overline{SU}$.

There are 5 points, M, R, S, T, U.

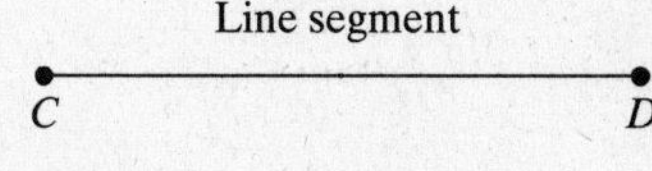

Intersecting lines have exactly one point in common. So $\overleftrightarrow{RU}$ and $\overleftrightarrow{TU}$ are intersecting lines.

Line $\overleftrightarrow{TU}$ never intersects line $\overleftrightarrow{RS}$, so $\overleftrightarrow{TU}$ and $\overleftrightarrow{RS}$ are parallel lines.

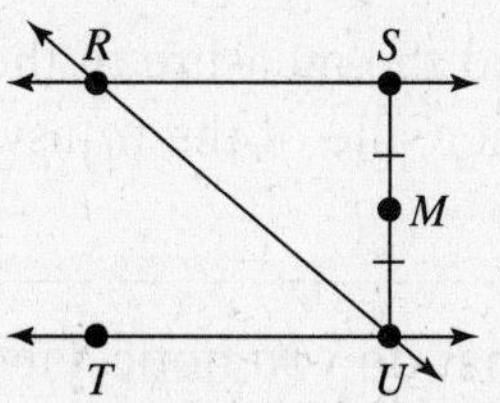

Use the figure to name each of the following.

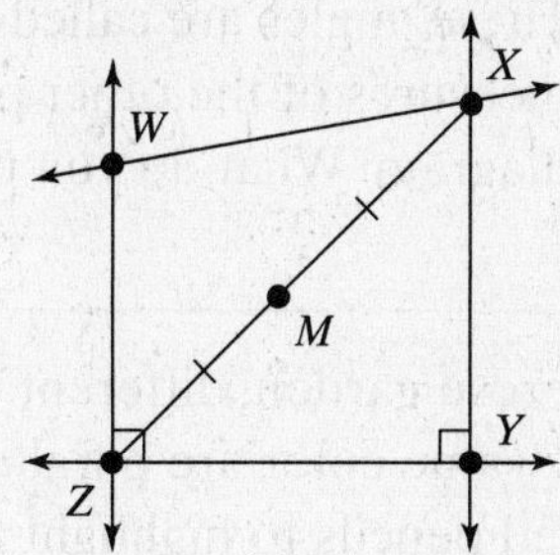

1. a line segment ______________________
2. a point ______________________
3. two pairs of intersecting lines ______________________
4. a pair of parallel lines ______________________
5. Sketch a rectangle to represent a bulletin board.

   a. Write *parallel* or *intersecting* to describe the lines formed by the left and right sides of a bulletin board.

   ____

   b. Write *parallel* or *intersecting* to describe the lines that meet at a corner of the bulletin board.

   ____

Use a straightedge to draw each figure.

6. a line $\overleftrightarrow{AB}$

7. a line segment $\overline{BC}$

Name ______________________ Class ______________ Date ______________

Enrichment 7-1

Lines and Planes

Critical Thinking

There is a relationship between the angles formed when a line, called a *transversal,* crosses one pair of parallel lines.

1. Draw two parallel lines. Then draw a transversal through them. Label the angles 1, 2, 3, . . . , 8. Measure one of the angles inside the two parallel lines with your protractor and write its measure on your diagram. This is called an interior angle.

2. Find the measure of the non-supplementary interior angle on the other side of the transversal.

____

3. What do you notice about the measures of these two angles?

____

4. These angles are called alternate interior angles. Find the measures of the other pair of alternate interior angles in your diagram. What do you notice?

____

For a rose garden, different colored roses are planted in rows. Rows of the same color are parallel. You may want to use colored pencils to highlight the rows.

5. Use what you know about alternate interior angles to list as many of the pairs of alternate interior angles in the diagram as you can.

____

____

____

____

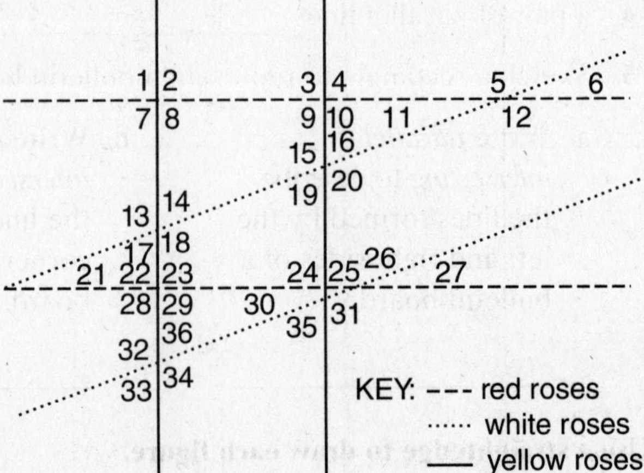

7A: Graphic Organizer

For use before Lesson 7-1

Study Skill Take notes while you study. Writing something down might help you remember it better. Go back and review your notes when you study for quizzes and tests.

Write your answers.

1. What is the chapter title? ______________________
2. How many lessons are there in this chapter? ______________________
3. What is the topic of the Test-Taking Strategies page? ______________________
4. Complete the graphic organizer below as you work through the chapter.
   - In the center, write the title of the chapter.
   - When you begin a lesson, write the lesson name in a rectangle.
   - When you complete a lesson, write a skill or key concept in a circle linked to that lesson block.
   - When you complete the chapter, use this graphic organizer to help you review.

Name ______________________ Class ______________ Date ______________

Puzzle 7-1

Lines and Planes

Draw the line, ray, or segment described in each of the exercises. The final picture you create should answer the question at the bottom of the page.

1. The ray $\overrightarrow{MF}$
2. A segment through two of the points that is parallel to $\overrightarrow{MF}$
3. $\overrightarrow{AC}$
4. A line that passes through points G, D, and J
5. $\overrightarrow{IB}$
6. A segment parallel to $\overline{AC}$ with G as one endpoint
7. $\overrightarrow{KD}$
8. A segment perpendicular to $\overrightarrow{MF}$ with N as one endpoint

D B E C F A H G L J K I M N

What is about one half the length of a tiger?

Its ______________________!

Name ______________________ Class ______________ Date ______________

Practice 7-2

Identifying and Classifying Angles

In exercises 1–6, classify each angle as *acute, right, obtuse,* or *straight.*

1.

2.

3.

______________ ______________ ______________

4. $m\angle A = 180°$

5. $m\angle B = 43°$

6. $m\angle D = 90°$

______________ ______________ ______________

Use the figure at the right to name the following.

7. two lines ______________

8. three segments ______________

9. a pair of congruent angles ______________

10. four right angles

____

11. two pairs of obtuse vertical angles

____

12. two pairs of adjacent supplementary angles

____

13. two pairs of complementary angles

____

Solve.

14. If $m\angle A = 23°$, what is the measure of its complement?

____

15. If $m\angle T = 163°$, what is the measure of its supplement?

____

16. If a 67° angle is complementary to $\angle Q$, what is the measure of $\angle Q$?

____

17. Use the dot grid to draw two supplementary angles, one of which is 45°. Do *not* use a protractor.

Name ______________________ Class ______________ Date ______________

7-2 • Guided Problem Solving

GPS Student Page 334, Exercise 26:

Writing in Math Can an angle ever have the same measure as its complement? Explain.

Understand

1. What are you being asked to do?

____

____

2. What do you have to do to explain your answer?

____

____

____

Plan and Carry Out

3. What is the definition of complementary angles?

____

4. If an angle and its complement have the same measure, explain the relationship between the angle and 90°.

____

5. Determine the measure of the angle. ______________

6. Can an angle ever have the same measure as its complement?

____

Check

7. Explain your answer.

____

____

Solve Another Problem

8. Can an angle ever have the same measure as its supplement? Explain.

____

____

Name ______________________ Class ______________ Date ______________

Practice 7-2

Identifying and Classifying Angles

In Exercises 1–6, classify each angle as *acute, right, obtuse,* or *straight.*

1. ______________

2. ______________

3. ______________

4. $m\angle A = 180°$ ______________

5. $m\angle B = 43°$ ______________

6. $m\angle D = 90°$ ______________

Use the figure below to name the following.

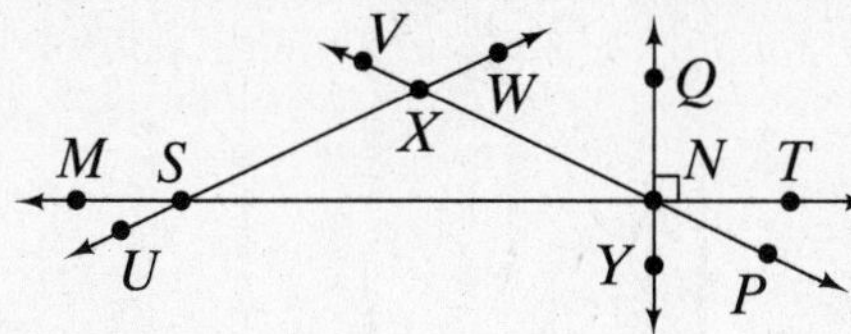

7. two lines ______________

8. three segments ______________

9. a pair of congruent angles ______________

10. four right angles ______________

11. two pairs of complementary angles ______________

Solve.

12. If $m\angle A = 23°$, what is the measure of its complement?

____

13. If $m\angle T = 163°$, what is the measure of its supplement?

____

14. Use the dot grid to draw two supplementary angles, one of which is 45°. Do *not* use a protractor.

Name ______________________ Class ______________ Date ____________

Activity Lab 7-2

Identifying and Classifying Angles

There is a relationship between the angles formed when a line crosses one pair of parallel lines. Complete the exercises to discover more about this relationship.

1. In the figure below, $\overleftrightarrow{AB}$ and $\overleftrightarrow{CD}$ are parallel. Measure angle $\angle FGB$ with a protractor and record your answer on the diagram.

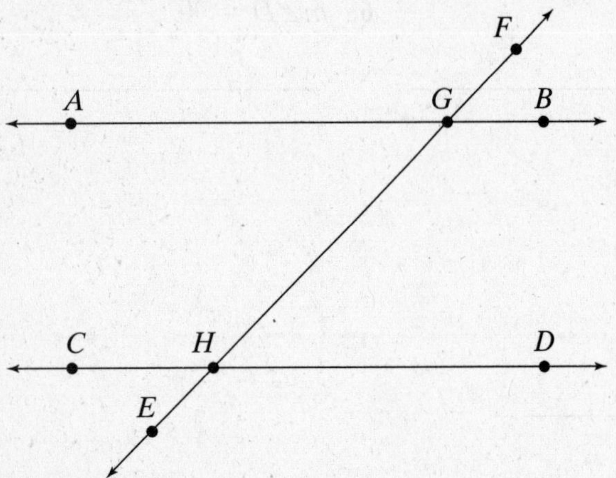

2. What is the relationship between $\angle AGH$ and $\angle FGB$? Write the measure of $\angle AGH$ in the diagram.

3. Use what you know about supplementary angles to find the measures of $\angle AGF$ and $\angle HGB$.

4. Now measure $\angle GHD$ with a protractor and record your answer on the diagram.

5. Find the measures of angles $\angle CHG$, $\angle CHE$, and $\angle EHD$.

6. What is the relationship between the first set of angles and the second?

For a rose garden, different colored roses are planted in rows. Rows of the same color are parallel. You may want to use colored pencils to highlight the rows.

Use what you know about angles to find the measure of:

7. The acute angle made by the red and white roses. ____________

8. The obtuse angle made by the red and white roses. ____________

9. The acute angle made by the white and yellow roses. ____________

10. The angle made by the red and yellow roses. ____________

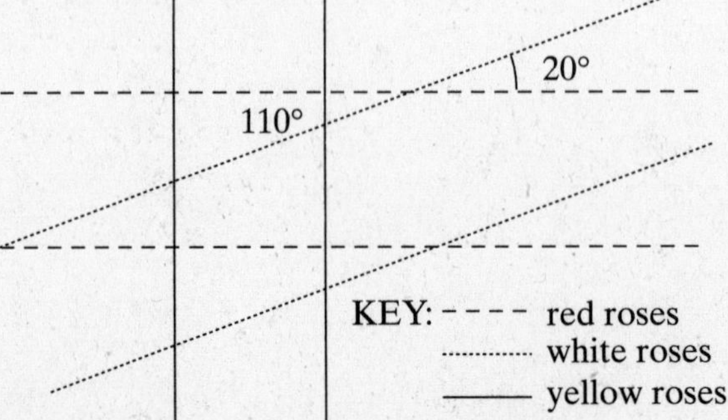

Name ______________________ Class ______________ Date ______________

Reteaching 7-2

Identifying and Classifying Angles

Acute angles have a measurement of less than 90°. In the diagram below, ∠1 and ∠2 are acute angles.

Obtuse angles have a measurement of more than 90°. In the diagram, ∠5 is an obtuse angle.

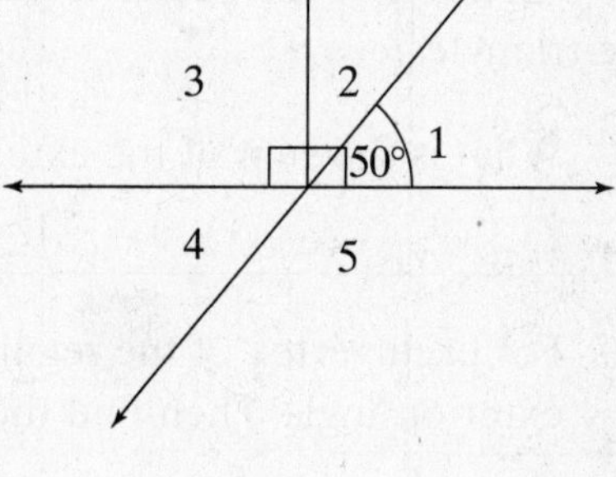

Vertical angles are formed across from each other where two lines intersect. They always have equal measurements. In the diagram, ∠1 and ∠4 are vertical angles. They both measure 50°.

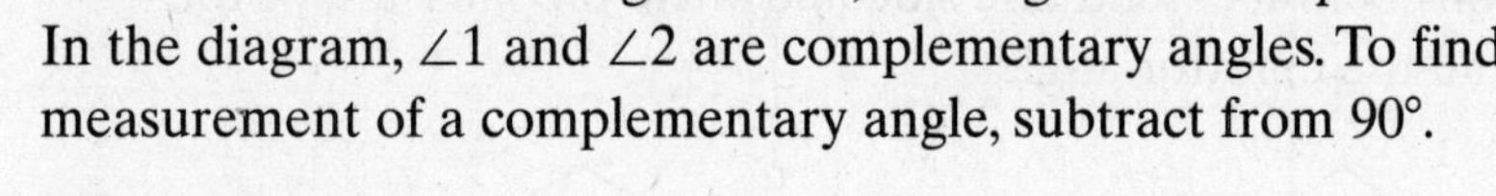

When the sum of two angles is 90°, the angles are *complementary.* In the diagram, ∠1 and ∠2 are complementary angles. To find the measurement of a complementary angle, subtract from 90°.

$90° - m\angle 1 = m\angle 2$

$90° - 50° = m\angle 2$

$40° = m\angle 2$

$m\angle 2 = 40°$

When the sum of two angles is 180°, the angles are *supplementary*. In the diagram, ∠4 and ∠5 are supplementary angles. To find the measurement of a supplementary angle, subtract from 180°.

$180° - m\angle 4 = m\angle 5$

$180° - 50° = m\angle 5$

$130° = m\angle 5$

$m\angle 5 = 130°$

Use the diagram to find the measurement of each angle. Then classify each angle as *obtuse, right,* or *acute.*

146° B A C D 40°

1. ∠*A* ______________
2. ∠*B* ______________
3. ∠*C* ______________
4. ∠*D* ______________

Name ______________________ Class ______________ Date ____________

Enrichment 7-2

Identifying and Classifying Angles

Patterns in Geometry

An exterior angle is the angle formed by one side of the triangle and the extension of the adjacent side. The exterior angles are marked in the triangle.

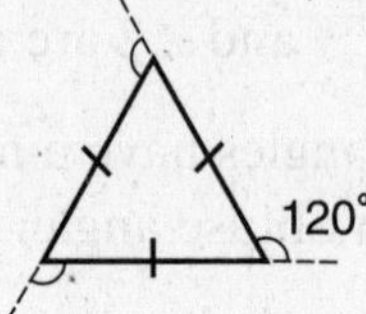

1. What is the sum of the exterior angles in the triangle?

____

2. For each vertex of the regular polygons below, extend one side and write the measure of the exterior angle. Then find the sum of all the exterior angles.

a. 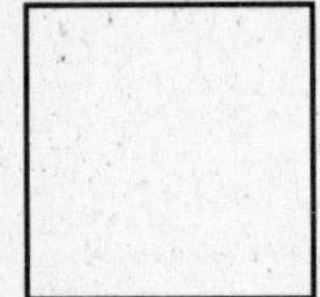

b. 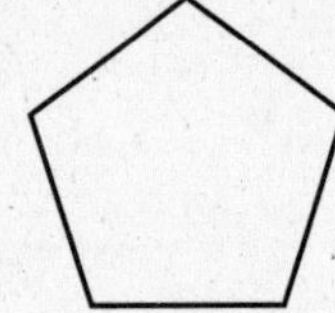

c. 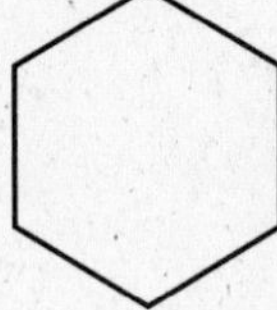

______________ ______________ ______________

3. What pattern did you discover? ____

____

4. Find the sum of the exterior angles for these nonregular polygons.

a. 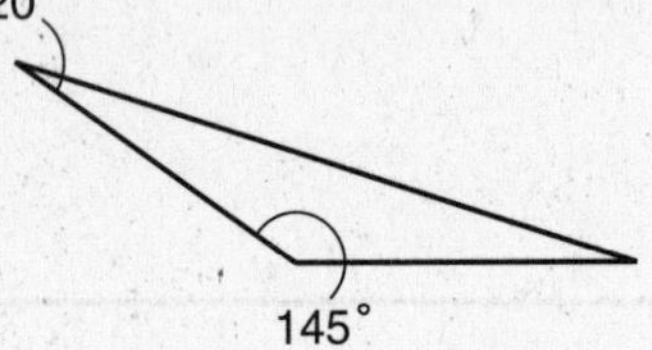

b. 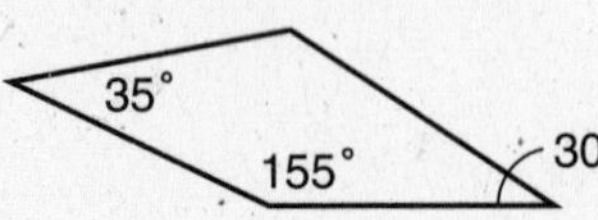

______________ ______________

c. 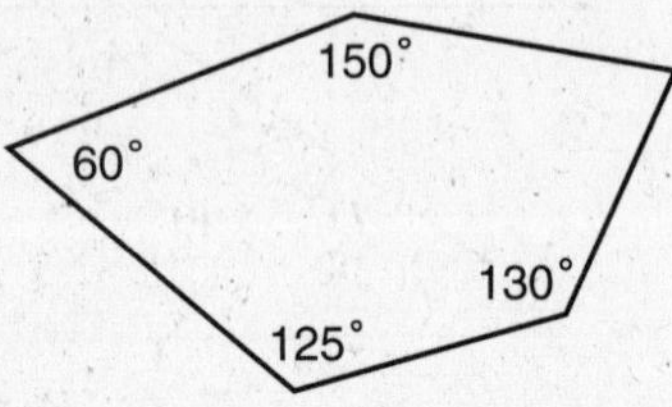

d. 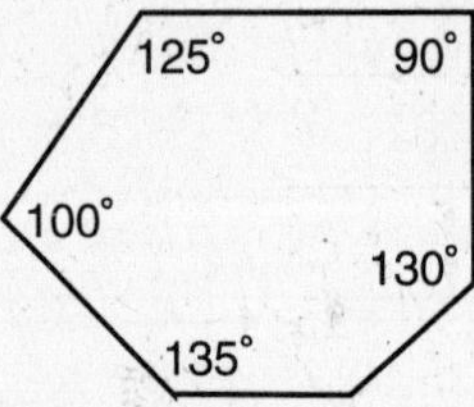

______________ ______________

5. Is the pattern the same or different? Why do you think this is true?

____

____

____

Name ______________________ Class ______________ Date ______________

Puzzle 7-2

Identifying and Classifying Angles

Use the diagram to complete the exercises.

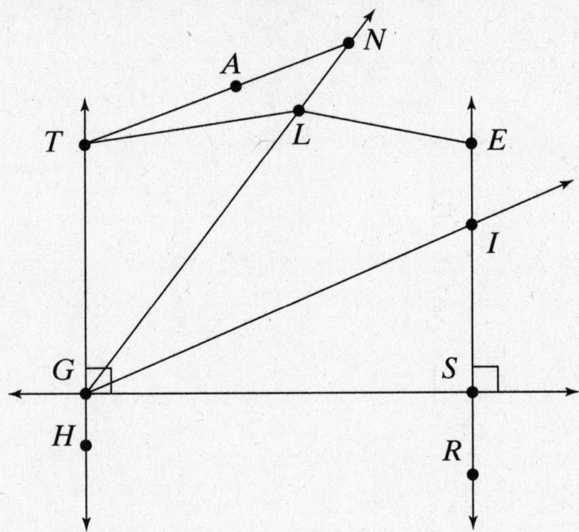

Answer each question by choosing values from the table.

Answer Box

$\angle TLG$	$\overleftrightarrow{TH}$	$\overline{TL}$	$\angle IGH$	$\angle GLE$	$\overrightarrow{GI}$
$\angle GSI$	$\angle HGS$	$\overleftrightarrow{ER}$	$\angle TAN$	$\overline{LE}$	$\overrightarrow{GN}$

1. A line parallel to $\overleftrightarrow{ER}$ is ____________.

2. $\overrightarrow{GI}$ intersects this line. ____________

3. ____________ and $\angle TGI$ are supplementary.

4. ____________ is a straight angle.

5. $\angle NLE$ and ____________ are supplementary.

Re-write your answers below to make sure you chose:

____ ____ ____ ____ ____ ____ ____ ____ ____ ____ ____ ____ ____

1 2 3 4 5

Name ______________________ Class ______________ Date ______________

Practice 7-3

Find the value of *x* in each triangle.

1. 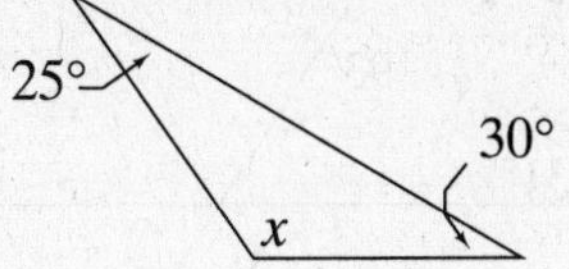

2. 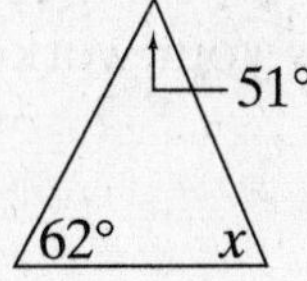

3. 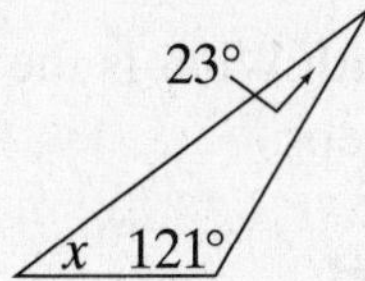

4. 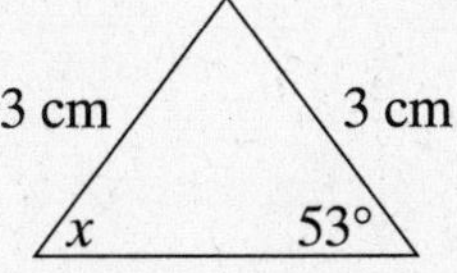

5. 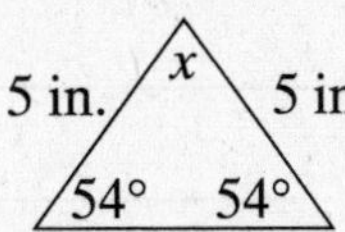

6. 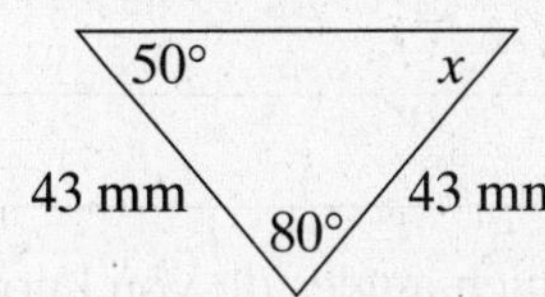

Classify each triangle.

7. The measures of two angles are 53° and 76°.

8. Two sides have the same length.

9. The measure of one angle is 90°.

10. All three sides have the same length.

11. The measures of the angles of a triangle are 40°, 50°, and 90°.
    a. Classify the triangle by its angles.
    b. Can the triangle be equilateral? Why or why not?
    c. Can the triangle be isosceles? Why or why not?
    d. Can you classify the triangle by its sides? Why or why not?

Name ______________________ Class ______________ Date ______________

7-3 • Guided Problem Solving

GPS Student Page 339, Exercise 19:

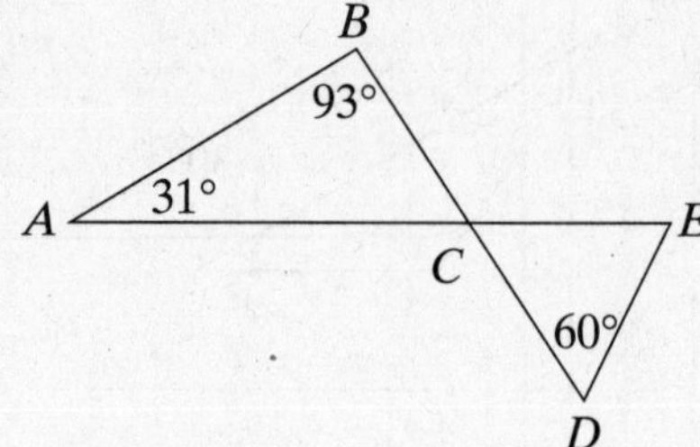

Writing in Math What is the measure of $\angle E$? Show your work and justify your steps.

Understand

1. What are you being asked to do?

____

____

2. Which angles do you know the measure of? What is their measure?

____

Plan and Carry Out

3. What is the sum of the measures of the angles in a triangle?

____

4. What is the sum of the measures of angles A and B?

____

5. Use the results from Steps 3 and 4 to determine the measure of $\angle ACB$. What is the measure of $\angle ECD$?

____

6. What is the sum of the measures of angles $\angle ECD$ and $\angle D$?

____

7. Use the results from Steps 3 and 6 to determine $m\angle E$.

____

Check

8. How do you justify using 180° to find the measure of the unknown angles?

____

Solve Another Problem

9. Suppose $m\angle A = 62°$, $m\angle B = 43°$, and $m\angle D = 73°$. Find the measure of $\angle E$.

____

____

Name ______________________ Class ______________ Date ____________

Practice 7-3

Triangles

Find the value of *x* in each triangle.

1. 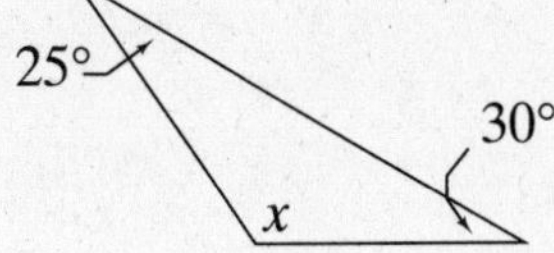

2. 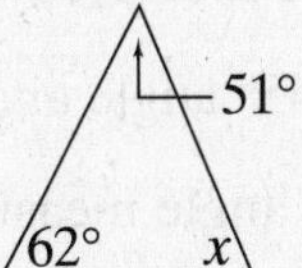

3. 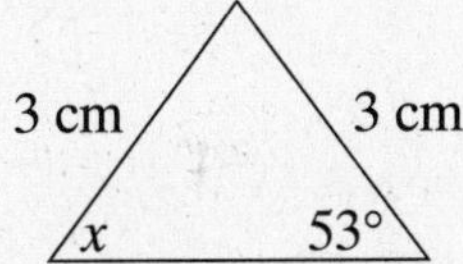

4. x
5 in. 5 in.
54° 54°

Classify each triangle.

5. The measures of two angles are 53° and 76°.

6. Two sides have the same length.

7. All three sides have the same length.

8. The measures of the angles of a triangle are 40°, 50°, and 90°.

   a. Classify the triangle by its angles.

   b. Can the triangle be equilateral? Why or why not?

   c. Can the triangle be isosceles? Why or why not?

Name ______________________ Class ______________ Date ______________

Activity Lab 7-3

Triangles

Without measuring, predict the measure of the third angle of each triangle. Use a protractor to check your predictions.

1. a. Draw a triangle with one 45° angle and one 35° angle.

   b. Classify the triangle by its angle measures.

   c. Classify the triangle by its sides. Use tick marks to indicate congruent sides.

2. a. Draw a triangle with one 50° angle and one 20° angle.

   b. Classify the triangle by its angle measures.

   c. Classify the triangle by its sides. Use tick marks to indicate congruent sides.

3. a. Draw a triangle with one 70° angle and one 40° angle.

   b. Classify the triangle by its angle measures.

   c. Classify the triangle by its sides. Use tick marks to indicate congruent sides.

4. a. Draw a triangle with one 52° angle and one 38° angle.

   b. Classify the triangle by its angle measures.

   c. Classify the triangle by its sides. Use tick marks to indicate congruent sides.

5. a. Draw a triangle with two 60° angles.

   b. Classify the triangle by its angle measures.

   c. Classify the triangle by its sides. Use tick marks to indicate congruent sides.

Name ______________________ Class ______________ Date ______________

Reteaching 7-3

Classifying Triangles by Angles	Classifying Triangles by Sides
Acute triangle: three acute angles	**Equilateral triangle:** three congruent sides
Right triangle: one right angle	**Isosceles triangle:** at least two congruent sides
Obtuse triangle: one obtuse angle	**Scalene triangle:** no congruent sides

The sum of the measures of the angles of a triangle is 180°.

Find the value of x in the triangle at the right.

$$x = m\angle A$$
$$m\angle A + 40° + 78° = 180°$$
$$m\angle A + 118° = 180°$$
$$m\angle A = 180° - 118°$$
$$m\angle A = 62°$$
$$x = 62°$$

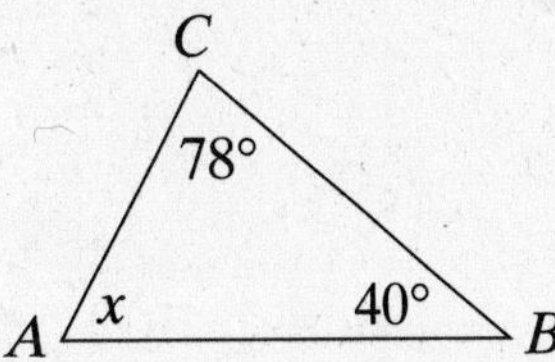

Classify each triangle by its sides and then by its angle measures.

1. 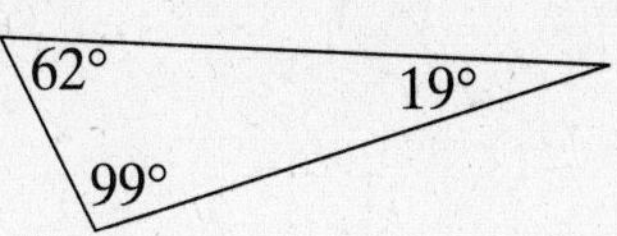

____

2. 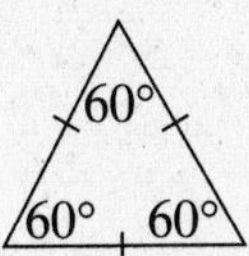

____

3. 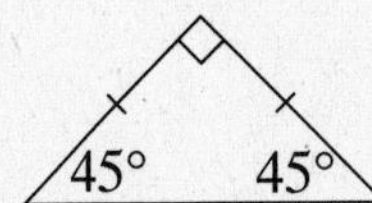

____

4. 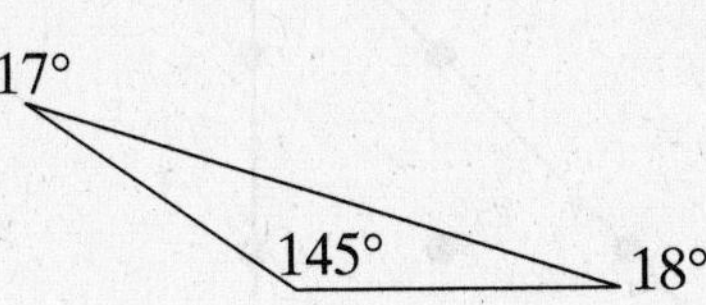

____

5. 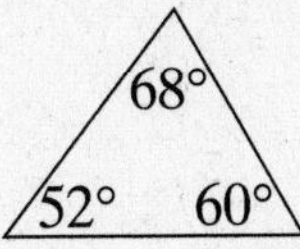

____

6. 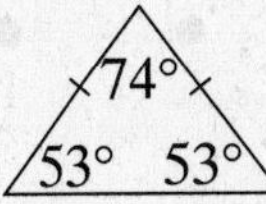

____

Find the value of x in each triangle.

7. 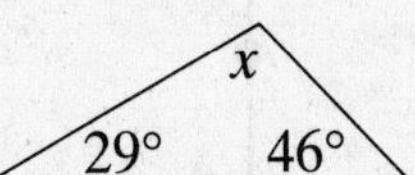

____

8. 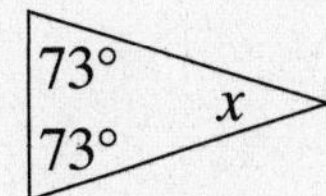

____

Name ______________________ Class ______________ Date ____________

Enrichment 7-3

Triangles

Visual Thinking

Each of the triangles below can be divided into congruent parts. Congruent parts have the same size and shape. Divide each triangle into a different number of congruent parts. The first one has been started for you.

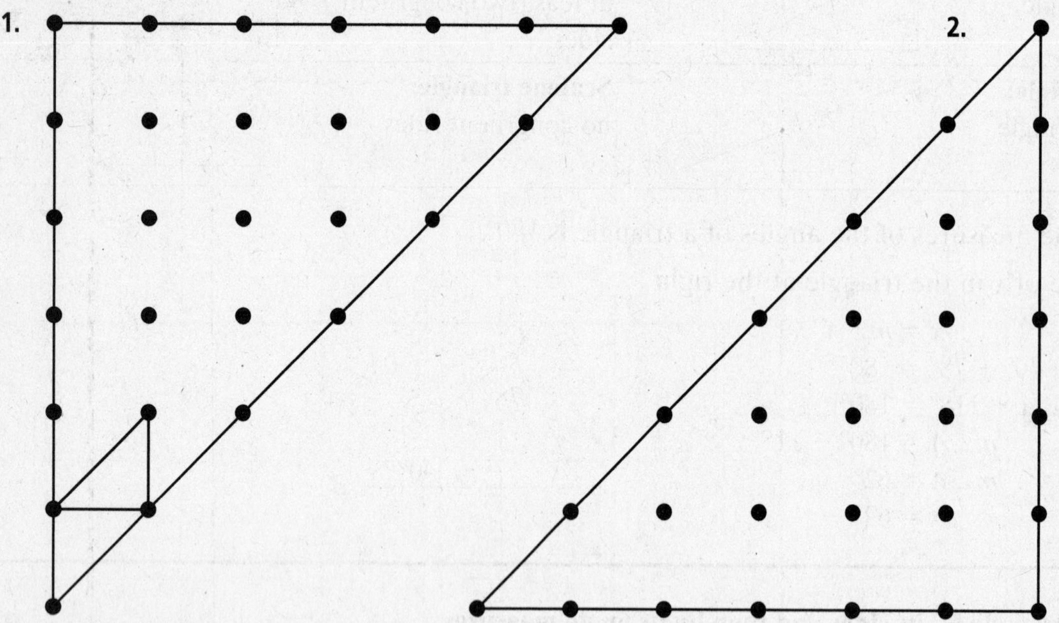

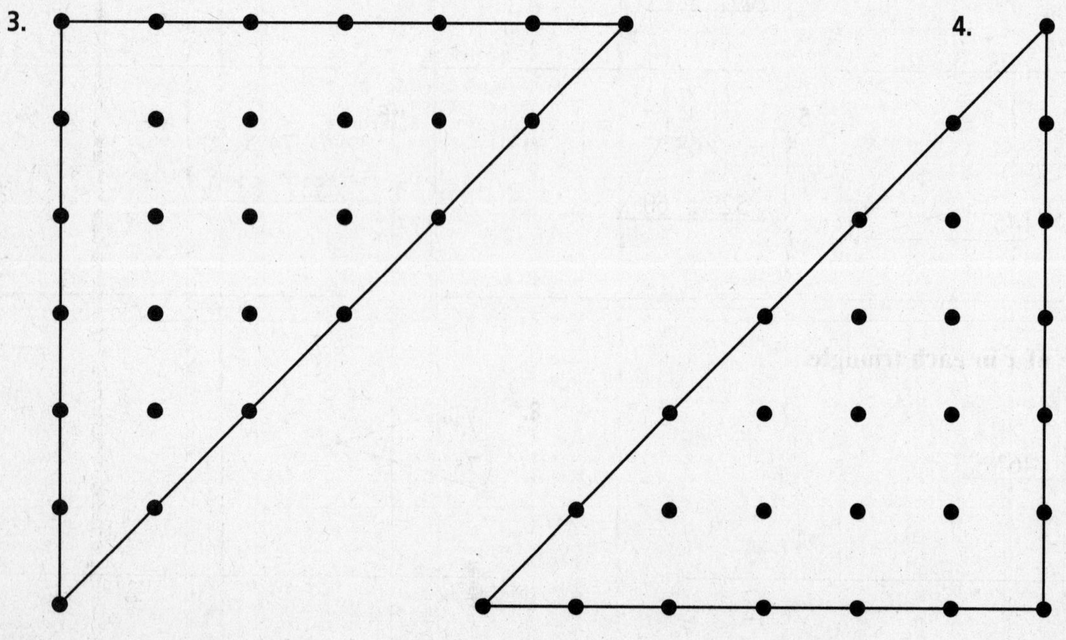

Name ______________________ Class ______________ Date ______________

Puzzle 7-3

Triangles

Look at the figure below.

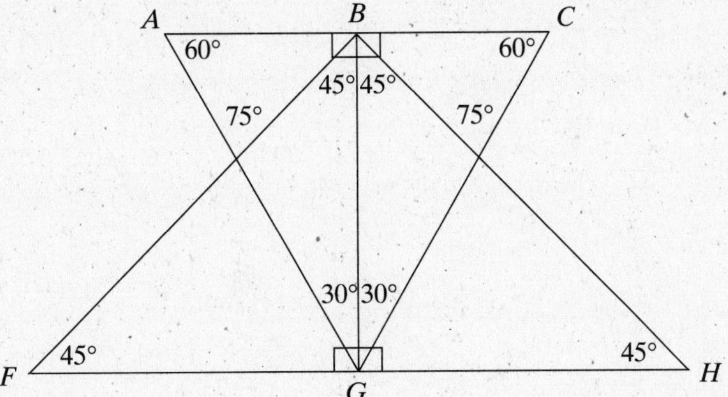

1. How many triangles do you find in all? ______________
2. How many scalene triangles do you find? ______________
3. How many isosceles triangles are there? ______________
4. How many right triangles? ______________
5. How many obtuse triangles? ______________
6. How many acute triangles are there? ______________
7. How many equilateral triangles do you find? ______________

Name ______________________ Class ______________ Date ______________

Practice 7-4

Quadrilaterals and Other Polygons

Identify each polygon and classify it as *regular* or *irregular.*

1. 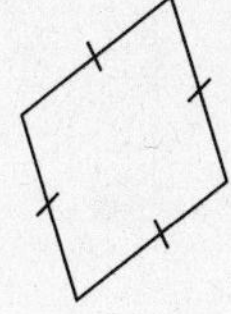

2. 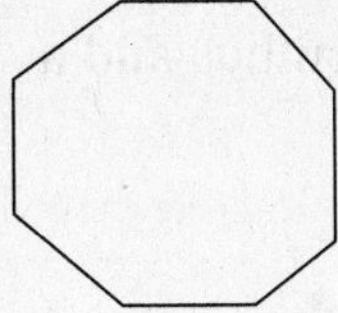

3. 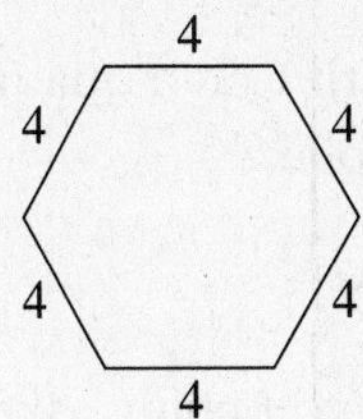

State all correct names for each quadrilateral. Then circle the best name.

4. 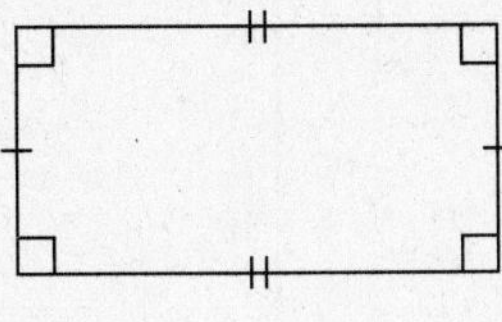

5. 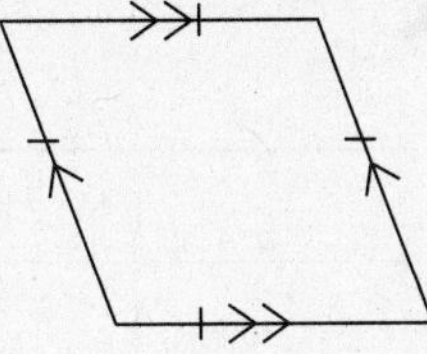

6. 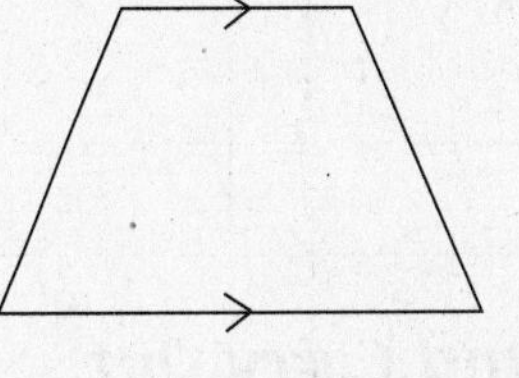

Use dot paper to draw each quadrilateral.

7. a rectangle that is not a square

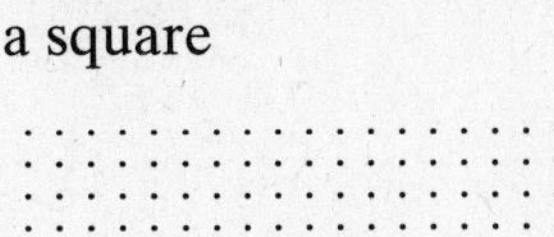

8. a rhombus with two right angles

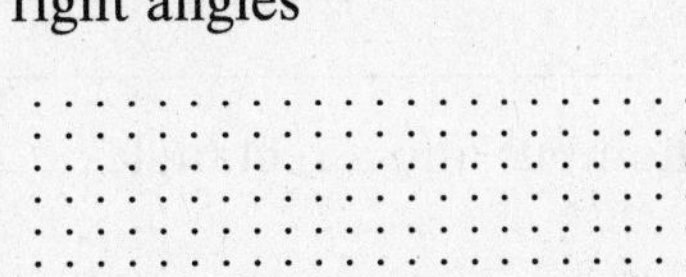

9. a trapezoid with no right angles

10. List all additional side lengths and angle measures you can find for the trapezoid *JKLM*, where $\overline{KL}$ is parallel to $\overline{JM}$, $\angle K$ is a right angle, and the length of $\overline{LM}$ is 10 cm.

____

Name ______________________ Class ______________ Date ____________

7-4 • Guided Problem Solving

GPS Student Page 344, Exercise 22:

Writing in Math Can a quadrilateral be both a rhombus and a rectangle? Explain.

Understand

1. What are you being asked to do?

____

____

2. In order to answer this question, what definitions do you need to know?

____

____

Plan and Carry Out

3. What is a quadrilateral?

____

4. What is a rhombus?

____

5. What is a rectangle?

____

6. Can a quadrilateral be both a rhombus and a rectangle?

____

Check

7. Explain your answer to Step 6 by giving an example of a shape that is both a rhombus and a rectangle.

____

____

____

Solve Another Problem

8. If all squares are types of rectangles, are all rhombuses types of rectangles? Explain.

____

Name ____________________ Class ____________ Date ____________

Practice 7-4

Quadrilaterals and Other Polygons

Identify each polygon and classify it as *regular* or *irregular.*

1.

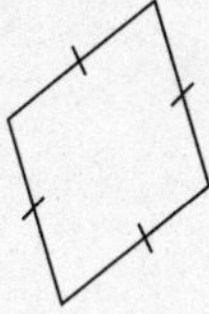

2.

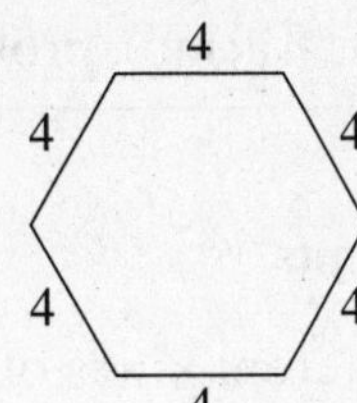

______________________________ ______________________________

____

State all correct names for each quadrilateral. Then circle the best name.

3.

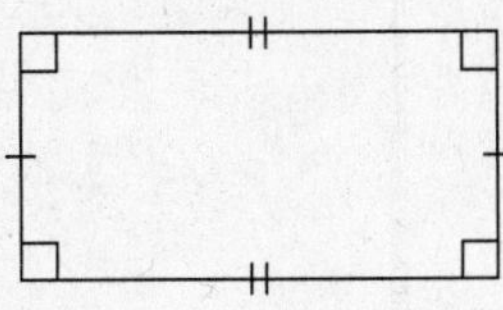

4.

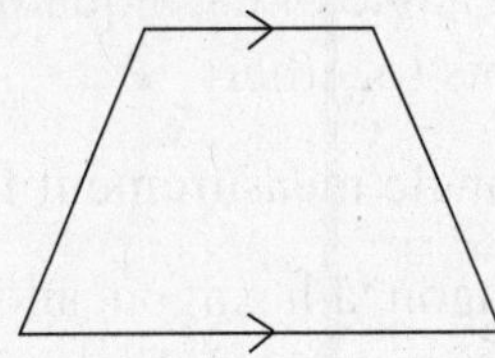

______________________________ ______________________________

______________________________ ______________________________

______________________________ ______________________________

Use dot paper to draw each quadrilateral.

5. a rectangle that is not a square

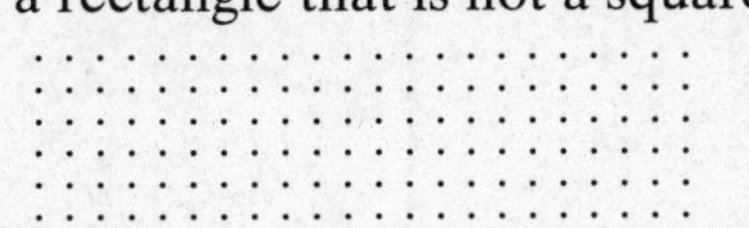

6. a rhombus with two right angles

7. a trapezoid with no right angles

Name ______________________ Class ______________ Date ____________

Activity Lab 7-4

Quadrilaterals and Other Polygons

Materials needed: pattern or attribute blocks and/or geometric shape templates (for tracing), protractor, dot paper

Work in small groups of 3–4 students.

1. a. Trace or draw as many different kinds of triangles as you can on the dot paper. Measure each angle of each triangle and add the three angle measurements together.

   b. What is the total angle measurement for each triangle?

2. a. Trace or draw as many different kinds of quadrilaterals as you can. Measure each angle of each quadrilateral and add the angle measurements together.

   b. What is the total angle measurement for each quadrilateral?

3. Trace or draw a pentagon, a hexagon, and an octagon. Measure the angles of each shape and add the angle measurements for each shape together.

   a. What is the total angle measurement for a pentagon?

   b. What is the total angle measurement for a hexagon?

   c. What is the total angle measurement for an octagon?

4. a. Write conclusions about angle measurements in triangles and polygons.

   b. Describe the patterns that relate these angle measures to the shapes.

5. a. Draw a triangle with one 50° angle and one 30° angle.

   b. Without measuring, how can you predict the measure of the third angle? Use a protractor to check your prediction.

6. The rule for determining the total angle measurement of a polygon with n sides is $(n - 2)(180)$.

   a. Predict the total angle measurement for a decagon.

   b. Draw a decagon on dot paper.

   c. Measure each angle and add the measurements together to confirm your prediction.

Name ______________________ Class ______________ Date ______________

Reteaching 7-4

Quadrilaterals and Other Polygons

You name polygons by the number of sides. A **quadrilateral** is a polygon with four sides. The table shows the names and properties of some special quadrilaterals.

Special Quadrilaterals

Quadrilateral	Figure	Only 1 Pair of Parallel Sides	2 Pairs of Parallel Sides	All Sides Must be Congruent	Opposite Sides Are Congruent	All Angles Must Be Right Angles
Square			✔	✔	✔	✔
Rectangle			✔		✔	✔
Rhombus			✔	✔	✔	
Parallelogram			✔		✔	
Trapezoid		✔				

Look at the rhombus. It is also a parallelogram, but the name rhombus is best because it gives the most information about the figure.

Write the best name for each quadrilateral.

1. 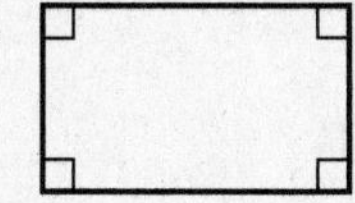

____

2. 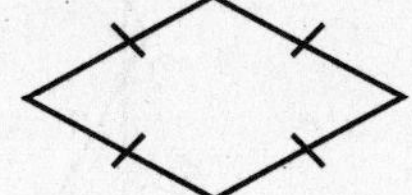

____

3. 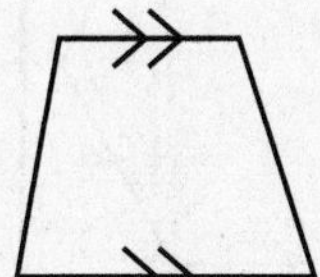

____

Draw each of the following.

4. a trapezoid with a right angle

5. a quadrilateral with opposite sides parallel and a right angle

6. a regular octagon

Name ______________________ Class ______________ Date ____________

Enrichment 7-4

Visual Thinking

A diagonal connects two non-adjacent vertices of a polygon. Draw only the diagonals needed to divide each figure into the smaller figures given.

1. 2 equilateral triangles
   2 rhombuses

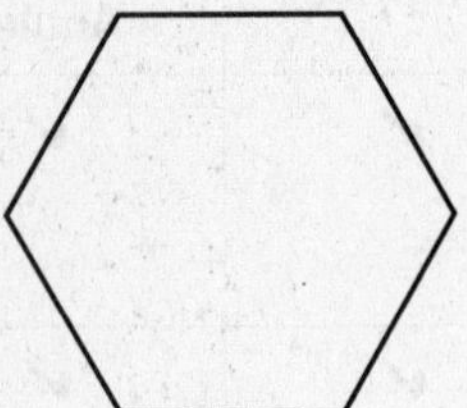

2. 2 right triangles
   2 isosceles triangles

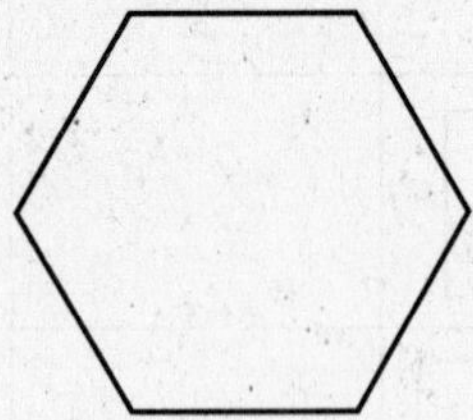

3. 1 trapezoid
   1 isosceles triangle
   1 scalene triangle

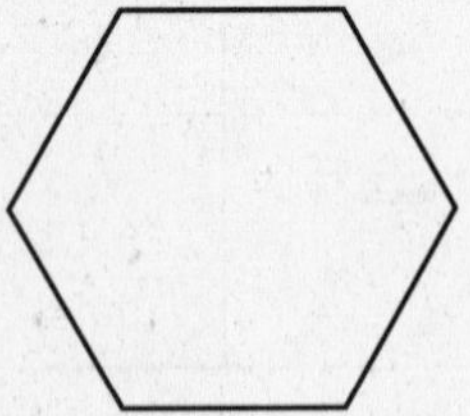

4. 3 isosceles triangles
   1 equilateral triangle

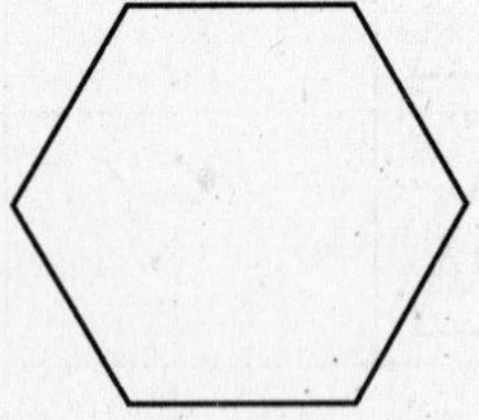

5. 1 pentagon
   1 isosceles triangle

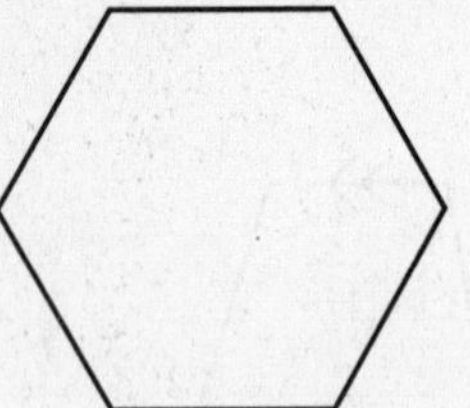

6. 1 quadrilateral
   2 isosceles triangles

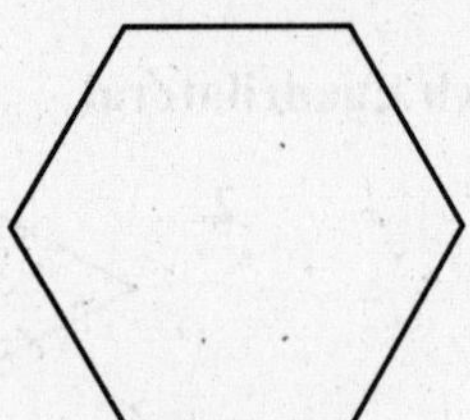

7. 4 equilateral triangles
   4 right triangles

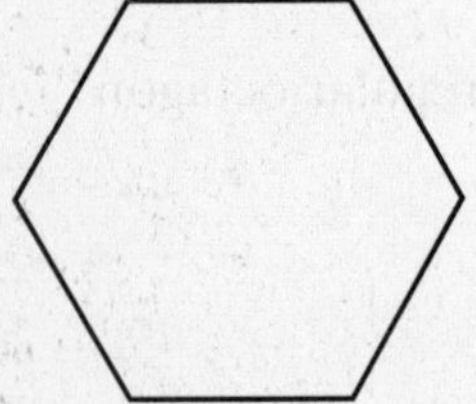

8. 2 rectangles
   4 right triangles

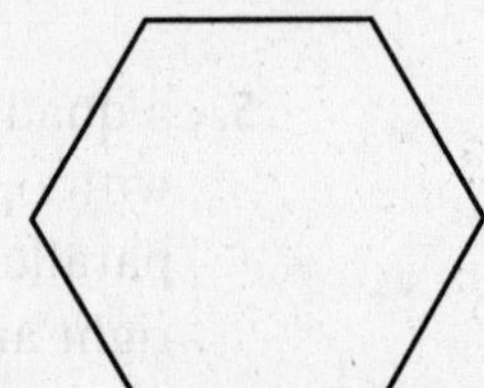

Name ______________________ Class ______________ Date ______________

Puzzle 7-4

Quadrilaterals and Other Polygons

1. I am a polygon with an odd number of sides. I have more sides than a quadrilateral but fewer than a hexagon. What am I?

___ ___ ___ ___ ___ ___ ___ ___
(blank 2: 4)

2. I am a quadrilateral with two pairs of parallel sides. What am I?

___ ___ ___ ___ ___ ___ ___ ___ ___ ___ ___ ___ ___
(blank 5: 7; blank 11: 2)

3. I am a polygon with twice as many sides as a triangle. All of my sides are the same length. What am I?

___ ___ ___ ___ ___ ___ ___   ___ ___ ___ ___ ___ ___ ___
(blank 1: 3; blank 11: 8)

4. I am a polygon with all of my sides congruent. I have the same number of sides as a trapezoid. I have two pairs of sides that are parallel. What am I?

___ ___ ___ ___ ___ ___ ___
(blank 6: 6)

5. I am a quadrilateral with one less set of parallel sides than a rectangle. What am I?

___ ___ ___ ___ ___ ___ ___ ___ ___
(blank 2: 9; blank 7: 5)

6. I am a polygon with an even number of sides. My number of sides is the cube of two. What am I?

___ ___ ___ ___ ___ ___ ___ ___
(blank 2: 4)

Fill in your answer to solve the puzzle.

A polygon with sides that are not all congruent or angles that are not all congruent is known as

___ ___ ___ ___ ___ ___ ___ ___ ___.
1 2 3 4 5 6 7 8 9

Name ______________________ Class ______________ Date ______________

Practice 7-5

Congruent Figures

Are the figures *congruent* or *not congruent*? Explain.

1\.

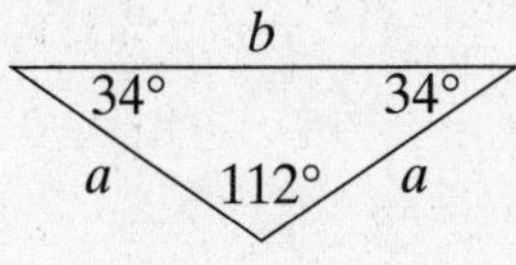

2\.

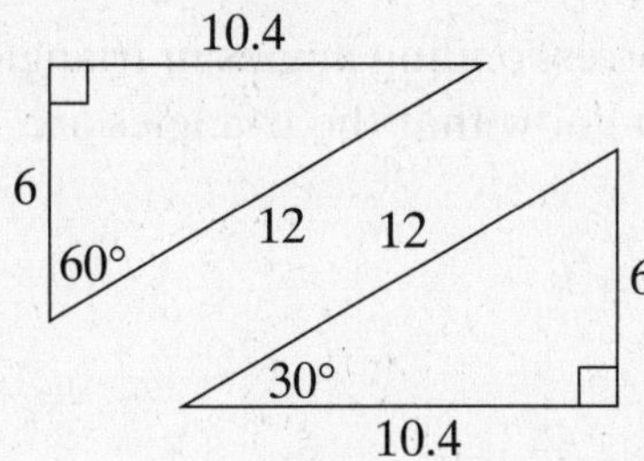

3\.

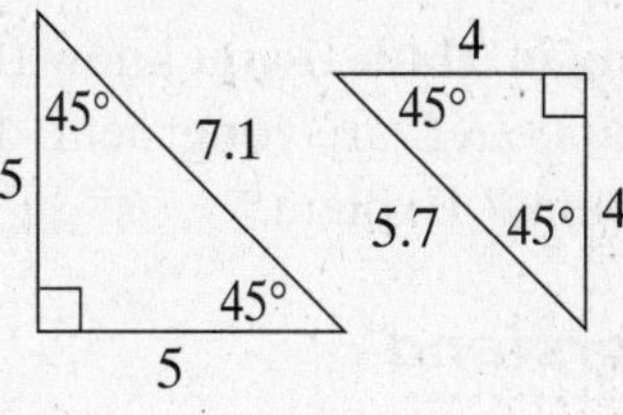

____

Complete each congruence statement.

4\. $\triangle ABC \cong$ ______________

5\. $\triangle ABC \cong$ ______________

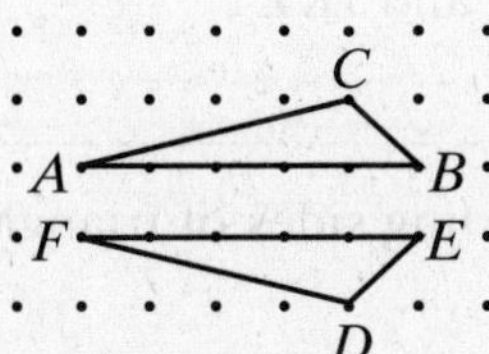

6\. $\triangle ABC \cong$ ______________

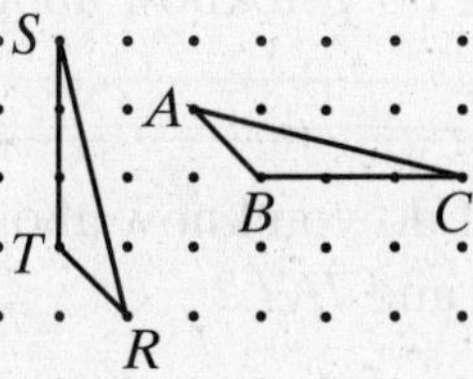

Write six congruences involving corresponding sides and angles for each pair of triangles.

7\. $\triangle ABC \cong \triangle DEF$

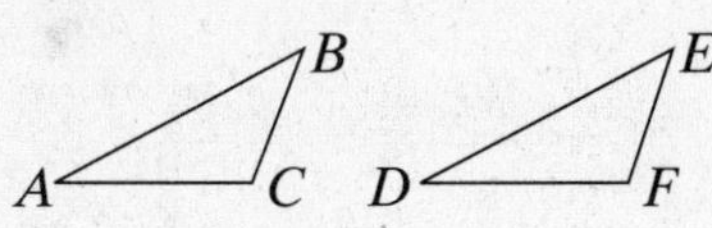

8\. $\triangle JKL \cong \triangle MNO$

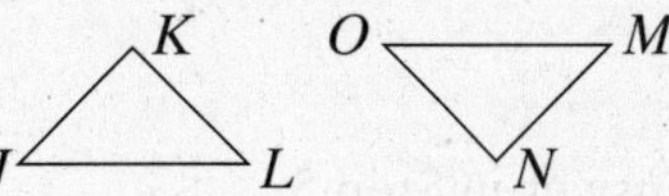

Use the diagram at the right to complete each of the following.

9\. **a.** $\angle ABC \cong$ ______________

b. $\overline{AB} \cong$ ______________

c. $\angle F \cong$ ______________

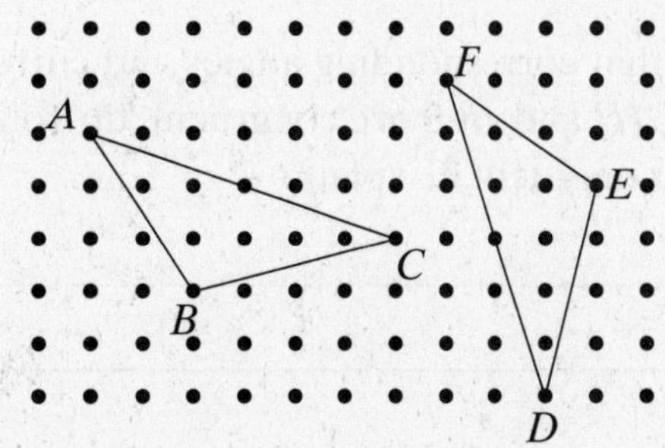

Name ______________________ Class ______________ Date ____________

7-5 • Guided Problem Solving

GPS Student Page 349, Exercise 13:

Writing in Math If you know that corresponding angles in triangles *GHI* and *JKL* are congruent, do you know that the triangles are congruent? Explain.

Understand

1. What are you being asked to do?

____

____

2. What proves that two triangles are congruent?

____

____

Plan and Carry Out

3. What do you know about triangles *GHI* and *JKL*?

____

4. What do you know about the corresponding sides of triangles *GHI* and *JKL*?

____

5. Do you know that the two triangles are congruent?

____

Check

6. Explain your answer in Step 5.

____

____

____

Solve Another Problem

7. If you know that corresponding angles and corresponding sides in triangles *GHI* and *JKL* are congruent, do you know that the triangles are congruent? Explain.

____

____

Practice 7-5

Congruent Figures

Are the figures *congruent* or *not congruent*? Explain.

1. 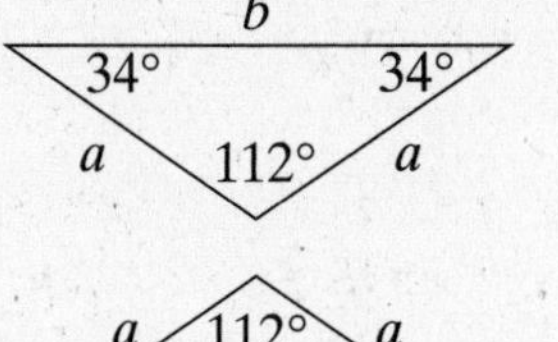

____

____

____

2. 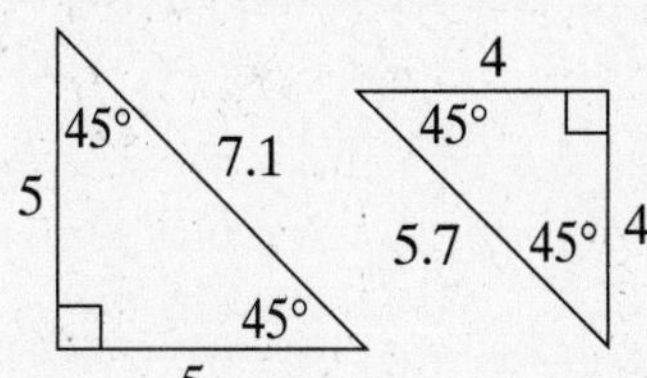

____

____

____

Complete each congruence statement.

3. $\triangle ABC \cong$ ______________

4. $\triangle ABC \cong$ ______________

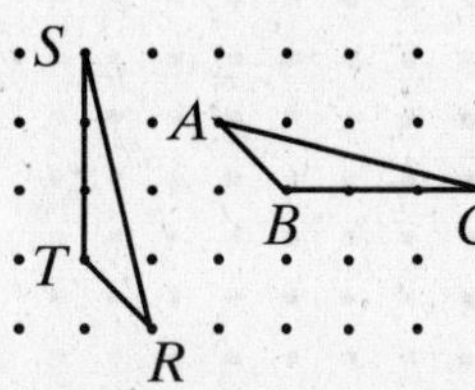

Write six congruences involving corresponding sides and angles for the triangles.

5. $\triangle ABC \cong \triangle DEF$

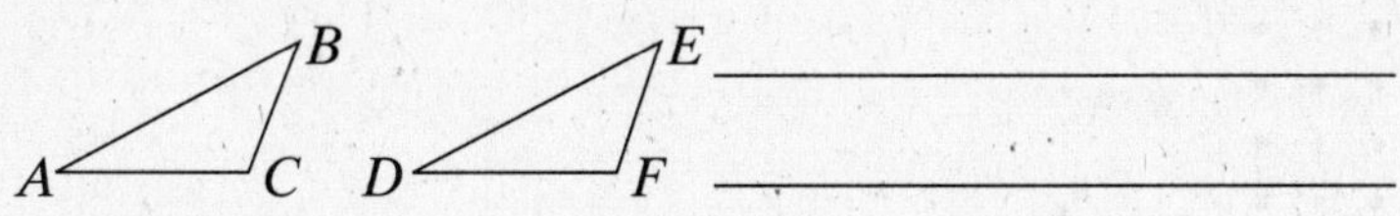

____

____

____

Use the diagram at the right to complete each of the following.

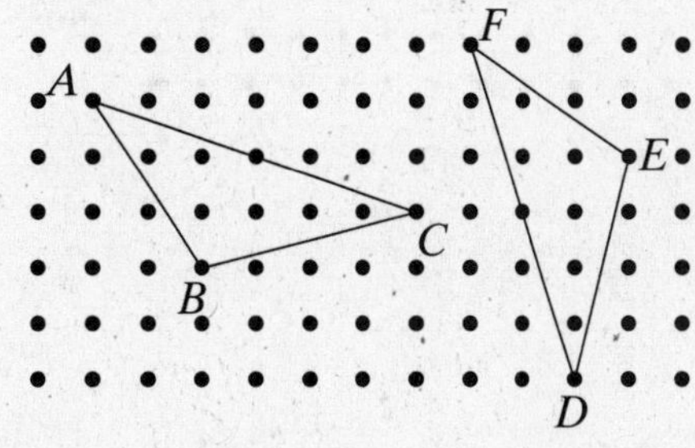

6. a. $\angle ABC \cong$ ______________

b. $\overline{AB} \cong$ ______________

c. $\angle F \cong$ ______________

Name ______________________ Class ______________ Date ______________

Activity Lab 7-5

Congruent Figures

1. Find the missing sides and angles of $\triangle ABC$.
2. Draw a congruent triangle on the dot grid below. Label the vertices D, E, and F.
3. Label the sides and angles of $\triangle DEF$. ______________________
4. List the pairs of congruent sides and angles. ______________________
5. How many did you find? ______________________
6. If you know that the triangles are congruent, can you conclude they are similar? Explain.

____

____

____

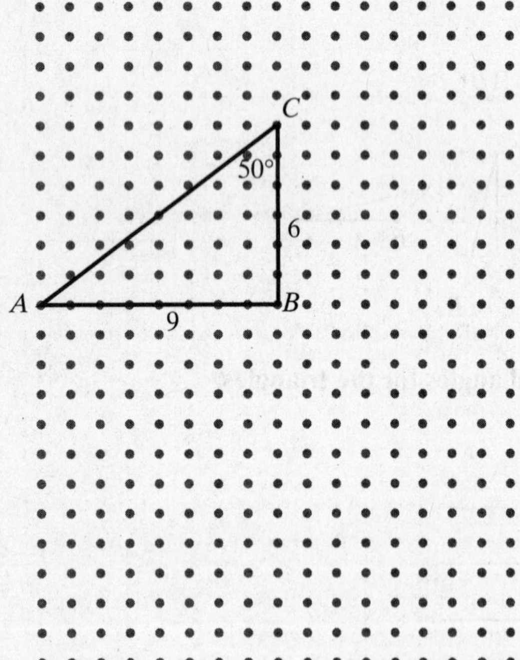

Name ______________________ Class ______________ Date ______________

Reteaching 7-5

Congruent Figures

Congruent polygons have congruent sides and angles. These are called the *corresponding parts* of the congruent figures.

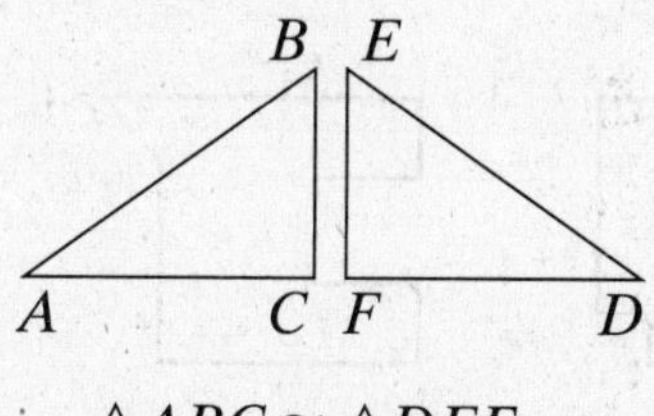

$\triangle ABC \cong \triangle DEF$

Corresponding Angles	Corresponding Sides
$\angle A \cong \angle D$	$BC \cong EF$
$\angle B \cong \angle E$	$CA \cong FD$
$\angle C \cong \angle F$	$AB \cong DE$

Complete each congruence statement.

1. $\triangle LMN \cong \triangle RPQ$

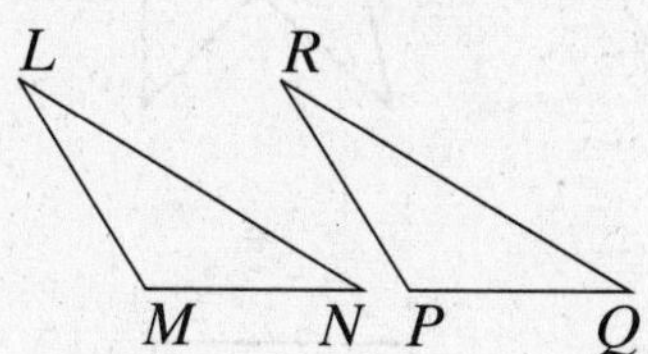

$\overline{MN} \cong \overline{PQ}$ $\angle M \cong \angle P$

$\overline{NL} \cong$ ________ $\angle L \cong$ ________

2. $\triangle FGJ \cong \triangle YWX$

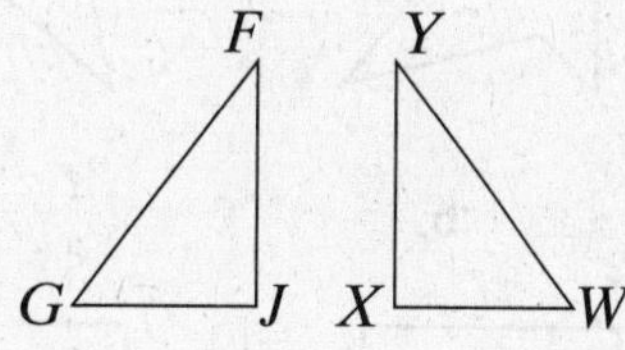

$\overline{JF} \cong \overline{XY}$ $\angle G \cong \angle W$

$\overline{FG} \cong$ ________ $\angle J \cong$ ________

Are the figures below *congruent* or *not congruent*? Explain.

3. 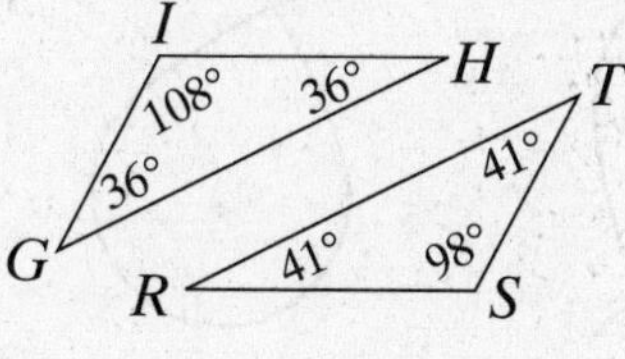

____

____

____

____

4. 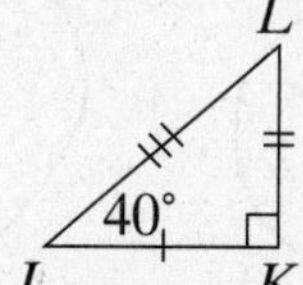

____

____

____

____

Name ______________________ Class ______________ Date ____________

Enrichment 7-5

Congruent Figures

Visual Thinking

Circle the letter of the figure in each row that is different from the others.

1.

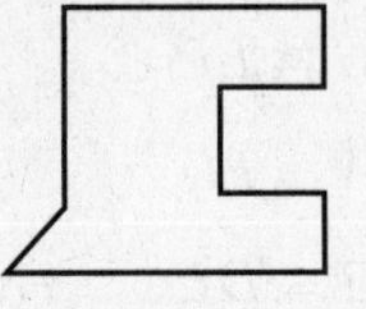
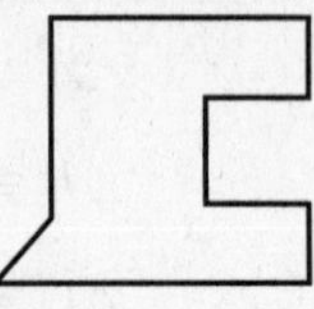
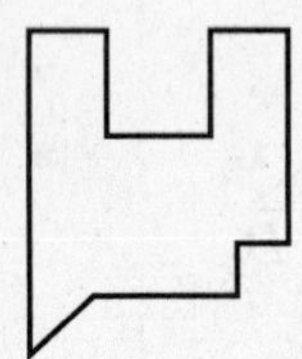
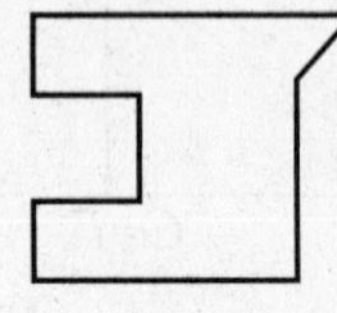

a. b. c. d. e.

2.

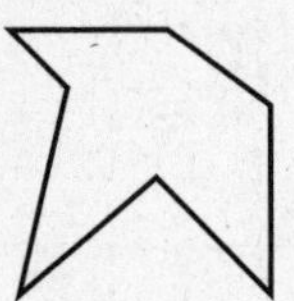

a. b. c. d. e.

3.

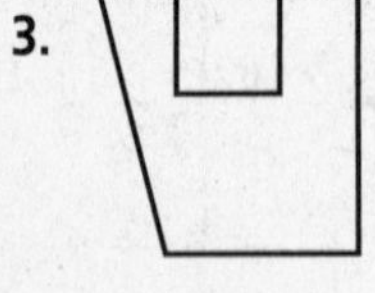
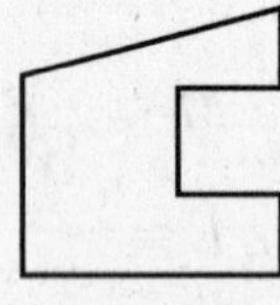
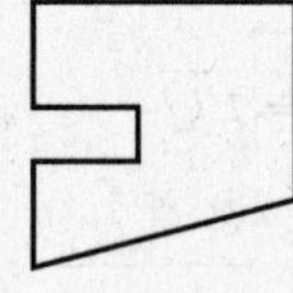

a. b. c. d. e.

4.

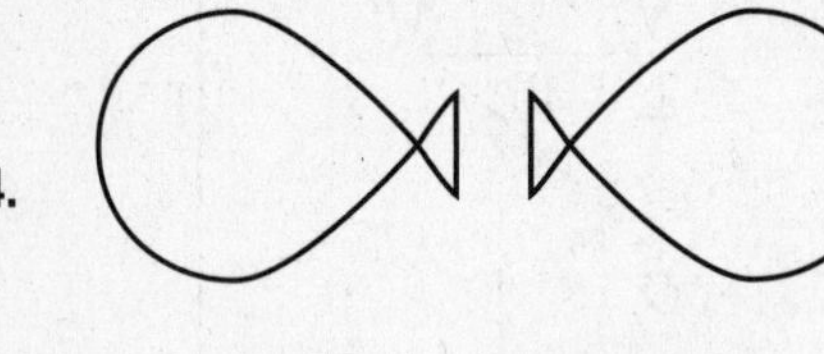
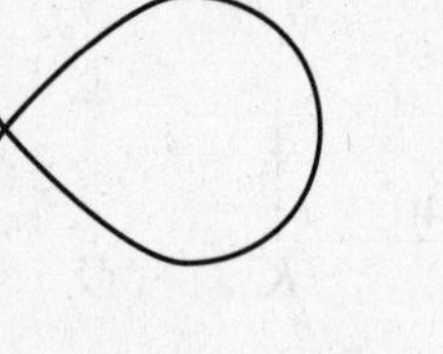

a. b. c. d. e.

5.

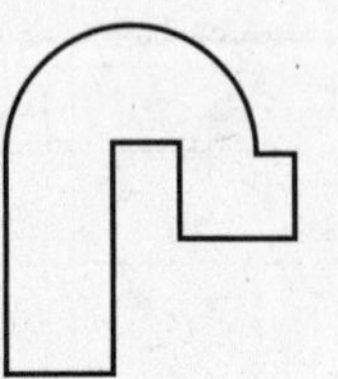

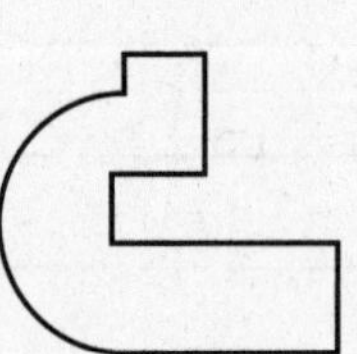
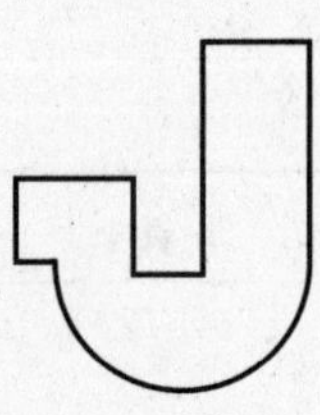

a. b. c. d. e.

Name ______________________ Class ______________ Date ______________

7C: Reading/Writing Math Symbols

For use after Lesson 7-5

Study Skill When you take notes, use abbreviations and symbols such as @ (at), # (number), and w/ (with) to save time and reduce writing.

Match the symbol in Column A with its meaning in Column B.

Column A	Column B
1. $\angle ABC$	**A.** the measure of angle ABC
2. $\overline{AB}$	**B.** the length of segment AB
3. $\overleftrightarrow{AB}$	**C.** triangle ABC
4. AB	**D.** segment AB
5. $\overrightarrow{AB}$	**E.** ray starting at A and passing through B
6. $m\angle ABC$	**F.** ray starting at B and passing through A
7. $\overrightarrow{BA}$	**G.** line AB
8. $\triangle ABC$	**H.** angle ABC

Write the meaning of each of the following mathematical statements.

9. $m\angle B = 80°$

____

10. $\triangle ABC \cong \triangle HIJ$

____

11. $\angle XYZ \cong \angle MNP$

____

12. $BC = 4$

____

13. $\overline{DJ} \cong \overline{KL}$

____

14. $DJ = KL$

____

15. $m\angle P = m\angle R$

____

16. $BC = \frac{1}{2}TU$

____

Name ______________________ Class ______________ Date ____________

Puzzle 7-5

Congruent Figures

Each figure that makes up the left square has a congruent part in the right square.

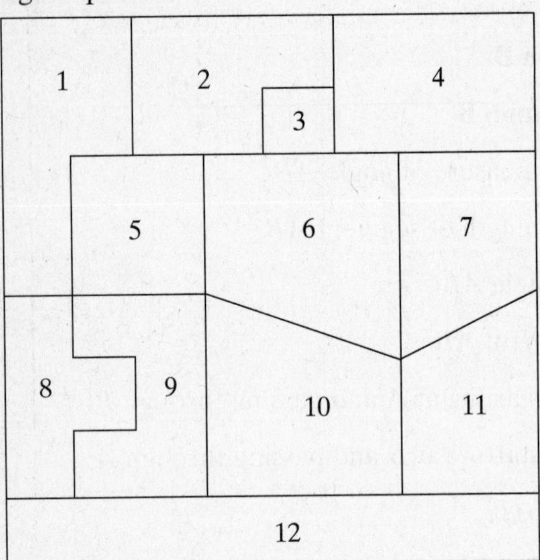

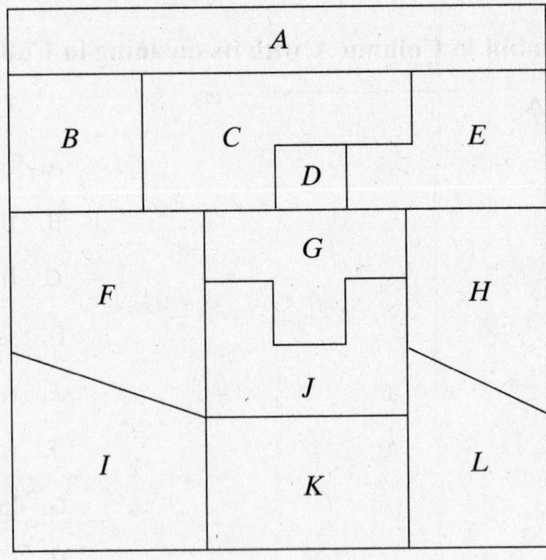

Write the letter of the figure in the right square that is congruent to the numbered figure in the left square.

1. ____________ **2.** ____________ **3.** ____________

4. ____________ **5.** ____________ **6.** ____________

7. ____________ **8.** ____________ **9.** ____________

10. ____________ **11.** ____________ **12.** ____________

13. Make up your own puzzle.

Name ______________________ Class ______________ Date ______________

Practice 7-6

Circles

Name each of the following for circle *O*.

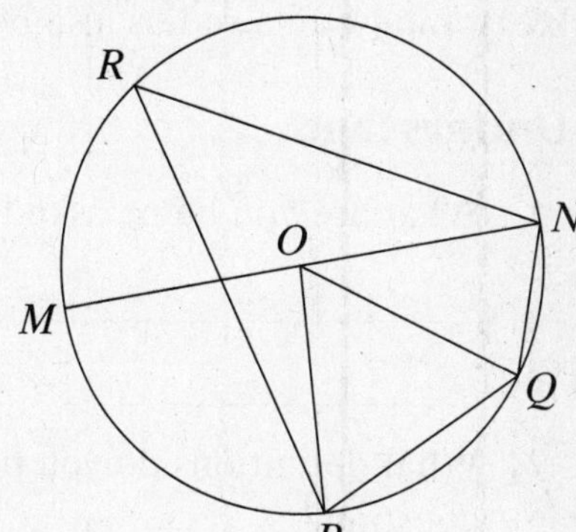

1. two chords ______________

2. three radii ______________

3. a diameter ______________

4. a central angle ______________

5. a semicircle ______________

6. two arcs ______________

7. the longest chord ______________

8. the shortest chord ______________

Name all of the indicated arcs for circle *Q*.

9. all arcs shorter than a semicircle ______________

10. all arcs longer than a semicircle ______________

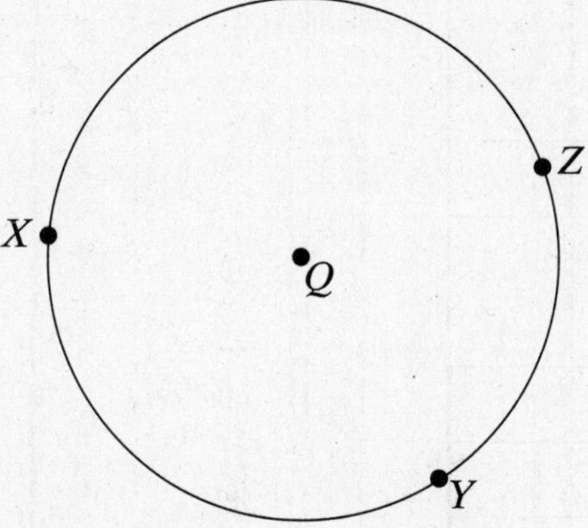

11. Use a compass to draw and label a circle Q. Label a semicircle $\widehat{ABC}$ and an arc $\widehat{AX}$.

7-6 • Guided Problem Solving

GPS Student Page 352, Exercise 25:

Reasoning Can a radius also be a chord? Explain.

Understand

1. What are you being asked to do?

____

____

2. What definitions do you need to know in order to answer the question?

____

Plan and Carry Out

3. What is a radius?

____

____

4. Where are the endpoints of a radius?

____

____

5. What is a chord?

____

____

6. Can a radius also be a chord? ____________________

Check

7. Explain your answer in Step 6.

____

____

____

Solve Another Problem

8. Can a diameter also be a chord? Explain.

____

____

Name ______________________ Class ______________ Date ______________

Practice 7-6

Circles

Name each of the following for circle *O*.

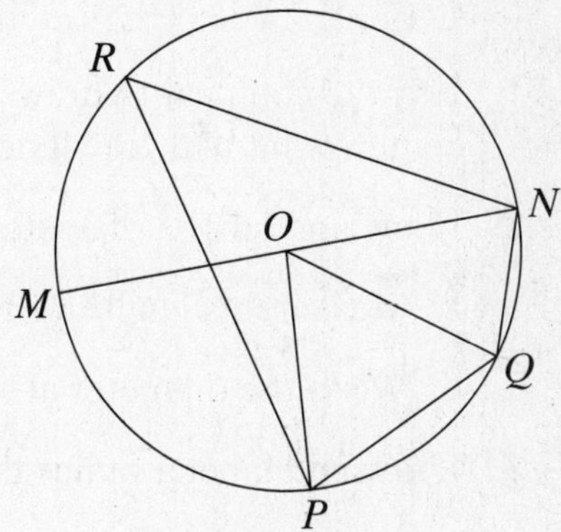

1. two chords ______________
2. three radii ______________
3. a diameter ______________
4. a central angle ______________
5. a semicircle ______________
6. two arcs ______________

Name all of the indicated arcs for circle *Q*.

7. all arcs shorter than a semicircle ______________
8. all arcs longer than a semicircle ______________

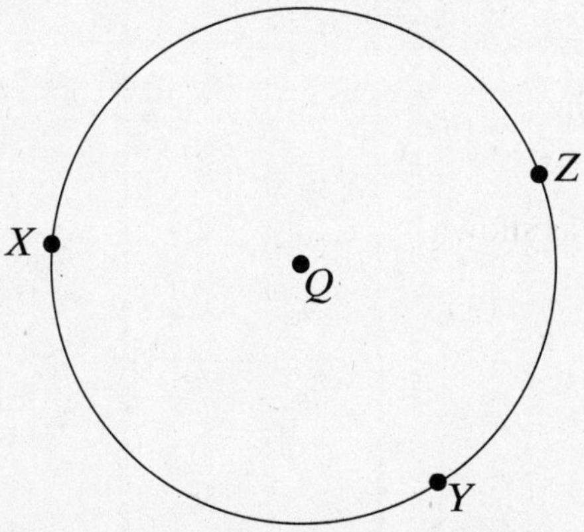

9. Use a compass to draw and label a circle *Q*. Label a semicircle $\overset{\frown}{ABC}$ and an arc $\overset{\frown}{AX}$.

Name ______________________ Class ______________ Date ______________

Activity Lab 7-6

Materials needed: compass, protractor, centimeter ruler

1. Use the compass to draw a circle on a sheet of paper. Label the center point with any letter.
2. Draw and label a diameter of the circle using different letters.
   a. Measure its length with a centimeter ruler.
   b. Write the diameter at the top of the paper.
3. Draw and label a radius that is perpendicular to the diameter.
   a. Name three of the circle's radii on your paper.
   b. What is the length of each radius?
4. Draw a chord from one end of the diameter to the outside point of the perpendicular radius.
   a. What kind of triangle is formed?
   b. Find the length of the third side of the triangle using the Pythagorean Theorem. Write it on your paper, too.
5. Draw a different point on the circumference of the circle, as shown.

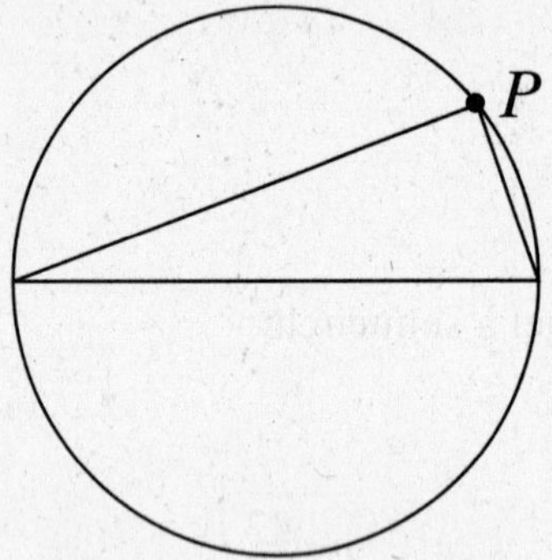

   a. Draw chords from this point to either end of the diameter as shown in the diagram.
   b. What kind of triangle is formed by the chords and the diameter? Explain.

Name ______________________ Class ______________ Date ______________

Reteaching 7-6

Circles

A **circle** is the set of points in a plane that are all the same distance from a point, called the *center.* This circle is called circle *A*.

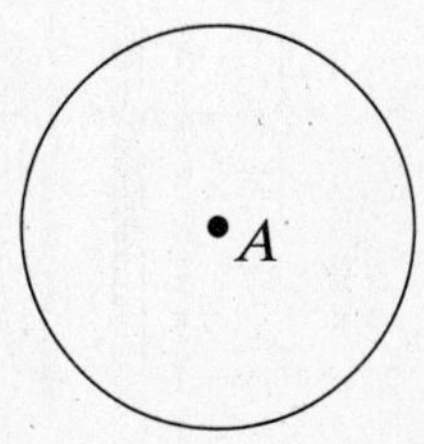

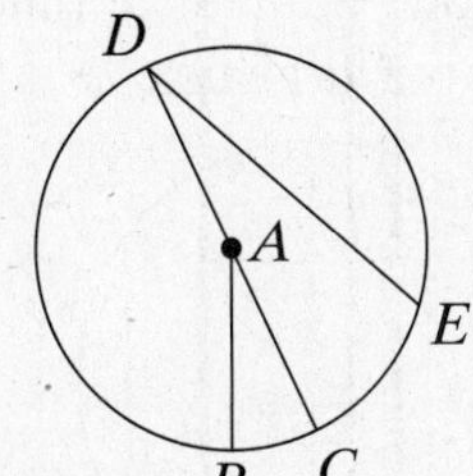

$\overline{AB}$ is a **radius** of circle *A*. It is a segment that has one endpoint on the circle and the other at the center. $\overline{AC}$ and $\overline{AD}$ are also *radii* of circle *A*.

$\overline{DC}$ is a **diameter** of circle *A*. It is a segment that passes through the center of the circle and has both endpoints on the circle.

$\overline{DE}$ is a chord of circle *A*. A **chord** is a segment that has both endpoints on the circle.

$\overset{\frown}{DB}$ is an arc of circle *A*. An **arc** is part of a circle.

$\angle DAB$ is a **central angle** of circle *A*. It is an angle with its vertex at the center of the circle.

$\overset{\frown}{DEC}$ is a **semicircle.** A semicircle is an arc that is half a circle.

Name each of the following for circle *P*.

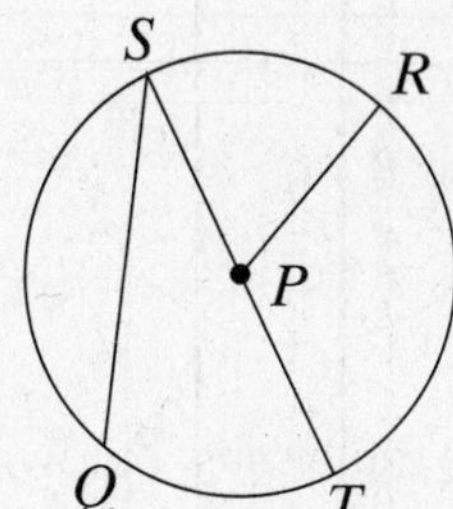
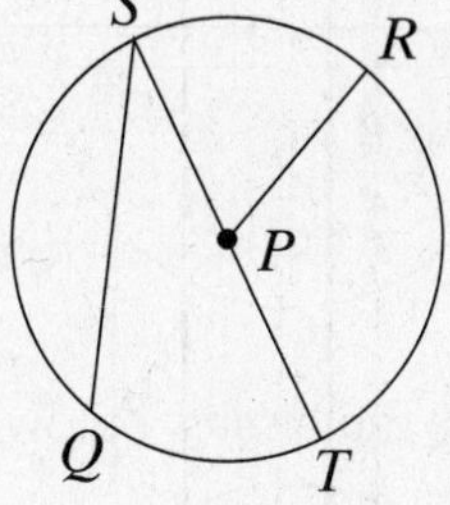

1. all radii ______________________

2. all chords ______________________

3. 3 arcs ______________________

Name each of the following shown for circle *M*.

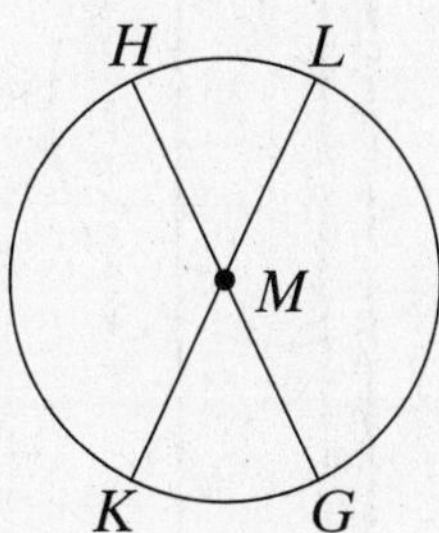

4. all diameters

____

5. 3 central angles

____

6. all chords

____

7. 2 semicircles

____

8. two radii

____

Name ______________________ Class ______________ Date ____________

Enrichment 7-6

Circles

Visual Thinking

1. Draw the figure that should appear in the center circle according to these rules: If a shape appears an even number of times in the other four circles, include it in your drawing. If a shape appears an odd number of times in the other four circles, do not include it in your drawing.

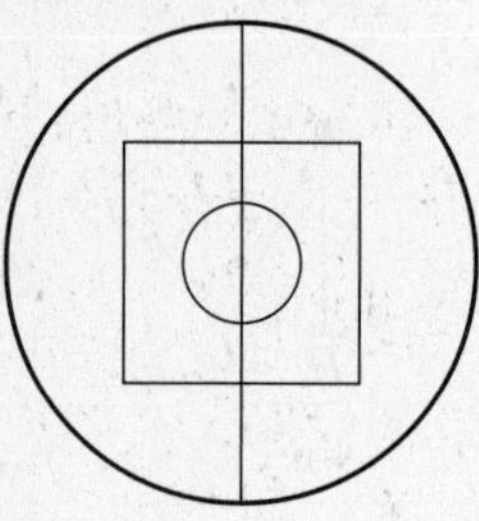

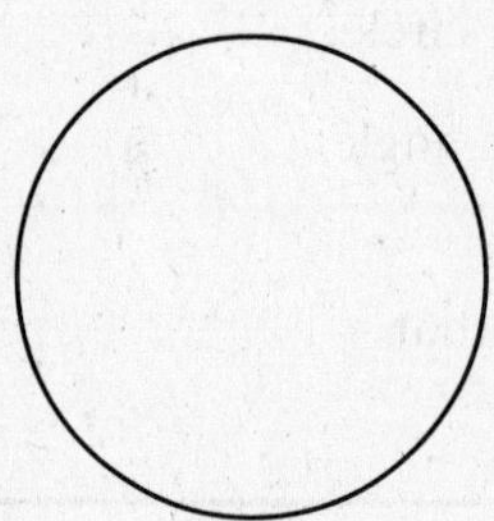

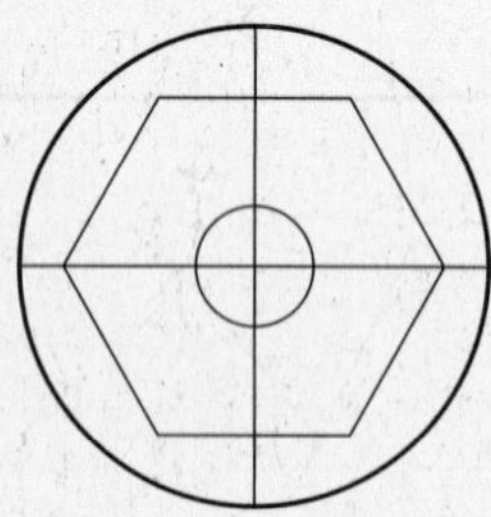

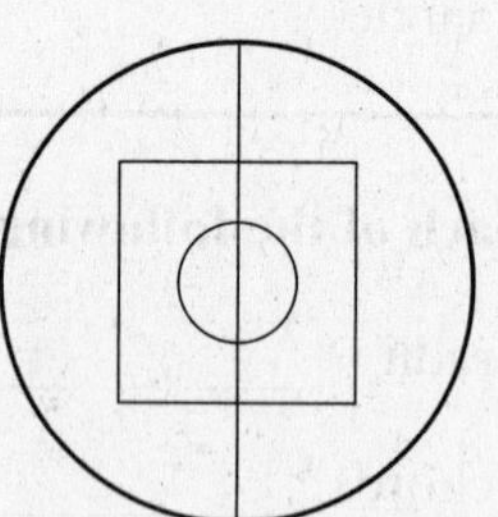

2. Use the circles below to create your own puzzle. Trade with a friend and solve.

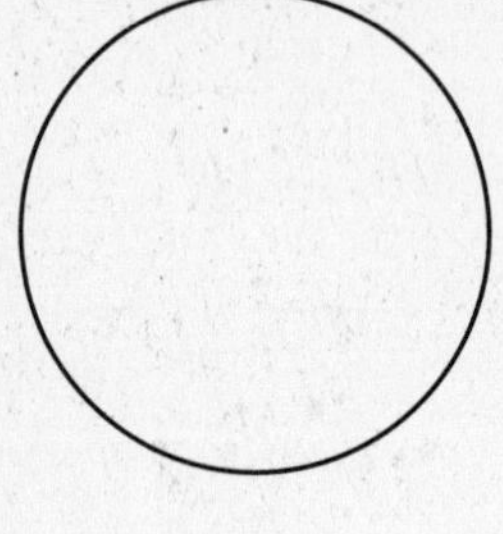

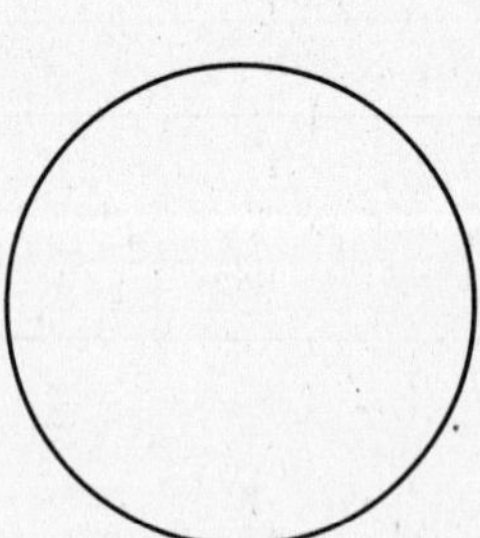

Name ______________________ Class ______________ Date ____________

7E: Vocabulary Check

For use after Lesson 7-6

Study Skill Strengthen your vocabulary. Use these pages and add cues and summaries by applying the Cornell Notetaking style.

Write the definition for each word or term at the right. To check your work, fold the paper back along the dotted line to see the correct answers.

______________________________	polygon
______________________________	parallel lines
______________________________	trapezoid
______________________________	acute angle
______________________________	circle

Name ______________________ Class ______________ Date ______________

7E: Vocabulary Check (continued) For use after Lesson 7-6

Write the vocabulary word or term for each definition. To check your work, fold the paper forward along the dotted line to see the correct answers.

a closed figure with sides formed by three or more line segments ______________________

lines in the same plane that never intersect ______________________

a quadrilateral with exactly one pair of parallel sides ______________________

an angle with measure between 0 and 90 degrees ______________________

the set of all points in the plane that are the same distance from a given point ______________________

Name ______________________ Class ______________ Date ______________

Puzzle 7-6

Circles

Study the figure below. Locate the area described by the clues. The correct answers will spell out the state where the Shoshone Falls, "The Niagara of the West," is located.

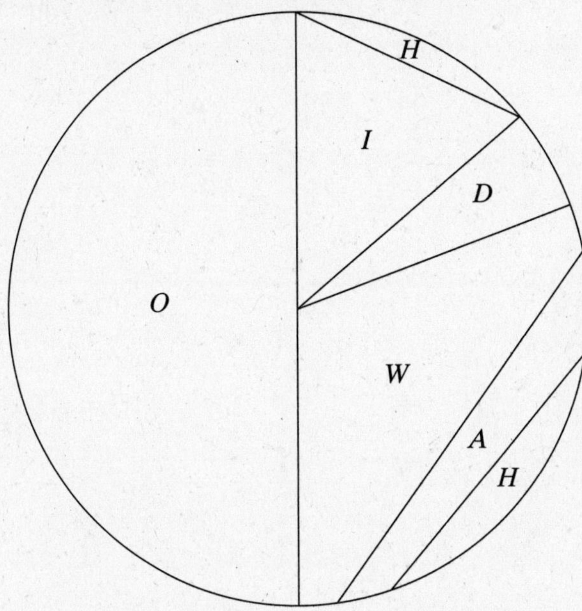

1. The area defined by two radii and one chord. ______________
2. The area defined by two radii and an arc of the circle. __________
3. The area defined by two chords and two arcs of the circle. ______
4. The area defined by one chord and the arc of the circle. ________
5. The area defined by a diameter and a semicircle. ______________

Name ______________________ Class ______________ Date ______________

Practice 7-7

Circle Graphs

Use the information in each table to create a circle graph.

1. The data show the total number of space vehicles that either successfully reached or exceeded orbit around Earth.

Years	Number of Successful United States Space Launches
1957–1959	15
1960–1969	470
1970–1979	258
1980–1989	153
1990–1995	146

2. The data represent the percent of private schools in the United States that have an annual tuition in each of the given ranges.

Annual Tuition	% of Private Schools
Less than $500	13
$500–$1,000	28
$1,001–$1,500	26
$1,501–$2,500	15
More than $2,500	18

3. The data represent a poll taken in a seventh-grade class.

Favorite Color for a Car	Number of Seventh Graders
Red	14
Blue	9
White	3
Green	1

a. What percent of seventh graders like blue cars? ______________

b. What percent of seventh graders like green cars? ______________

c. What percent of seventh graders like either red *or* blue cars?

____

d. What percent of seventh graders like a car color *other than* white?

____

Name ____________________ Class ____________ Date ____________

7-7 • Guided Problem Solving

GPS Student Page 357, Exercise 17:

The table shows how many days each week students do volunteer work. Use the table to make a circle graph.

Days	1	2	3	4	5
Students	11	5	5	2	2

Understand

1. What are you being asked to do?

____

2. How many students total volunteered?

____

Plan and Carry Out

3. Use a proportion to find the angle of measure for the number of students who volunteered on Day 1.

____

4. Repeat Step 3 for Day 2.

____

5. Repeat Step 3 for Day 3.

____

6. Repeat Step 3 for Day 4.

____

7. Repeat Step 3 for Day 5.

____

8. Use the central angles you found in Steps 3–7 to draw the circle graph.

Check

9. Does the section for 1 day take up a large portion of the circle?

____

Solve Another Problem

10. You are in charge of the activities page in the school yearbook. You want to show how many students are participating in each activity. Use the data in the table to make a circle graph.

Activity	Sports	Band	Student Council	Horticulture	Clubs
Students	28	15	5	3	10

Name ______________________ Class ______________ Date ______________

Practice 7-7

Use the information in each table to create a circle graph.

1. The data show the total number of space vehicles that either successfully reached or exceeded orbit around Earth.

Years	Number of Successful United States Space Launches
1957–1959	15
1960–1969	470
1970–1979	258
1980–1989	153
1990–1995	146

2. The data represent the percent of private schools in the United States that have an annual tuition in each of the given ranges.

Annual Tuition	% of Private Schools
Less than $500	13
$500–$1,000	28
$1,001–$1,500	26
$1,501–$2,500	15
More than $2,500	18

3. The data represent a poll taken in a seventh-grade class.

Favorite Color for a Car	Number of Seventh Graders
Red	14
Blue	9
White	3
Green	1

What percent of seventh graders like blue cars? __________

Name ______________________ Class ______________ Date ______________

Activity Lab 7-7

Circle Graphs

Materials needed: protractor, compass

The data below represents the results of a survey in which 20 students were asked to name as many state capitals as possible. Each number represents the number of correctly named capitals from one student.

9	20	15	4	48	30	10	12	8	5
22	28	34	16	13	41	29	11	33	19

1. Arrange the data in a table like the one shown below. Set interval ranges for the number of correct responses, for instance 1 to 5 correct responses, 6 to 10 correct responses, etc., and enter the intervals in the first column of your table. Make sure your intervals are equal.

Number of Correct Responses	Tally of Students	Tally Totals	%	Central Angle

2. Count the tallies for each interval range. Record the totals in your table.
3. Calculate the percent of students within each interval range. For example, in an interval of 1 to 5 correct responses, you would divide the number of students (2) by the total (20) and multiply by 100 to get $\frac{2}{20} \times 100 = 10\%$
4. To calculate the central angle for each interval, multiply the percent by 360°. For example, $10\% \times 360° = 0.10 \times 360° = 36°$. Record your calculations.
5. Construct a circle graph to display the results. Use a compass to draw a circle like the one at the right. Then, use a protractor to construct each of the central angles you found. Be sure to label each sector of the circle graph with the correct percentage and the corresponding interval.

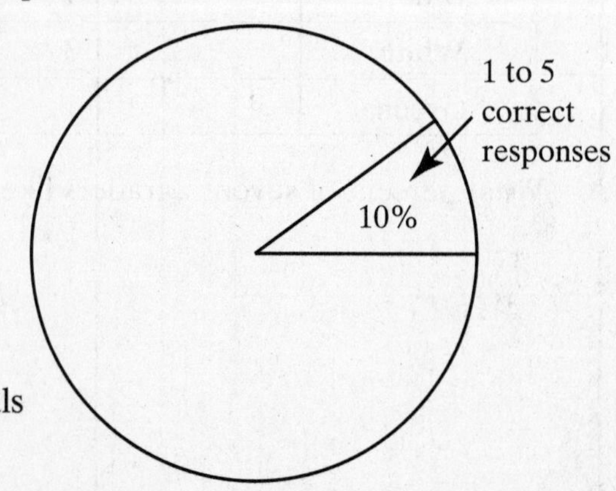

   a. What should be the total of the percents?

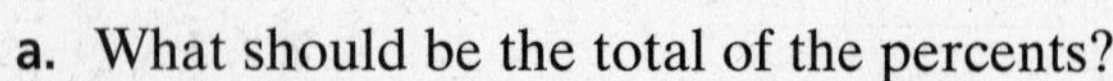

   b. What should be the total of your angles?

   c. Compare your graph to other students'. Did you choose the same intervals? How do different intervals affect the appearance of your graphs?

Reteaching 7-7

Circle Graphs

Use the information in the table to create a circle graph.

The class took a survey of what time students usually go to sleep. To make a circle graph:

① Find the total number of students.

② Use a proportion to find the measure of each central angle. Round to the nearest degree.

③ Use a compass. Draw a circle. Use a protractor. Draw the central angles. Label each sector.

Time Students Go to Sleep	Number of Students	② Central Angle Measure
Before 9 P.M.	2	$\frac{2}{28} = \frac{a}{360°}$ $a \approx 26°$
9 P.M.–10 P.M.	3	$\frac{3}{28} = \frac{b}{360°}$ $b \approx 39°$
10 P.M.–11 P.M.	9	$\frac{9}{28} = \frac{c}{360°}$ $c \approx 116°$
After 11 P.M.	14	$\frac{14}{28} = \frac{d}{360°}$ $d = 180°$
① Total	28	

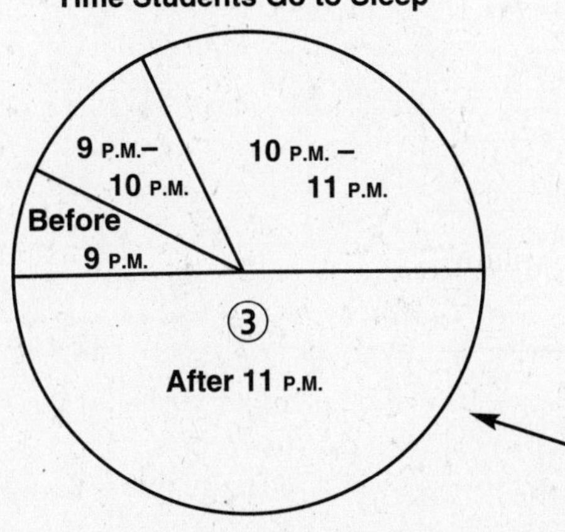

The central angle measures add to 361° because of rounding, but the difference does not show in the graph.

1. Complete the table. Draw a circle graph of the data.

Tuesday's Music CD Sales

Type of Music	Number of CDs Sold	Central Angle Measure
Country	10	
Rock	8	
Jazz	16	
Rap	14	
Total		

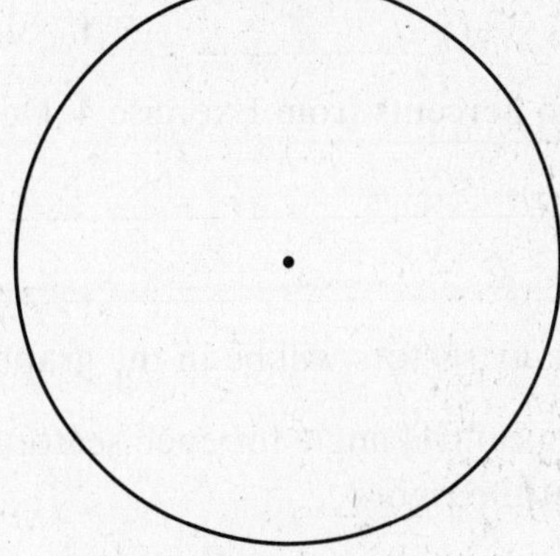

Name ______________________ Class ______________ Date ______________

Enrichment 7-7

Circle Graphs

Patterns in Data

The value of most computer equipment decreases each year. Some people use general guidelines to determine the value of their equipment.

Suppose a monitor was purchased for $450. Using one rule of thumb, the monitor will be worth $225 after one year, $112.50 after two years, and $56.25 after three years.

1. What pattern do you see in the value of the monitor for each successive year?

____

2. If the pattern continues, will the value of the monitor ever be $0.00? Explain.

____

____

3. In actuality, will the value of the monitor ever be $0.00? Explain.

____

Use the data in Exercises 4–7 to draw a circle graph.

4. Give the decrease in value of the monitor as a percent of the original price.

   a. First year ________ b. Second year ________

   c. Third year ________ d. Fourth year ________

   e. Fifth year ________ f. Sixth year ________

5. Add the percents from Exercise 4. Do they total 100%? Explain.

____

____

6. How many sectors will be in the graph? ________________

7. Find the central angle for each sector. Then draw the circle graph at the right.

   a. First year ________ b. Second year ________

   c. Third year ________ d. Fourth year ________

   e. Fifth year ________ f. Sixth year ________

Name ______________________ Class ______________ Date ______________

7B: Reading Comprehension

For use after Lesson 7-7

Study Skill Review notes that you have taken in class as soon as possible to clarify any points you missed. Be sure to ask questions if you need extra help.

Here is a circle graph for a monthly household budget. Use the graph to answer the questions that follow.

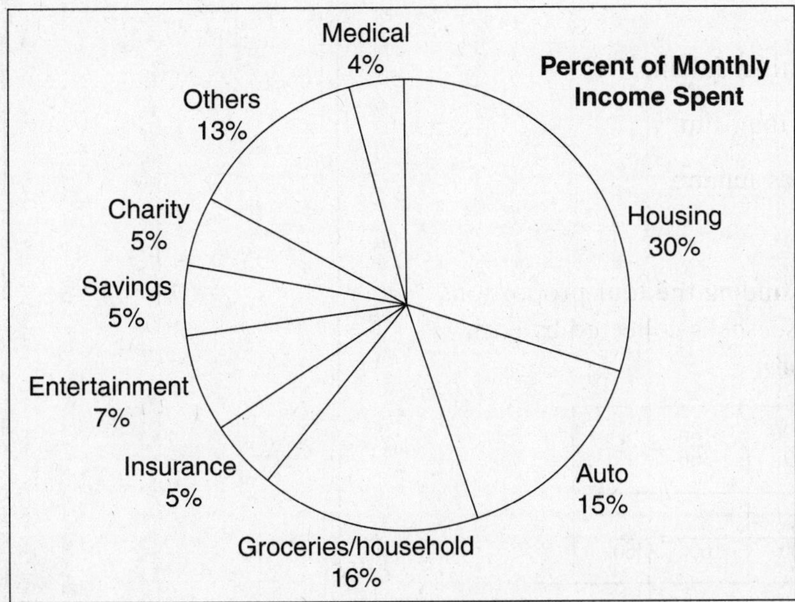

1. On which category was the largest percent of income spent? ______________
2. On which category was the smallest percent of income spent? ______________
3. Why are the insurance, savings, and charity sectors the same size?

   ____

4. What is the total of the percents listed in the circle graph? ______________
5. If the monthly income is $2,400, how much should be spent on an automobile?

   ____

6. How much of a $1,900 monthly income should be saved? ______________
7. If $60 is the amount budgeted for entertainment, what is the monthly income?

   ____

8. **High-Use Academic Words** What does it mean to *review*, as mentioned in the study skill?

   a. to put in order

   b. to study again

Name ______________________ Class ______________ Date ____________

Puzzle 7-7

Circle Graphs

Four friends spent the day collecting seashells at the beach. At the end of the day, they counted the number of shells each had collected. The friends decided to create a circle graph showing how many shells each collected.

Facts:

- Julian collected 40 seashells
- Jim found seven more seashells than Julian.
- Wilson collected six more shells than Jim.
- Jorge found half as many shells as Julian.

Help the friends create their graph by finding the four proportions that correctly relate to the number of seashells collected by each person, and solving each proportion for n.

$\frac{20}{100} = \frac{n}{160}$	$\frac{40}{160} = \frac{n}{360}$	$\frac{53}{160} = \frac{n}{360}$	$\frac{160}{360} = \frac{n}{47}$
$\frac{47}{160} = \frac{n}{100}$	$\frac{53}{160} = \frac{n}{160}$	$\frac{20}{160} = \frac{n}{100}$	$\frac{n}{160} = \frac{40}{360}$

Julian's proportion: ______________

Jim's proportion: ______________

Wilson's proportion: ______________

Jorge's proportion: ______________

Now, choose the section of the circle that matches each proportion. The correct pieces will fit together to form a circle.

A.

12.5%

B.

12.5°

C.

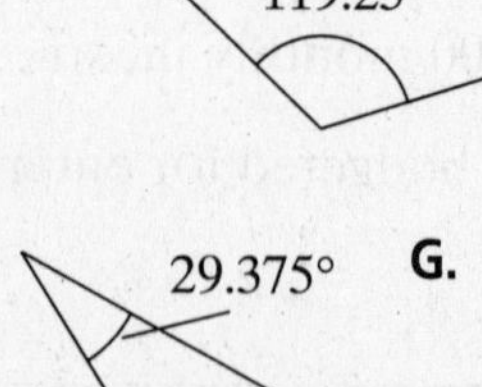

D.

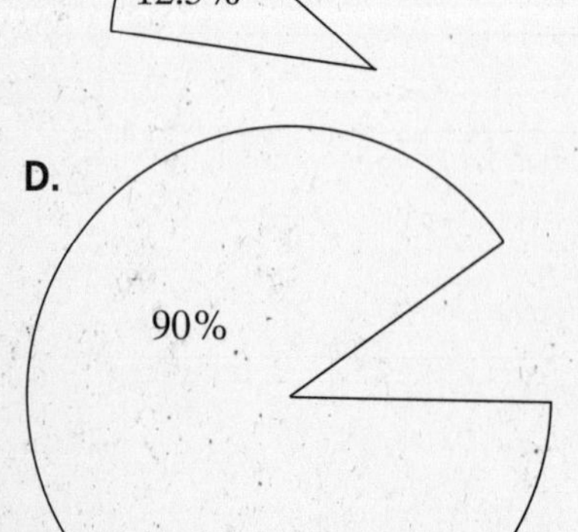

E.

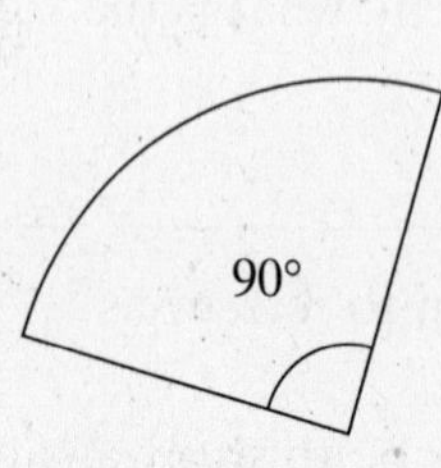

F.

29.375°

G.

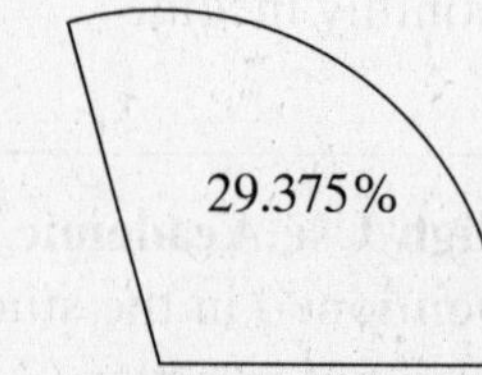

Name ______________________________ Class ________________ Date ______________

Practice 7-8

Constructions

Construct the perpendicular bisector of each segment.

1.

2.

Construct a congruent segment.

3.

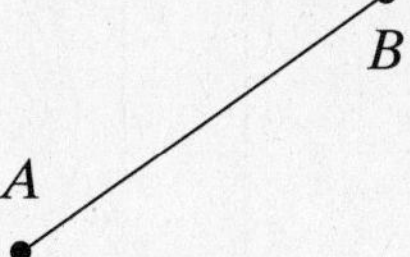

4.

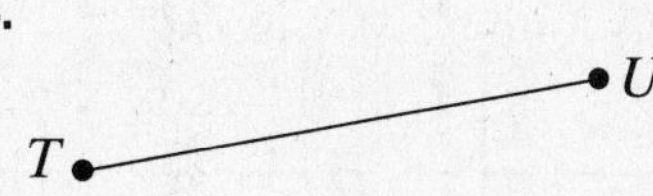

Construct each angle or segment.

5. Construct a segment with measure $\frac{3}{4}$ that of $\overline{TU}$.

6. Construct the perpendicular bisector of $\overline{XY}$. Then make the perpendicular bisector congruent to segment $\overline{XY}$.

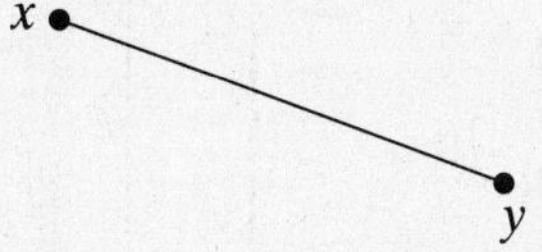

Point D is the midpoint of $\overline{BC}$. Complete.

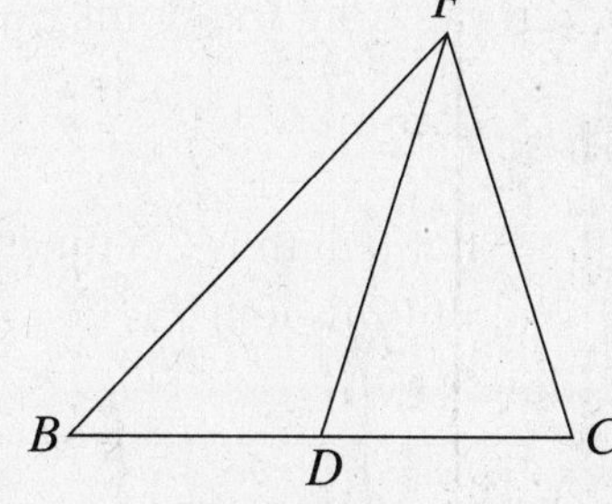

7. $\overline{BC}$ = 10 in., $\overline{CD}$ = ________

8. $\overline{DC}$ = 9 mm, $\overline{BD}$ = ________

9. $\overline{BD}$ = 2 cm, $\overline{BC}$ = ________

10. $\overline{BC}$ = 12 yd, $\overline{DC}$ = ________

Name ______________________ Class ______________ Date ______________

7-8 • Guided Problem Solving

GPS Student Page 363, Exercise 16:

Draw $\overline{MN}$ about 4 in. long. Then construct $\overline{JK}$ two and one half times as long as $\overline{MN}$.

Understand

1. How many times as long as $\overline{MN}$ is $\overline{JK}$?

   ____

2. What two constructions will you need to know how to perform to draw $\overline{JK}$?

   ____

Plan and Carry Out

3. Draw $\overline{MN}$ so that it is about 4 inches long.
4. Next, draw a ray with endpoint *J* that looks at least two and one half times as long as $\overline{MN}$.
5. Use your compass to mark a point on your ray that is exactly the length of $\overline{MN}$ from *J*.
6. Now use your compass to mark a point the length of $\overline{MN}$ away from the point you marked in Step 5.
7. Construct the bisector for $\overline{MN}$. Use this to find half the length of $\overline{MN}$.
8. Use your compass to mark endpoint *K* half the length of $\overline{MN}$ away from the point you marked in Step 6.

Check

9. What length is 2.5 times as long as 4 in.? Is your line segment about this long?

   ____

Solve Another Problem

10. Draw $\overline{AB}$ about 1.5 in. long. Then construct $\overline{CD}$ two and one half times as long as $\overline{AB}$.

Name ______________________ Class ______________ Date ______________

Practice 7-8

Constructions

Construct the perpendicular bisector of the segment.

1.

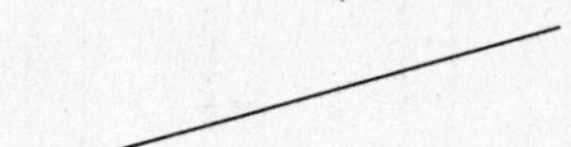

Construct a congruent segment.

2.

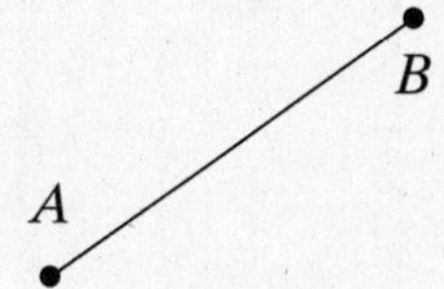

3. Construct the perpendicular bisector of $\overline{XY}$. Then make the perpendicular bisector congruent to segment $\overline{XY}$.

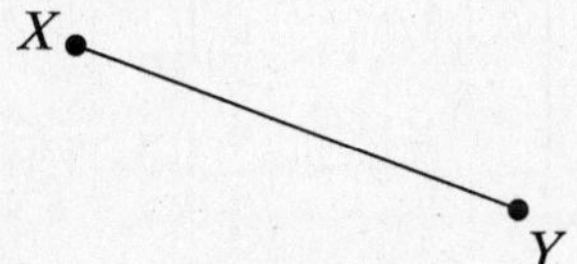

Point D is the midpoint of $\overline{BC}$. Complete.

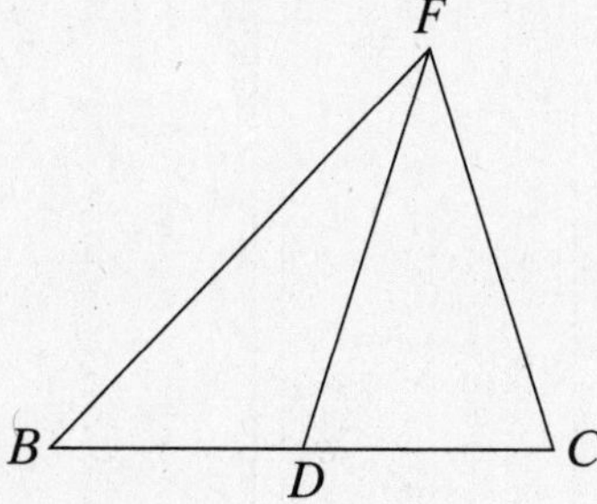

4. $\overline{BC} = 10$ in., $\overline{CD} =$ ________

5. $\overline{DC} = 9$ mm, $\overline{BD} =$ ________

6. $\overline{BD} = 2$ cm, $\overline{BC} =$ ________

7. $\overline{BC} = 12$ yd, $\overline{DC} =$ ________

Name ____________________ Class ____________ Date ____________

Activity Lab 7-8

Constructions

Materials needed: compass, straightedge (an unmarked ruler)

Construct the perpendicular bisector of a given segment.

1. In the space below, draw a 2.5 in. segment and label the segment $\overline{EF}$. Construct the perpendicular bisector of $\overline{EF}$.

2. Label the points where the arcs intersect, G and H.

3. Label the intersection of $\overline{EF}$ and $\overline{GH}$ point M.

4. Is $\overline{EM}$ congruent to $\overline{MF}$?

   ____

5. What angle is formed where the perpendicular segments intersect?

   ____

6. If $\overline{EF}$ is 2.5 in., what is $\overline{EM}$?

   ____

7. Name the perpendicular bisector.

   ____

Name ______________ Class ______________ Date ______________

Reteaching 7-8

Constructions

To construct a segment that is congruent to $\overline{AB}$:

① Open the compass to the length of $\overline{AB}$. Draw a ray with endpoint C that is at least as long as $\overline{AB}$.

② Place the end of the compass on C and draw an arc that intersects the ray. Label the point of intersection as endpoint D. $\overline{CD}$ is congruent to $\overline{AB}$.

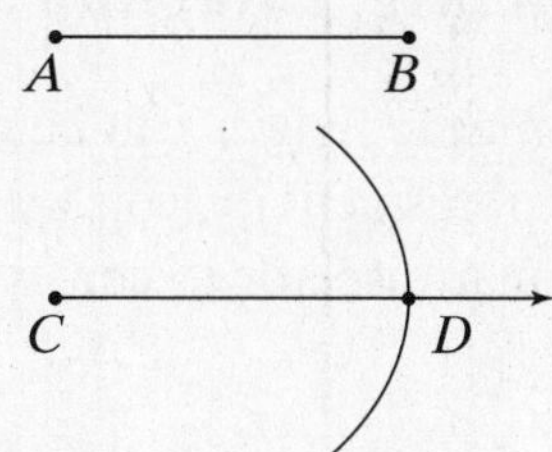

To bisect $\overline{AB}$:

① Open the compass more than half the length of $\overline{AB}$. With the compass tip on A, draw an arc.

② Without changing the opening, move the compass tip to B. Draw another arc.

③ Draw $\overleftrightarrow{CD}$ through the intersections of the arcs. $\overleftrightarrow{CD}$ is the bisector of $\overline{AB}$. Point M is the midpoint of $\overline{AB}$.

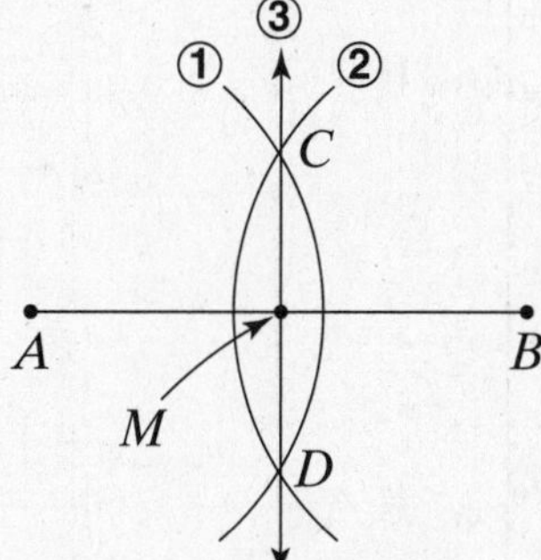

---

1. Complete the construction of a segment congruent to $\overline{JK}$.

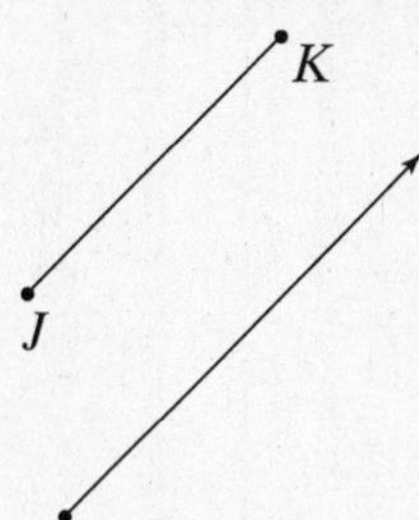

2. Complete the construction to bisect $\overline{ST}$.

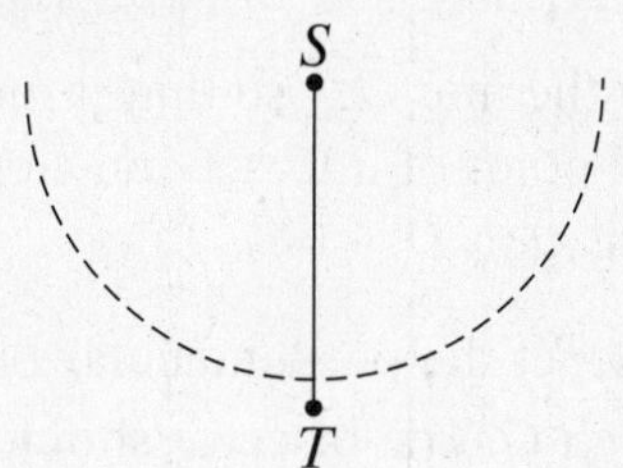

Make the indicated constructions.

3. Construct a segment congruent to $\overline{MN}$.

4. Bisect $\overline{XY}$.

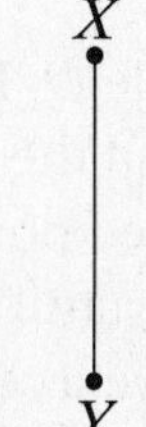

5. Bisect $\overline{PQ}$ with a congruent segment.

Enrichment 7-8

Constructions

Constructing a Regular Octagon

Many geometric figures can be constructed using a straightedge and compass. In this activity, you will use the construction of a perpendicular bisector to construct a regular octagon.

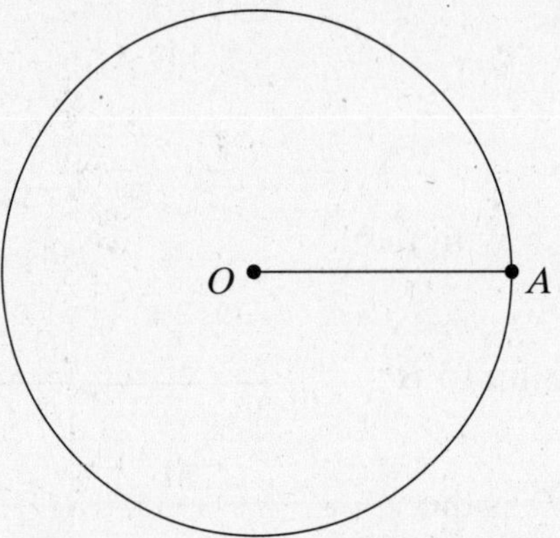

1. Construct the perpendicular bisector of $\overline{OA}$. Label the midpoint M.
2. Set the radius of your compass to the length of $\overline{OM}$. Draw an arc centered at M that intersects the perpendicular bisector of $\overline{OA}$. Label the point of intersection P.
3. Draw the line $\overleftrightarrow{OP}$ so that it intersects circle O twice. Label point C, the point of intersection closest to A. Label the other point of intersection D.
4. Construct the perpendicular bisector of $\overline{CD}$. It should pass through O. The bisector should intersect circle O twice. Label the points of intersection E and F.
5. Extend OA so that it intersects circle O on the other side. Label the point of intersection B.
6. Construct the perpendicular bisector of $\overline{AB}$. It will intersect circle O twice. Label the points of intersection G and H.
7. Now you have 8 labeled points on circle O. Draw a line segment connecting A and C. Continuing around the circle, draw a line segment between C and the next labeled point. Repeat the process as you move around the circle, until you come back to A. When you are finished, you should have a regular octagon!
8. What other geometric figures do you think you could construct using the constructions you know? Try some!

____

____

Name ____________________ Class ____________ Date ____________

7D: Visual Vocabulary Practice

For use after Lesson 7-8

Study Skill Use Venn Diagrams to understand the relationship between words whose meanings overlap, such as squares, rectangles, and quadrilaterals or real numbers, integers, and counting numbers.

Concept List

obtuse angle	right triangle	adjacent angles
chord	equilateral triangle	perpendicular bisector
midpoint	hexagon	pentagon

Write the concept that best describes each exercise. Choose from the concept list above.

1.

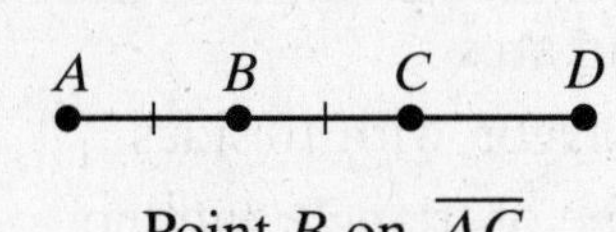

Point B on $\overline{AC}$

____

2.

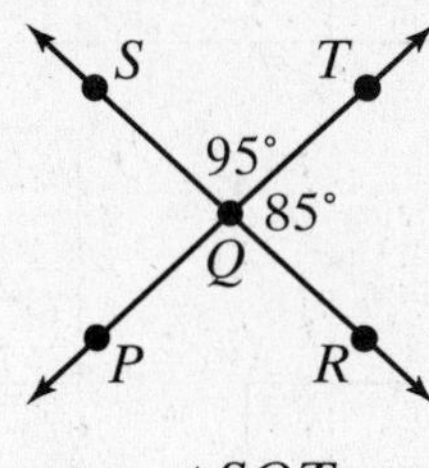

$\angle SQT$

____

3.

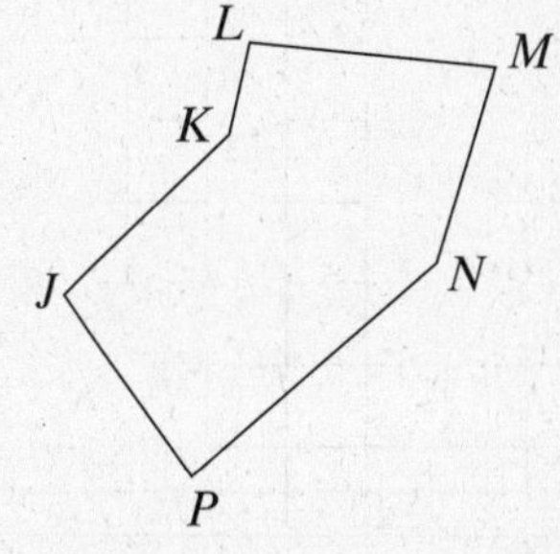

____

4.

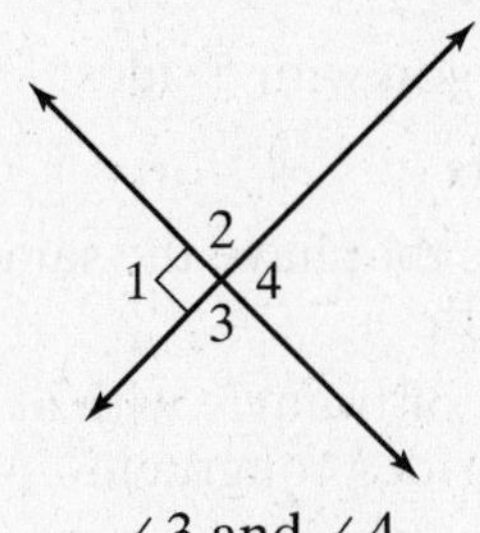

$\angle 3$ and $\angle 4$

____

5.

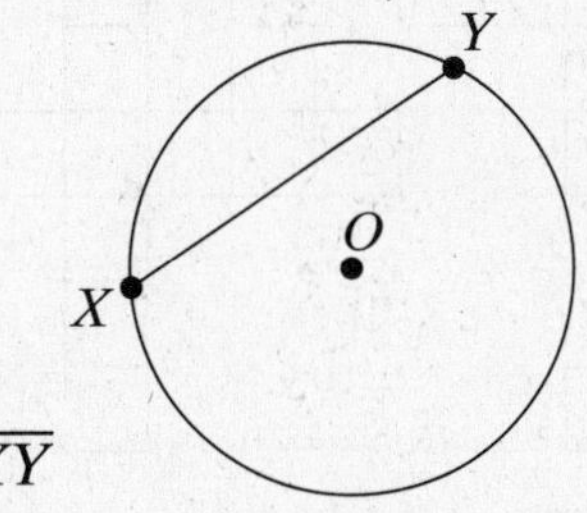

$\overline{XY}$

____

6.

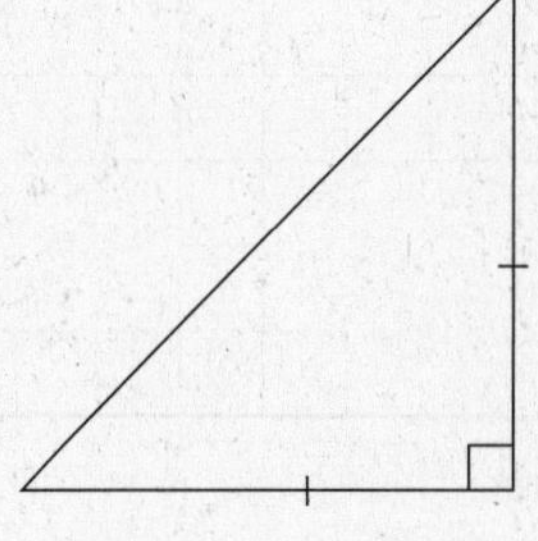

____

7.

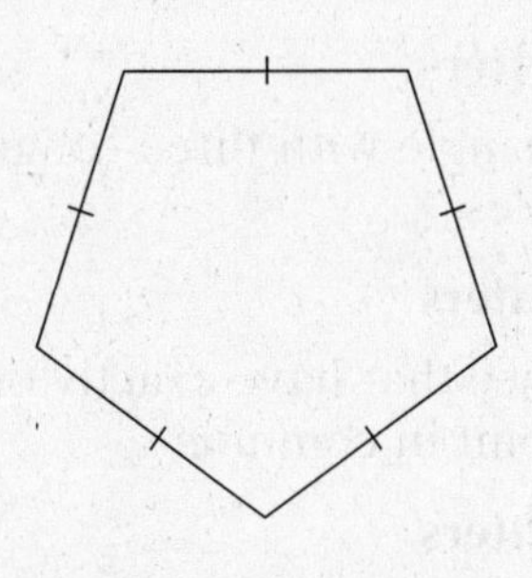

____

8.

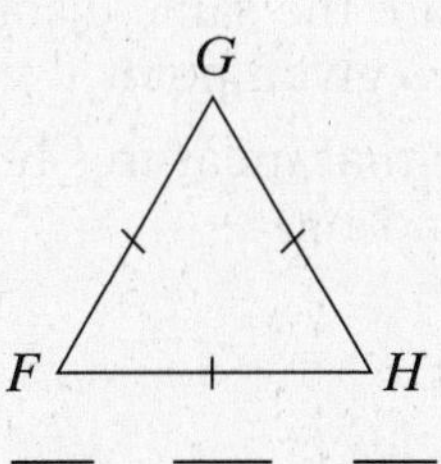

$\overline{FG} \cong \overline{GH} \cong \overline{FH}$

____

9.

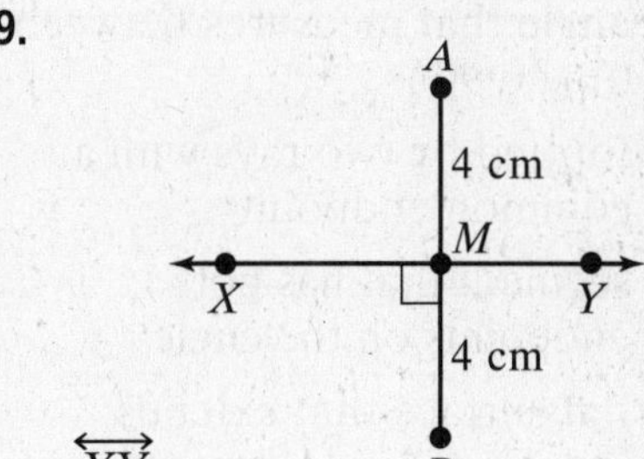

$\overleftrightarrow{XY}$

____

Name ______________________ Class ______________ Date ____________

7F: Vocabulary Review Puzzle

For use with the Chapter Review

Study Skill Write assignments down; do not rely only on your memory.

Below is a list of clues grouped by the number of letters in the answer. Identify the word each clue represents, and fit each word into the puzzle grid.

3 letters
- part of a circle

5 letters
- angle that measures between 0° and 90°
- formed by two rays with a common endpoint
- segment that has both endpoints on the circle
- flat surface that extends indefinitely in all directions

6 letters
- point of intersection of two sides on an angle or figure
- set of all points in a plane that are the same distance from a given point
- angle that measures between 90° and 180°

7 letters
- tool used to draw circles and arcs
- polygon with 10 sides
- type of triangle with no congruent sides
- polygon with all sides and angles congruent

8 letters
- point that divides a segment into two segments of equal length
- polygon with 5 sides

9 letters
- sides that have the same length
- type of triangle with at least two sides congruent
- parallelogram with four right angles
- quadrilateral with exacly one pair of parallel sides

11 letters
- triangle with three congruent sides

12 letters
- lines that have exactly one point in common

13 letters
- two angles whose sum is 180°
- two angles whose sum is 90°

Name ______________________ Class ______________ Date ____________

Puzzle 7-8

Constructions

Unscramble the steps below to construct a segment congruent to $\overline{AB}$ and the perpendicular bisector of $\overline{AB}$. Number the steps in the correct order in the spaces provided. To check your answers, follow the steps and draw each construction.

Constructing a Congruent Segment:

_____ Draw a ray with endpoint *C*.

_____ Keep the compass open to the same width.

_____ Label the point of intersection *D*.

_____ Open the compass to the length of $\overline{AB}$.

_____ Put the compass at point *C*.

_____ Draw an arc that intersects the ray.

A *B*

Constructing the Perpendicular Bisector:

_____ Draw $\overleftrightarrow{CD}$.

_____ Put the tip of the compass at *A* and draw an arc intersecting $\overline{AB}$.

_____ Points *C* and *D* are where the arcs intersect.

_____ Keeping the compass set at the same width, put the tip at *B* and draw another arc intersecting $\overline{AB}$.

_____ Points *C* and *D* are where the arcs intersect.

_____ Set the compass to more than half the length of $\overline{AB}$.

_____ The intersection of $\overline{AB}$ and $\overleftrightarrow{CD}$ is point *M*.

A *B*

Name ________________ Class ________________ Date ________________

Chapter 7 Project: Raisin' the Roof

Build a Tower

Beginning the Chapter Project

Look around you. Triangles are everywhere in construction! You see them in bridges, in buildings, in scaffolding, even in bicycle frames!

This project will give you a greater appreciation of the importance of triangles in construction. You also develop a taste for raisins!

In this chapter project, you will use toothpicks and raisins to build geometric shapes. Your final product will be a tower strong enough to support a baseball.

Activities

Activity 1: Researching

Find pictures of structures such as bridges and towers that use triangles in their construction. Use the pictures to get ideas for the design of your tower.

Activity 2: Analyzing

Use toothpicks and raisins to build a triangle and a square. Gently wiggle each figure. Which is more rigid? Add toothpicks to strengthen the weaker one. Describe how you did it.

Activity 3: Creating

Use toothpicks and raisins to build a cube. How many of each are needed? Use additional toothpicks to strengthen the cube. Describe how you did it.

Activity 4: Measuring

Sketch a design of a tower that is at least 4 in. tall. How many toothpicks are needed? Build the tower using glue instead of raisins. Test it by gently placing a baseball on it. If your tower starts to buckle, reinforce it.

Chapter 7 Project: Raisin' the Roof (continued)

Finishing the Project

Try to make your tower attractive as well as strong. Demonstrate to the class that your tower will support a baseball.

Be sure your work is neat and clear. Write any explanations you think are necessary.

Reflect and Revise

Show your tower to a friend, and discuss its design. Demonstrate its strength. Can you use fewer toothpicks without losing strength? If necessary, revise the design.

Write a paragraph explaining what changes you needed to make to your design and why.

Compare your design to that of your peers. In your paragraph include ideas of what you might do in a future design to make your tower better.

Extending the Project

Use note cards to build as tall a note-card house as possible.

- *How many inches tall is your note-card house?*
- *What type of geometric properties are displayed in your note-card house?*

Draw a sketch of your note-card house in the space provided.

Visit PHSchool.com for information and links you might find helpful as you complete your project.

Name ______________________ Class ______________ Date ______________

Chapter Project Manager

Getting Started

Read about the project. As you work on it, you will need several sheets of paper. If available, a spreadsheet program also can be used. Keep all your work for the project in a folder, along with this Project Manager.

Checklist	Suggestions
❑ Activity 1: researching	❑ Check out architecture magazines or books on construction. They will have a lot of ideas and examples.
❑ Activity 2: analyzing	❑ Wood toothpicks work a little better than the plastic. The raisins do not tend to slide off.
❑ Activity 3: creating	❑ Take pictures of each step of your construction, or take notes on how you are constructing the cube. This way you can learn from your mistakes and fix them.
❑ Activity 4 : measuring	❑ Compare the tower you created with the cube you built.

Scoring Rubric

3 You provide several sample pictures showing the use of triangles in construction. You draw and describe how you strengthened your toothpick-and-raisin constructions. You sketch and build a tower that is at least four inches tall and can support a baseball. Your explanations, drawings, and construction are neat and clean.

2 You provide a picture showing triangles in construction. You explain how you strengthened your toothpick-and-raisin constructions, and you build a tower that is at least four inches tall and can support a baseball.

1 You build a tower but you do not provide any evidence that you tested toothpick-and-raisin constructions beforehand.

0 Your preliminary tests and your tower are incomplete or missing.

Your Evaluation of Project Evaluate your work, based on the Scoring Rubric.

Teacher's Evaluation of Project

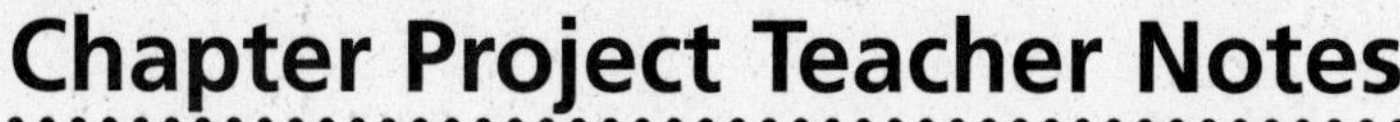
Name ______ Class ______ Date ______

Chapter Project Teacher Notes

About the Project

Students will have an opportunity to apply their knowledge of geometry to make a tower with toothpicks and raisins that is strong enough to hold a baseball.

Introducing the Project

Ask students:

- *Have you ever built a tower before?*
- *How can you make sure the tower is sturdy?*
- *How can you use geometry in building a structure?*

Activity 1: Researching

Have architecture magazines or books on construction for students to look through and see how triangles are used in construction.

Activity 2: Analyzing

Have models in the classroom that you have created with toothpicks and raisins so they understand the construction.

Activity 3: Creating

Before students begin building their cubes, challenge them to predict how many toothpicks and raisins they will need by imagining the finished cube.

Activity 4: Measuring

Encourage students to see how tall they can construct their tower. Perhaps, in addition to the project, have a contest to see who can build the tallest toothpick tower that holds a baseball.

Finishing the Project

You may wish to plan a project day on which students share their completed projects. Encourage students to explain their process as well as their products.

Have students review their methods for designing, building, testing, and improving their towers for the project.

Visit PHSchool.com for information and links you might find helpful as you complete your project.

Name ______________________ Class ______________ Date ______________

✔ Checkpoint Quiz 1

Use with Lessons 7-1 through 7-4.

Measure each angle. Then classify the angle.

1. 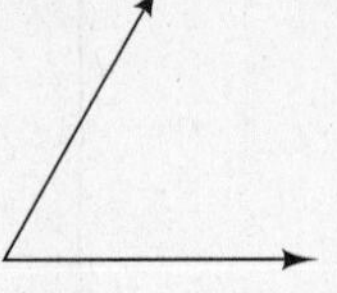

2. 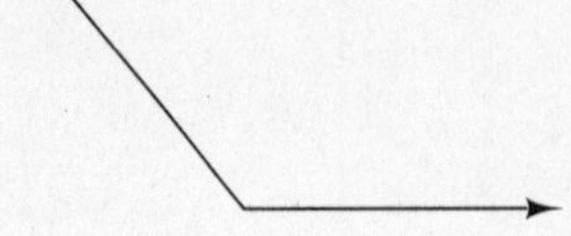

3. 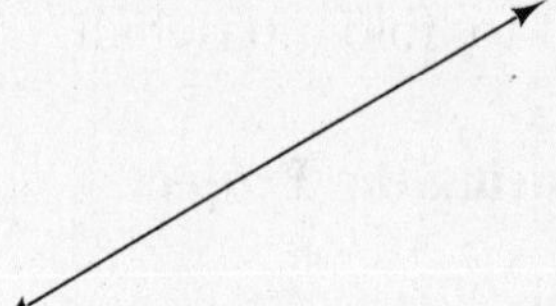

______________ ______________ ______________

4. The measures of two angles of a triangle are 45° and 45°. Name the type of triangle it is. ______________

Find the measures of the complement and supplement of each angle.

5. m/Q = 428 ______________ 6. m/H = 188 ______________ 7. m/B = 748 ______________

Draw each polygon.

8. pentagon 9. parallelogram 10. octagon 11. rectangle

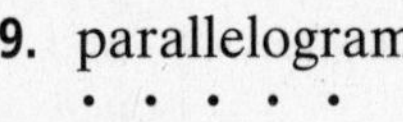

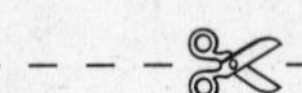

Name ______________________ Class ______________ Date ______________

✔ Checkpoint Quiz 2

Use with Lessons 7-5 through 7-7.

1. Draw a circle graph to display the following results of a survey of favorite automobile colors.

   Red: 72 Black: 63

   Blue: 27 All others: 18

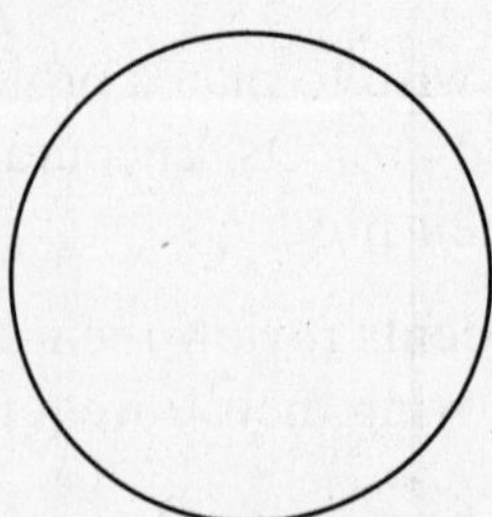

Use circle X for Exercises 2–5. Name each of the following.

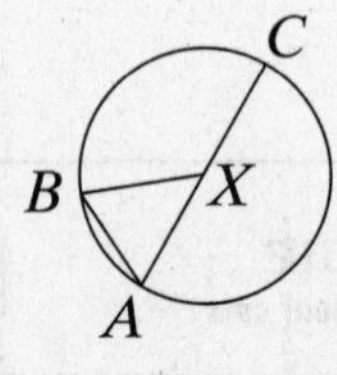

2. a chord ______________________

3. a diameter ______________________

4. a central angle ______________________

5. If $\triangle DEF \cong \triangle XYZ$, then $\angle E \cong$ ________ and $\overline{EF} \cong$ ________.

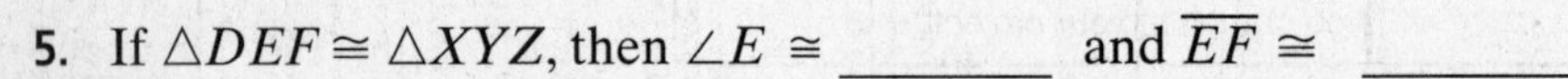

Name ______________________ Class ______________ Date ______________

Chapter Test — Form A

Chapter 7

Use the diagram to the right for excercises 1–3.

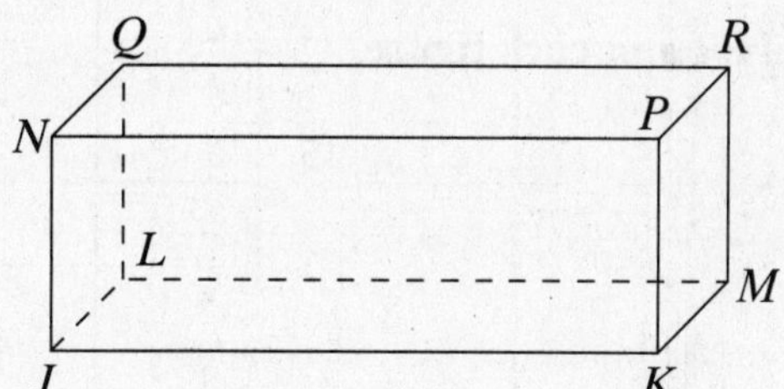

1. Name all the segments parallel to $\overline{NP}$.

____

2. Name all the segments intersecting $\overline{PK}$.

____

3. Name all the segments skew to $\overline{QR}$.

____

Measure each angle below.

4. ______________________

5. ______________________

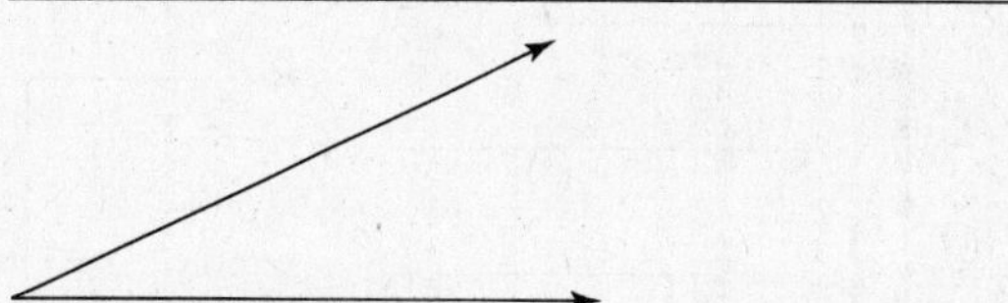

Find the measures of the complement and supplement of each angle.

6. $m\angle A = 38°$ ______________________

7. $m\angle J = 72°$ ______________________

8. $m\angle C = 12°$ ______________________

9. $m\angle K = 51°$ ______________________

Construct the perpendicular bisector of each segment.

10.

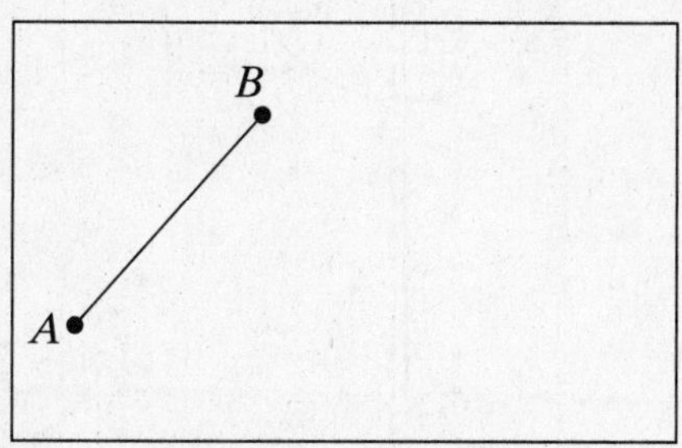

11.

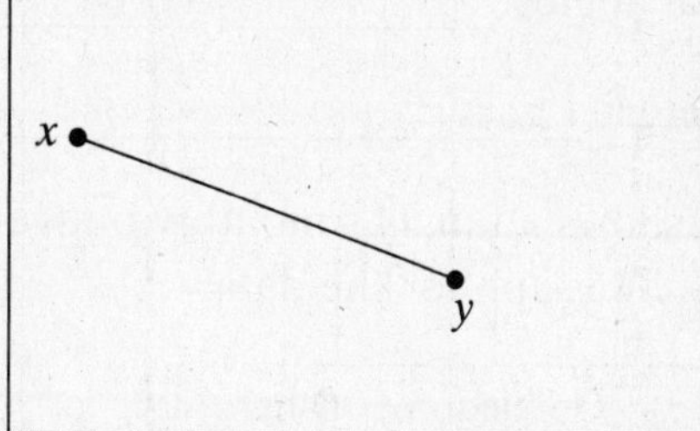

Find the value of *x* in each triangle. Then classify each triangle by its side lengths and angle measures.

12. ______________________

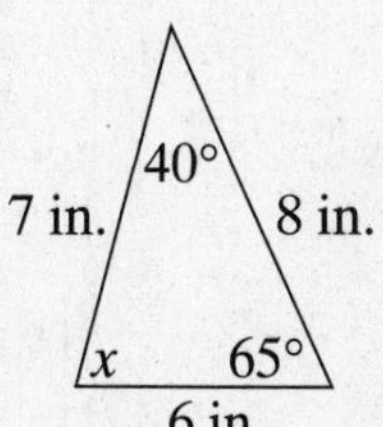

13. ______________________

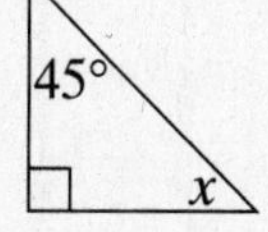

Name ________________ Class ________________ Date ________________

Chapter Test (continued) Form A

Chapter 7

Name the polygon in each figure.

14. ________________ **15.** ________________ **16.** ________________

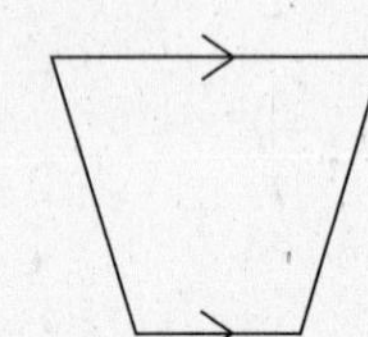

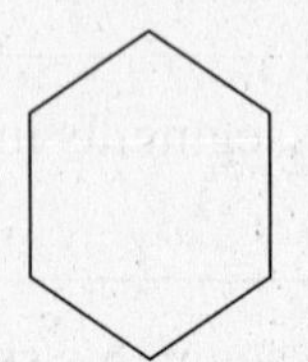

In the diagram $\triangle PQR \cong \triangle STU$. Complete each statement.

17. $\overline{PR} \cong$ ________________

18. ________________ $\cong \overline{UT}$

19. $\angle P \cong$ ________________

20. $PQ =$ ________________

21. $m\angle T =$ ________________

P 13 100° R Q

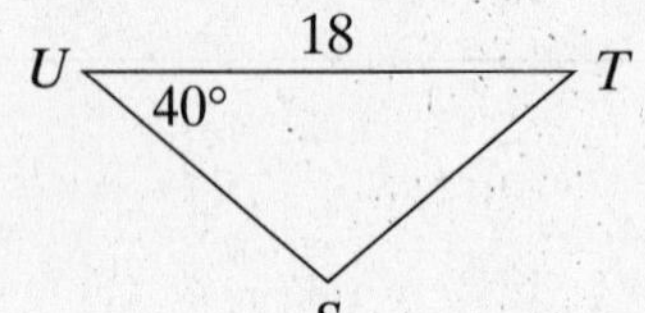

Name the following for circle *S*.

22. three radii ________________

23. two chords ________________

24. two central angles ________________

25. one diameter ________________

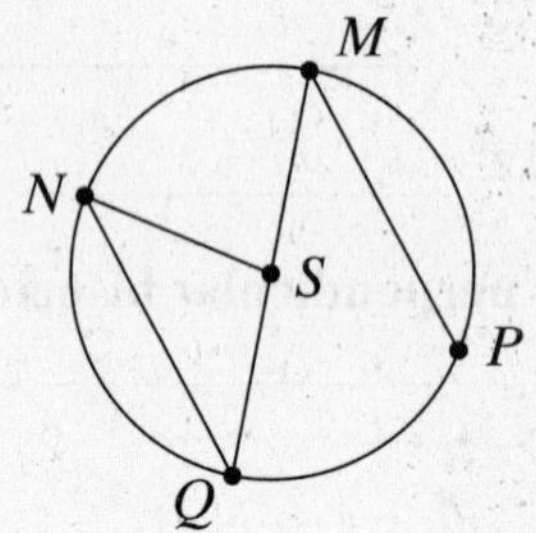

26. The table shows a family's monthly budget of $2,350. Make a circle graph for the data.

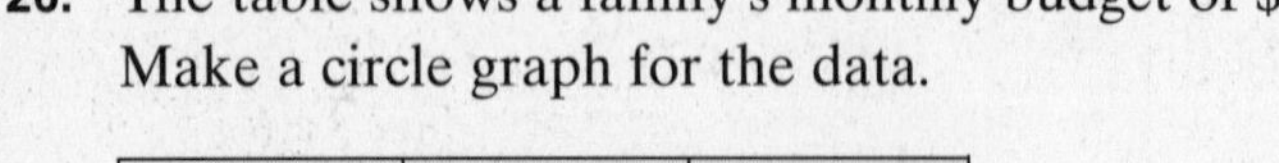

Food	Clothing	Other
$400	$750	$1,200

Name ______________________ Class ______________ Date ______________

Chapter Test Form B

Chapter 7

Use the diagram to the right for exercises 1–3.

1. Name all the segments parallel to $\overline{NP}$.

____

2. Name all the segments skew to $\overline{QR}$.

____

Measure each angle below.

3. ______________________

4. ______________________

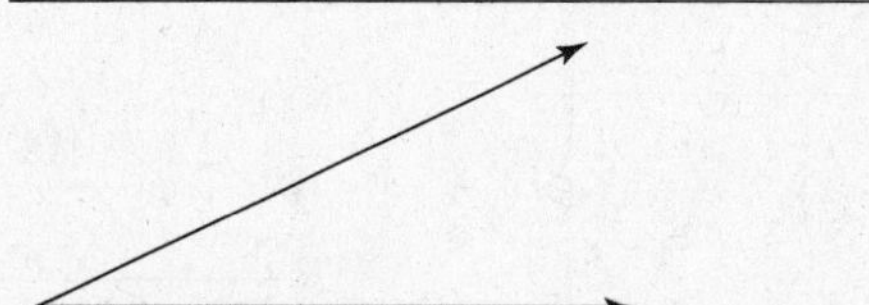

Find the measures of the complement and supplement of each angle.

5. $m\angle A = 38°$ ______________________

6. $m\angle J = 72°$ ______________________

Construct the perpendicular bisector of the segment.

7.

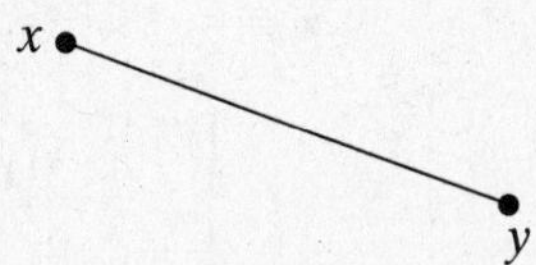

Find the value of *x* in each triangle. Then classify each triangle by its side lengths and angle measures.

8. ______________________

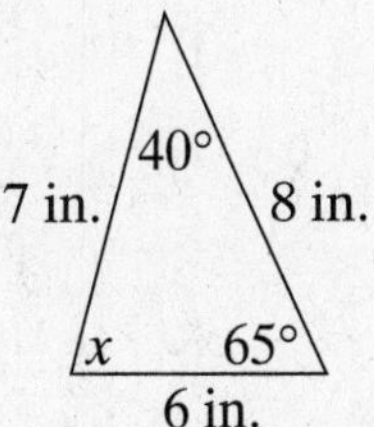

9. ______________________

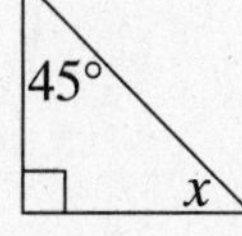

Chapter Test (continued) Form B

Chapter 7

Name the polygon in each figure.

10. ______________________

11. ______________________

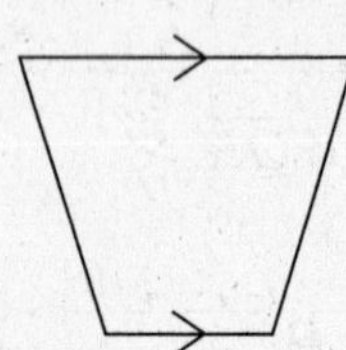

In the diagram $\triangle PQR \cong \triangle STU$. Complete each statement.

12. $\overline{PR} \cong$ ____________

13. $\angle P \cong$ ____________

14. $PQ =$ ____________

15. $m\angle T =$ ____________

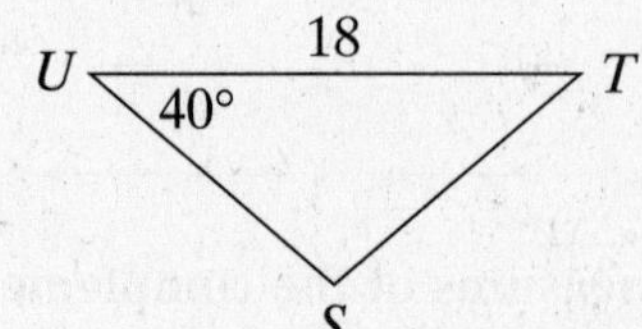

Name the following for circle *S*.

16. three radii ______________________

17. two central angles ______________

18. one diameter ______________________

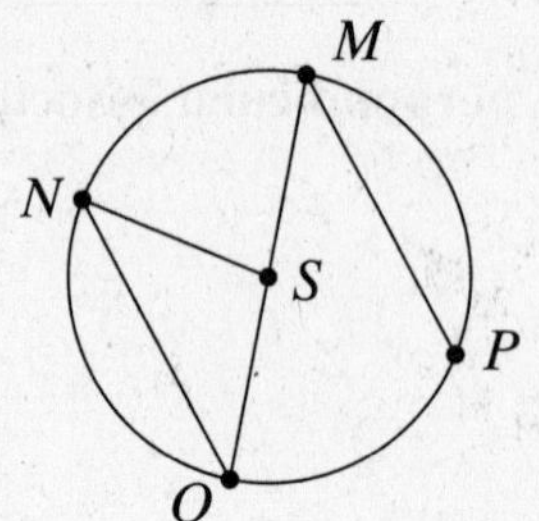

19. The table shows a family's monthly budget of \$2,350. Make a circle graph for the data.

Food	Clothing	Other
\$400	\$750	\$1,200

Alternative Assessment

Form C

Chapter 7

POLYGONS TO WEAR

An art class is making T-shirt designs. The teacher has given the following guidelines:

- Create your design by repeating *one regular polygon.*
- The polygons that make up your design must completely cover the design area; there may not be any space between the polygons. In other words, the sides of each polygon must meet exactly with the sides of other polygons.
- Do not worry about the edges of the patterns because fabrics will be cut where necessary.

Show all of your work on a separate sheet of paper.

1. Tamika drew the design shown below. On dot paper, make a *different* design, using the same type of polygon that Tamika used.

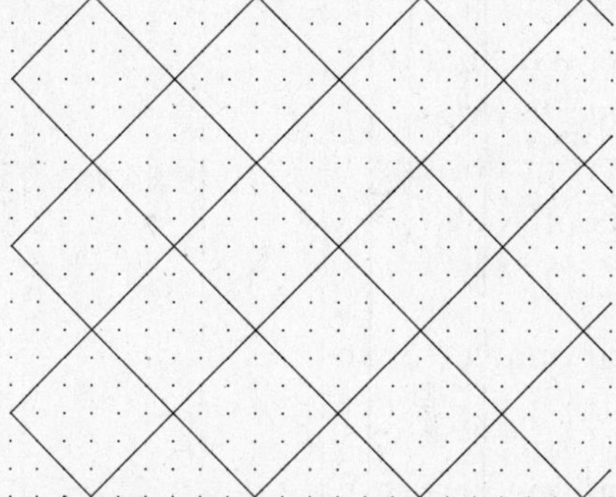

2. Travis decided to pattern his design after Tamika's by adding vertical lines to her pattern, as shown below. Did Travis's design meet the teacher's requirements? Explain.

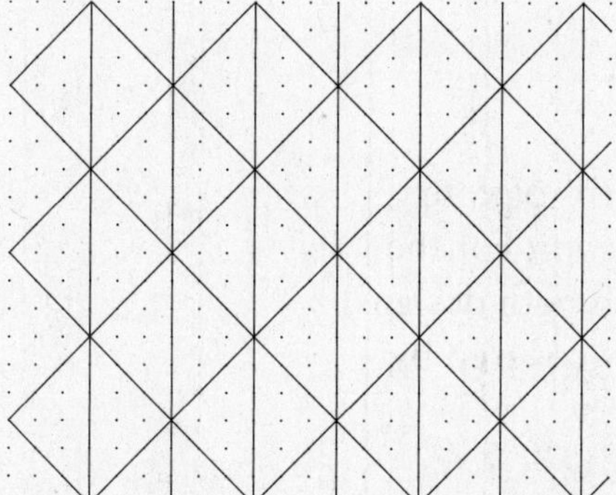

Alternative Assessment (continued) Form C

Chapter 7

3. Ira made the design below. Change Ira's design by using polygons that have one-fourth the area of each of Ira's polygons. Make your changes right on Ira's design.

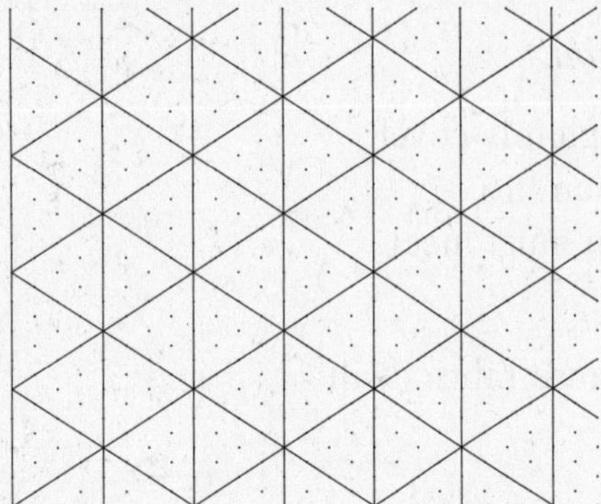

4. Is it possible to make a design using pentagons that meets the teacher's requirements? If so, draw such a design.

5. Is it possible to make a design using hexagons that meets the teacher's requirements? If so, draw such a design.

6. Jerry wanted to predict which polygons could make a design that meets the requirements. The teacher gave him a clue, saying, "Add the measures of the angles at each vertex of your design. Remember, a vertex is any point where the corners of your polygons meet."

   a. What is the sum of the measures of the angles at one vertex in Tamika's pattern?

   b. What is the sum of the measures of the angles at one vertex in Ira's pattern?

   c. What is the sum of the measures of the angles at one vertex in the patterns you drew in Exercises 1, 3, and 5?

7. What should Jerry have concluded? Explain.

Excursion

Now it's your turn to design two different T-shirt patterns of your own. For the first design, *use two different regular polygons*. For the second design, *use three different regular polygons*. With both designs, follow the rule that the design area must be completely covered by your polygons.

Name ______________________ Class ______________ Date ______________

Cumulative Review

Chapter 1–7

Multiple Choice. Choose the letter of the best answer.

1. Compare. -14×10 __?__ $-28 + (-102)$

   A. $<$ B. $>$

   C. $\geq$ D. $=$

2. What is the value of $5 \times 6 - 7 \times 3$?

   F. –15 G. 9

   H. 51 J. 69

3. What is $\frac{19}{25}$ written as a decimal?

   A. 0.91 B. 0.1925

   C. 0.25 D. 0.76

4. John has $4\frac{1}{2}$ lb of halibut. He wants each person to get a 6-oz serving. How many people can he feed?

   F. 6 people G. 12 people

   H. 27 people J. 75 people

5. What is the value of 1^{20}?

   A. 1 B. 5

   C. 10 D. 20

6. What is the range of the data given below?
   13.4, 24.2, 33.0, 11.5, 21.0, 35.9, 40.2

   F. 22.5 G. 26.8

   H. 27.0 J. 28.7

7. Which fraction is equivalent to $\frac{8}{12}$?

   A. $\frac{2}{6}$ B. $\frac{10}{15}$

   C. $\frac{3}{4}$ D. $\frac{16}{20}$

8. Solve $-3m - 1 = -25$.

   F. –24 G. –8

   H. 3 J. 8

9. Complete. 153 in. = ______ ft

   A. 4.25 B. 12.75

   C. 51 D. 459

10. What is the prime factorization for 210?

    F. $2 \times 3 \times 5 \times 7$ G. $5 \times 6 \times 7$

    H. $2 \times 7 \times 15$ J. $2 \times 5 \times 21$

11. $\triangle FGH$ has angle measures of 78° and 54°. What is the measure of the third angle?

    A. 12° B. 36°

    C. 48° D. 96°

12. A scale on a map is 1.5 in. : 200 mi. The map distance from Miami to Chicago is 9 in. What is the actual distance between the cities?

    F. 600 mi G. 1,200 mi

    H. 1,800 mi J. 2,700 mi

13. Which one of the following is a regular quadrilateral?

    A. trapezoid B. triangle

    C. square D. pentagon

Name ______________________ Class ______________ Date ______________

Cumulative Review (continued)

Chapter 1–7

14. The mean of five numbers is 20. Four of the numbers are 24, 19, 25, and 22. What is the fifth number?

F. 18 **G.** 10

H. 21 **J.** 24

15. According to the graph, how many families have more than two cars?

Number of Cars Owned by Families

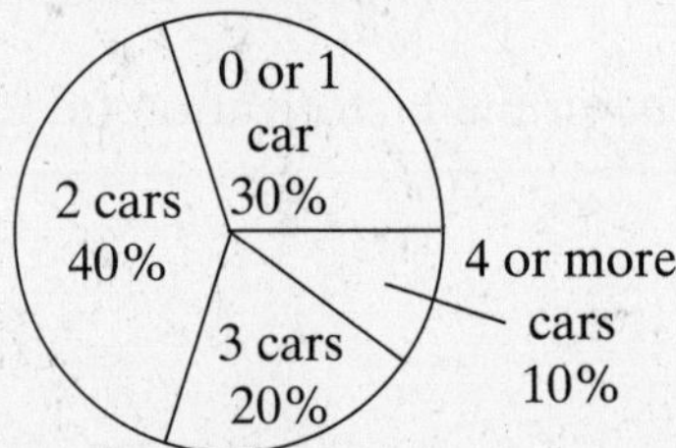

Total Families: 150

A. 15 families **B.** 45 families

C. 60 families **D.** 105 families

16. Find the value of n in $\frac{32}{n} = \frac{4}{9}$ that makes the proportion true.

F. 4 **G.** 8

H. 36 **J.** 72

17. What is 60% of 60?

A. 36 **B.** 60

C. 100 **D.** 360

18. A computer costs $2,800 on sale. The original price was $3,500. Find the percent of change.

F. 20% decrease

G. 20% increase

H. 25% decrease

J. 25% increase

Short Answer

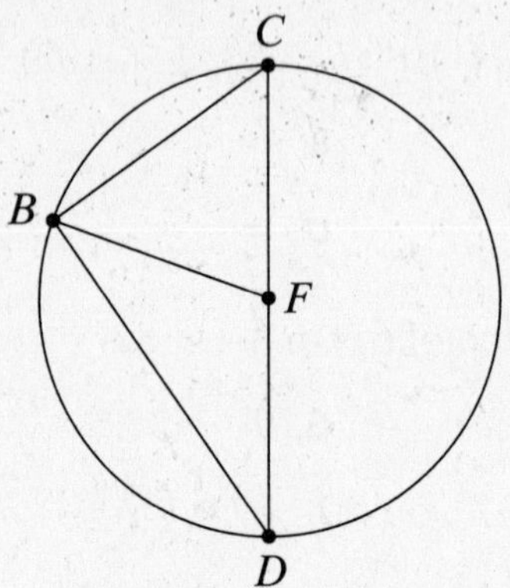

19. Use the circle above. Name all the radii labeled in circle *F*.

____

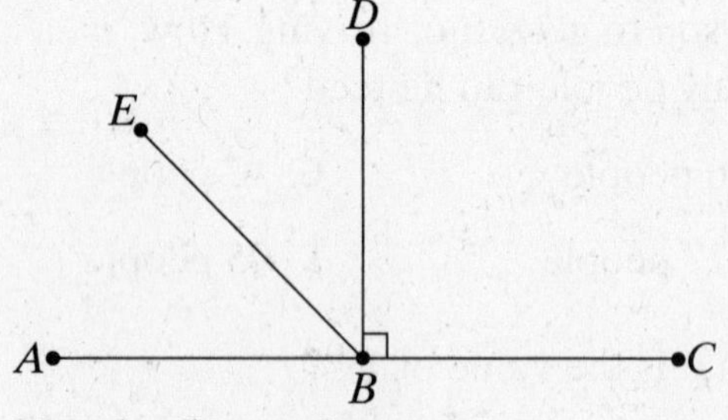

20. Use the figure above.

a. Name a pair of complementary angles.

____

b. Name a pair of supplementary angles.

____

Name ______________________ Class ______________ Date ____________

Practice 8-1

Estimating Perimeter and Area

Estimate the perimeter of each figure. The length of one side of each square represents 1 yd.

1. 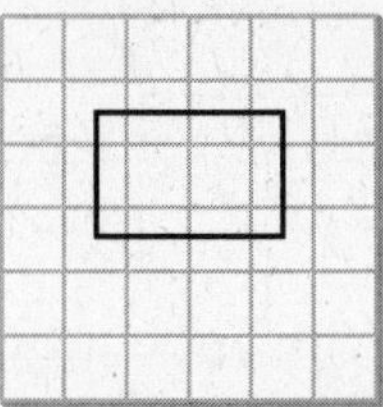

2. 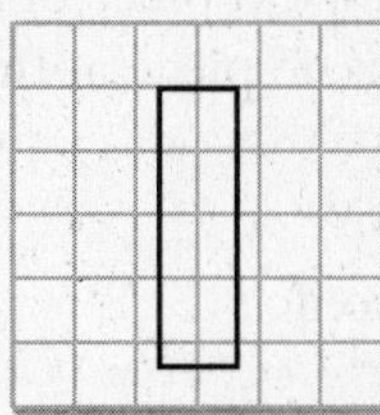

3. 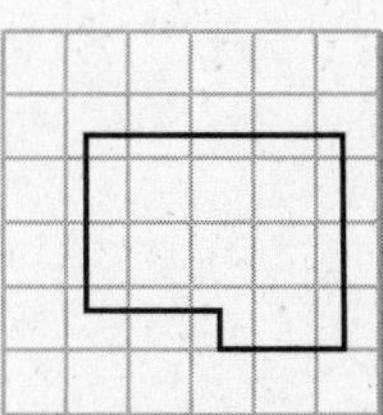

4. 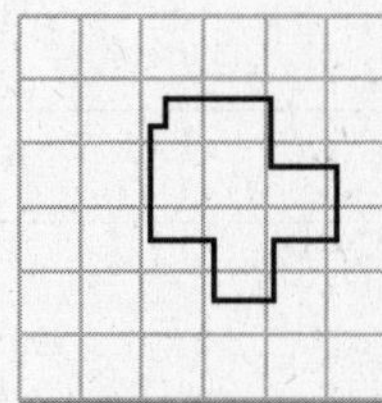

Choose a reasonable estimate. Explain your choice.

5. height of a truck cab: 12 in. or 12 ft ______________________
6. width of a book: 8 in. or 8 ft ______________________
7. diameter of a pizza: 8 in. or 8 ft ______________________
8. depth of a bathtub: 2 ft or 2 yd ______________________

Suppose each square on the grids below is 1 cm by 1 cm. Estimate the area of each figure.

9. 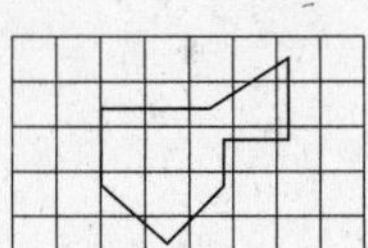

10. 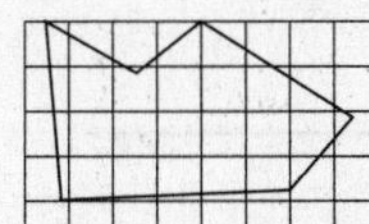

11. 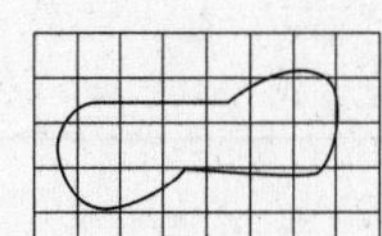

12. 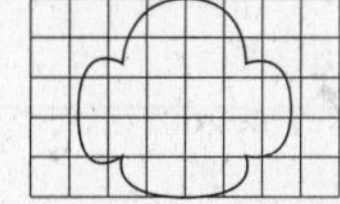

Choose the unit of measure you would use to estimate the given length or area.

13. the height of a tree: in., ft, yd, mi

14. the perimeter of the cover of a book: in., ft, yd, mi

15. the area of an ocean: ft^2, yd^2, $in.^2$, mi^2

Name ______________________ Class ______________ Date ______________

8-1 • Guided Problem Solving

GPS Student Page 378, Exercise 25:

Writing in Math How could you use a piece of string to estimate the perimeter of the puzzle piece at the right?

Understand

1. What are you being asked to do?

____

____

2. Define *perimeter*.

____

____

Plan and Carry Out

3. What do you have to do with the string?

____

4. How do you use the string to get a measurement?

____

____

5. Why would the measurement be an estimate?

____

____

Check

6. Why might using a piece of string to measure the perimeter of the puzzle piece be a good idea?

____

____

Solve Another Problem

7. How could you estimate the area of the puzzle piece with the string?

____

____

____

____

Name ______________________ Class ______________ Date ______________

Practice 8-1

Estimating Perimeter and Area

Estimate the perimeter of each figure. The length of one side of each square represents 1 yd.

1. 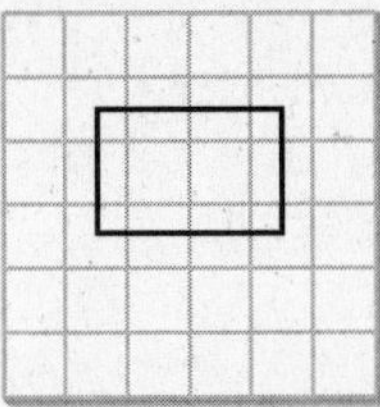

2. 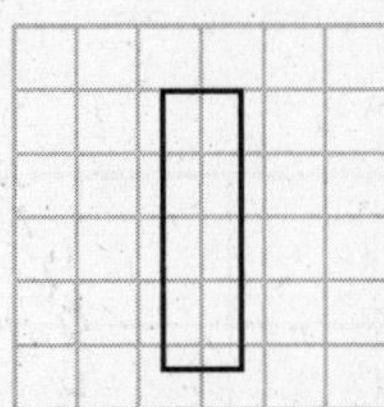

3. 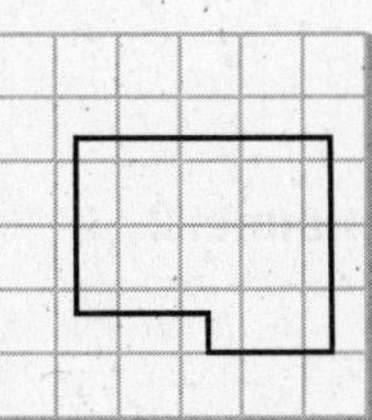

4. 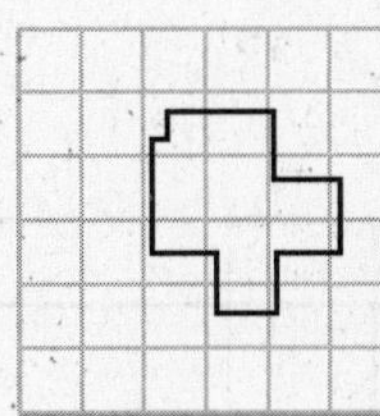

Choose a reasonable estimate. Explain your choice.

5. height of a truck cab: 12 in. or 12 ft ______________________

6. depth of a bathtub: 2 ft or 2 yd ______________________

Suppose each square on the grids below is 1 cm by 1 cm. Estimate the area of each figure.

7. 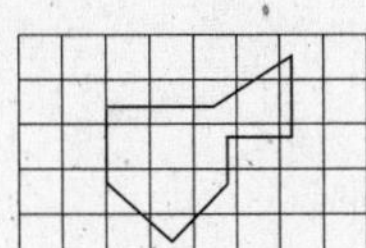

8. 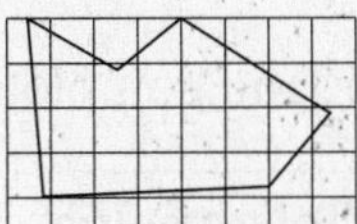

9. 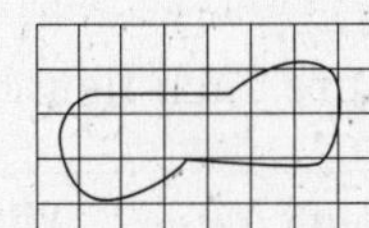

Choose the unit of measure listed that you would use to estimate the given length or area.

10. the height of a tree:
in., ft, yd, mi

11. the area of an ocean:
ft^2, yd^2, $in.^2$, mi^2

Name ______________________ Class ______________ Date ______________

Activity Lab 8-1

Estimating Perimeter and Area

Which of these figures do you think will have the greatest area? The greatest perimeter? The least area? The least perimeter? Record your estimates below.

1.

Estimate: 1.

Area: _____

Perimeter: _____

2.

Estimate: 2.

Area: _____

Perimeter: _____

3.

Estimate: 3.

Area: _____

Perimeter: _____

4. Now measure each figure with a metric ruler, and complete the table.

Figure	Length (cm)	Width (cm)	Area (cm^2)	Perimeter (cm)
1				
2				
3				

In the table, circle the greatest and least areas and the greatest and least perimeters.

5. How do these values compare to your initial estimates?

____

Reteaching 8-1

Estimating Perimeter and Area

To choose a reasonable estimate, determine if the measurement is small (like inches or centimeters) or big (like feet, yards, or meters).

Choose a reasonable estimate. Explain your choice.

Which is a better estimate for the height of an office building: 20 in. or 20 yd?
An office building is tall, so 20 yd is the better estimate.

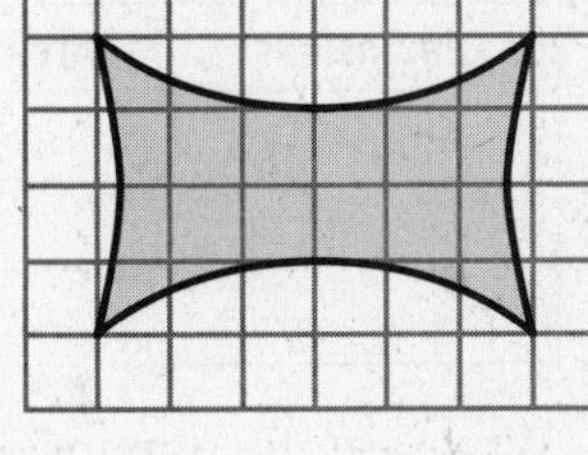

To estimate the area of a figure, estimate the number of square units contained in the figure.

Each square unit represents 1 ft^2 Estimate the area.

8 whole squares
partial squares ≈ 6 whole squares

8 + 6 = 14

The area is about 14 ft^2.

To estimate the perimeter of a figure, estimate the length of each side of the figure and add.

Each side of each square represents 1 ft.

Estimate the perimeter of this figure.

top side	≈ 6 ft
bottom side	≈ 6 ft
left side	≈ 4 ft
right side	≈ 4 ft

6 + 6 + 4 + 4 = 20

The perimeter is about 20 ft.

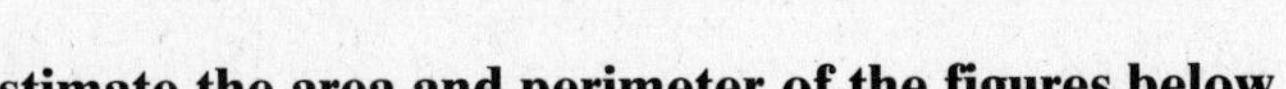

Choose a reasonable estimate. Explain your choice.

1. height of a refrigerator: 6 in. or 6 ft

____

____

2. height of a stop sign: 8 ft or 8 yd

____

____

Estimate the area and perimeter of the figures below.

3. 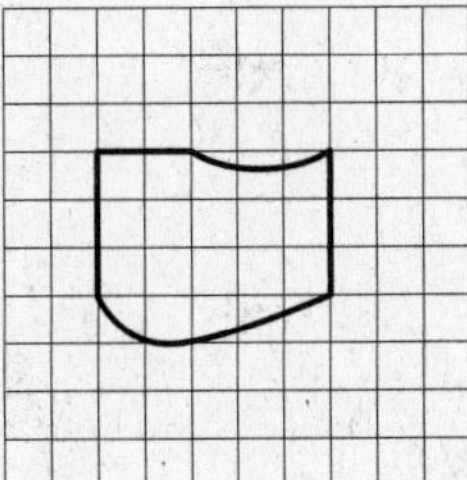

Area ≈ ______________

Perimeter ≈ ______________

4. 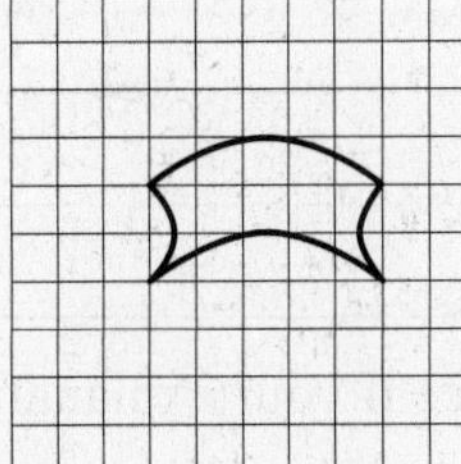

Area ≈ ______________

Perimeter ≈ ______________

Name ______________________ Class ______________ Date ______________

Enrichment 8-1

Estimating Perimeter and Area

Critical Thinking

Figures with the same perimeter can have different areas. Likewise, figures with the same area can have different perimeters. For all the questions below, use only whole numbers to complete the tables.

1. Complete the table to show all possible whole-number dimensions for a rectangle with a perimeter of 36 in. Then find each area.

Dimensions	Area	Dimensions	Area	Dimensions	Area
1 ×					

2. What are the dimensions of the figure with the largest area?

____

3. Name the figure with the largest area. ______________

4. Complete the table to show all possible whole-number dimensions for a rectangle with an area of 36 in.^{2}. Then find each perimeter.

Dimensions	Perimeter	Dimensions	Perimeter	Dimensions	Perimeter

5. What are the dimensions of the figure with the shortest perimeter?

____

6. Name the figure with the shortest perimeter. ______________

7. Explain the relationship between perimeter and area shown above.

____

____

____

8. How could you test to see if your explanation is correct?

____

____

____

Name ______________________ Class ______________ Date ______________

8A: Graphic Organizer

For use before Lesson 8-1

Study Skill Take a few minutes to relax before and after studying. Your mind will absorb and retain more information if you alternate studying with brief rest intervals.

Write your answers.

1. What is the chapter title? ______________________
2. How many lessons are there in this chapter? ______________________
3. What is the topic of the Test-Taking Strategies page? ______________________
4. Complete the graphic organizer below as you work through the chapter.
   - In the center, write the title of the chapter.
   - When you begin a lesson, write the lesson name in a rectangle.
   - When you complete a lesson, write a skill or key concept in a circle linked to that lesson block.
   - When you complete the chapter, use this graphic organizer to help you review.

Name ______________________ Class ______________ Date ____________

Puzzle 8-1

Estimating Perimeter and Area

Estimate the area of each shaded figure, and record your answers below.

U.

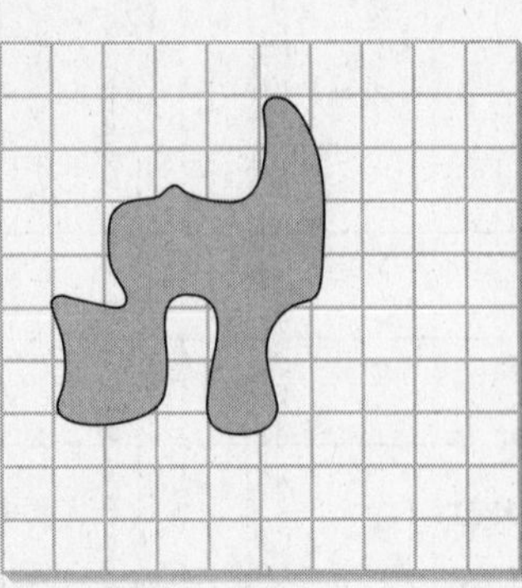

Each square represents 2 ft^2

C.

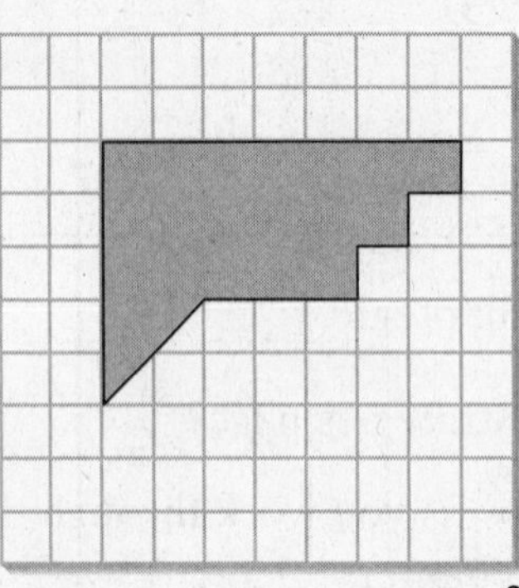

Each square represents 1 ft^2

K.

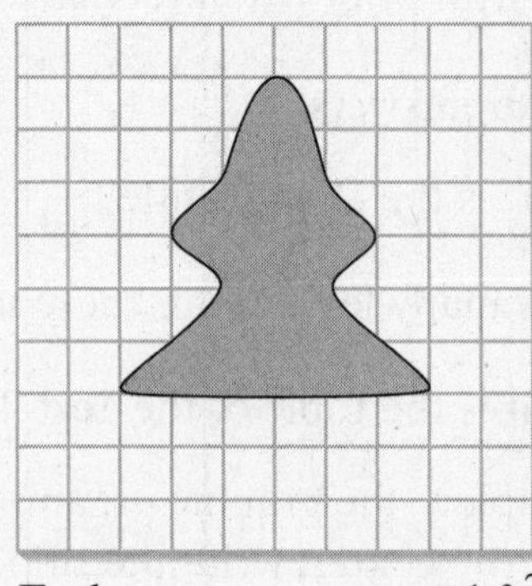

Each square represents 1 ft^2

L.

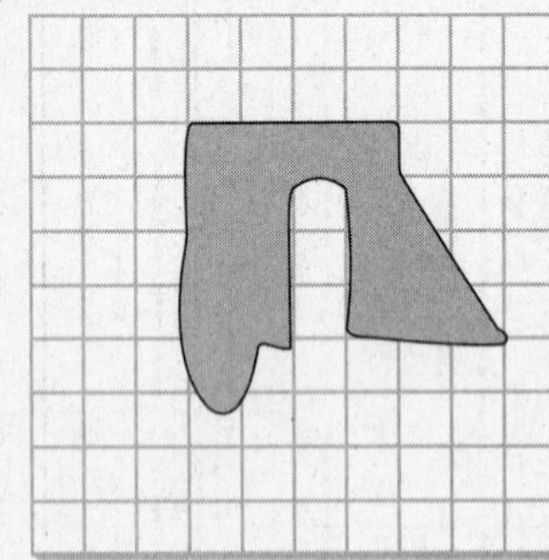

Each square represents 3 ft^2

Y.

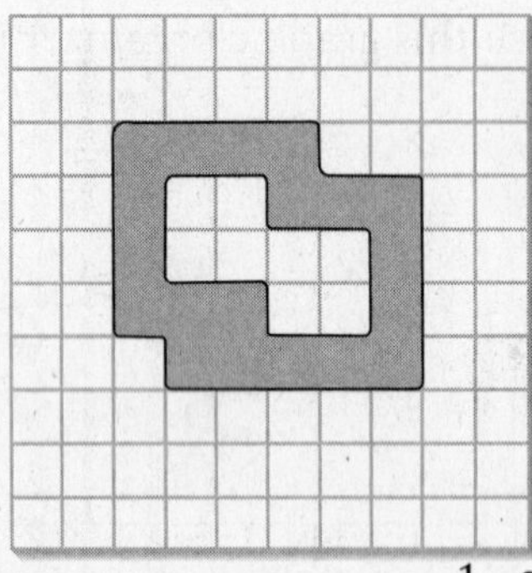

Each square represents $\frac{1}{2}$ ft^2

U ≈ __________ ft^2

C ≈ __________ ft^2

K ≈ __________ ft^2

L ≈ __________ ft^2

Y ≈ __________ ft^2

Find the missing word by ordering your answers from greatest to least, and writing each corresponding letter in the blank spaces below.

A good estimate is always worth more than a ____ ____ ____ ____ ____ guess.

Name ______________________ Class ______________ Date ______________

Practice 8-2

Area of a Parallelogram

Find the area of each parallelogram.

1. 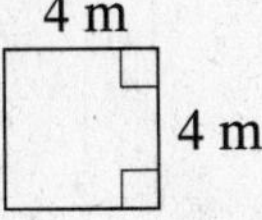

2. 5 cm
23 cm

3. 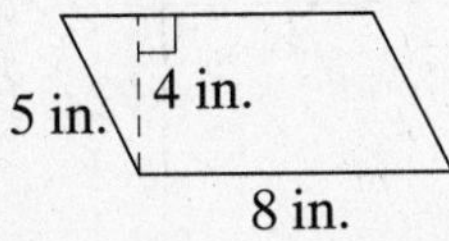

4. 8 mm
10 mm
10 mm

Find the area of each parallelogram with base b and height h.

5. $b = 16$ mm, $h = 12$ mm

6. $b = 23$ km, $h = 14$ km

7. $b = 65$ mi, $h = 48$ mi

8. $b = 19$ in., $h = 15$ in.

Solve.

9. The area of a parallelogram is 6 square units. Both the height and the length of the base are whole numbers. What are the possible lengths and heights?

10. The perimeter of a rectangle is 72 m. The width of the rectangle is 16 m. What is the area of the rectangle?

11. The area of a certain rectangle is 288 yd^2. The perimeter is 68 yd. If you double the length and width, what will be the area and perimeter of the new rectangle?

12. If you have 36 ft of fencing, what are the areas of the different rectangles you could enclose with the fencing? Consider only whole-number dimensions.

Name ______________________ Class ______________ Date ____________

8-2 • Guided Problem Solving

Student Page 383, Exercise 22:

Geography The shape of the state of Tennesee is similar to a parallelogram. Estimate the area of Tennessee.

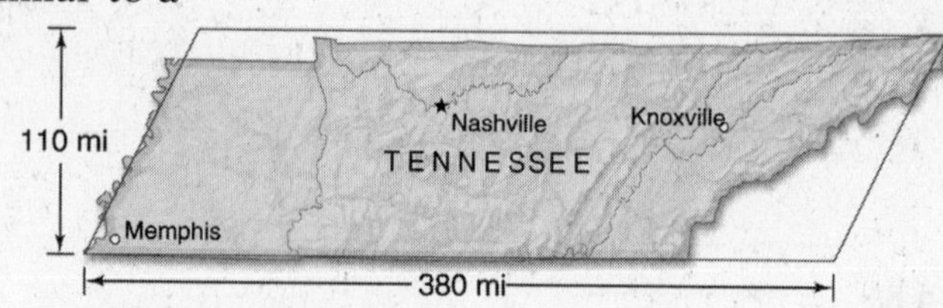

Understand

1. What are you being asked to do?

____

____

2. What shape is Tennessee similar to?

____

____

3. How do you find the area of a parallelogram?

____

____

____

Plan and Carry Out

4. What is the height of Tennessee? ____________
5. What is the length of the base of Tennessee? ____________
6. Substitute the values into the formula $A = bh$. ____________
7. What is the approximate area of Tennessee? ____________

Check

8. Is this estimate more or less than the actual area of Tennessee? Explain.

____

____

Solve Another Problem

9. Tamika's yard is similar to the shape of a parallelogram. Estimate the area of Tamika's yard.

____

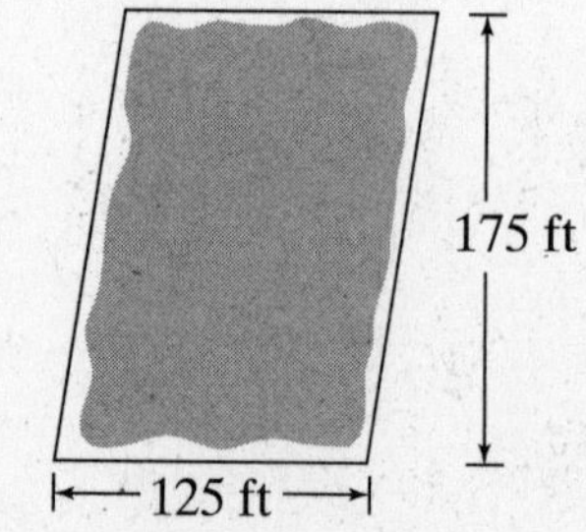

Practice 8-2

Area of a Parallelogram

Find the area of each parallelogram.

1. 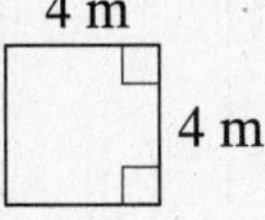

2. 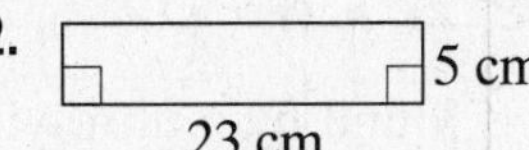

3. 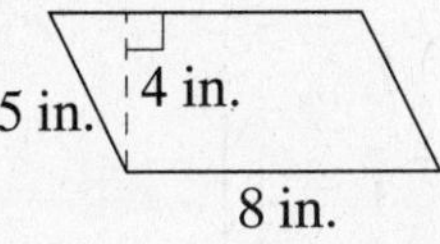

4. 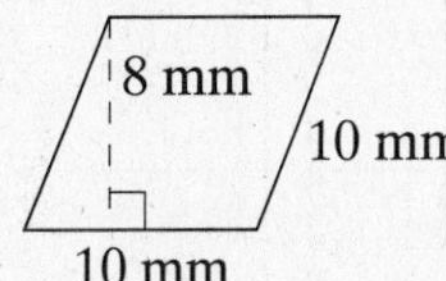

Find the area of each parallelogram with base *b* and height *h*.

5. $b = 16$ mm, $h = 12$ mm
6. $b = 23$ km, $h = 14$ km

Solve.

7. The area of a parallelogram is 6 square units. Both the height and the length of the base are whole numbers. What are the possible lengths and heights?

8. The perimeter of a rectangle is 72 m. The width of the rectangle is 16 m. What is the area of the rectangle?

9. The area of a certain rectangle is 288 yd^2. The perimeter is 68 yd. If you double the length and width, what will be the area and perimeter of the new rectangle?

Activity Lab 8-2

Area of a Parallelogram

Materials needed: ruler, paper, tape

The area of a parallelogram is found by multiplying its base by its height.

$$A = bh$$

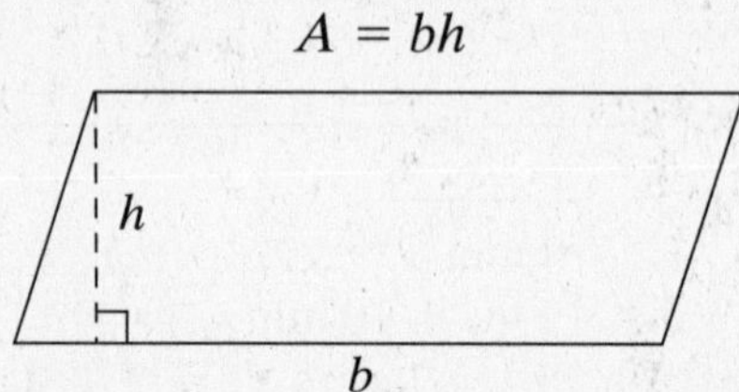

Many parallelograms can have the same area. For example, compare the area of a parallelogram with $b = 10$ cm and $h = 6$ cm to the area of a parallelogram with $b = 20$ cm and $h = 3$ cm. Both parallelograms have an area of 60 cm^2.

1. Using only whole number measurements for the bases and heights, how many different parallelograms have an area of 12 cm^2? Sketch them below and write their measurements.

2. On a separate sheet of paper, use a ruler to construct the parallelograms you thought of in Exercise 1.

3. Do any of the parallelograms you drew look larger than the others? Are they actually larger?

____

____

4. Tape together three sheets of notebook paper end-to-end to make one large sheet of paper. On this sheet, use the ruler to construct as many parallelograms as you can that have an area of 48 cm^2. Again, use only whole number measurements for the bases and heights. Label all of the bases and heights.

Name ______________________ Class ______________ Date ______________

Reteaching 8-2

Area of a Parallelogram

You can use the area of a rectangle to find the area of a parallelogram.

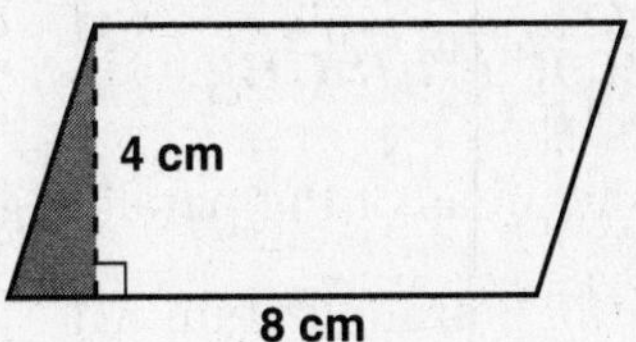

① Draw a perpendicular segment from one vertex to the opposite side to form a triangle.

② Move the triangle to the right side of the parallelogram to form a rectangle.

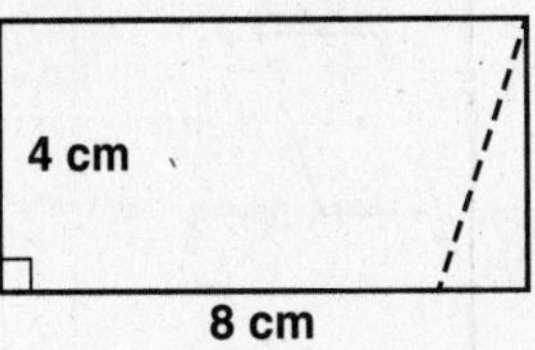

③ Find the area of the rectangle.
A = length × width = base × height = bh

The parallelogram has the same base, height, and area as the rectangle.

$$A = bh$$
$$= 8 \cdot 4$$
$$= 32 \text{ cm}^2$$

Find the area of each figure.

1.
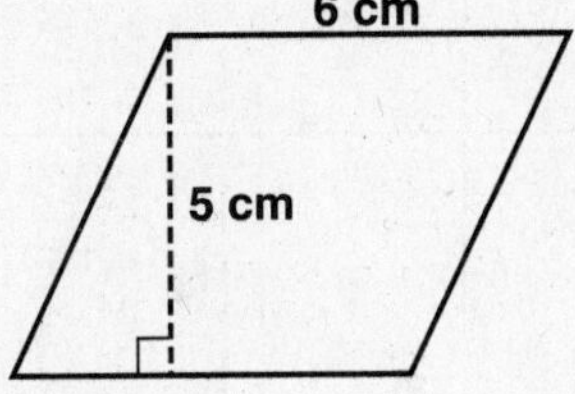

____

2.
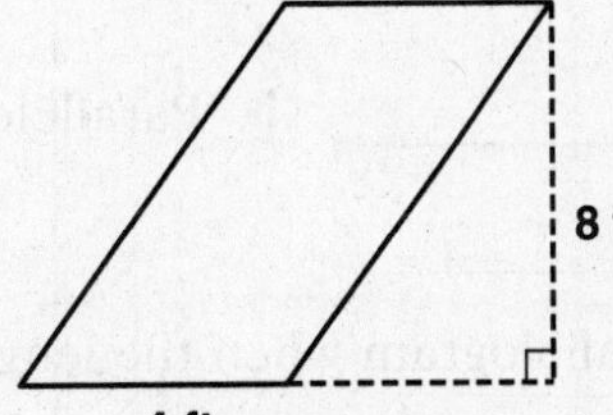

____

3.
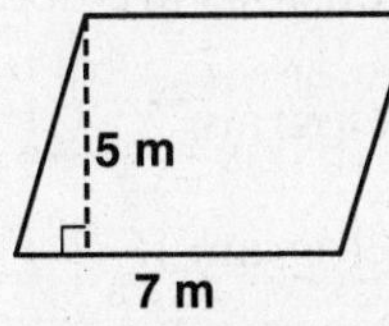

____

4.
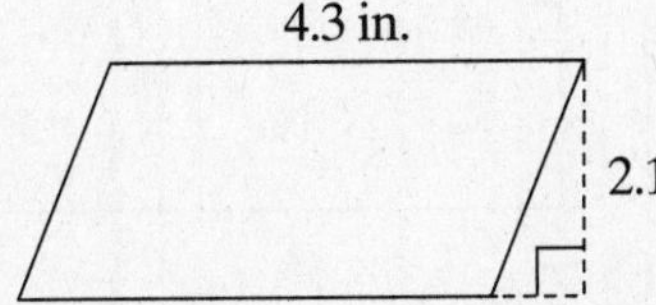

____

5.
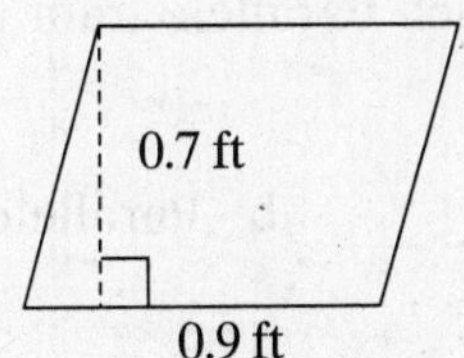

____

6.
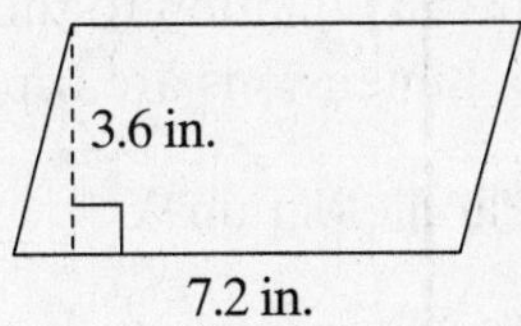

____

Find the area of a parallelogram with base length b and height h.

7. b =7 in., h = 4 in. ______________

8. b =9 m, h = 1.5 m ______________

9. b =1.25 cm, h = 2 cm ______________

Name ______________________ Class ______________ Date ______________

Enrichment 8-2

Area of a Parallelogram

Critical Thinking

Find the areas of the parallelograms below.

Parallelogram *X*

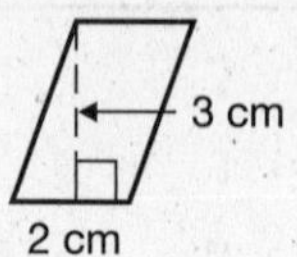

Parallelogram *Y*

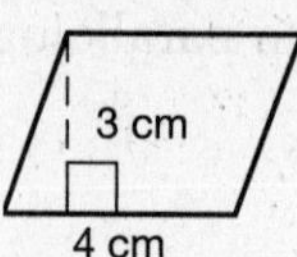

Parallelogram *Z*

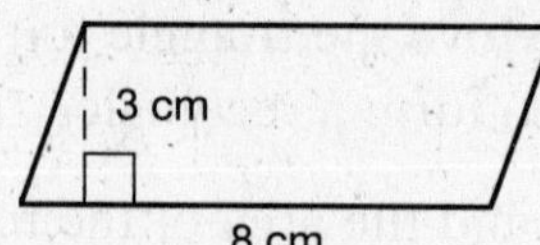

______________ ______________ ______________

1. What happens to the area of a parallelogram when the length of one dimension is doubled?

____

2. Write an equation to show the area of each parallelogram when both dimensions are doubled.

   a. Parallelogram *X* ______________ b. Parallelogram *Y* ______________

   c. Parallelogram *Z* ______________

3. What happens to the area of a parallelogram when the lengths of both dimensions are doubled?

____

4. Write an equation to show the area of each parallelogram when both dimensions are tripled.

   a. Parallelogram *X* ______________ b. Parallelogram *Y* ______________

   c. Parallelogram *Z* ______________

5. What happens to the area of a parallelogram when the lengths of both dimensions are tripled?

____

____

6. What pattern do you see in how the area of a parallelogram changes when both dimensions are multiplied by the same factor?

____

____

Name ______________________ Class ______________ Date ______________

Puzzle 8-2

Area of a Parallelogram

Use the four parallelograms to answer the questions below.

A.

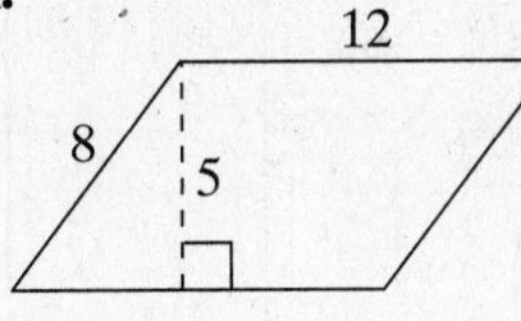

B.

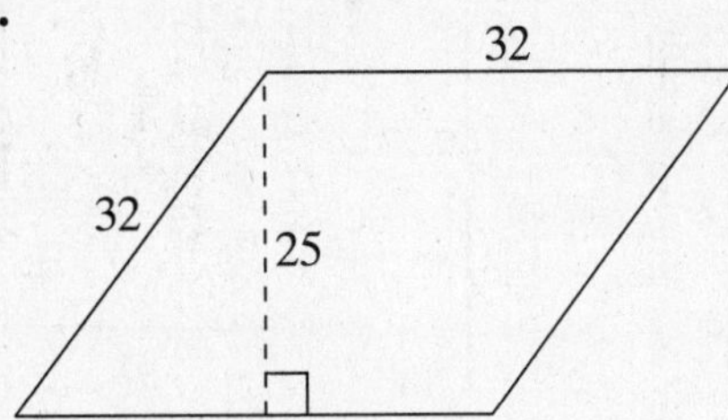

C.

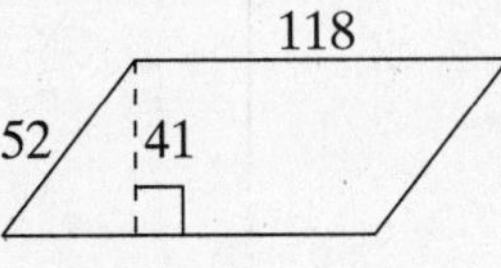

D.

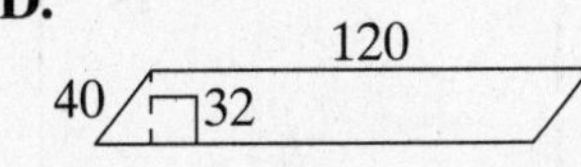

1. The area of parallelogram *C* ______________________

2. The perimeter of parallelogram *A* ______________________

3. The perimeter of parallelogram *D* ______________________

4. The area of parallelogram *B* ______________________

5. The area of parallelogram *A* ______________________

6. The area of parallelogram *D* ______________________

7. The perimeter of parallelogram *B* ______________________

8. The perimeter of parallelogram *C* ______________________

Name ______________________ Class ______________ Date ______________

Practice 8-3

Perimeter and Area of a Triangle

Find the perimeter of each triangle.

1.

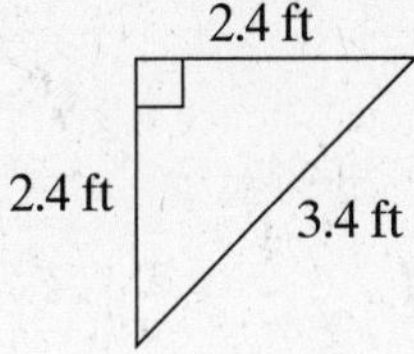

____

2.

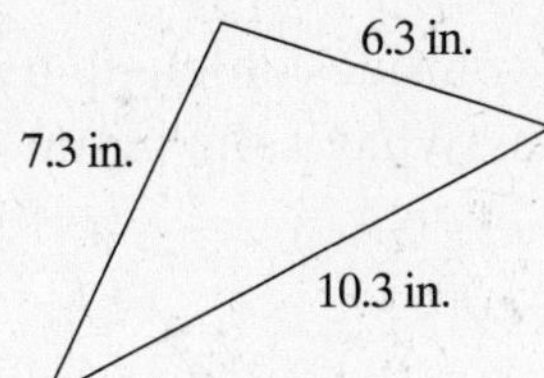

____

3.

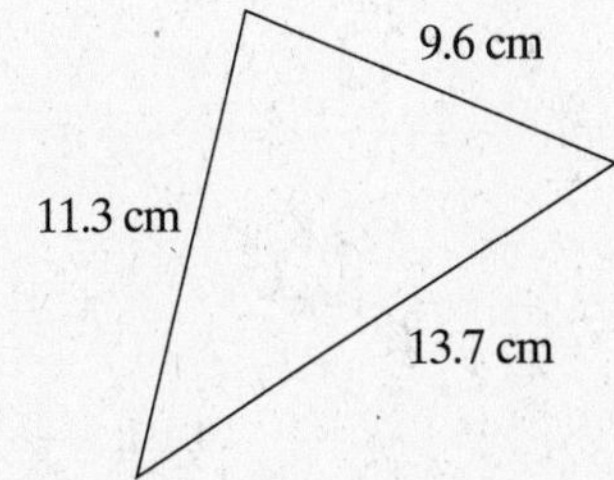

____

4.

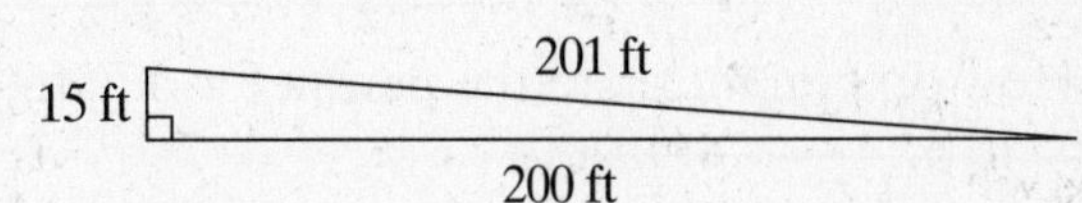

____

Find the area of each triangle.

5.

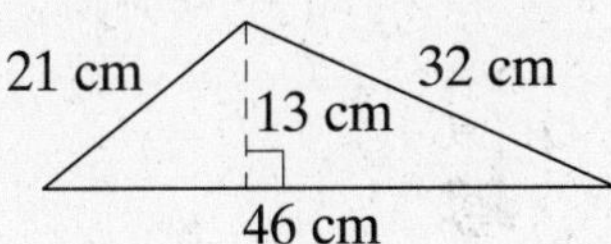

____

6.

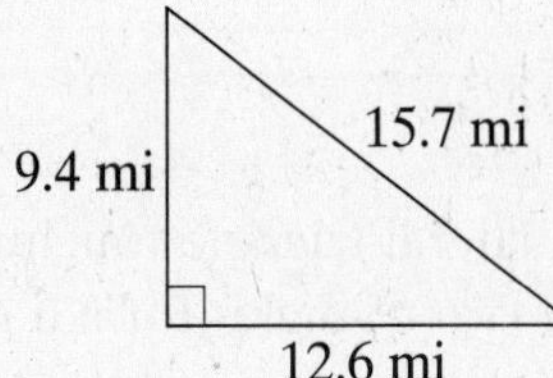

____

7.

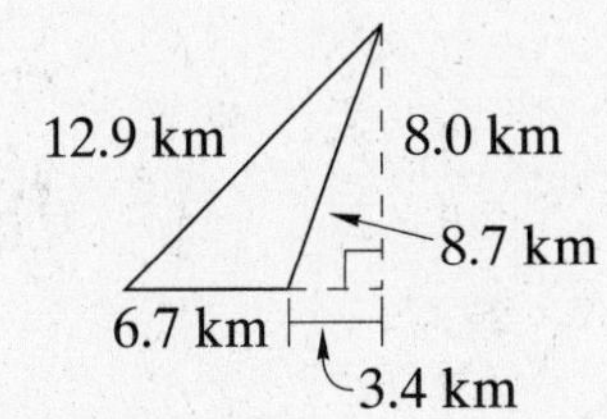

____

8.

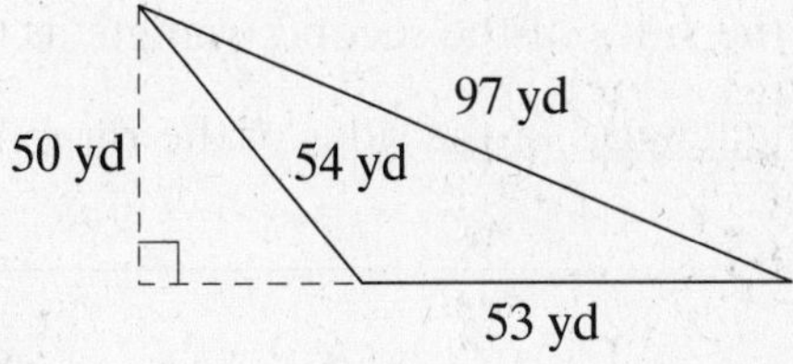

____

Solve.

9. The perimeter of an isosceles triangle is 12 in. What are the possible whole-number lengths of the legs?

____

10. The side of an equilateral triangle has a length of 5.4 m. The height of the triangle is approximately 4.7 m. What are the perimeter and area of this triangle? Round your answers to the nearest tenth.

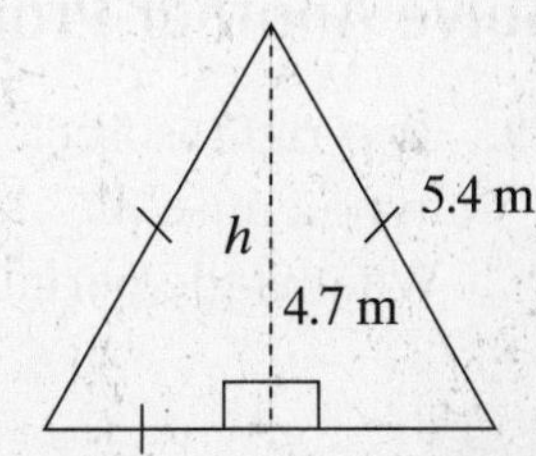

____

Name ______________________ Class ______________ Date ______________

8-3 • Guided Problem Solving

GPS Student Page 387, Exercise 26:

Two equilateral triangles with sides of length 6 inches are joined together to form a rhombus. What is the perimeter of the rhombus?

Understand

1. What are you being asked to do?

 ____

2. How do you measure the perimeter of a figure?

 ____

3. What is an equilateral triangle?

 ____

Plan and Carry Out

4. In the space to the right, draw an equilateral triangle. Label all of its sides as 6 in.

5. Draw another equilateral triangle touching the first equilateral triangle so that the two triangles form a rhombus.

6. Label the sides of the second triangle as 6 in.

7. Add the lengths of the sides of the rhombus to find the perimeter.

 ____

Check

8. Count the number of sides that the rhombus has. Multiply this number by the length of the sides. Is this number the same as your answer?

 ____

Solve Another Problem

9. Two right isosceles triangles with legs of 5 in. length and a hypotenuse of 7.1 in. are joined together to make a square. What is the perimeter of the square?

 ____

Name ______________________ Class ______________ Date ____________

Practice 8-3

Perimeter and Area of a Triangle

Find the perimeter of each triangle.

1.
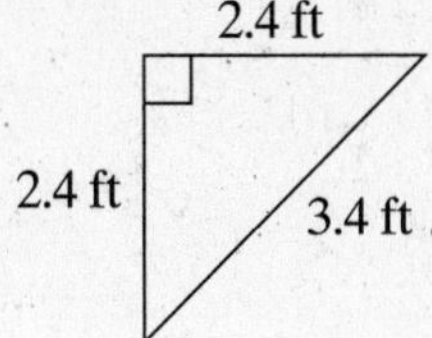

2.
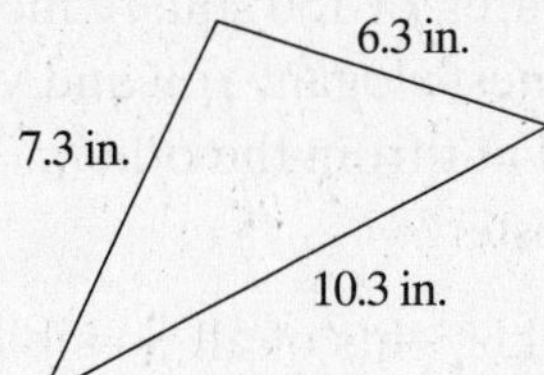

3.
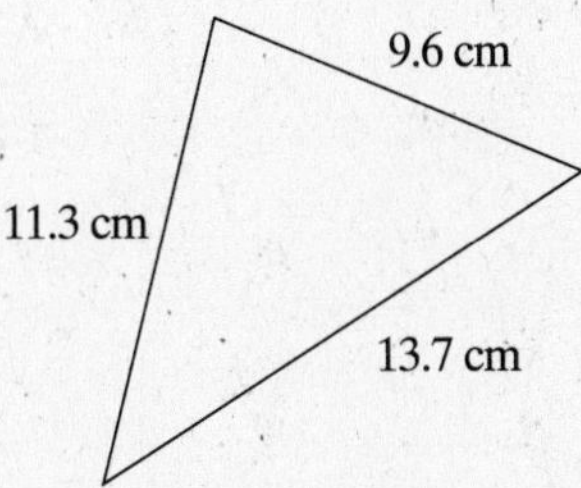

4.
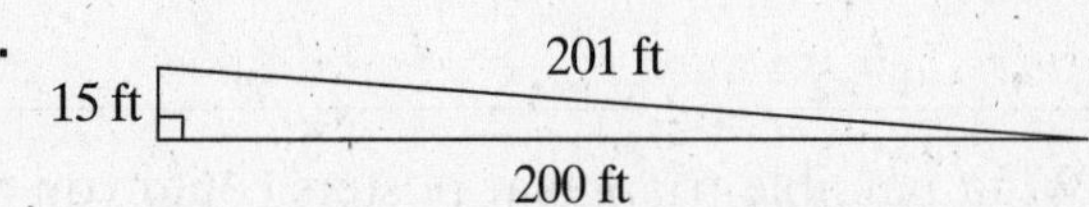

Find the area of each triangle.

5.
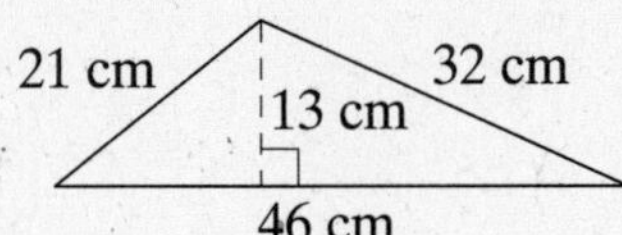

6.
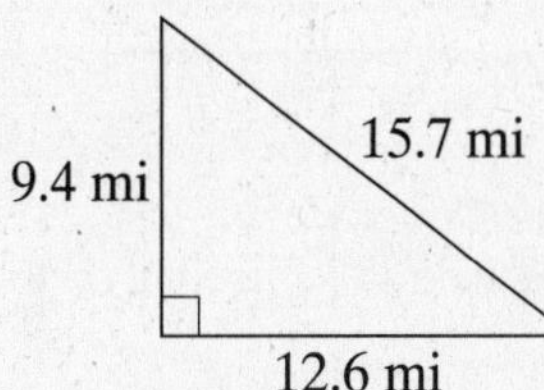

7.
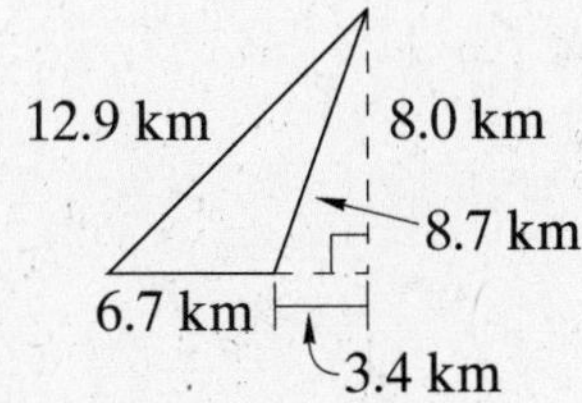

8.
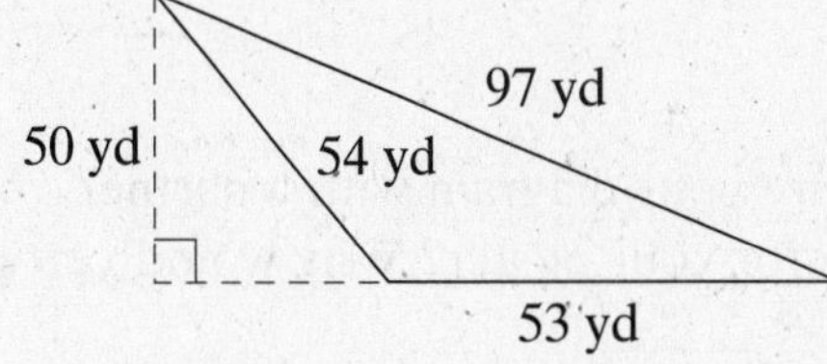

Solve.

9. The perimeter of an isosceles triangle is 12 in. What are the possible whole-number lengths of the legs?

Name ______________________________ Class ____________ Date ____________

Activity Lab 8-3

Perimeter and Area of a Triangle

You are entering a poster contest with your friends. The posters for the contest must have an area of 150 square inches, and must be large enough to display the contest slogan. You and your friends really want your poster to stand out from the others! What dimensions could you use for your poster?

1. Record the bases and heights of all possible rectangular posters if the dimensions are integers.

____

____

2. What possible triangular posters could you make? Record the bases and heights.

____

____

3. Draw a diagram of an irregularly shaped poster that covers an area of 150 square inches.

4. Compare your diagram with a partner's. Which shape would you choose for your poster? Why would you choose it?

____

____

Name ______________________ Class ______________ Date ______________

Reteaching 8-3

Perimeter and Area of a Triangle

To find the perimeter of a triangle, add the lengths of the sides together.

$5 + 5 + 7 = 17$

This triangle has a perimeter of 17 cm.

You can use the area of a parallelogram to find the area of a triangle. Two identical triangles, together as shown, form a parallelogram. Each triangle has half the area of the parallelogram.

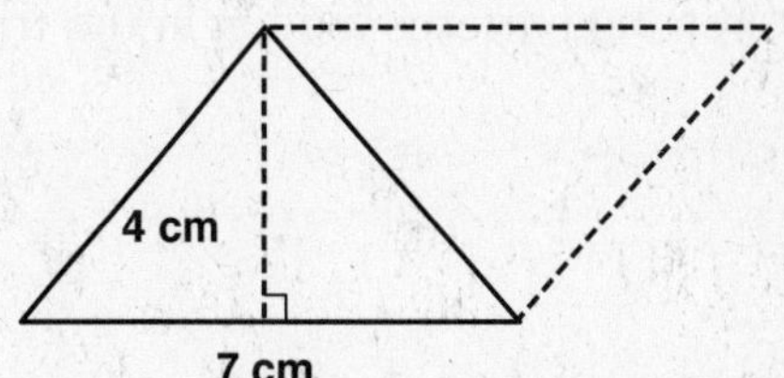

Area of parallelogram: $A = bh$

Area of triangle: $A = \frac{1}{2}bh = \frac{1}{2} \cdot 7 \cdot 4 = 14 \text{ cm}^2$

This triangle has an area of 14 cm^3.

Find the perimeter of each triangle.

1. 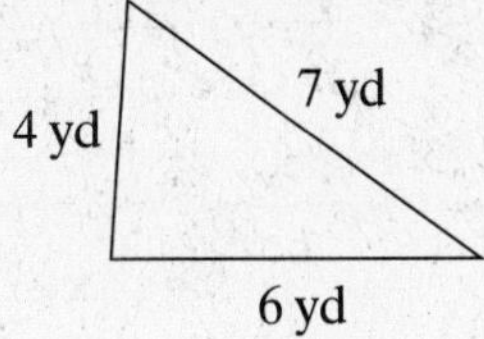

2. 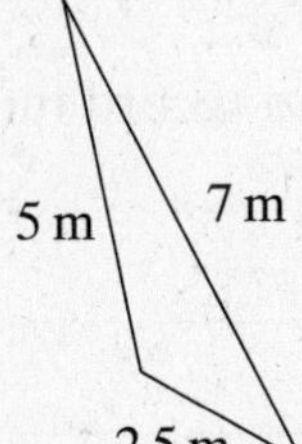

3. 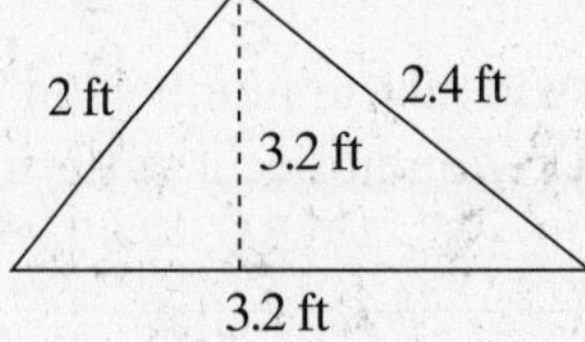

______________ ______________ ______________

Find the area of each triangle.

4. 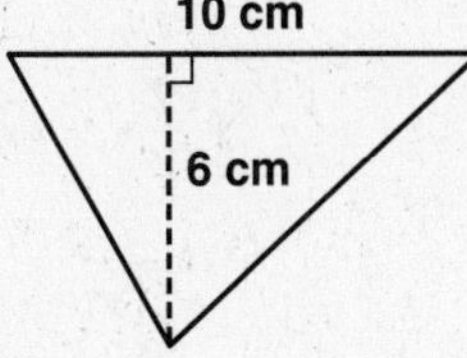

5. 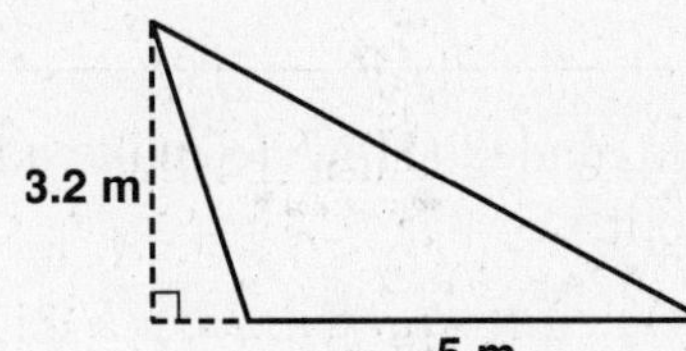

6. 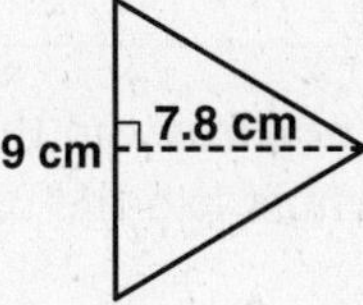

______________ ______________ ______________

Solve.

7. Ryan took measurements of his new kite and made the drawing shown on the right.

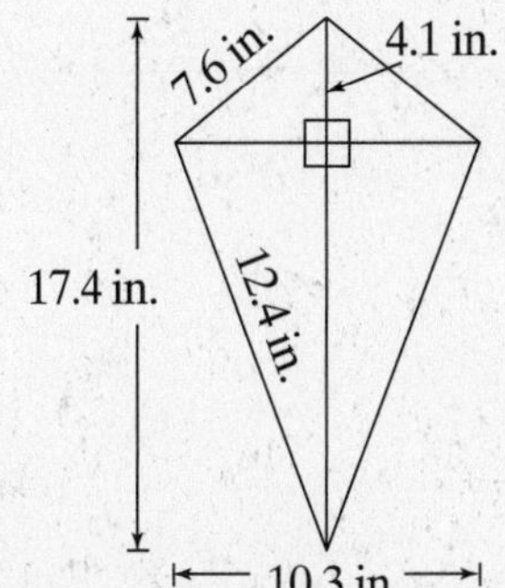

   a. What is the largest perimeter of any triangle in Ryan's drawing?

   ____

   b. What is the area of Ryan's kite? ______________

Name ______________________ Class ______________ Date ____________

Enrichment 8-3

Area and Perimeter of a Triangle

Visual Thinking

Pascal's Triangle is a number pattern based on a triangle, originally developed by ancient Chinese mathematicians. It is named after mathematician Blaise Pascal because he discovered several interesting patterns hidden in the triangle.

1
1 1
1 2 1
1 3 3 1
1 4 6 4 1
1 5 10 10 5 1
1 6 15 20 15 6 1
? ? ? ? ? ? ? ?

1. Add all the numbers in each horizontal row and record the totals. Do you notice a pattern?

____

____

2. Begin looking at diagonal rows in the triangle. Do you notice any patterns?

____

____

3. How are new rows in the triangle made? (Hint: To make a new row, you must use the row above it.)

____

____

4. Write the values for the next row in the triangle.

____

Name ______________________ Class ______________ Date ______________

Puzzle 8-3

Perimeter and Area of a Triangle

Find the missing value for each figure described. Use the letters of the correct answers to solve the puzzle at the bottom of the page.

Formula Box

The areas of a parallelogram can be found by the formula $A = bh$.

The area of a trapezoid can be found by the formula $A = \frac{1}{2}h(b_1 + b_2)$.

1. trapezoid: $b_1 = 8; b_2 = 10; h = 7$ **A.** $A = 560$ **B.** $A = 280$ **C.** $A = 63$

2. trapezoid: $b_1 = 7; b_2 = 9; A = 48$ **A.** $h = 6$ **B.** $h = 7$ **C.** $h = 8$

3. trapezoid: $b_2 = 12; h = 3; A = 24$ **A.** $b_1 = 2$ **B.** $b_1 = 3$ **C.** $b_1 = 4$

4. parallelogram: $b = 9; h = 7$ **S.** $A = 56$ **T.** $A = 63$ **U.** $A = 72$

5. parallelogram: $h = 3; A = 36$ **S.** $b = 8$ **T.** $b = 10$ **U.** $b = 12$

6. parallelogram: $b = 8; A = 48$ **S.** $h = 6$ **T.** $h = 7$ **U.** $h = 8$

The world's largest _____ _____ _____ _____ _____ _____ plantation is found
1 2 3 4 5 6
in Edwards, Mississippi.

Name ______________________ Class ______________ Date ______________

Practice 8-4

Areas of Other Figures

Find the area of each trapezoid.

1. 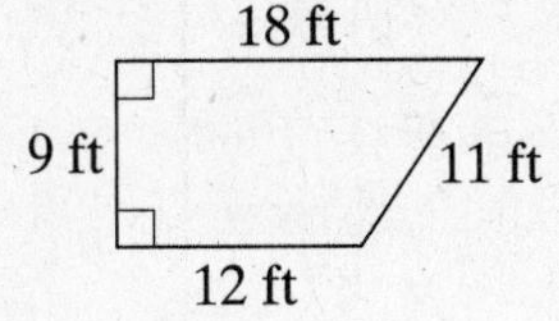

2. 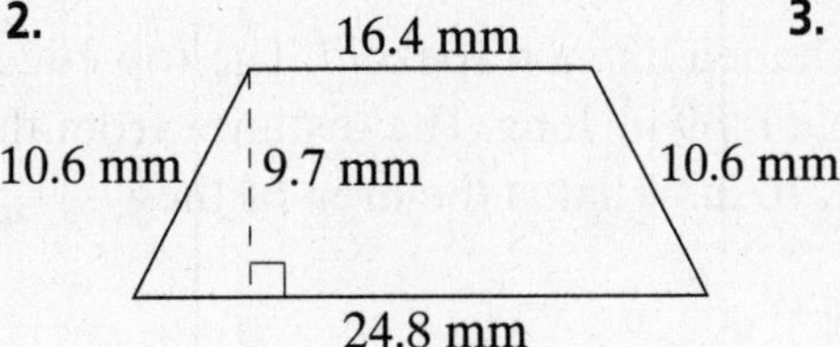

3. 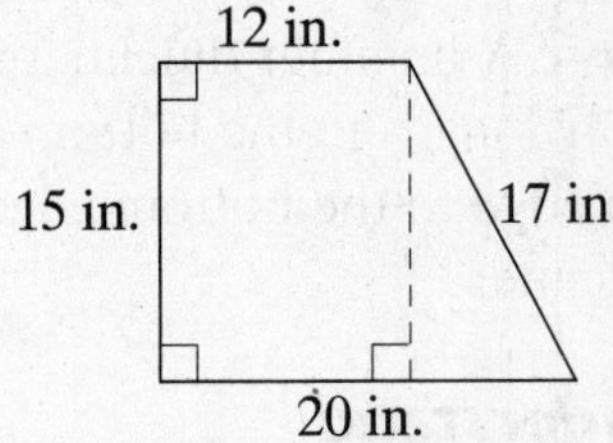

4. 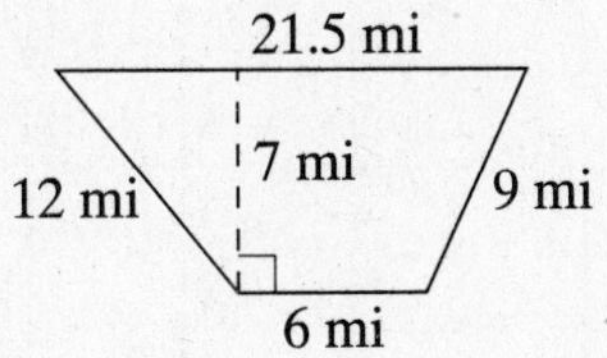

5. 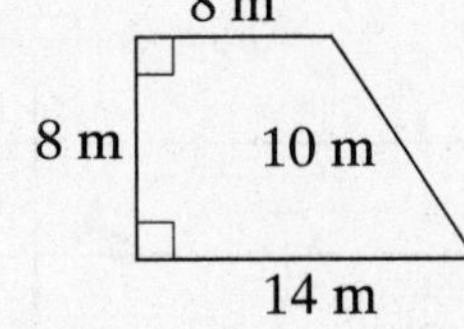

6. 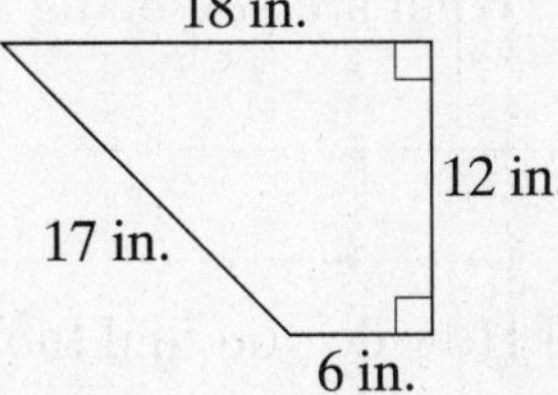

Find the area of each irregular figure.

7. 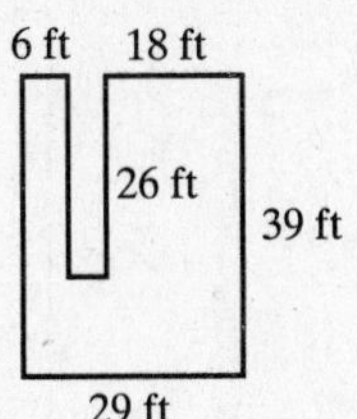

8. 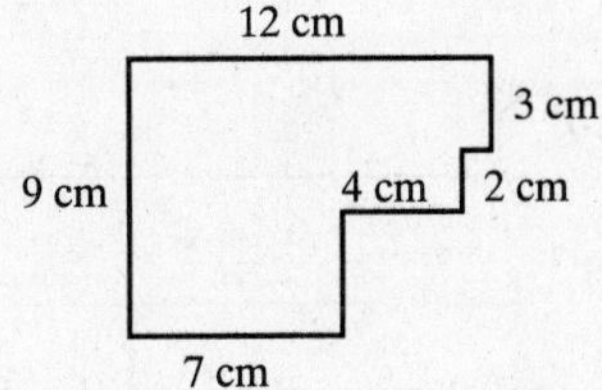

9. 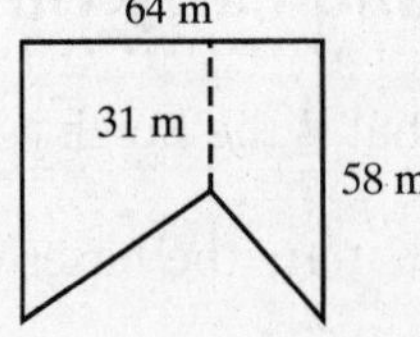

Solve.

10. The flag of Switzerland features a white cross on a red background.

a. Each of the 12 sides of the cross has a length of 15 cm. Find the area of the white cross.

b. The flag has dimensions 60 cm by 60 cm. Find the area of the red region.

11. A trapezoid has an area of 4 square units, and a height of 1 unit. What are the possible whole-number lengths for the bases?

Name ______________________ Class ______________ Date ______________

8-4 • Guided Problem Solving

GPS Student Page 392, Exercise 17:

Music A hammer dulcimer is shaped like a trapezoid. The top edge is 17 in. long, and the bottom edge is 39 in. long. The distance from the top edge to the bottom edge is 16 in. What is the area of the dulcimer?

Understand

1. Circle the information you will need to solve the problem.
2. What are you being asked to do?

____

____

3. How do you find the area of a trapezoid?

____

____

Plan and Carry Out

4. What is the height of the dulcimer? ______________
5. What are the bases of the dulcimer? ______________
6. Substitute the values for the bases and the height into the formula for area.

____

7. What is the area of the dulcimer? ______________

Check

8. Explain how you chose which measurements are the bases.

____

____

Solve Another Problem

9. Suppose the dulcimer had bases of 20 in. and 36 in. with the same height. What would be the area of the dulcimer? How do the areas compare? Explain.

____

____

Name ______________________ Class ______________ Date ____________

Practice 8-4

Areas of Other Figures

Find the area of each trapezoid.

1.

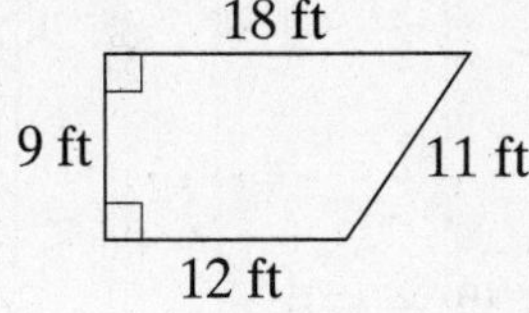

2.

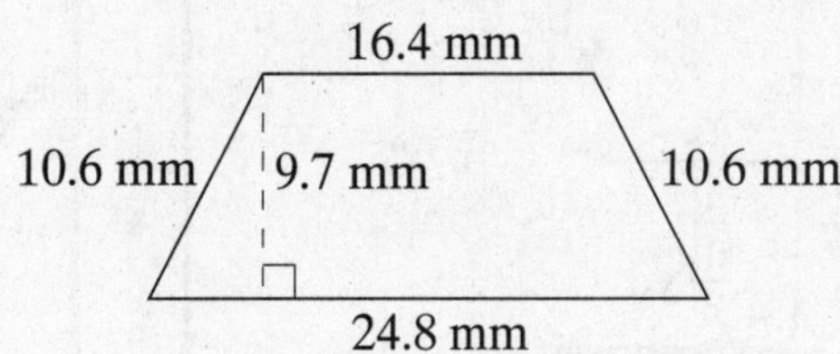

3.

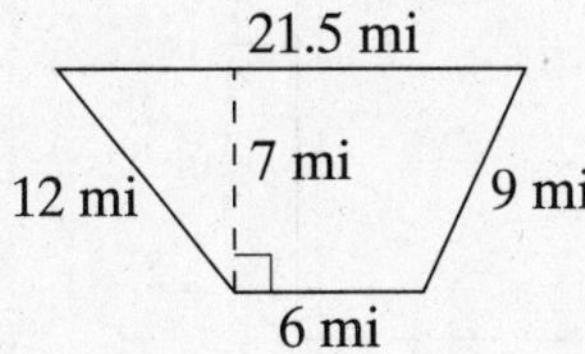

4.

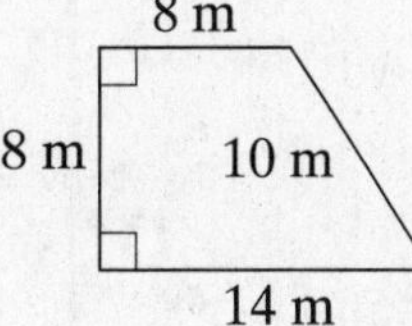

Find the area of each irregular figure.

5.

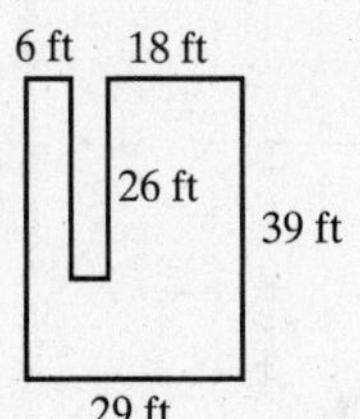

6.

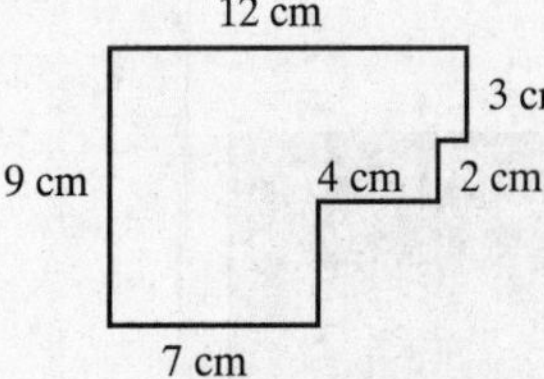

Solve.

7. The flag of Switzerland features a white cross on a red background.

a. Each of the 12 sides of the cross has a length of 15 cm. Find the area of the white cross.

____

b. The flag has dimensions 60 cm by 60 cm. Find the area of the red region.

____

8. A trapezoid has an area of 4 square units, and a height of 1 unit. What are the possible whole-number lengths for the bases?

____

Name ______________________ Class ______________ Date ______________

Activity Lab 8-4

Find the area of each shaded part.

1. ____________

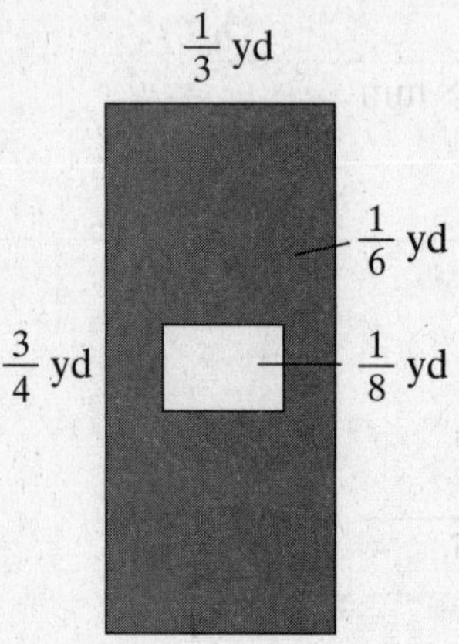

2. ____________

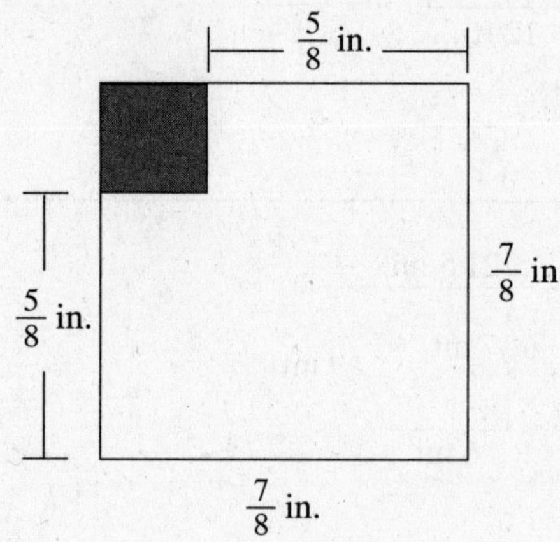

3. ____________

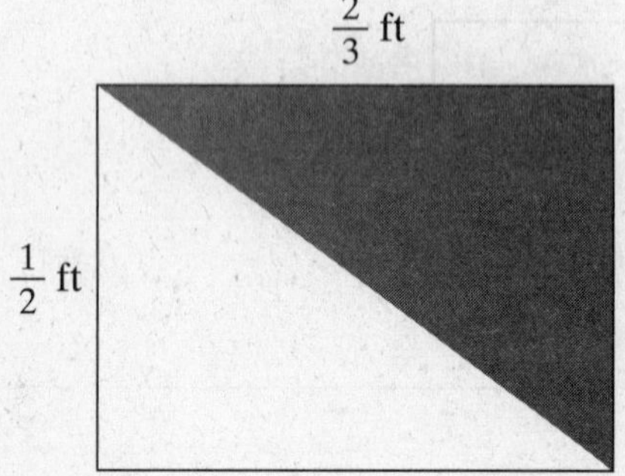

4. ____________

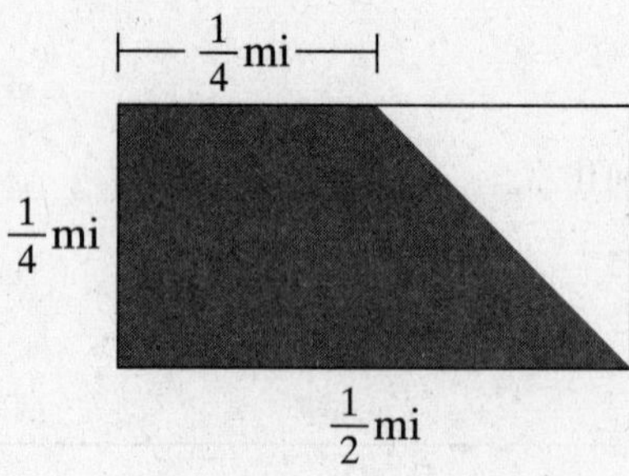

5. Did you use the same method and formulas to solve all four area problems? Explain.

____

____

____

Name ______________ Class ______________ Date ______________

Reteaching 8-4

Areas of Other Figures

Trapezoid

Two identical trapezoids, together as shown, form a parallelogram. The trapezoid has half the area of the parallelogram.

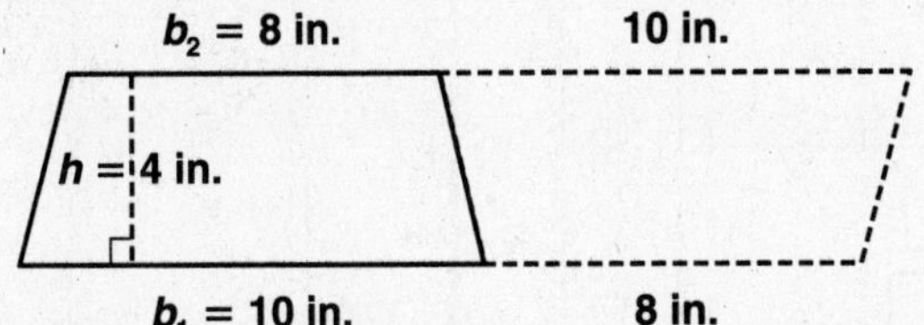

Area of parallelogram: $A = (b_1 + b_2)h$

Area of trapezoid: $A = \frac{1}{2}h(b_1 + b_2)$

$= \frac{1}{2}(4)(10 + 8)$

$= 2(18) = 36 \text{ in.}^2$

Irregular Figures

Not all geometric figures are shapes with which you are familiar. Some of them, however, can be divided into familiar shapes.

Find the area of the figure.

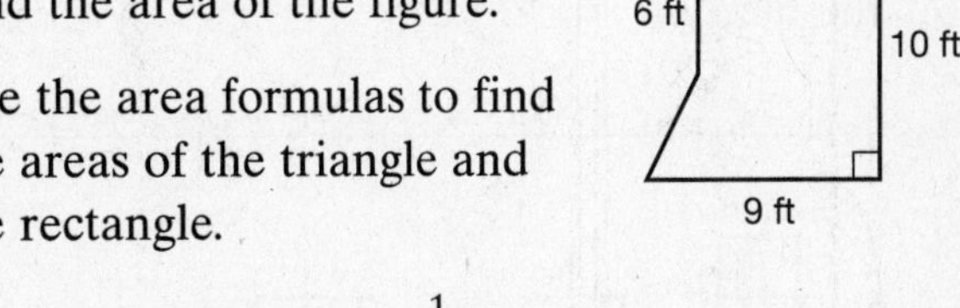

Use the area formulas to find the areas of the triangle and the rectangle.

Area of a triangle $= \frac{1}{2}bh$

$= \frac{1}{2}(2)(4)$

$= \frac{1}{2}(8)$

$= 4 \text{ ft}^2$

4 ft
2 ft

Area of a rectangle $= bh$

$= (7)(10)$

$= 70 \text{ ft}^2$

7 ft
10 ft

Find the total area by adding the area of each figure.

Total area = area of triangle + area of rectangle

$= 4 + 70$

$= 74$

The total area is 74 ft^2.

Based on appearance, find the area of each figure.

1.

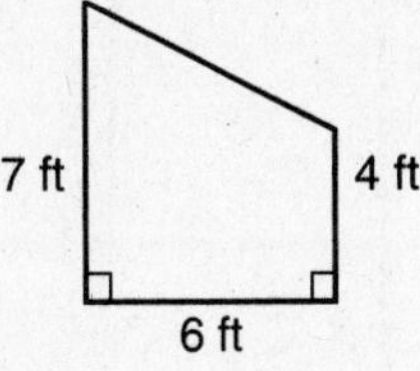

____

2.

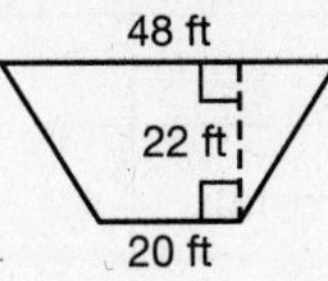

____

3. $3\frac{1}{2}$ in.
$9\frac{1}{2}$ in.

____

4.

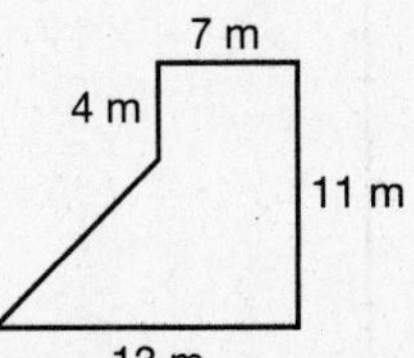

____

5.

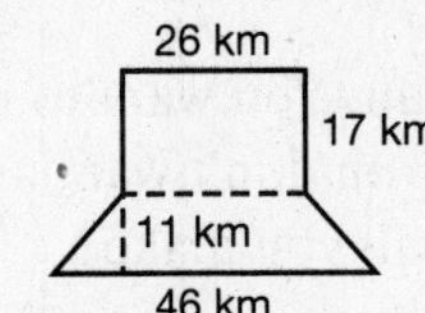

____

6.

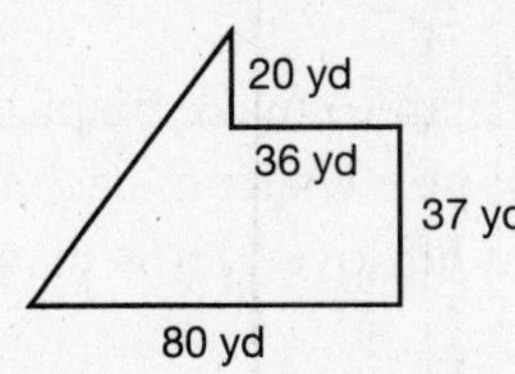

____

Name ______________________ Class ______________ Date ______________

Enrichment 8-4

Areas of Other Figures

Decision Making

The students in a woodworking class are making toddlers' puzzles to sell at a craft fair.

1. Find the area of each puzzle piece. Then find the total area of the puzzle.

____

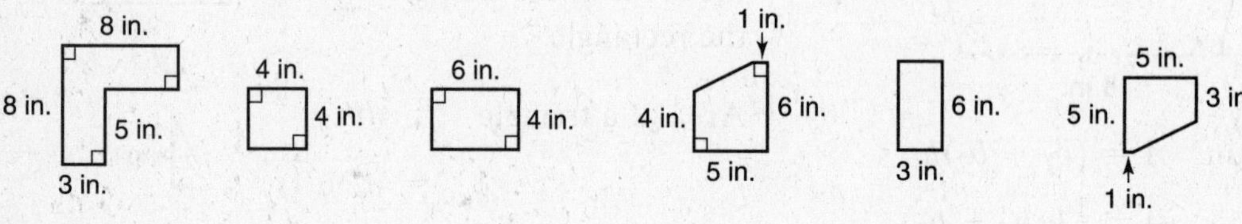

______ ______ ______ ______ ______ ______

2. The prices of different types of wood are given in the table below. The supplier sells the wood in either 4- or 8-board-foot sections. One board foot measures 1 square foot.

Type of Wood	Cost per board foot	Board feet per section	Cost per section	Puzzles per section
Cherry	$5.50	4		
Maple	$3.80	8		
Red Oak	$4.00	8		
White Oak	$3.50	4		

3. What things in addition to cost would you consider when setting a price for each puzzle?

____

____

4. What price would you set for each puzzle? Explain.

____

____

5. You plan to make 52 puzzles to sell at the fair. You want to make some puzzles from each type of wood, and you don't want any wood left over. How many of each puzzle will you make?

____

Puzzle 8-4

Areas of Other Figures

1. Find the area of each shape, and record your answers below.

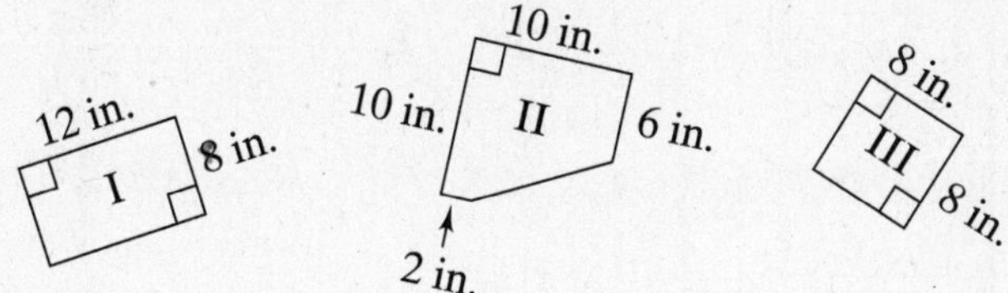

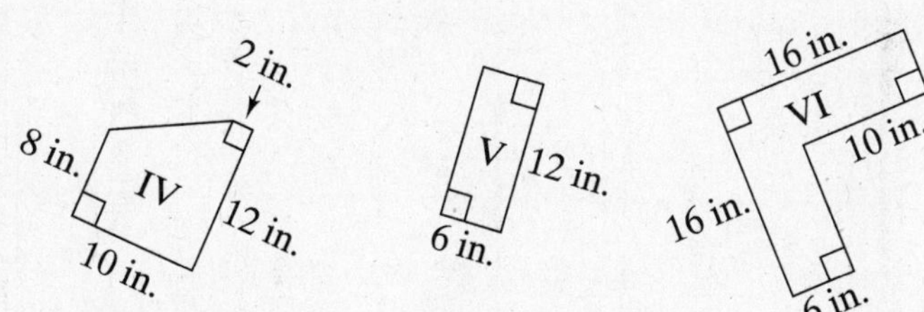

Area of Shape I: ______________ Area of Shape II: ______________

Area of Shape III: ______________ Area of Shape IV: ______________

Area of Shape V: ______________ Area of Shape VI: ______________

2. Find the sum of the areas you calculated in Exercise 1. ______________

3. Each shape is a piece of a puzzle. When assembled properly, the shapes fit together to form a square. Cut out the shapes and assemble the puzzle below.

4. Find the area of the square. ______________

5. How does the area of the square compare to the areas of the pieces?

Name ______________________ Class ______________ Date ______________

Practice 8-5

Circumference and Area of a Circle

Find the circumference and area of each circle. Round your answers to the nearest tenth.

1.

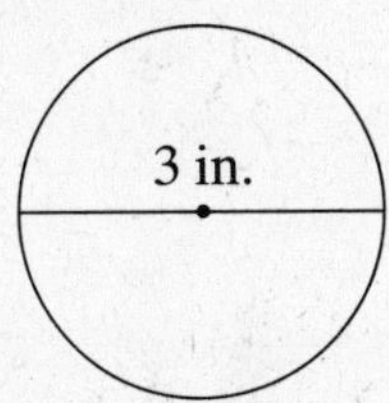

2.

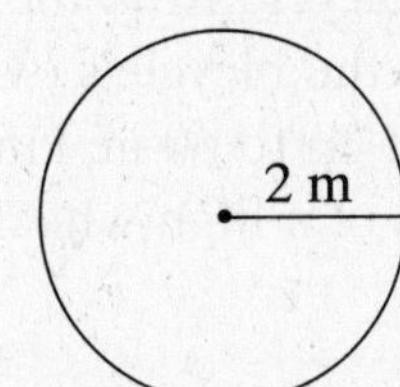

3.

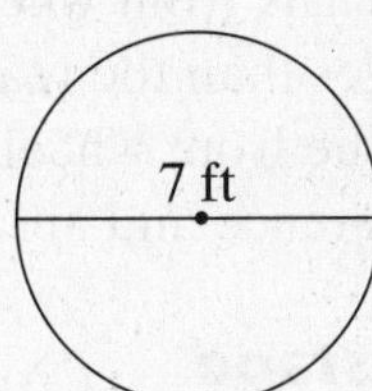

4.

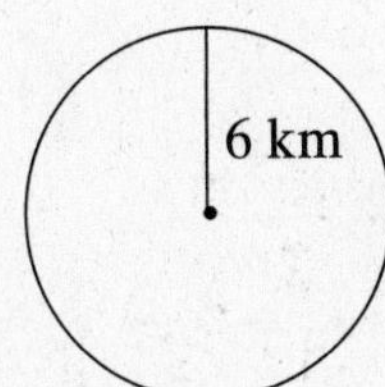

5.

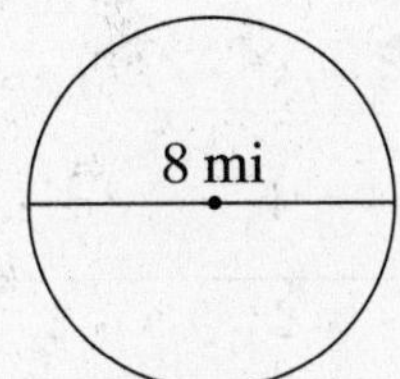

6.

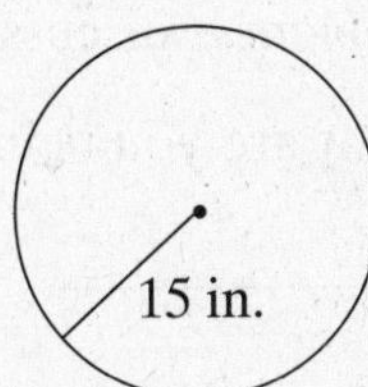

7.

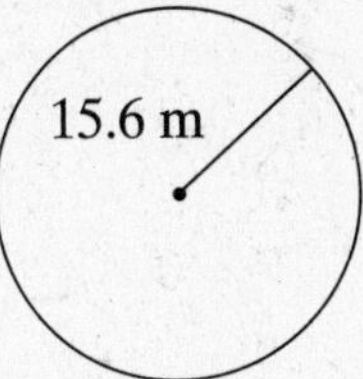

8.

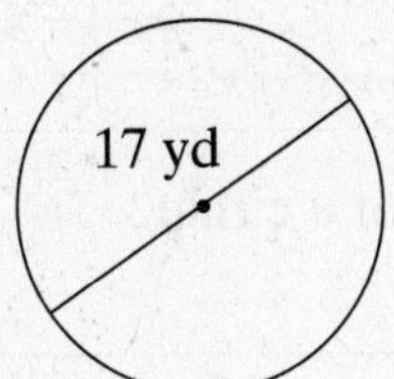

9.

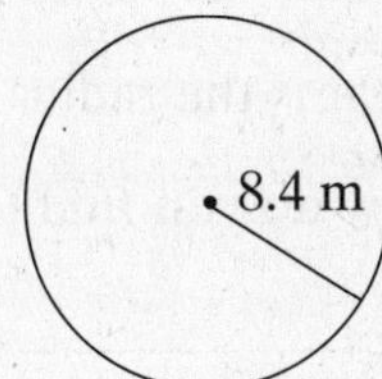

Estimate the radius of each circle with the given circumference. Round your answer to the nearest tenth.

10. 80 km

11. 92 ft

12. 420 in.

13. In the diagram at the right, the radius of the large circle is 8 in. The radius of each of the smaller circles is 1 in. Find the area of the shaded region to the nearest square unit.

____

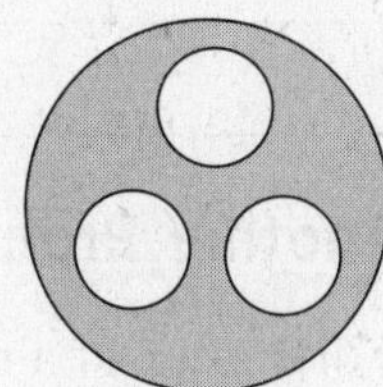

Name ______________________ Class ______________ Date ______________

8-5 • Guided Problem Solving

GPS Student Page 397, Exercise 25:

Bicycles The front wheel of a high-wheel bicycle from the late 1800s was larger than the rear wheel to increase the bicycle's overall speed. The front wheel measured in height up to 60 in. Find the circumference and area of the front wheel of a high-wheel bicycle.

Understand

1. Circle the information you will need to solve.
2. In the space to the right, draw a sketch of the bicycle that the problem is discussing.
3. What are you being asked to do?

____

____

Plan and Carry Out

4. What is the diameter of the front wheel? ______________
5. What is the radius of the front wheel? ______________
6. How do you find the circumference of a circle?

____

7. What is the circumference of the front wheel? ______________
8. How do you find the area of a circle?

____

9. What is the area of the front wheel? ______________

Check

10. How do you determine the radius if you know the area and circumference of a circle?

____

____

Solve Another Problem

11. The diameter of a normal front wheel on a bicycle is 24 in. Find the circumference and area of the front wheel.

____

Name ____________________ Class ____________ Date ____________

Practice 8-5

Circumference and Area of a Circle

Find the circumference and area of each circle. Round your answers to the nearest tenth.

1.

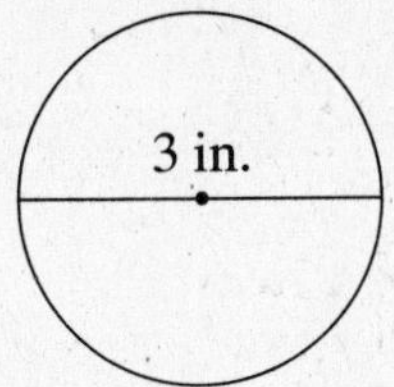

2.

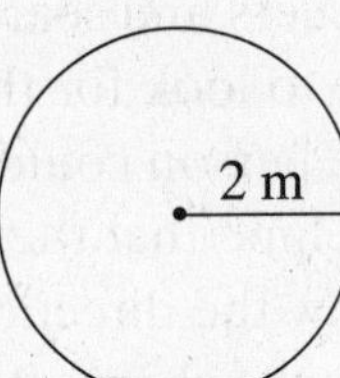

3.

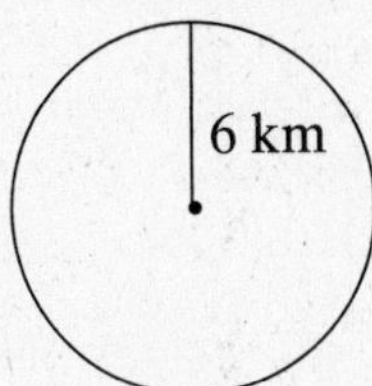

4.

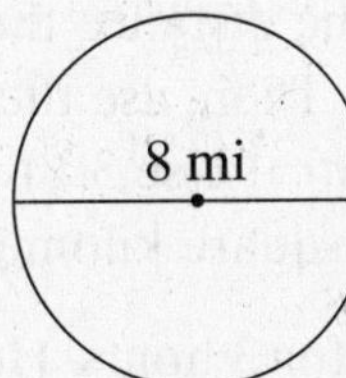

5.

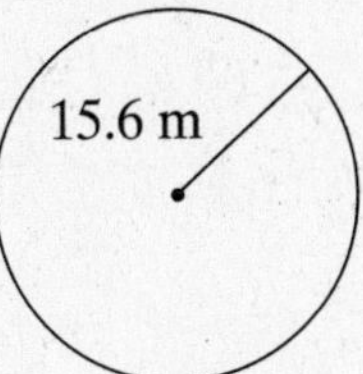

6.

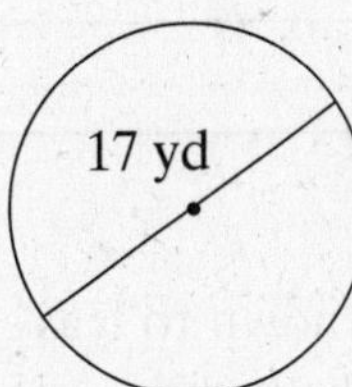

Estimate the radius of each circle with the given circumference. Round your answers to the nearest tenth.

7. 80 km

8. 420 in.

9. The radius of the large circle is 8 in. The radius of each of the smaller circles is 1 in. Find the area of the shaded region to the nearest square unit.

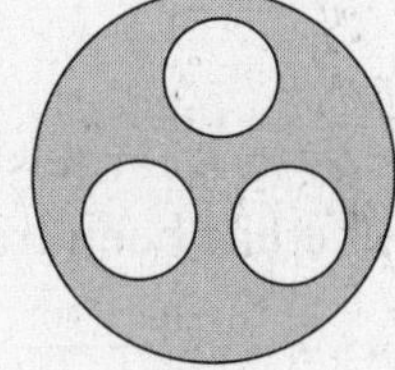

Activity Lab 8-5

Circumference and Area of a Circle

Search Area

When a person is lost, rescuers and search teams must define a search area before they go to look for the person. The search area is determined by how far the person could have gone from their last known location within the time that they have been missing. Because searchers do not often know the direction in which the person has gone, the search area takes the shape of a circle, the center of which is the person's last known location.

To calculate the search area in each situation below, find the radius of the circle by determining the distance the person could have traveled (distance = speed × time). Then, use the radius to find the area of the circular search area. ($A = \pi r^2$) Use 3.14 for π. Round your answers to the nearest square mile or square kilometer.

1. A hiker has been lost for 3 hours. He can hike at an average rate of 5 miles per hour.

Radius	Search area

2. A mountain biker is known to travel at an average speed of 10.5 miles per hour. She has been lost for 6 hours.

Radius	Search area

3. A swimmer has been lost for 30 minutes. She normally swims at an average speed of 4 kilometers per hour.

Radius	Search area

4. A man in a car has been missing for 4 hours. Searchers assume that he has been traveling at an average of 75 miles per hour.

Radius	Search area

Name ______________________ Class ______________ Date ______________

Reteaching 8-5

Circumference and Area of a Circle

The **circumference** of a circle is the distance around it. To find the circumference of a circle with radius r and diameter d, use either the formula $C = 2\pi r$ or $C = \pi d$. Use 3.14 for π.

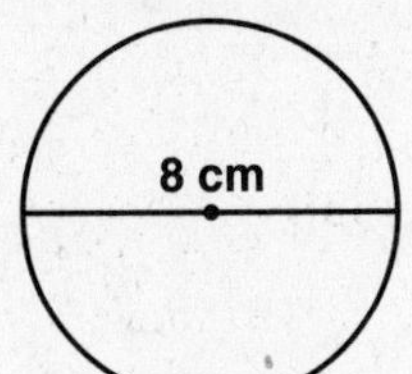

$d = 8$ cm
$C = \pi d$
$\approx 3.14 \cdot 8$
$= 25.12$ cm

To the nearest centimeter, the circumference is 25 cm.

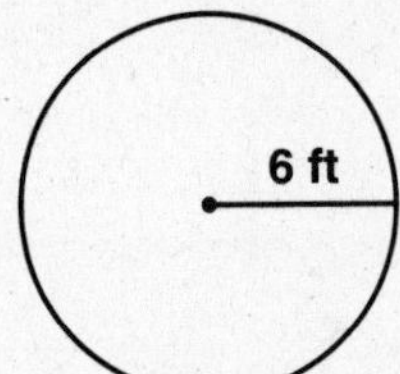

$r = 6$ ft
$C = 2\pi r$
$\approx 2 \cdot 3.14 \cdot 6$
$= 37.68$ ft

To the nearest foot, the circumference is 38 ft.

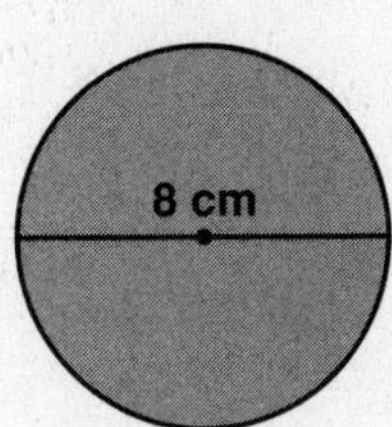

To find the area of a circle, use $A = \pi r^2$.
The diameter of the circle is 8 cm, so the radius is 4 cm.

$A = 5\ \pi r^2$
$\approx 3.14 \cdot 4 \cdot 4$
$= 50.24\ \text{cm}^2$

To the nearest square centimeter, the area is 50 cm^2.

Find the circumference and area of each circle. Round your answer to the nearest whole unit.

1. 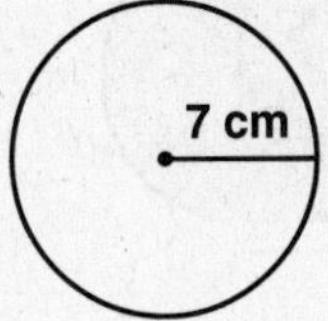

____

2. 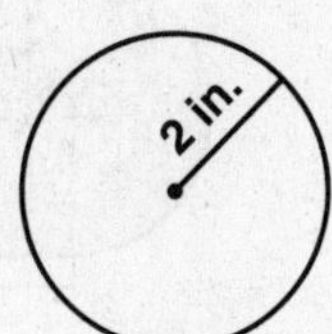

____

3. 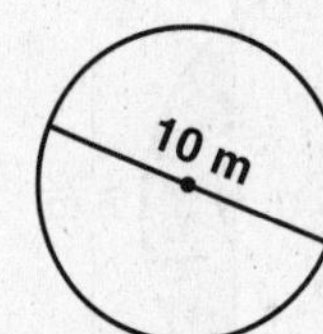

____

4. 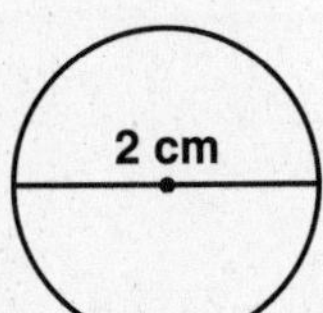

____

5. 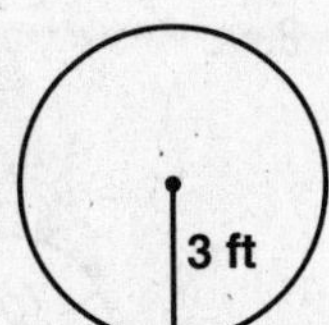

____

6. 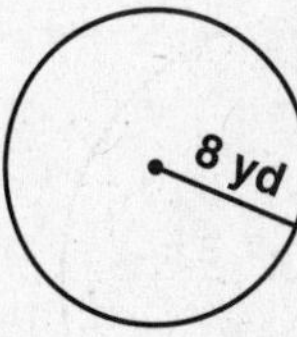

____

Name ______________________ Class ______________ Date ______________

Enrichment 8-5

Circumference and Area of a Circle

Critical Thinking

Find the area of the shaded portion in each region.

1.

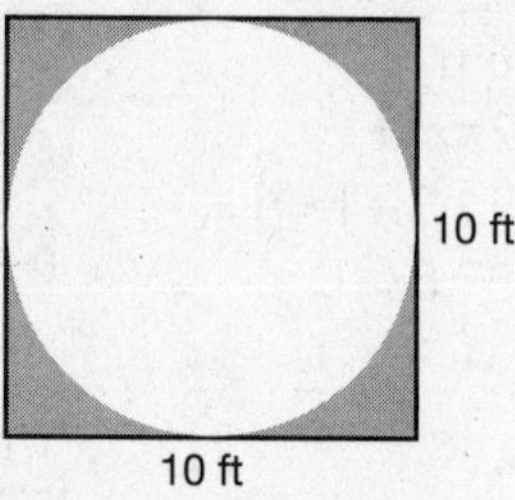

____

2.

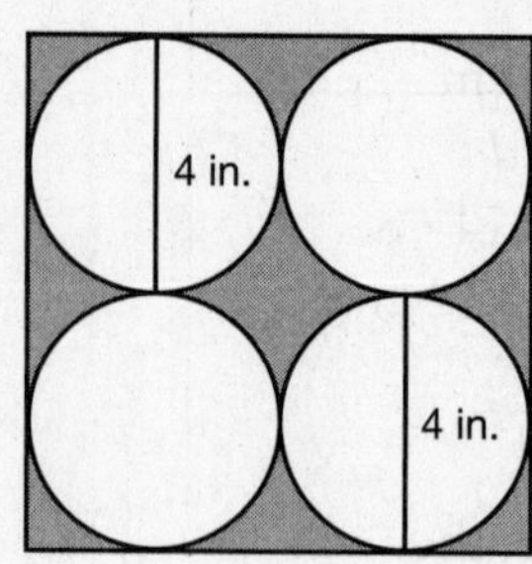

____

3.

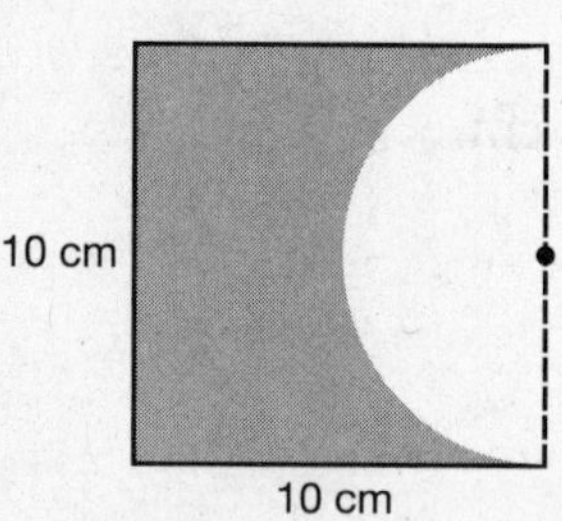

____

4.

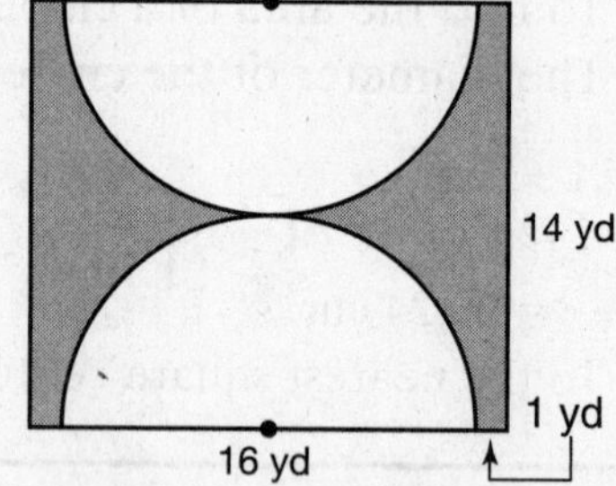

____

5.

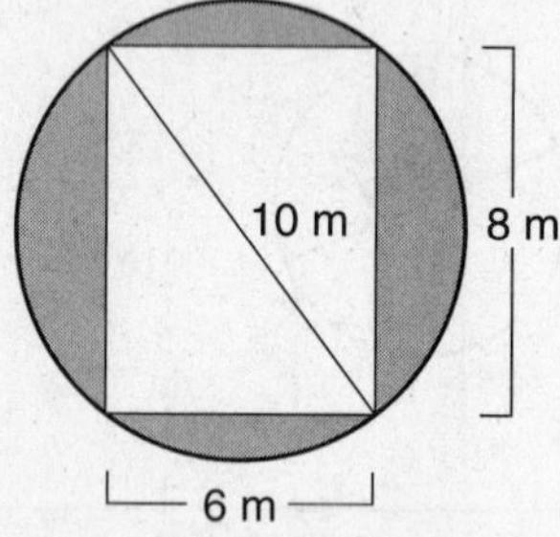

____

6.

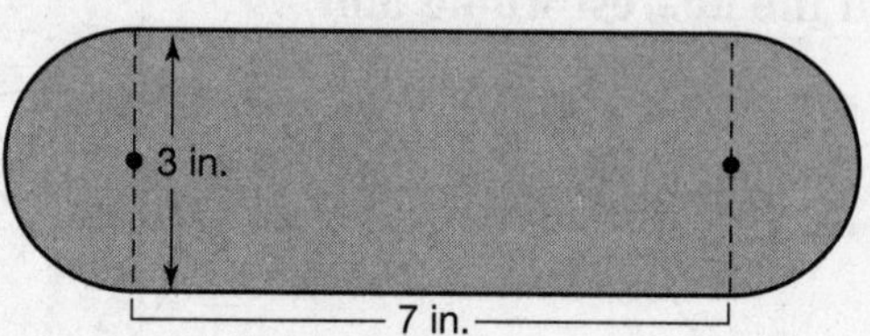

____

7.

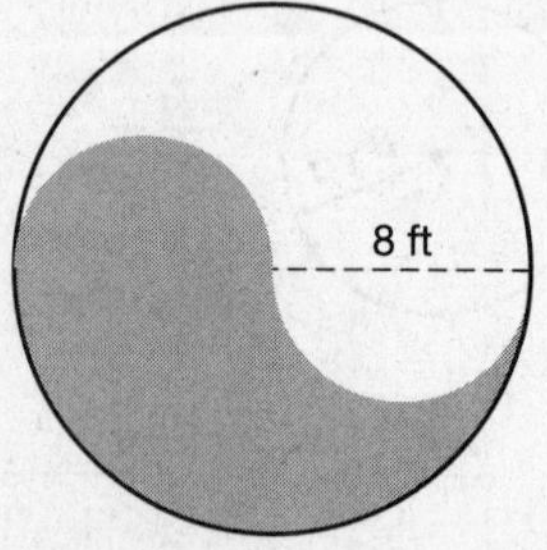

____

8.

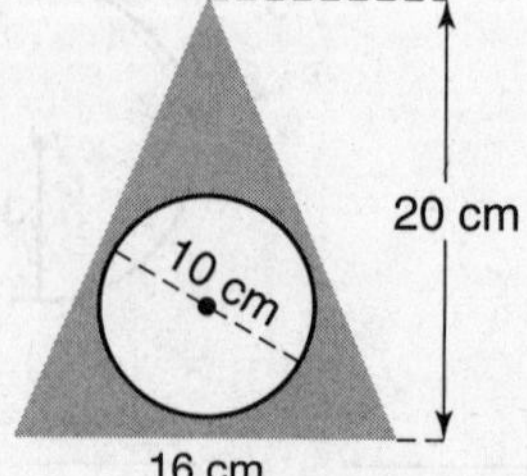

____

Name ______________________ Class ______________ Date ______________

Puzzle 8-5

Circumference and Area of a Circle

Find the area of the shaded portion of each figure. Use 3.14 for π.
Then check your answers by locating them in the number-puzzle below.

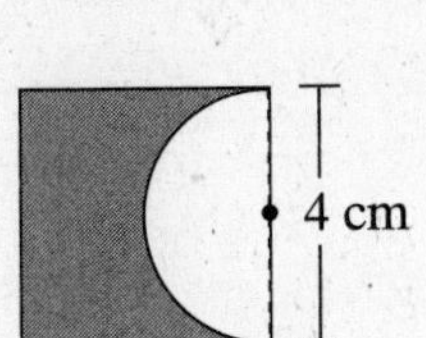

$A =$ ______________

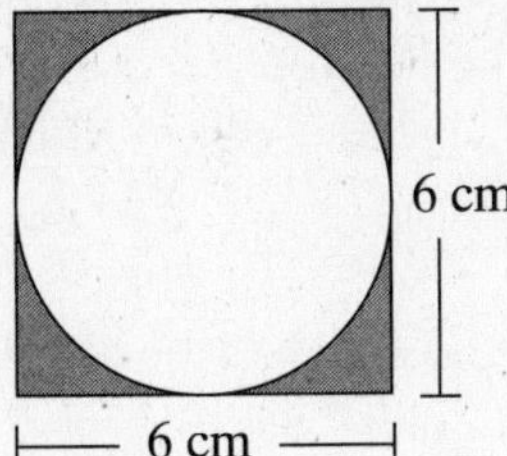

$A =$ ______________

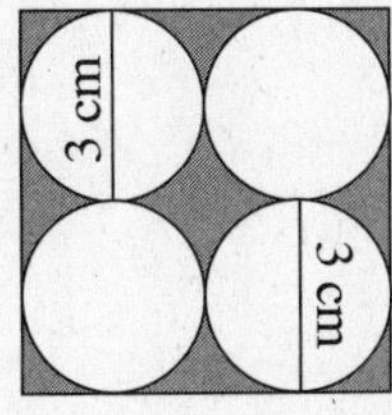

$A =$ ______________

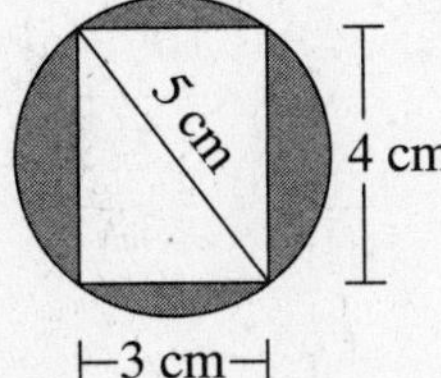

$A =$ ______________

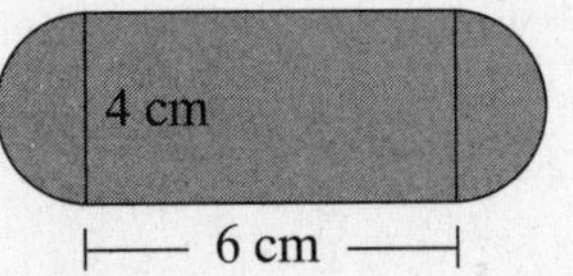

$A =$ ______________

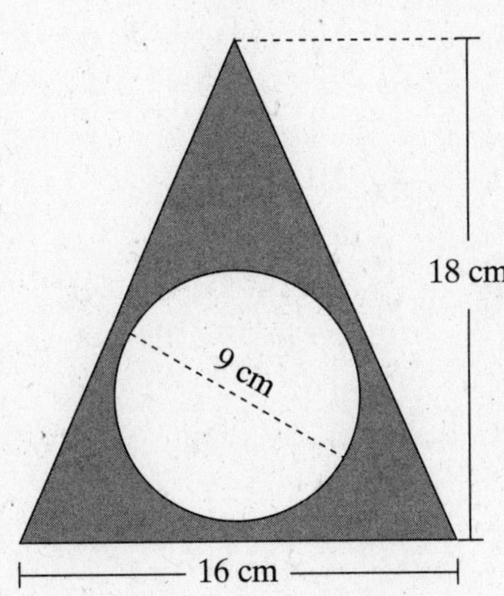

$A =$ ______________

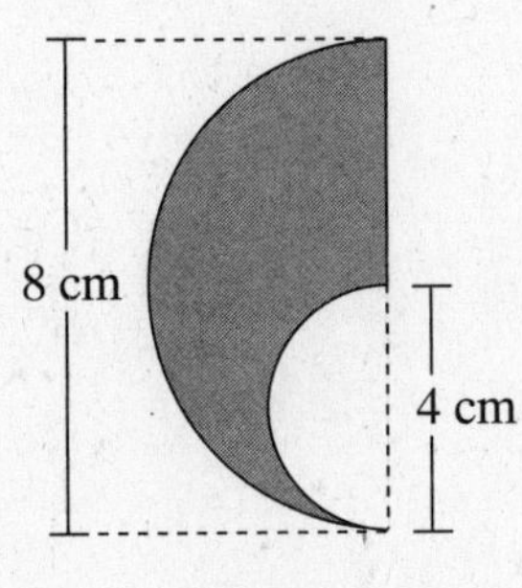

$A =$ ______________

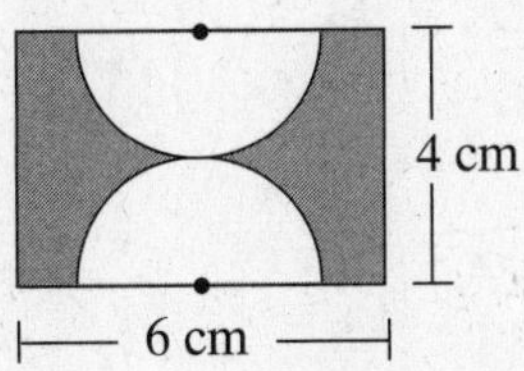

$A =$ ______________

2	c	1	.	8	2	c	m^2	9	6
5	4	1	.	8	6	9	1	.	3
1	8	.	8	4	c	m^2	8	7	5
7	c	4	0	6	1	3	.	2	c
.	m^2	4	3	6	.	5	6	c	m^2
7	9	c	m^2	1	3	.	3	m^2	5
4	c	m^2	0	8	7	.	6	8	c
c	m^2	4	8	.	3	9	c	m^2	6
m^2	m^2	6	1	7	c	3	m^2	9	.
4	8	0	.	4	1	5	c	m^2	9
3	6	1	8	c	m^2	c	m^2	6	3
8	7	.	7	4	c	m^2	1	9	5

Name ______________________ Class ______________ Date ____________

Practice 8-6

Square Roots and Irrational Numbers

Simplify each square root.

1. $\sqrt{64}$ ______ **2.** $\sqrt{81}$ ______ **3.** $\sqrt{100}$ ______

4. $\sqrt{121}$ ______ **5.** $\sqrt{1}$ ______ **6.** $\sqrt{36}$ ______

7. $\sqrt{25}$ ______ **8.** $\sqrt{16}$ ______ **9.** $\sqrt{256}$ ______

10. $\sqrt{196}$ ______ **11.** $\sqrt{49}$ ______ **12.** $\sqrt{225}$ ______

Identify each number as rational or irrational.

13. 0.363636 . . . ______ **14.** $\sqrt{10}$ ______ **15.** $-\frac{1}{9}$ ______

For each number, write all the sets to which it belongs. Choose from rational number, irrational number, whole number, and integer.

16. $\frac{3}{8}$ ______ **17.** $\sqrt{49}$ ______ **18.** $\sqrt{98}$ ______

Find the length of the side of a square with the given area.

19. 64 km^2 ______ **20.** 81 m^2 ______ **21.** 121 ft^2 ______

22. 225 $in.^2$ ______ **23.** 196 yd^2 ______ **24.** 169 cm^2 ______

Solve.

25. The square of a certain number is the same as three times the number. What is the number?

______

26. The area of a square lawn is 196 yd^2. What is the perimeter of the lawn?

______

Find two consecutive whole numbers that each number is between.

27. $\sqrt{80}$ ______ **28.** $\sqrt{56}$ ______ **29.** $\sqrt{130}$ ______

30. $\sqrt{70}$ ______ **31.** $\sqrt{190}$ ______ **32.** $\sqrt{204}$ ______

Name ______________________ Class ______________ Date ____________

8-6 • Guided Problem Solving

Student Page 402, Exercise 32:

Open-Ended Write three irrational numbers between 4 and 5.

Understand

1. What are you being asked to do?

2. What is an irrational number?

Plan and Carry Out

3. Find 4^2 and 5^2. Use these values to find an irrational number between 4 and 5 using square roots.

4. Name a decimal between 4 and 5 that has a pattern but does not repeat.

5. Based on Step 3 or Step 4, write one more irrational number between 4 and 5.

6. How many irrational numbers do you think there are between 4 and 5?

Check

7. Is the number you chose in Step 3 irrational? Do the decimals you chose repeat or terminate?

Solve Another Problem

8. Write three irrational numbers between 2 and 3.

Name ______________________ Class ______________ Date ______________

Practice 8-6

Square Roots and Irrational Numbers

Simplify each square root.

1. $\sqrt{64}$ ______ 2. $\sqrt{81}$ ______ 3. $\sqrt{100}$ ______

4. $\sqrt{121}$ ______ 5. $\sqrt{1}$ ______ 6. $\sqrt{36}$ ______

7. $\sqrt{25}$ ______ 8. $\sqrt{16}$ ______ 9. $\sqrt{256}$ ______

Identify each number as rational or irrational.

10. 0.363636 . . . ______ 11. $\sqrt{10}$ ______ 12. $-\frac{1}{9}$ ______

For each number, write all the sets to which it belongs. Choose from rational number, irrational number, whole number, and integer.

13. $\frac{3}{8}$ ______

14. $\sqrt{49}$ ______

Find the length of the side of a square with the given area.

15. 64 km^2 ______ 16. 81 m^2 ______ 17. 121 ft^2 ______

Solve.

18. The area of a square lawn is 196 yd^2. What is the perimeter of the lawn? ______

Find two consecutive whole numbers that each number is between.

19. $\sqrt{80}$ ______ 20. $\sqrt{56}$ ______ 21. $\sqrt{130}$ ______

Name ______________________ Class ______________ Date ____________

Activity Lab 8-6

Square Roots and Irrational Numbers

Use your calculator to find the square root of each integer below. Round each answer to the nearest thousandth. The first ten are done for you.

N	$\sqrt{N}$	N	$\sqrt{N}$	N	$\sqrt{N}$
2	1.414	12		22	
3	1.732	13		23	
4	2.000	14		24	
5	2.236	15		25	
6	2.449	16		26	
7	2.646	17		27	
8	2.828	18		28	
9	3.000	19		29	
10	3.162	20		30	
11	3.317	21		31	

1. Use the square roots in the table to find each product. Round the product to the nearest thousandth.

a. $\sqrt{2} \times \sqrt{3}$ ________ **b.** $\sqrt{2} \times \sqrt{4}$ ________ **c.** $\sqrt{2} \times \sqrt{5}$ ________

d. $\sqrt{3} \times \sqrt{4}$ ________ **e.** $\sqrt{3} \times \sqrt{5}$ ________ **f.** $\sqrt{2} \times \sqrt{13}$ ________

2. Look at your answers in Exercise 1. Compare them to the square roots of other numbers in the table. What pattern do you see?

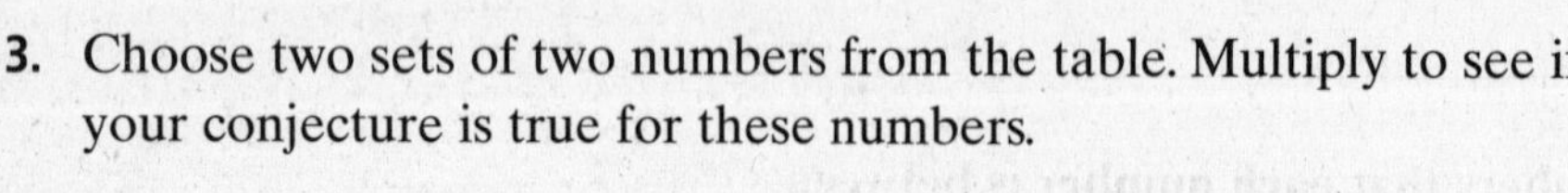

3. Choose two sets of two numbers from the table. Multiply to see if your conjecture is true for these numbers.

____

____

Name ______________________ Class ______________ Date ____________

Reteaching 8-6

Square Roots and Irrational Numbers

The number 25 is a **perfect square.**

It is the square of the whole number 5. $5^2 = 25$
5 is the **square root** of 25. $5 = \sqrt{25}$

You can find the length of a side of a square by finding the square root of the area.

$s^2 = A = 225$

$s = \sqrt{A} = \sqrt{225} = 15$

The length of each side is 15 in.

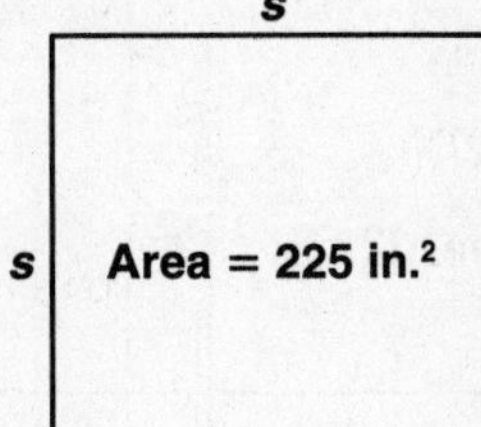

You can use patterns to find the square roots of some larger numbers.

$9^2 = 81 \rightarrow 90^2 = 8{,}100$

$9 = \sqrt{81} \rightarrow 90 = \sqrt{8{,}100}$

A **rational number** is a ratio of two integers, $\frac{a}{b}$, where $b \neq 0$. Since terminating decimals and repeating decimals can be written as ratios, they are rational. Irrational numbers are numbers that cannot be written as ratios. Decimals that do not end or repeat are irrational numbers.

Find each of the following.

1. $\sqrt{144}$ ______ **2.** $\sqrt{36}$ ______ **3.** $\sqrt{100}$ ______

4. $\sqrt{2{,}500}$ ______ **5.** $\sqrt{324}$ ______ **6.** $\sqrt{400}$ ______

Find the length of a side of a square with the given area.

7. $A = 49 \text{ cm}^2$
side = $\sqrt{49}$ = ______

8. $A = 81 \text{ in.}^2$
side = $\sqrt{81}$ = ______

9. $A = 144 \text{ cm}^2$
side = $\sqrt{144}$ = ______

10. $A = 625 \text{ in.}^2$ ______

11. $A = 676 \text{ ft}^2$ ______

12. $A = 3{,}600 \text{ yd}^2$ ______

Identify each number as rational or irrational.

13. $1\frac{1}{3}$ ______ **14.** $\sqrt{15}$ ______ **15.** 7 ______ **16.** $\sqrt{144}$ ______

Name ____________________ Class ____________ Date ____________

Enrichment 8-6

Square Roots and Irrational Numbers

Critical Thinking

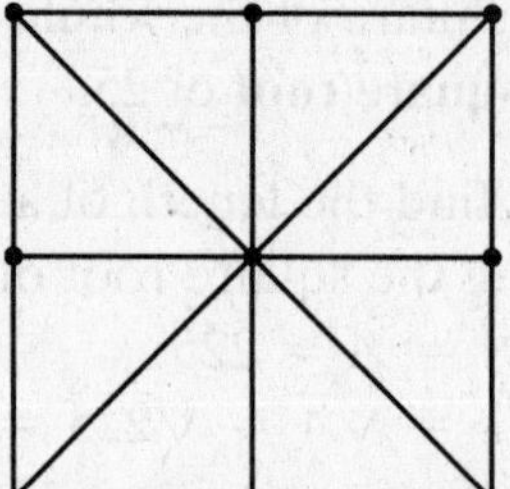

Schoolchildren in Ghana play the game of Achi on a board like the one shown. If the perimeter of an Achi board is 192 cm, what is its area?

1. Underline the perimeter above.
2. What polygon is the Achi board?

   ____
3. What is the formula to find the perimeter of this figure?

   ____
4. How can you use the formula to find the length of one side?

   ____
5. How can you find the area once you know the length of one side?

   ____
6. What is the length of one side?

   ____
7. What is the area of the Achi board?

   ____
8. How can you work backward from your answer to find the perimeter?

   ____

Solve these problems involving area and perimeter.

9. Butch has a square checkerboard. If the perimeter of the checkerboard is 160 cm, what is the area?

   ____
10. If the area of the checkerboard is 256 cm^2, how wide is one square on the board?

   ____

Name ______________________ Class ______________ Date ______________

Puzzle 8-6

Square Roots and Irrational Numbers

When the numbers below are arranged from least to greatest, their corresponding letters will form the answer to the question. Identify each number as rational or irrational. To complete the puzzle, place the corresponding letters on the number line. Estimate the value of each square root. The first exercise has been completed for you.

Y. 5.232323... *rational*

G. $\sqrt{9}$

B. $\sqrt{62}$

N. $\sqrt{15}$

I. $\sqrt{1}$

R. $\sqrt{75}$

M. 7

A. 4.0687

N. $\sqrt{38}$

E. 8

I. $\sqrt{10}$

U. $\sqrt{45}$

M. $\sqrt{2}$

A. 2.1

R. $\sqrt{20}$

What do mathematicians call $\sqrt{-1}$?

An: ____ ____ ____ ____ ____ ____ ____ ____ ____

____ ____ ____ ____ ____ ____

Y

0 1 2 3 4 5 6 7 8 9 10

Name ______________________ Class ______________ Date ______________

Practice 8-7

The Pythagorean Theorem

The lengths of two sides of a right triangle are given. Find the length of the third side to the nearest tenth of a unit.

1. legs: 5 ft and 12 ft
2. legs: 13 cm and 9 cm
3. leg: 7 m; hypotenuse: 14 m

Find each missing length. Round to the nearest tenth of a unit, if necessary.

4. 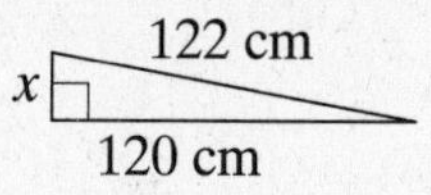

5. 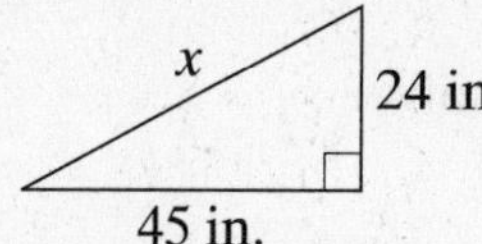

6. 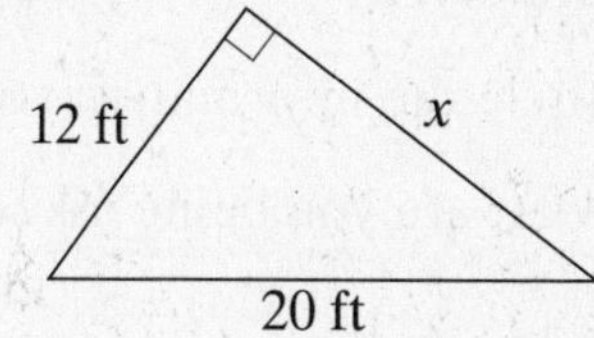

7. 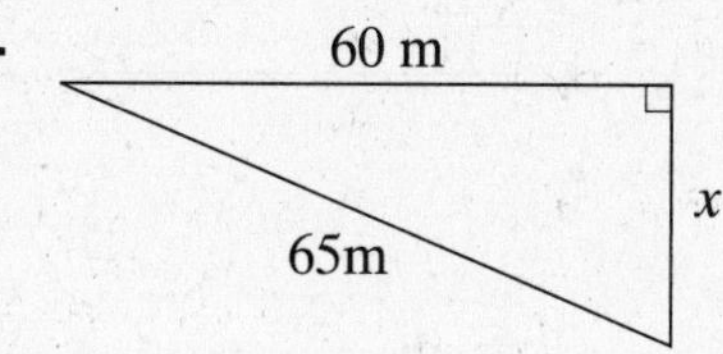

8. 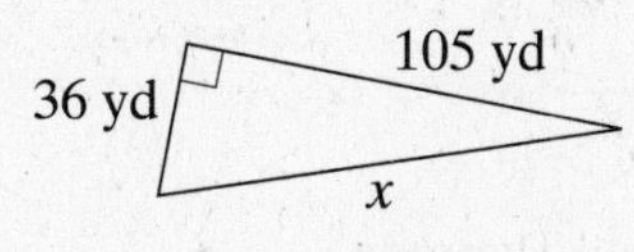

9. 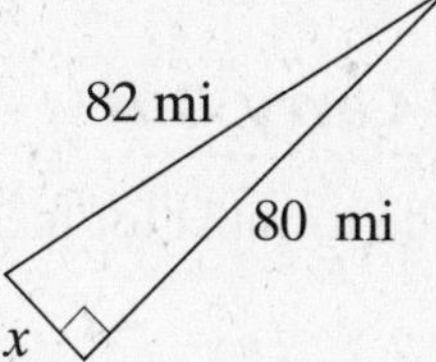

10. 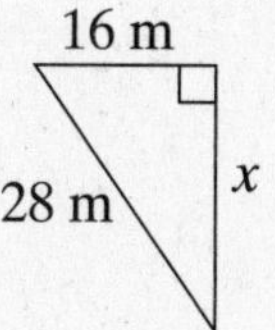

11. 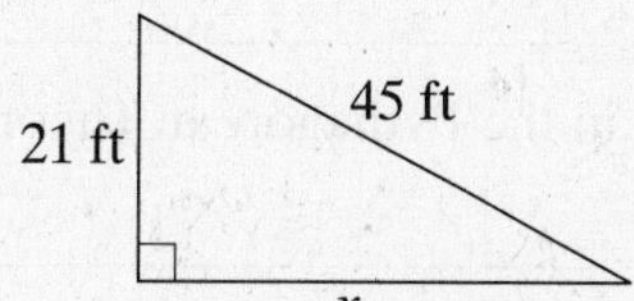

12. 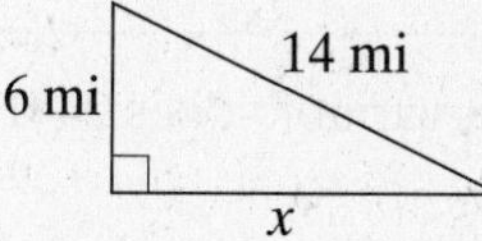

Solve.

13. A playground is 50 yd by 50 yd. Amy walked across the playground from one corner to the opposite corner. How far did she walk?

14. A 70-ft ladder is mounted 10 ft above the ground on a fire truck. The bottom of the ladder is 40 ft from the wall of a building. The top of the ladder is touching the building. How high off the ground is the top of the ladder?

Name ______________________ Class ______________ Date ______________

8-7 • Guided Problem Solving

GPS Student Page 408, Exercise 21:

Camping A large tent has an adjustable center pole. A rope 26 ft long connects the top of the pole to a peg 24 ft from the bottom of the pole. What is the height of the pole? Round to the nearest hundredth if necessary.

Understand

1. Circle the information you will need to solve.
2. What are you being asked to do?

   ____
3. The right triangle shown models the tent pole and rope. Label it with the correct values.

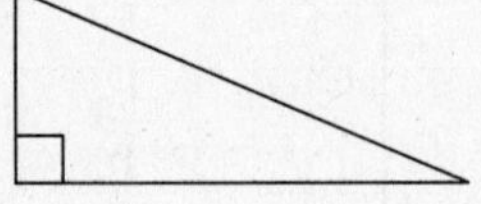

Plan and Carry Out

4. Write the formula for the Pythagorean Theorem.

   ____
5. What variable does 26 ft represent in the Pythagorean Theorem?

   ____
6. What variable does 24 ft represent in the Pythagorean Theorem?

   ____
7. Substitute these values into the Pythagorean Theorem formula and find the height of the pole.

   ____

Check

8. Substitute your answer from Step 7 and 24 ft into the Pythagorean Theorem formula for *a* and *b*. Do you get a true statement?

   ____

Solve Another Problem

9. You're building a right-triangular brace for a basketball hoop. You have the piece for the hypotenuse and for one of the legs. The hypotenuse measures 10 in. long, and the leg measures 6 in. long. How long must the other leg of the brace be?

   ____

Name ______________________ Class ______________ Date ____________

Practice 8-7

The Pythagorean Theorem

The lengths of two sides of a right triangle are given. Find the length of the third side to the nearest tenth of a unit.

1. legs: 5 ft and 12 ft

2. leg: 7 m; hypotenuse: 14 m

Find each missing length. Round to the nearest tenth of a unit, if necessary.

3. 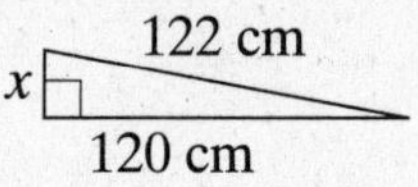

4. 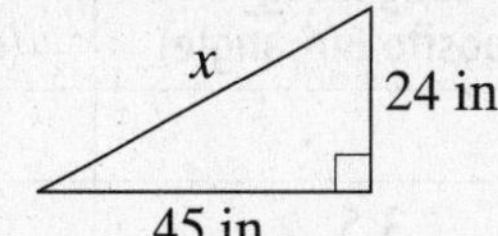

5. 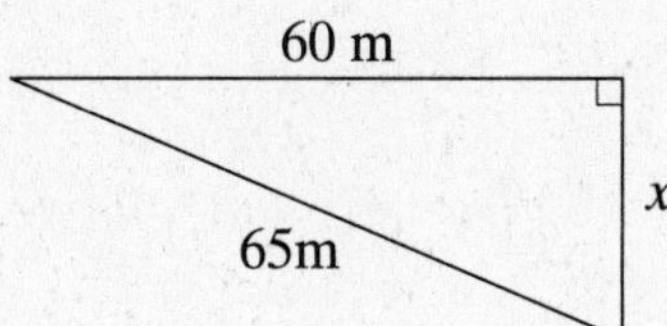

6. 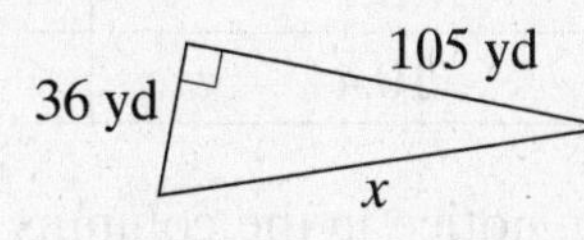

7. 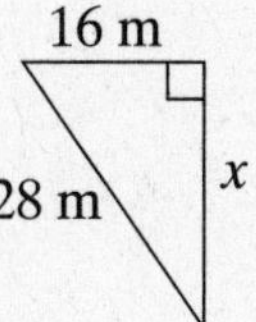

8. 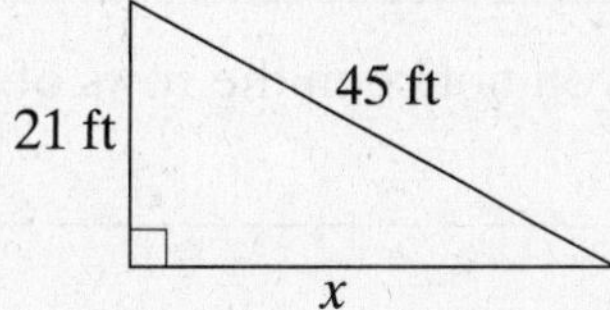

Solve.

9. A playground is 50 yd by 50 yd. Amy walked across the playground from one corner to the opposite corner. How far did she walk?

10. A 70-ft ladder is mounted 10 ft above the ground on a fire truck. The bottom of the ladder is 40 ft from the wall of a building. The top of the ladder is touching the building. How high off the ground is the top of the ladder?

Name ____________________ Class ____________________ Date ____________________

Activity Lab 8-7

The Pythagorean Theorem

A right triangle with angle measures of 30° and 60° is called a 30-60-90 triangle. A 30-60-90 triangle is actually one half of an equilateral triangle.

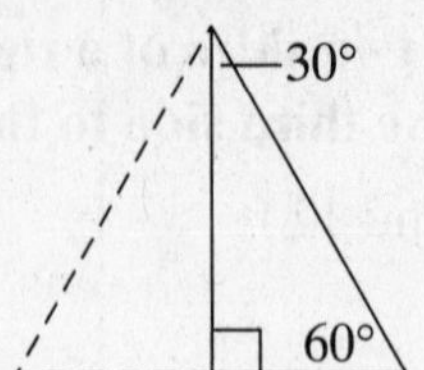

1. Use the Pythagorean Theorem to find the missing side of each triangle. Round your answer to the nearest tenth if necessary.

Shorter leg (opposite 30° angle)	Longer leg (opposite 60° angle)	Hypotenuse (opposite 90° angle)
1		2
2	3.5	
	5.2	6
4		8
5	8.7	
	10.4	12

2. What pattern do you notice in the columns of the table above?

____

____

____

3. What pattern do you notice in the rows of the table above?

____

____

____

The lengths of the sides of any 30-60-90 triangle are x, $x\sqrt{3}$ and $2x$. See how that compares to your answers to Exercises 2 and 3. Use this relationship to give the answers to the questions below in terms of y.

4. What is the length of the shorter leg? ______________

5. What is the length of the longer leg? ______________

6. Label the legs of the triangle.

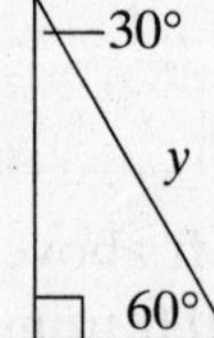

Name ______________________ Class ______________ Date ______________

Reteaching 8-7

The Pythagorean Theorem

Pythagorean Theorem

$a^2 + b^2 = c^2$

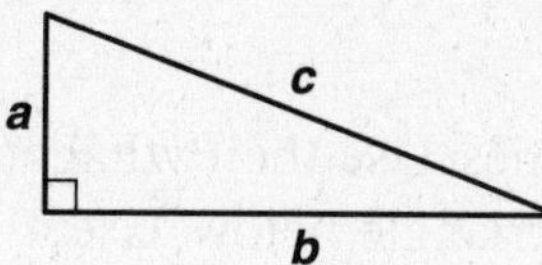

If you know the lengths of two sides of a right triangle, you can find the length of the third side.

Find the length of *a*.

$$\begin{aligned} a^2 + b^2 &= c^2 \\ a^2 + 12^2 &= 13^2 \\ a^2 + 144 &= 169 \\ a^2 &= 169 - 144 \\ a^2 &= 25 \\ a &= 5 \end{aligned}$$

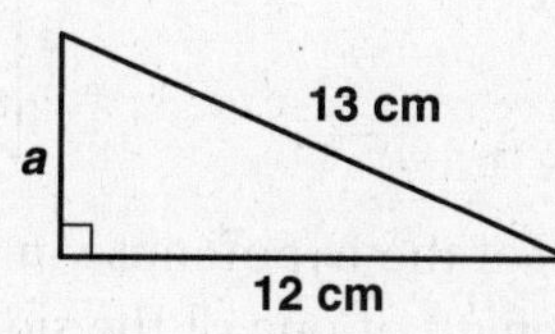

If $a^2 + b^2 = c^2$, then the triangle is a right triangle.

Is this triangle a right triangle?

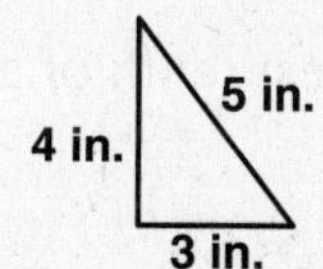

$3^2 + 4^2 = 9 + 16 = 25 = 5^2$

Yes, the triangle is a right triangle.

Find each missing length. Round your answer to the nearest tenth of a unit.

1. 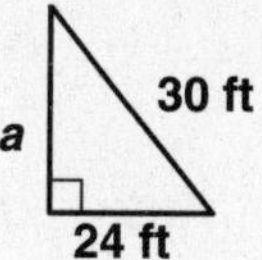

____

2. 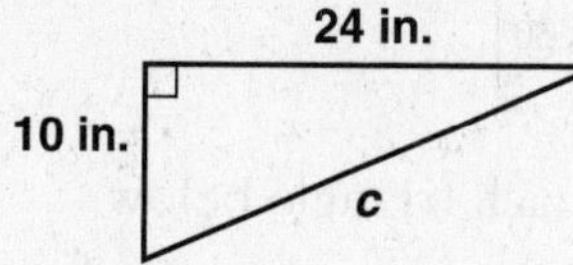

____

3. 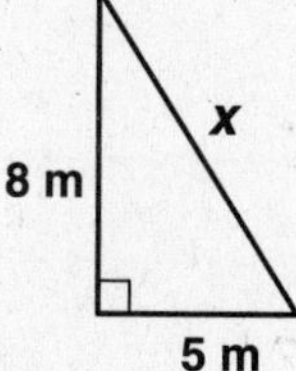

____

4. 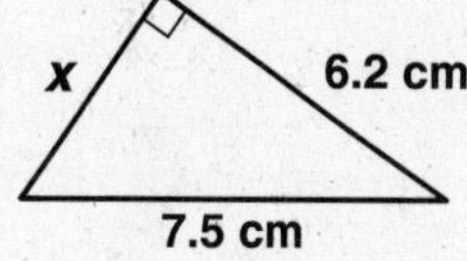

____

5. A ladder leans against a wall 6 ft above the ground. The base of the ladder is 3 ft from the wall. How long is the ladder?

____

6. A small rectangular tray measures 16 cm by 18 cm. How long is the diagonal?

____

Name ______________________ Class ______________ Date ______________

Enrichment 8-7

The Pythagorean Theorem

Patterns in Geometry

Some right triangles have special properties. Use the Pythagorean Theorem to find the missing leg in each triangle below. Use a calculator to check, and round all your answers to the nearest tenth.

1. $a =$ ______________________

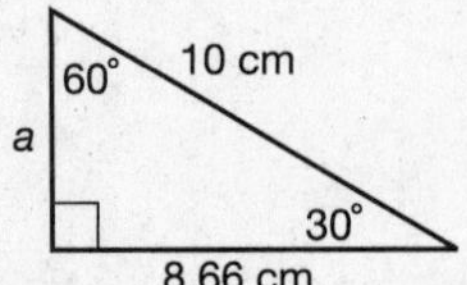

2. $a =$ ______________________

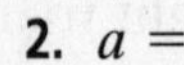

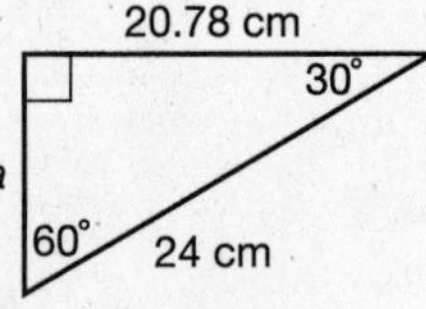

3. What do you notice about the length of the hypotenuse in each of the 30°-60°-90° triangles above and the length of one of the sides?

____

____

Use your observation to give the length to the nearest tenth of a unit of the missing sides below.

4. $a =$ ______________________

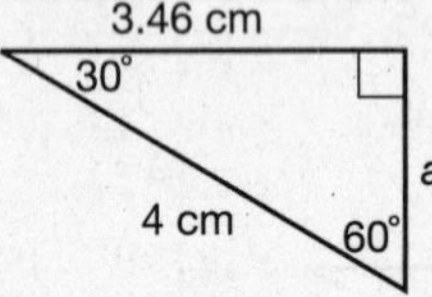

5. $a =$ ______________________

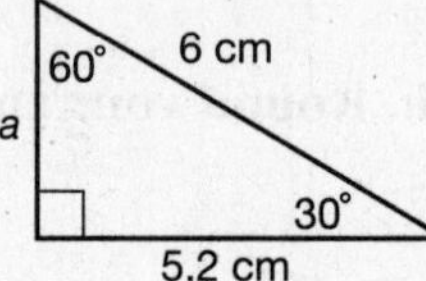

Find the missing leg in each triangle below.

6. $a =$ ______________________

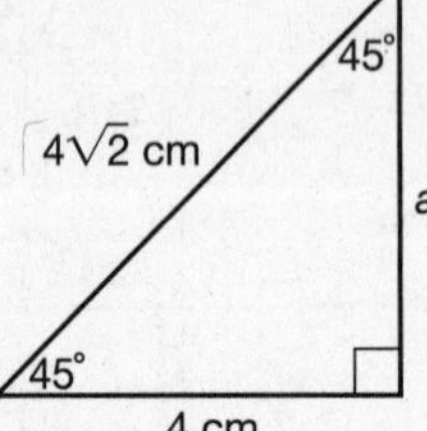

7. $a =$ ______________________

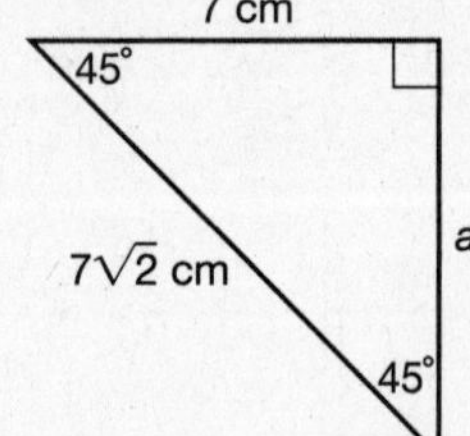

8. What do you notice about the length of the hypotenuse in each 45°-45°-90° triangle and the length of one of the sides?

____

____

Name ______________________ Class ______________ Date ______________

Puzzle 8-7

The Pythagorean Theorem

The Homecoming Committee was assigned the task of designing a crown for the Homecoming King. They created a design consisting of triangles that were symmetrical from the center of the crown out. Help the committee find the missing measurements for their design.

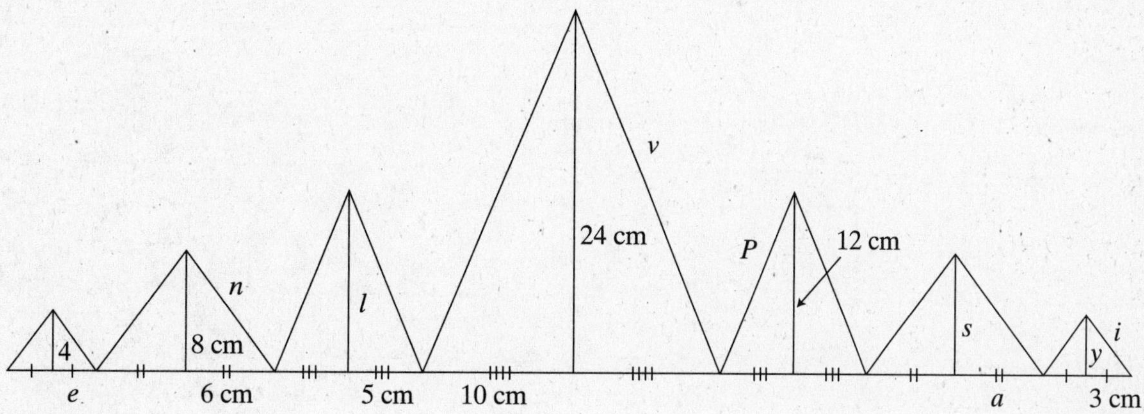

Use your answers to find out which state, which was one of the original thirteen colonies, is not bordered by the Atlantic Ocean.

___	___	___	___	___	___	___	___	___	___	___	___
13	3	10	10	8	4	12	26	6	10	5	6

Name ______________________ Class ______________ Date ____________

Practice 8-8

Three-Dimensional Figures

Describe the base and name the figure.

1. 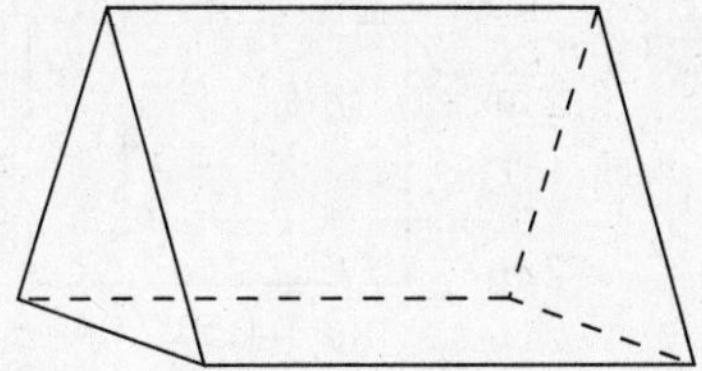

2. 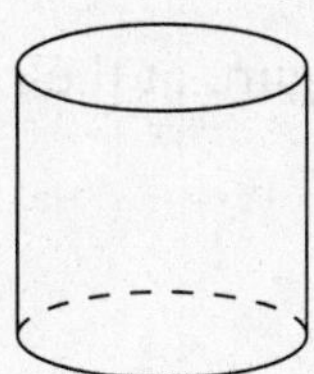

3. 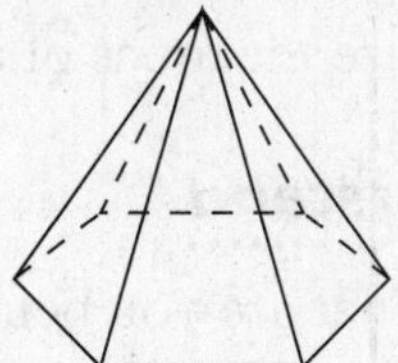

4. 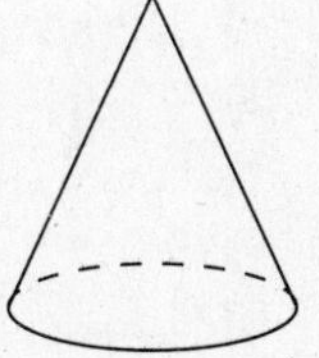

5. 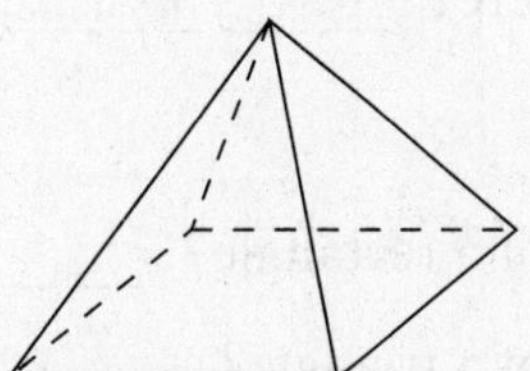

6. 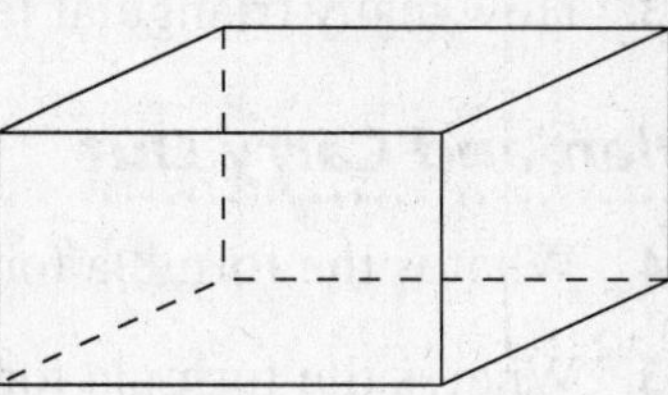

Draw each figure named.

7. a triangular pyramid

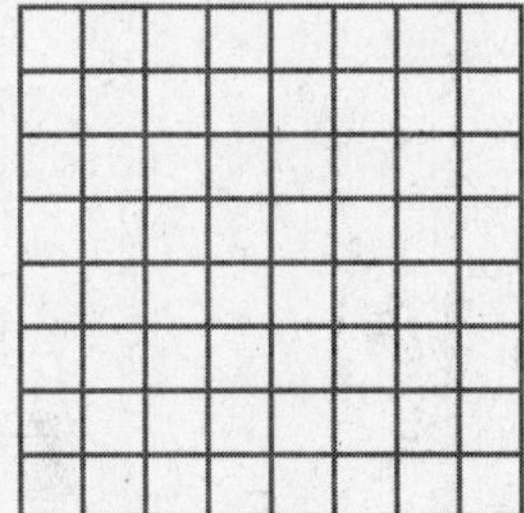

8. a square prism

9. a cone

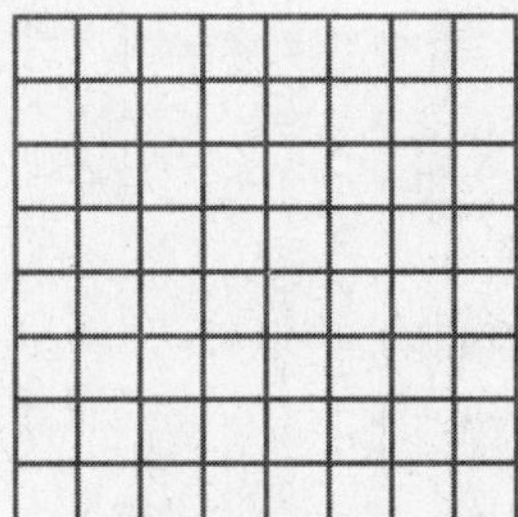

10. a pentagonal pyramid

Name ______________________ Class ______________ Date ______________

8-8 • Guided Problem Solving

GPS Student Page 413, Exercise 23:

What are the areas of all the faces of the figure at the right?

3.5 m 4 m 2 m 6 m

Understand

1. What are you being asked to do?

____

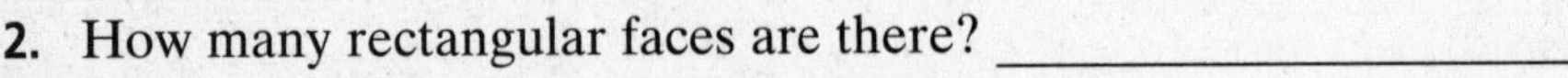

2. How many rectangular faces are there? ______________

3. How many triangular faces are there? ______________

Plan and Carry Out

4. What is the formula for the area of a rectangle? ______________

5. What is the formula for the area of a triangle? ______________

6. What are the dimensions of the triangular faces?

____

7. What is the area of one triangular face? ______________

8. What is the area of all the triangular faces? ______________

9. What are the dimensions of each rectangular face?

____

10. What is the area of each rectangular face?

____

11. Find the total area of the base and faces of the figure.

____

Check

12. Did you find the area of each face? How many faces are there?

____

Solve Another Problem

13. A rectangular solid has a base 11 in., height 15 in., and a length of 6 in. Find the total area of all faces.

____

____

Name ______________________ Class ______________ Date ______________

Practice 8-8

Three-Dimensional Figures

Describe the base and name the figure.

1. 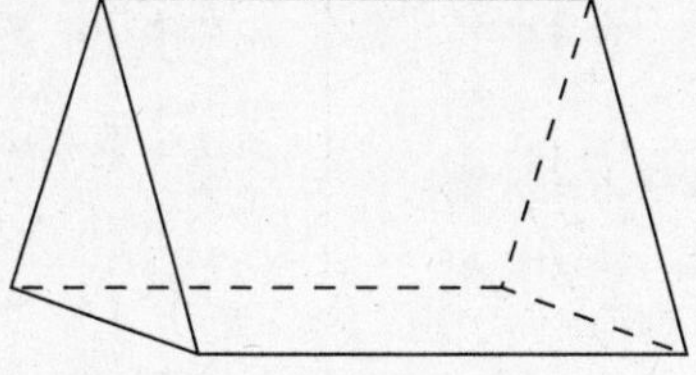

____

____

2. 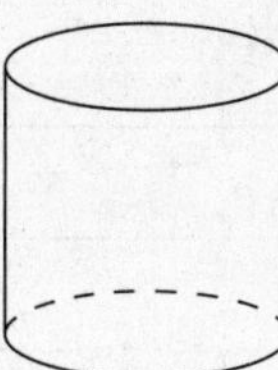

____

____

3. 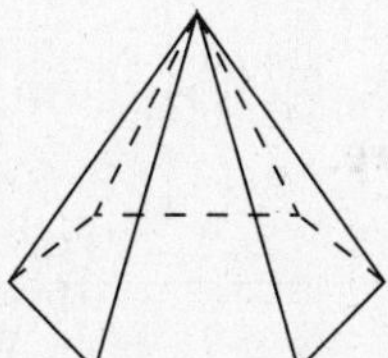

____

____

4. 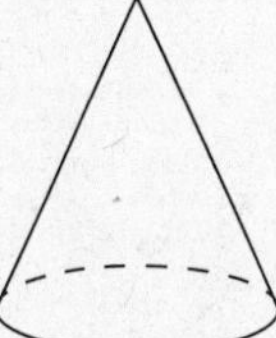

____

____

Draw each figure named.

5. a triangular pyramid

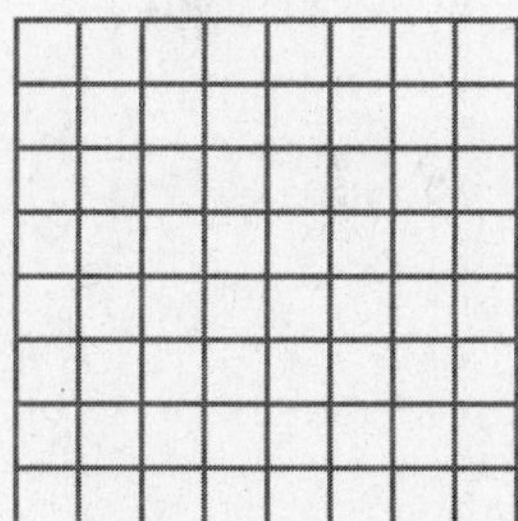

6. a square prism

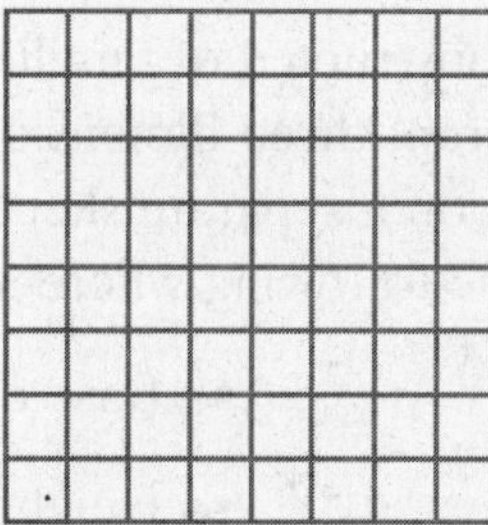

7. a cone

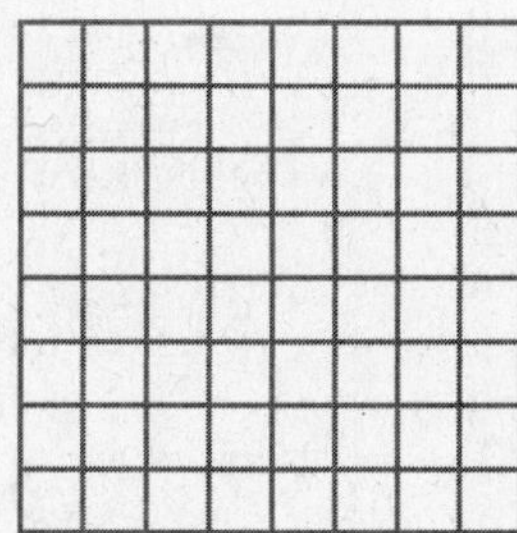

8. a pentagonal pyramid

Name ______________________ Class ______________ Date ____________

Activity Lab 8-8

Three-Dimensional Figures

Shade the bases of the figure.

Name the figure: ______________

Find the number of edges: ______________

Find the number of faces: ______________

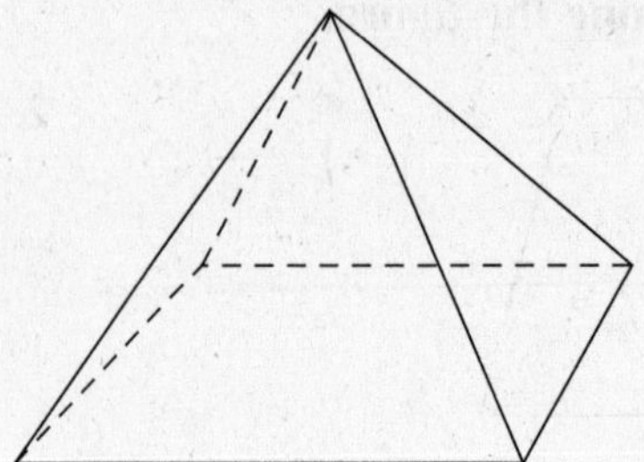

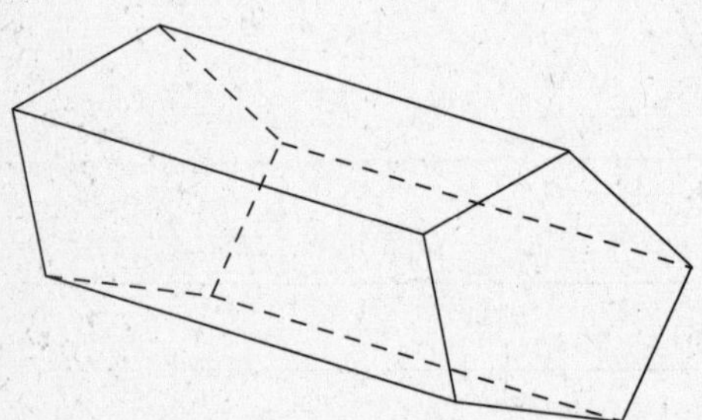

Shade the bases of the figure.

Name the figure: ______________

Find the number of edges: ______________

Find the number of faces: ______________

The locomotive below is constructed of familiar three-dimensional objects. Choose three different three-dimensional objects from the drawing. Draw each object on a separate sheet of paper, name the object, and label each of the following where applicable:

- Edges
- Vertex or Vertices
- Faces
- Base or Bases
- Height

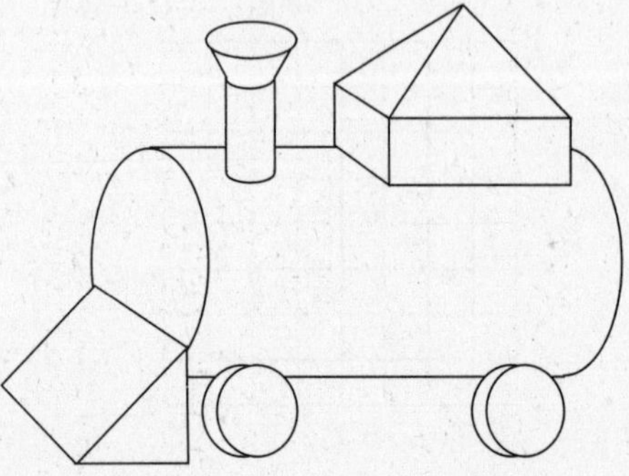

Name ______________________ Class ______________ Date ____________

Reteaching 8-8

Three-Dimensional Figures

A **prism** is a three-dimensional figure with two parallel and congruent polygonal **bases.** It is named by the shape of a base.

Rectangular prism
The bases are rectangles.

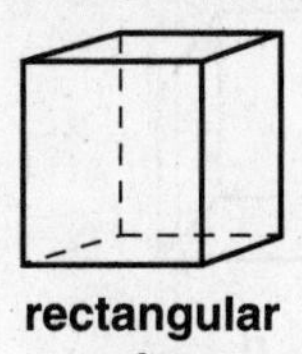

rectangular prism

Triangular prism
The bases are triangles.

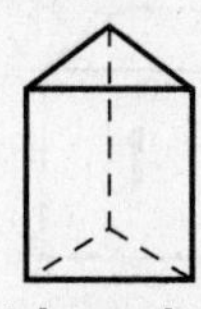

triangular prism

Hexagonal prism
The bases are hexagons.

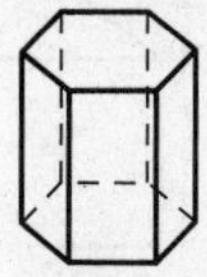

hexagonal prism

A **pyramid** is a three-dimensional figure with only one base.

Triangular pyramid
The base is a triangle.

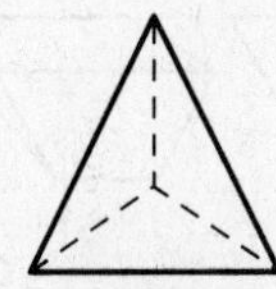

triangular pyramid

Square pyramid
The base is a square.

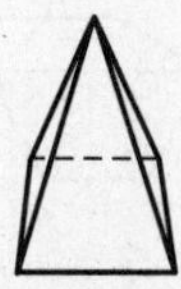

square pyramid

The **cylinder, cone,** and **sphere** are also three-dimensional figures.

cylinder

cone

sphere

Give the best name for each figure.

1. 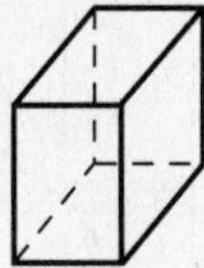

____

2. 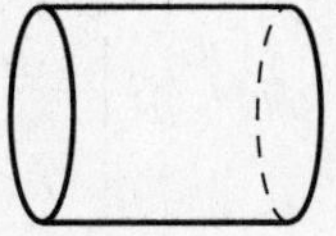

____

3. 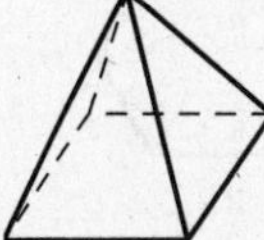

____

4. 

____

5. 

____

6. 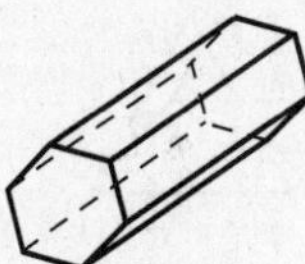

____

7. 

____

8. 

____

9. 

____

Name ________________________ Class ______________ Date ____________

Enrichment 8-8

Three-Dimensional Figures

Geometric Patterns

Circle the letter under the figure at the right that is the mirror image of the figure at the left.

1.

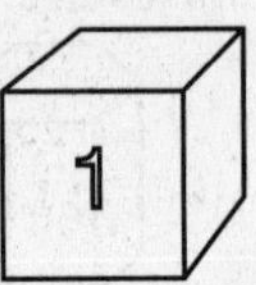

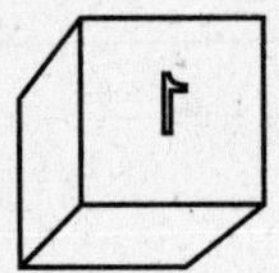

a. **b.** **c.** **d.**

2.

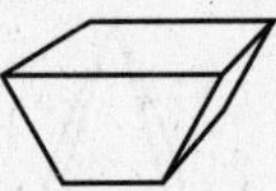

a. **b.** **c.** **d.**

3.

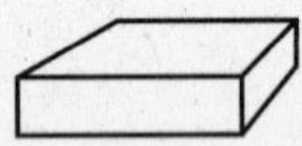

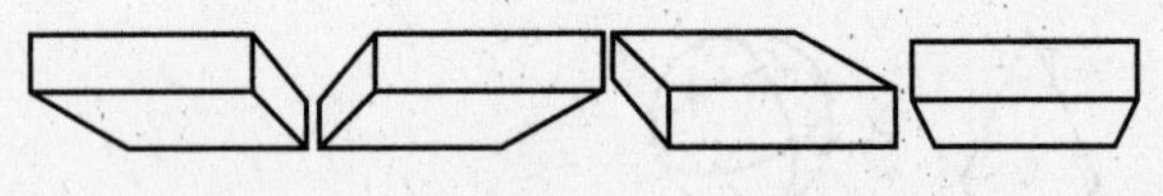

a. **b.** **c.** **d.**

Draw a bottom view of the figure on the left.

4.

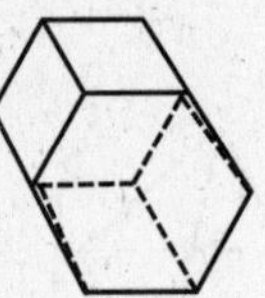

5.

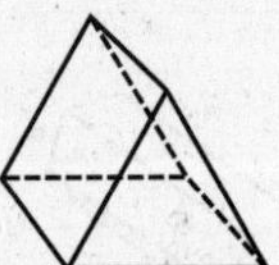

6.

Name ______________________ Class ______________ Date ____________

8D: Visual Vocabulary Practice

For use after Lesson 8-8

Study Skill When interpreting an illustration, look for the most specific concept represented.

Concept List

circumference	base	cone
Pythagorean Theorem	perfect square	edges
vertices	prism	pyramid

Write the concept that best describes each exercise. Choose from the concept list above.

1.

$AB^2 = 6^2 + 8^2$

$AB^2 = 36 + 64 = 100$

$AB = \sqrt{100} = 10$

B, 6 cm, A, 8 cm, C

____

2.

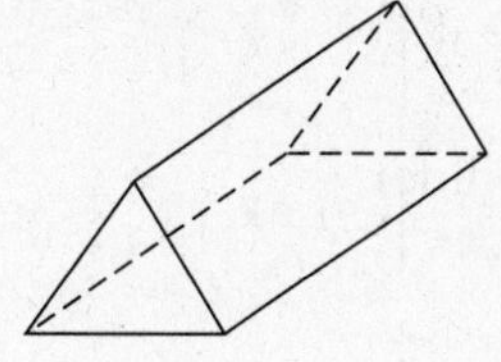

____

3.

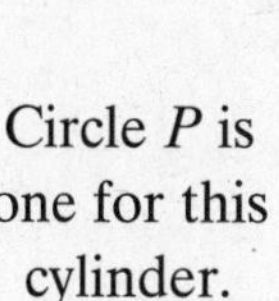

Circle P is one for this cylinder.

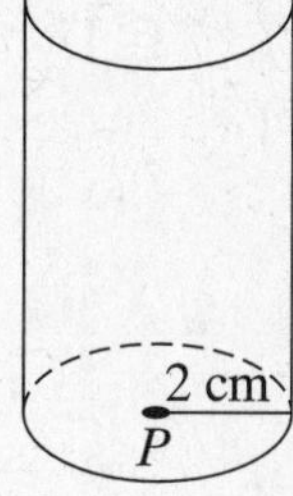

____

4.

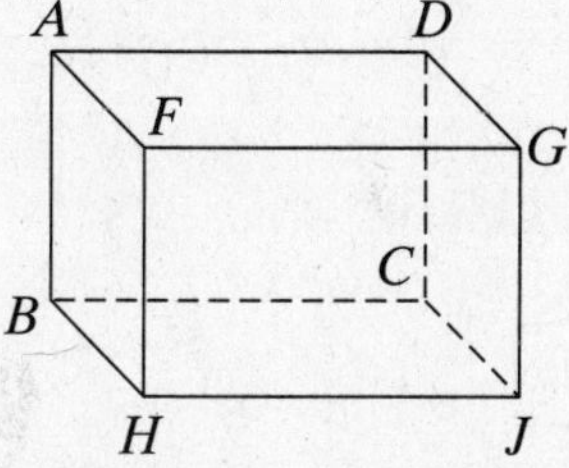

$\overline{AB}$ and $\overline{CJ}$ are examples.

____

5.

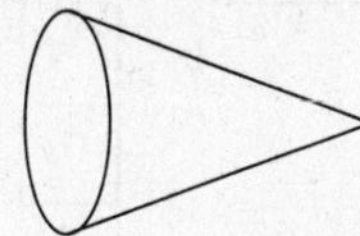

____

6.

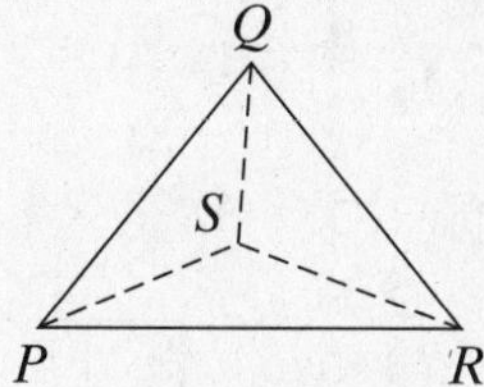

There are four of these in this three-dimensional figure.

____

7.

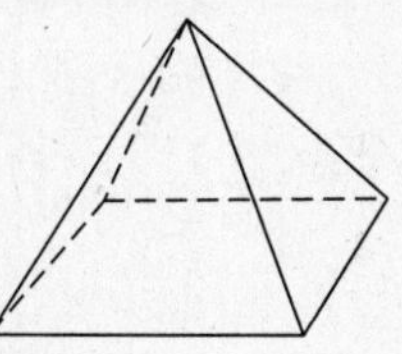

____

8.

576, since $24^2 = 576$.

____

9.

$C \approx 25.1$ cm

____

Name ______________________ Class ______________ Date ______________

Puzzle 8-8

Three-Dimensional Figures

Use the clues below to complete the crossword puzzle.

Across:

2. A three-dimensional figure in which every point is the same distance from the center.
4. A rectangular prism with six identical faces is called a _______.
6. Two identical six-sided polygons form the bases of this solid.
7. Two faces of a solid intersect to form an _______.
8. Two circles form the ______s of a cylinder.

Down:

1. The shape of a face of 6 across.
2. In Giza, the ancient Egyptians built monumental tombs in the shape of this solid.
3. All of the triangular faces of a pyramid intersect at the ________.
5. A can of soup is roughly the shape of a ________.

Name ______________________ Class ______________ Date ______________

Practice 8-9

Surface Areas of Prisms and Cylinders

Find the surface area of each prism.

1.

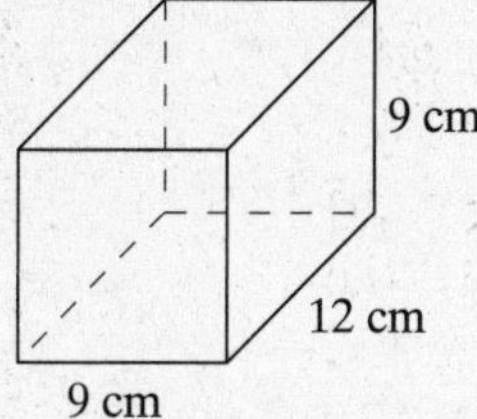

2.

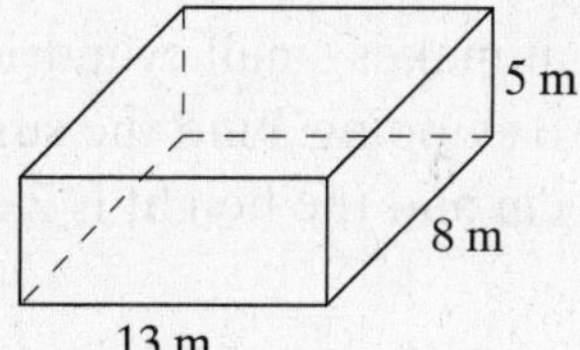

3.

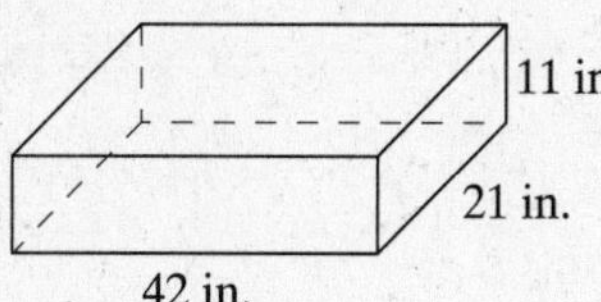

4.

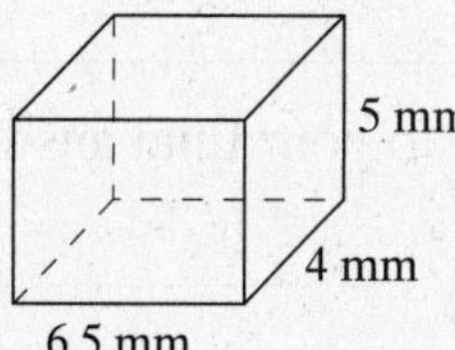

Find the surface area of each cylinder. Round to the nearest whole number.

5.

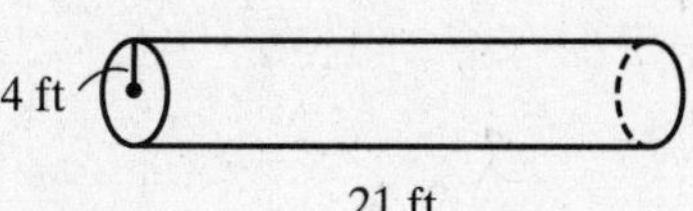

6.

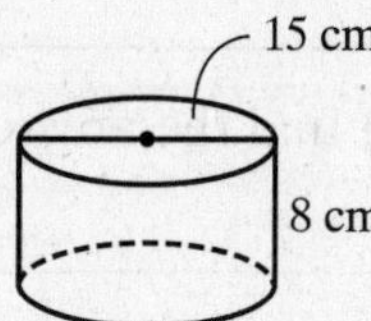

7.

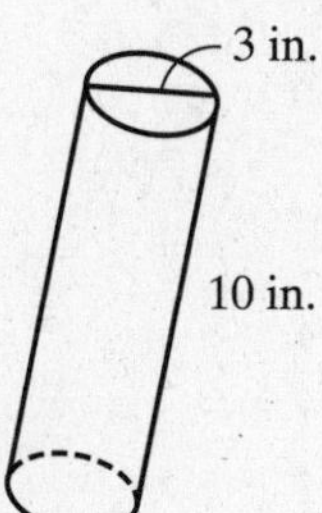

8.

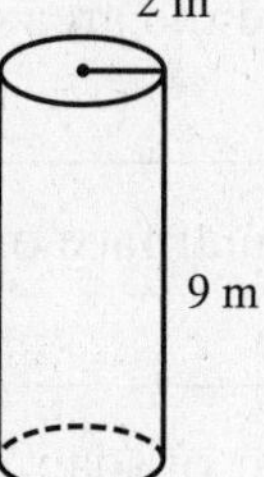

Draw a net for each three-dimensional figure.

9.

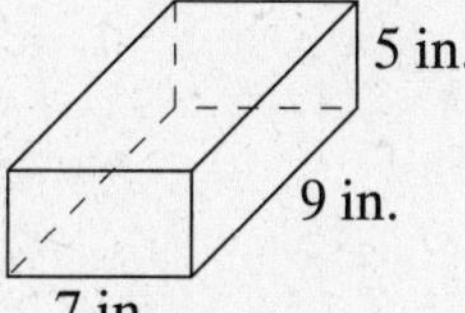

10.

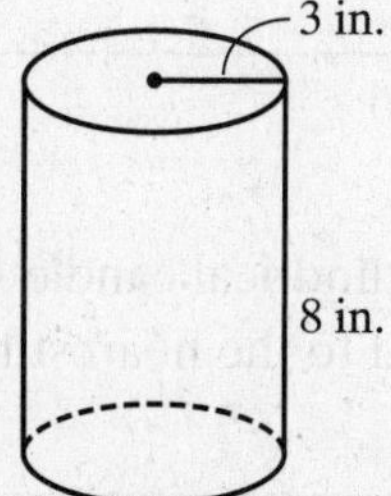

Name ______________ Class ______________ Date ______________

8-9 • Guided Problem Solving

GPS Student Page 418, Exercise 22:

A cosmetics company that makes small cylindrical bars of soap wraps the bars in plastic prior to shipping. Find the surface area of a bar of soap if the diameter is 5 cm and the height is 2 cm. Round to the nearest tenth.

Understand

1. What are you being asked to do?

____

2. What do you need to do to your final answer?

____

Plan and Carry Out

3. How do you find the surface area of a cylinder?

____

____

4. What formula do you use to find the area of a circular face?

____

5. What is the total area of the circular faces of a bar of soap?

____

6. What formula do you use to find the area of the rectangular face?

____

7. What is the area of the rectangular face of a bar of soap?

____

8. What is the surface area of a bar of soap? ______________

Check

9. Did you find the area of all the surfaces of a bar of soap? Does your answer check?

____

Solve Another Problem

10. Find the surface area of a cylindrical candle if the diameter is 6 in. and the height is 8 in. Round to the nearest tenth.

____

Name ______________________ Class ______________ Date ____________

Practice 8-9

Surface Areas of Prisms and Cylinders

Find the surface area of each prism.

1.

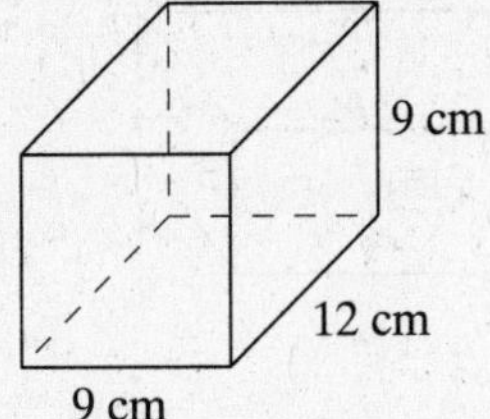

2.

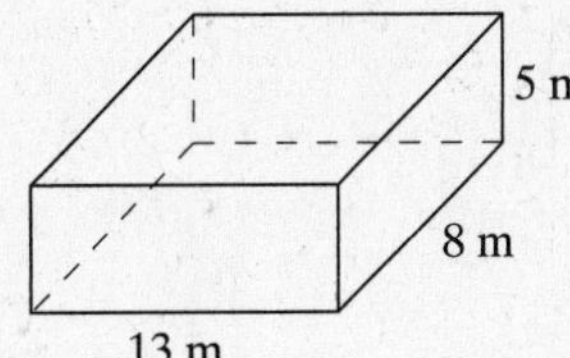

3.

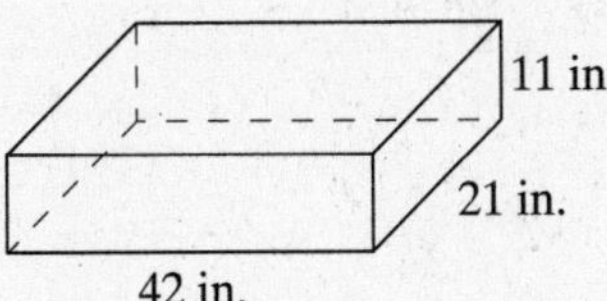

4.

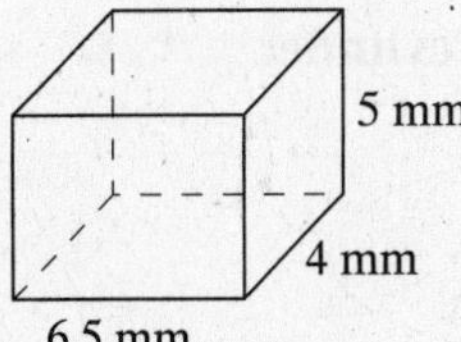

Find the surface area of each cylinder. Round to the nearest whole number.

5.

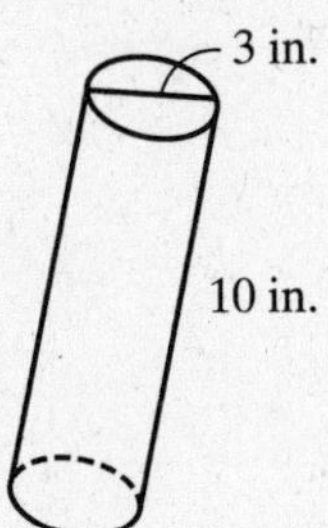

6.

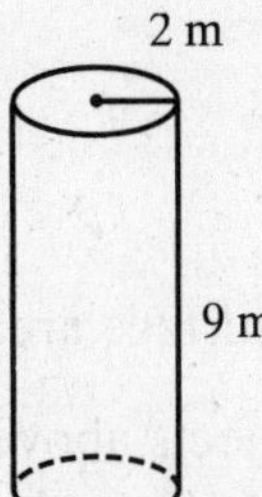

Draw a net for each three-dimensional figure.

7.

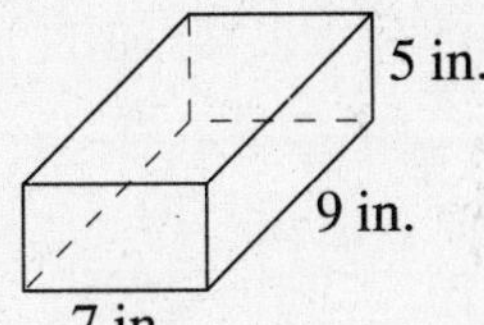

8.

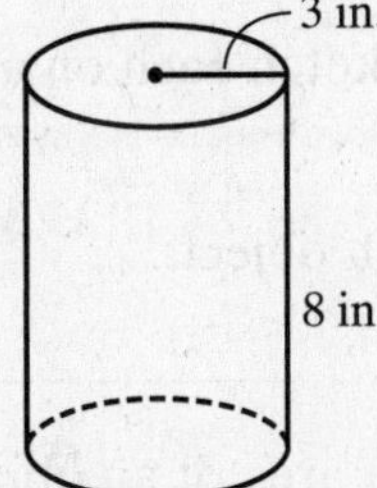

Activity Lab 8-9

Surface Areas of Prisms and Cylinders

Find the surface area of each rectangular prism:

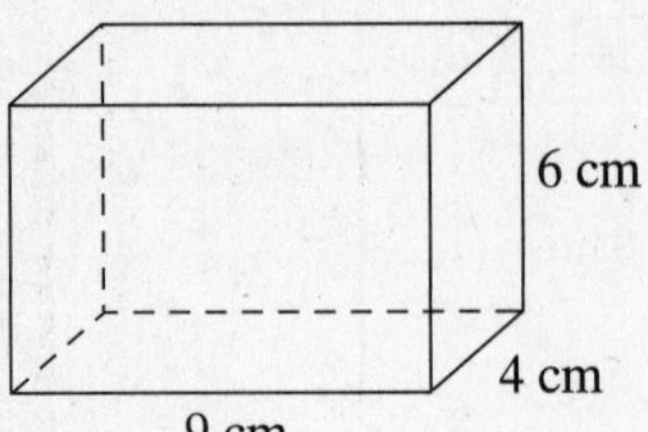

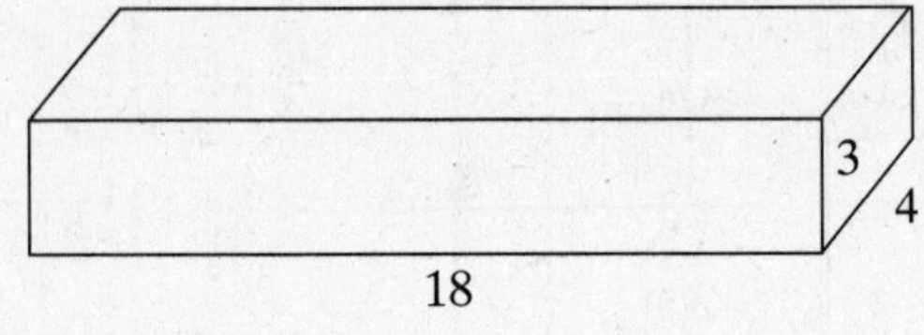

1. Which figure has the greater surface area? ________________

Find the suface area of each cylinder.

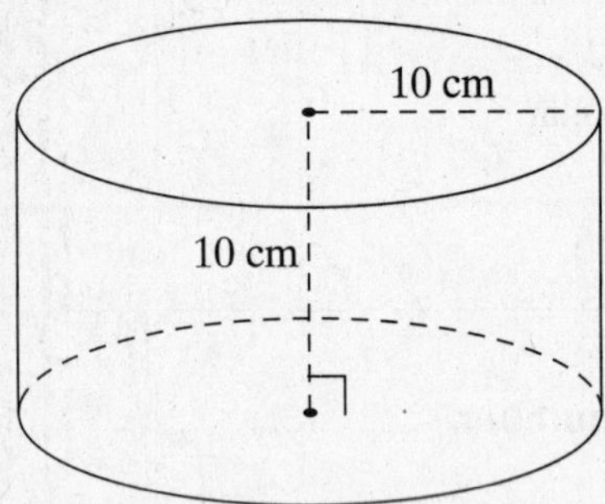

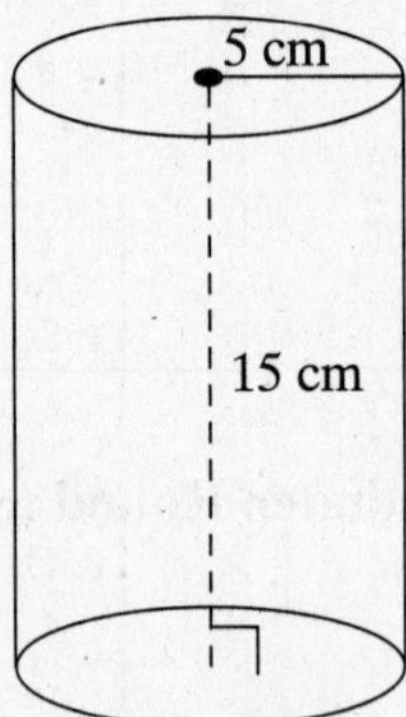

2. Which cylinder has the greater surface area? ________________

Notice that the dimensions of the objects above have relatively close measurements. Chose a pair of objects from the classroom that are in the shape of either cylinders or rectangular prisms. Ensure that the two objects are approximately the same size, but not identical.

3. Predict which of your objects will have a greater surface area.

   ____

4. Measure your objects and sketch each on a separate sheet of paper. Label all dimensions.
5. Find the surface area of each object.
6. Was your prediction correct? ________________
7. When predicting the surface area of an object, what must you consider? What estimation techniques did you use to make predictions about surface area?

   ____

   ____

Name ______________________ Class ______________ Date ______________

Reteaching 8-9

Surface Areas of Prisms and Cylinders

The **surface area** of a prism is the sum of the areas of its faces. You can use a **net,** or pattern, for the prism to help you find its surface area.

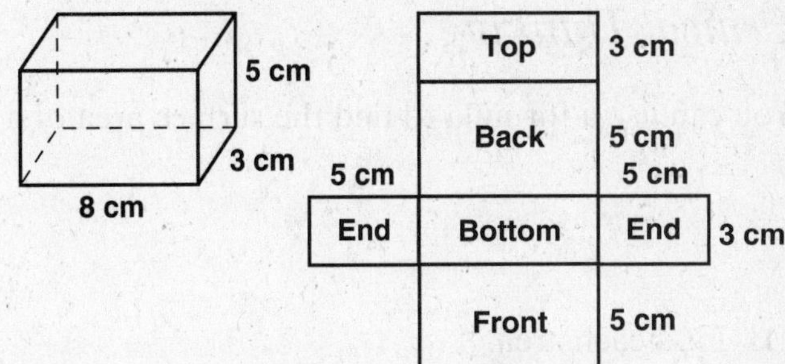

- Add the areas of all the surfaces.

Surface Area
= front + back + top + bottom + end + end
= $(8 \cdot 5) + (8 \cdot 5) + (8 \cdot 3) + (8 \cdot 3) + (5 \cdot 3) + (5 \cdot 3)$
= $40 + 40 + 24 + 24 + 15 + 15$
= 158 cm^2

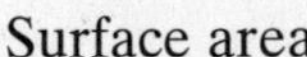

- To find the surface area of a cylinder, add the area of the rectangle and the areas of the bases. Use 3.14 for π.

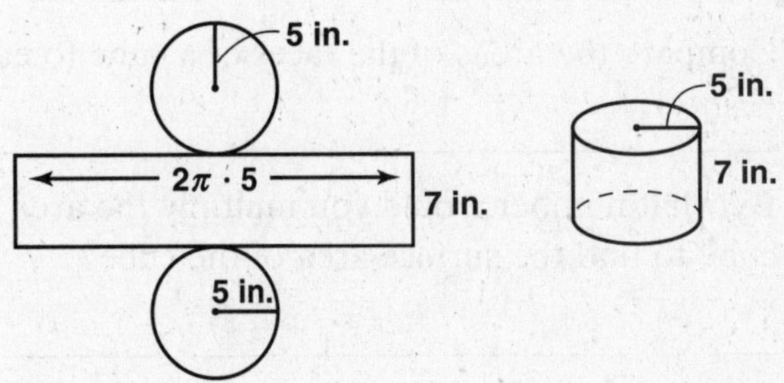

Surface area
= top + bottom + side (rectangle)
= $(\pi \cdot 5 \cdot 5) + (\pi \cdot 5 \cdot 5) + (2\pi \cdot 5 \cdot 7)$
= $(25\pi) + (25\pi) + (70\pi)$
$\approx 120 \cdot 3.14 = 376.8 \text{ in.}^2$

Use the net to find the surface area. Round your answers to the nearest whole unit.

1.

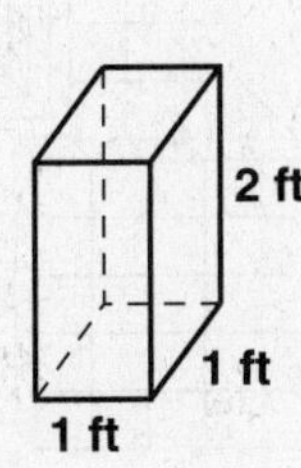

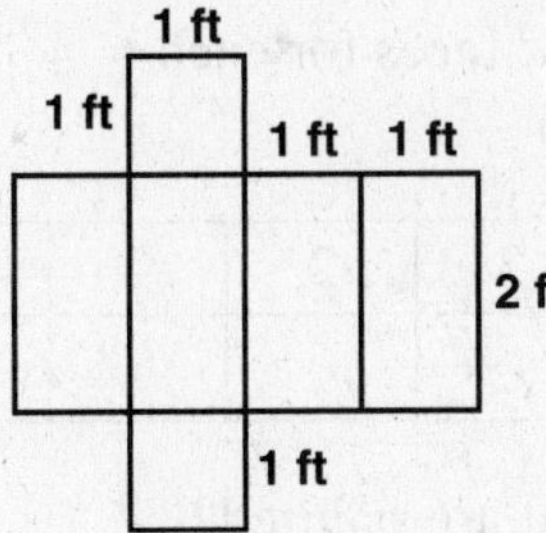

2.

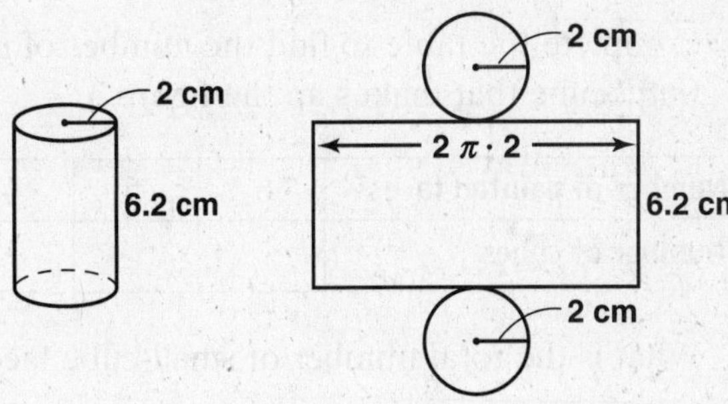

______________________ ______________________

Draw a net for each figure. Then find the surface area to the nearest tenth of a unit.

3.

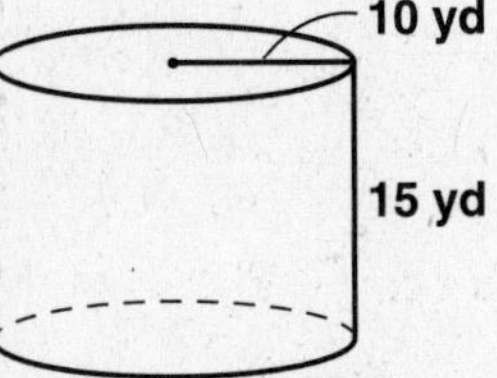

4.

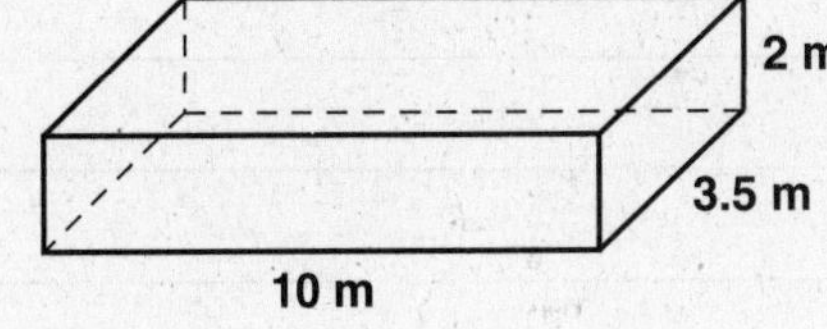

______________________ ______________________

Name ______________________ Class ______________ Date ____________

Enrichment 8-9

Surface Areas of Prisms and Cylinders

Critical Thinking

You can use a formula to find the surface area of a cube.

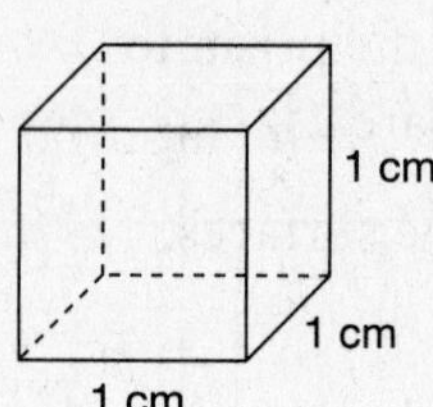

1. Find each area.

   a. Face 1 ________ b. Face 2 ________ c. Face 3 ________ d. Face 4 ________

   e. Face 5 ________ f. Face 6 ________ g. Surface area ________

2. Compare the areas of the faces of a cube to each other.

   ____

3. By what number would you multiply the area of one face of a cube to find the surface area of the cube?

   ____

4. Write the formula to find the surface area of a cube.

   ____

You are asked to paint each face, except the base, of the figure at right.

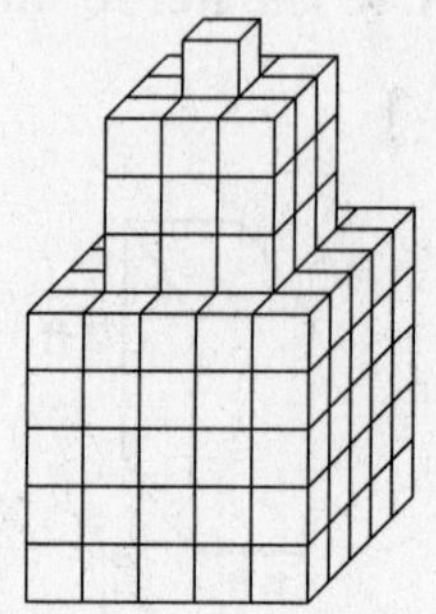

5. Complete the table to find the number of *painted* faces for each *small* cube that makes up the figure.

Number of painted faces	6	5	4	3	2	1	0
Number of cubes							

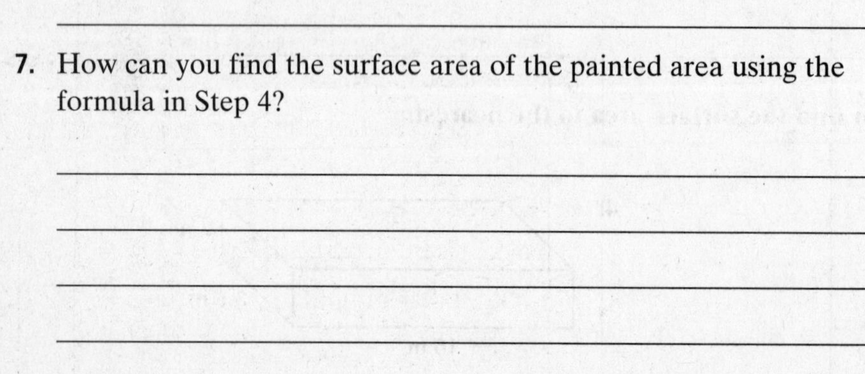

6. What is the total number of small-cube faces that are painted?

   ____

7. How can you find the surface area of the painted area using the formula in Step 4?

   ____

Name ______________________ Class ______________ Date ______________

8B: Reading Comprehension

For use after Lesson 8-9

Study Skill Learning to read for detail takes practice. As you read your notes, underline or highlight important information.

Read the paragraph and answer the questions.

The Grand Canyon was formed by the Colorado River in Arizona. It is estimated to be nearly 10 million years old. With a length of 277 miles, the Grand Canyon is nearly 18 miles wide at its widest point and one mile deep in some places. Arizona, called the Grand Canyon State, has a total land area of approximately 113,000 square miles.

1. What is the paragraph about?

____

2. How old is the Grand Canyon?

____

3. What dimensions are given for the Grand Canyon?

____

4. Use these dimensions to calculate the approximate area of the bottom of the Grand Canyon.

____

5. What percent of the land area in Arizona is occupied by the Grand Canyon?

____

6. Why is the area determined in Exercise 4 a maximum area?

____

____

7. What is the approximate volume of the Grand Canyon?

____

8. **High-Use Academic Words** In Exercise 4, what does it mean to *calculate?*

   a. to determine by mathematical processes
   b. to show that you recognize something

Name ______________________ Class ____________ Date ____________

Puzzle 8-9

Surface Areas of Prisms and Cylinders

Match the description of each solid in the left column with its surface area in the right column. Answers are rounded to the nearest hundredth. When you are finished, write the letter of the correct answer above the exercise number in the letter-code at the bottom of the page.

1. I am a prism with three rectangular faces. My bases are equilateral triangles with 6 cm edges, and I am 10 cm long.	**R.** 136 cm^2
2. I am a cylinder with a height of 5 cm. The radius of my base is also 5 cm.	**V.** 211.18 cm^2
3. I am a rectangular prism. My dimensions are 4 cm by 2 cm by 10 cm.	**O.** 603.19 cm^2
4. One of my faces is 2 cm wide, and I am a cube.	**A.** 314.16 cm^2
5. I am a cylinder with a height of 10 cm. My base diameter is 12 cm.	**D.** 144 cm^2
6. I am a prism with square bases. Each base is 4 cm wide, and I am 7 cm long.	**G.** 24 cm^2

6.023×10^{23} might seem like a very strange number, but it is very important to the study of chemistry. It is called

___ ___ ___ ___ ___ ___ ___ ___'s Number.

2 1 5 4 2 6 3 5

Name ______________________ Class ______________ Date ______________

Practice 8-10

Volumes of Prisms and Cylinders

Find each volume. Round to the nearest cubic unit.

1. 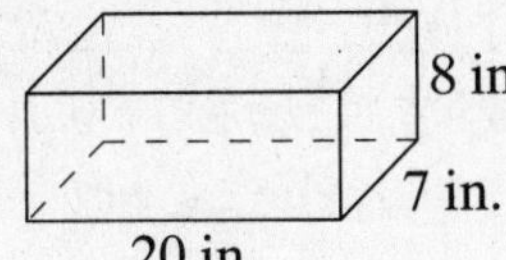

2. 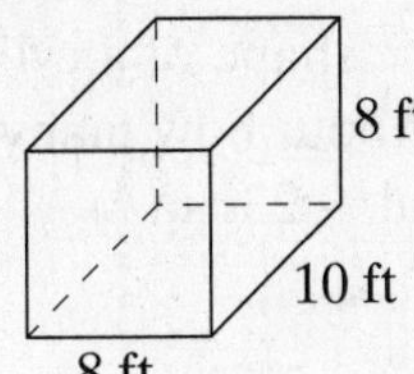

3. 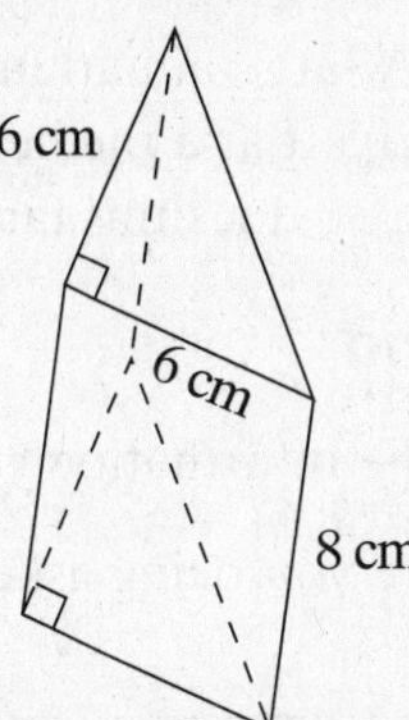

______________ ______________ ______________

4. 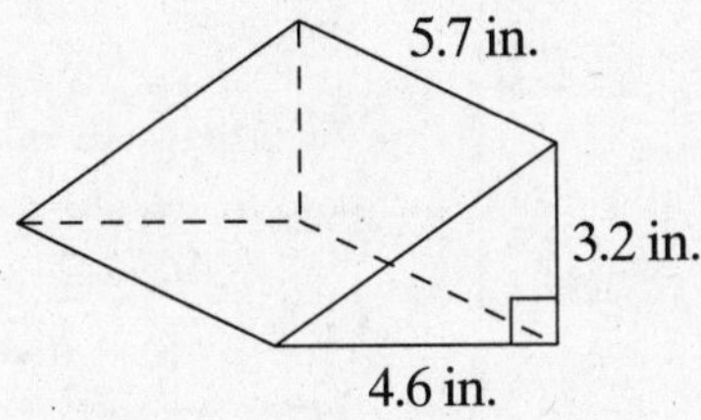

5. 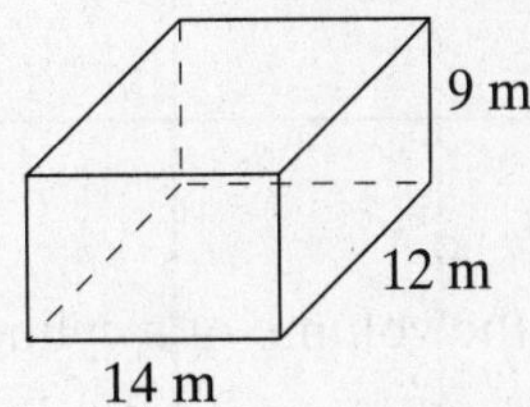

6. 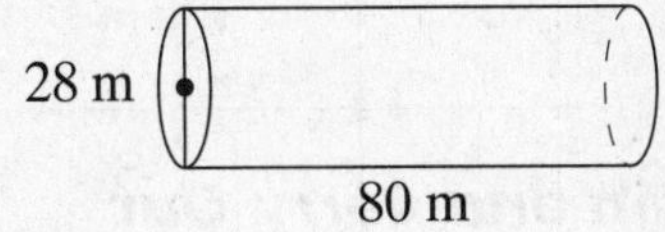

______________ ______________ ______________

7. 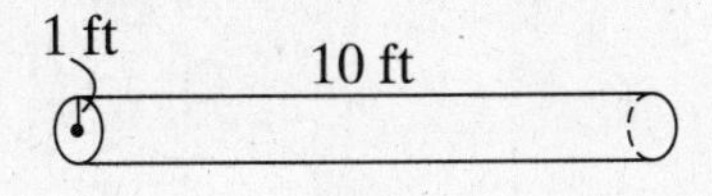

8. 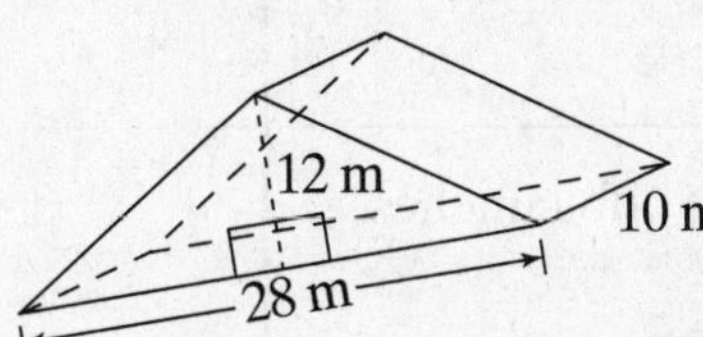

9. 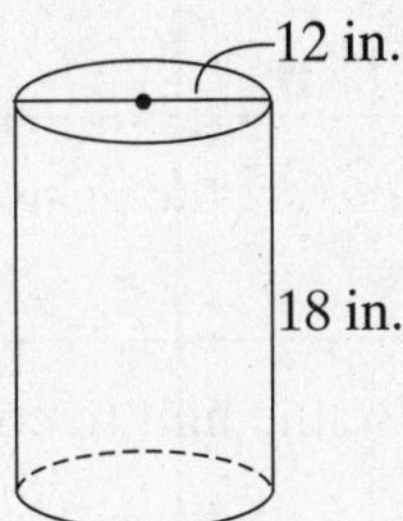

______________ ______________ ______________

Find the height of each rectangular prism given the volume, length, and width.

10. $V = 122{,}500 \text{ cm}^3$
$l = 50$ cm
$w = 35$ cm

11. $V = 22.05 \text{ ft}^3$
$l = 3.5$ ft
$w = 4.2$ ft

12. $V = 3{,}375 \text{ m}^3$
$l = 15$ m
$w = 15$ m

______________ ______________ ______________

Name ______________________ Class ______________ Date ______________

8-10 • Guided Problem Solving

GPS Student Page 425, Exercise 21:

Aquariums A large aquarium is built in the shape of a cylinder. The diameter is 203 ft and the height is 25 ft. About how many million gallons of water does this tank hold? (1 gal ≈ 231 in.^{3})

Understand

1. Circle the information you will need to solve.

2. What are you being asked to do?

____

____

3. What do you need to do to the units in your final answer?

____

Plan and Carry Out

4. Write the formula you use to find the volume of a cylinder.

____

5. Find the volume of the aquarium in cubic feet.

____

6. Convert the answer in Step 4 to cubic inches.

____

7. Use the hint to convert the answer in Step 5 to gallons.

____

8. About how many million gallons does the tank hold?

____

Check

9. Estimate the answer by using 3 for π, 200 ft for the diameter, and 1 gal ≈ 230 in.^{3}. Does your answer make sense? Check.

____

____

Solve Another Problem

10. The diameter of a tank is 26 cm, and the height is 58 cm. About how many liters of fuel oil can this steel tank hold? (1,000 cm^3 = 1L)

____

Name ______________________ Class ______________ Date ______________

Practice 8-10

Volumes of Prisms and Cylinders

Find each volume. Round to the nearest cubic unit.

1.

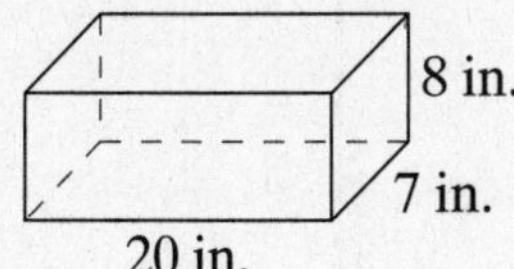

2.

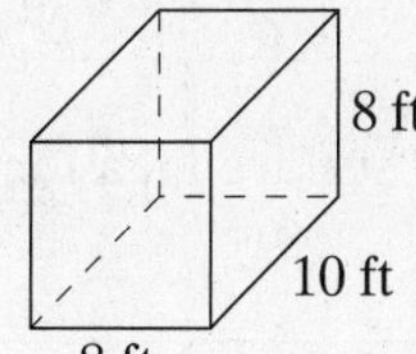

3.

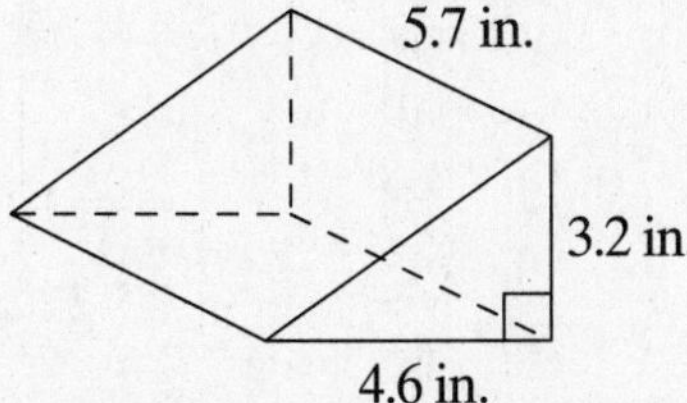

4.

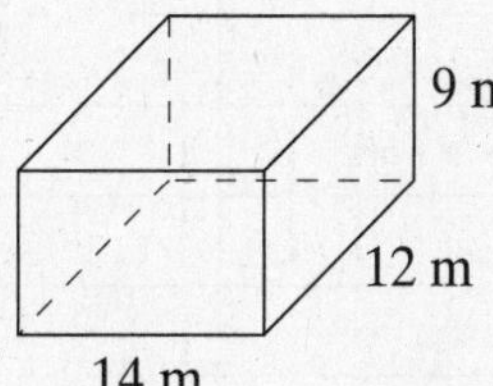

5.

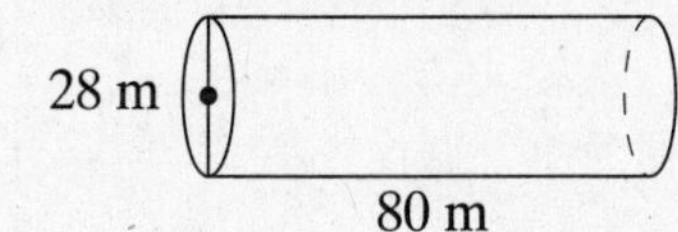

6.

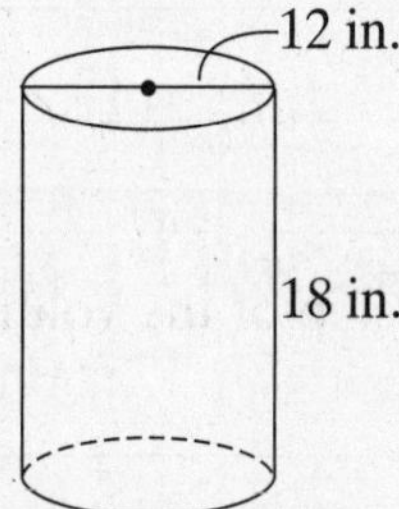

Find the height of each rectangular prism given the volume, length, and width.

7. $V = 122{,}500 \text{ cm}^3$
   $l = 50$ cm
   $w = 35$ cm

8. $V = 22.05 \text{ ft}^3$
   $l = 3.5$ ft
   $w = 4.2$ ft

9. $V = 3{,}375 \text{ m}^3$
   $l = 15$ m
   $w = 15$ m

Name ______________________ Class ______________ Date ____________

Activity Lab 8-10

Volumes of Prisms and Cylinders

Use your knowledge of volume and surface area to find the relationship between the rectangular prisms described in the table below.

1. Find the volume and surface area for each set of dimensions of the prisms below.

Base		Height	Volume (units^3)	Surface Area (units^2)
length	width			
1	36	6		
2	18	6		
3	12	6		
4	9	6		
6	6	6		

2. What pattern do you notice in the dimensions of the prisms?

____

____

____

3. What is the relationship of the volume and surface area?

____

____

____

4. Repeat the analysis for four sets of dimensions with a volume of 384 units^3. Was your outcome the same?

____

____

____

____

Name ______________________ Class ______________ Date ____________

Reteaching 8-10

Volumes of Prisms and Cylinders

The **volume** of a three-dimensional figure is the number of cubic units needed to fill the space inside the figure. A **cubic unit** is a cube whose edges are 1 unit long. You can find the volume of a prism or a cylinder by finding the *area of the base* (B) and multiplying by the *height* (h). Use 3.14 for π.

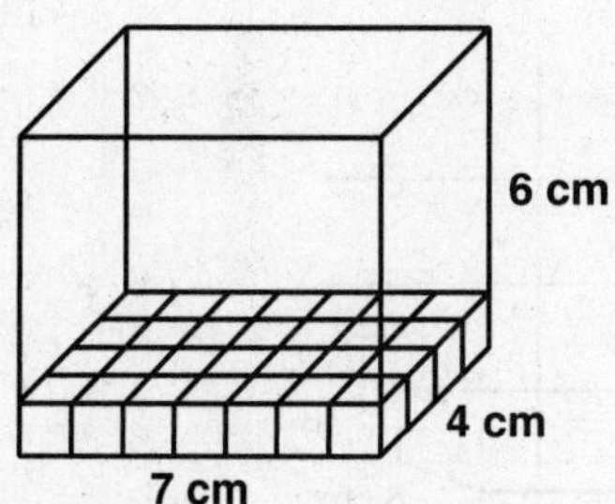

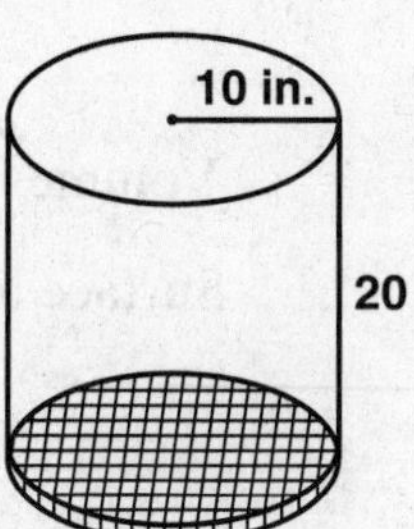

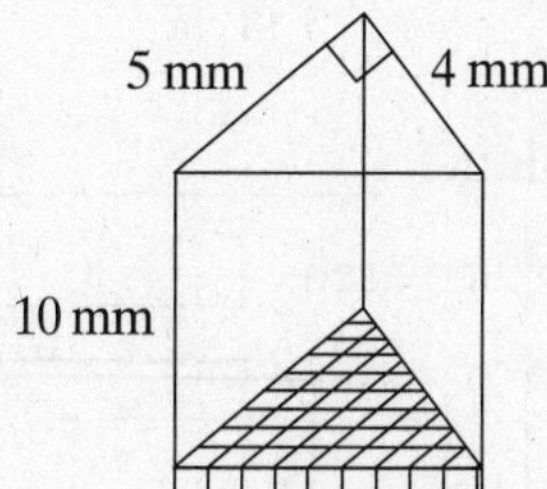

$B = lw$
$B = 7 \cdot 4 = 28 \text{ cm}^2$
$V = Bh$
$V = 28 \cdot 6 = 168 \text{ cm}^3$
The volume is 168 cubic centimeters.

$B = \pi r^2$
$B \approx 3.14 \cdot 10 \cdot 10 = 314 \text{ in.}^2$
$V = Bh$
$V \approx 314 \cdot 20 = 6{,}280 \text{ in.}^3$
The volume is 6,280 cubic inches.

$B = \frac{1}{2}bh$
$B = \frac{1}{2} \cdot 5 \cdot 4$
$B = 10$
$V = Bh$
$V = 10 \cdot 10 = 100 \text{ mm}^3$
The volume is 100 cubic millimeters.

Complete to find the volume to the nearest tenth of a unit.

1. 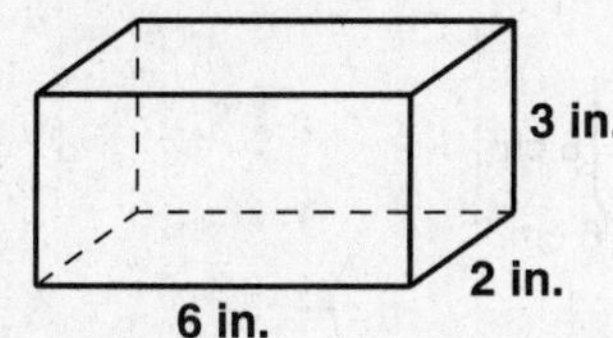

$V = Bh = lwh$

$= \_\_\_\_ \cdot \_\_\_\_ \cdot \_\_\_\_$

$= \_\_\_\_\_\_\_\_$

2.  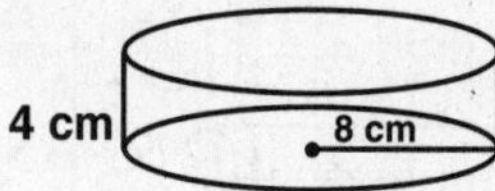

$V = Bh = \pi r^2 h$

$\approx 3.14 \cdot \_\_\_\_ \cdot \_\_\_\_ \cdot \_\_\_\_$

$= \_\_\_\_\_\_\_\_$

Find the volume. Round to the nearest cubic unit.

3. 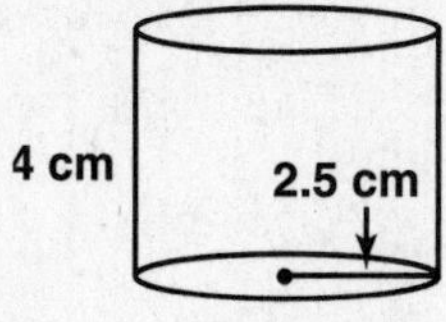

4. 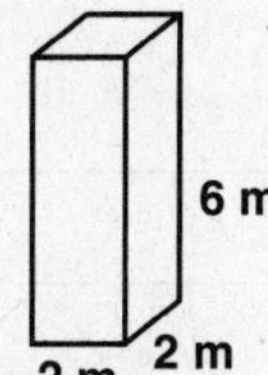

5. 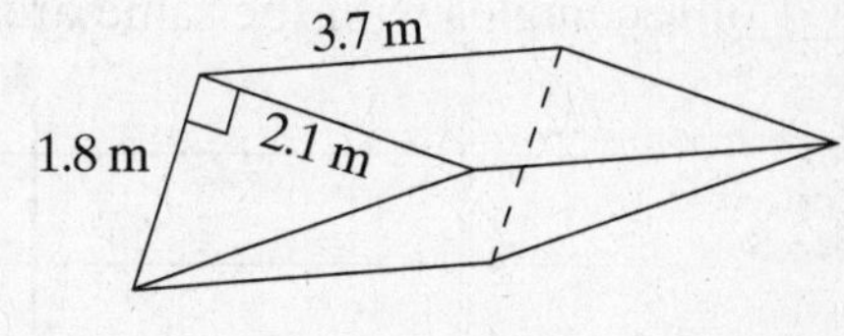

________ ________ ________

Name ______________ Class ______________ Date ______________

Enrichment 8-10

Geometric Calculations

Find the volume and surface area for each rectangular prism.

1.

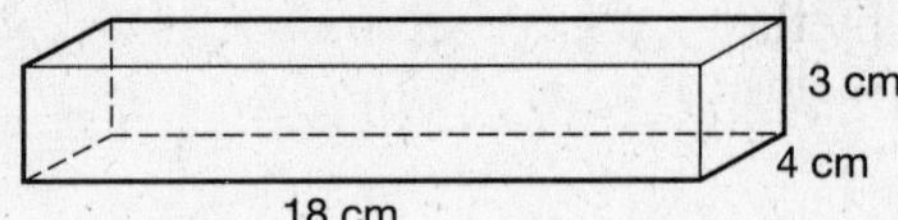

Volume ______________

Surface area ______________

2.

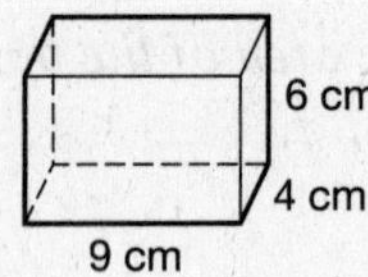

Volume ______________

Surface area ______________

3.

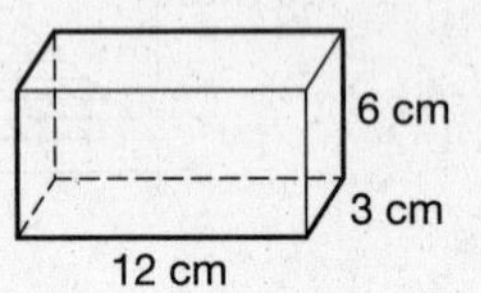

Volume ______________

Surface area ______________

4.

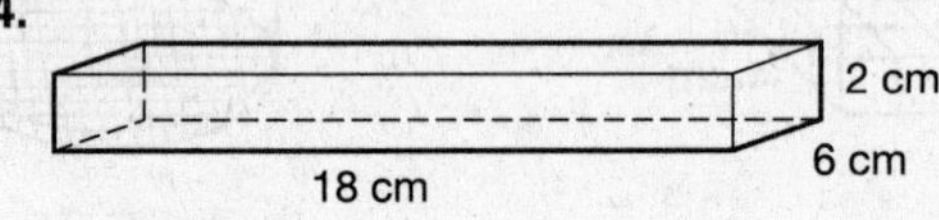

Volume ______________

Surface area ______________

5.

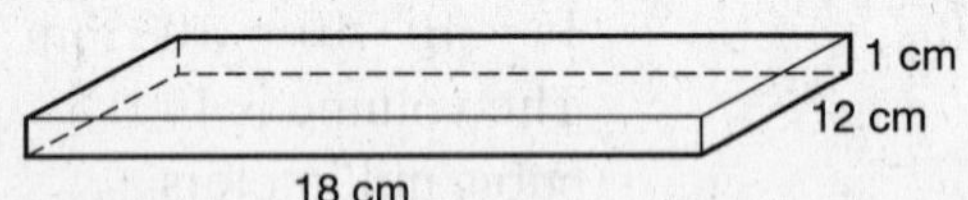

Volume ______________

Surface area ______________

6.

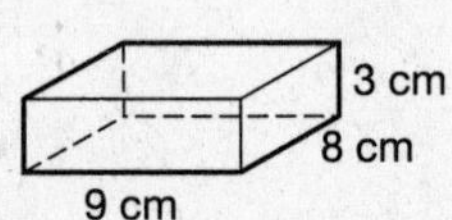

Volume ______________

Surface area ______________

7.

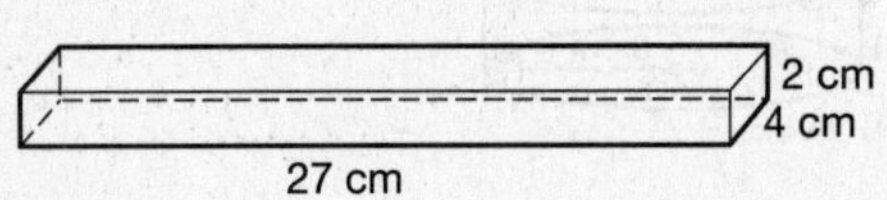

Volume ______________

Surface area ______________

8.

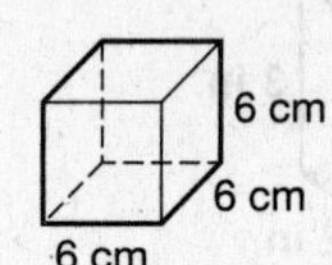

Volume ______________

Surface area ______________

9. Which figure has the smallest surface area?

____

10. Describe the relationship between volume and surface area. How does this compare with the relationship between the perimeters of rectangles with the same area?

____

____

____

Name ______________________ Class ______________ Date ______________

8E: Vocabulary Check

For use after Lesson 8-10

Study Skill Strengthen your vocabulary. Use these pages and add cues and summaries by applying the Cornell Notetaking style.

Write the definition for each word or term at the right. To check your work, fold the paper back along the dotted line to see the correct answers.

Definition	Term
______________________	irrational numbers
______________________	face
______________________	area
______________________	volume
______________________	prism

Name ______________________ Class ______________ Date ______________

8E: Vocabulary Check (continued)

For use after Lesson 8-10

Write the vocabulary word or term for each definition. To check your work, fold the paper forward along the dotted line to see the correct answers.

a number that cannot be written as the ratio of two integers	______________________
a flat surface of a three-dimensional figure that is shaped like a polygon	______________________
the number of square units a figure encloses	______________________
the number of cubic units needed to fill the space inside a three-dimensional figure	______________________
a three-dimensional figure with two parallel and congruent polygonal faces, called bases	______________________

Name ______________ Class ______________ Date ______________

8C: Reading/Writing Math Symbols

For use after Lesson 8-10

Study Skill After completing an assignment, take a break. Then, come back and check your work.

State whether each of the following units represents length, area or volume.

1. cm^2 ______________
2. $in.^3$ ______________
3. mi ______________
4. ft^2 ______________
5. km ______________
6. mm^3 ______________

State whether each expression can be used to calculate length, area, or volume and to what shapes they apply.

7. $\frac{1}{2}bh$ ______________
8. lwh ______________
9. bh ______________
10. πd ______________
11. πr^2 ______________
12. s^2 ______________
13. $\sqrt{a^2 + b^2}$ ______________
14. $\frac{1}{2}h(b_1 + b_2)$ ______________
15. $\pi r^2 h$ ______________
16. $2\pi r$ ______________

Name ______________________ Class ______________ Date ______________

8F: Vocabulary Review

For use with the Chapter Review

Study Skill Participating in class discussions will help you remember new material. Do not be afraid to express your thoughts when your teacher asks for questions, answers, or discussion.

Circle the word that best completes the sentence.

1. The longest side of a right triangle is the (*leg, hypotenuse*).
2. (*Parallel, Perpendicular*) lines lie in the same plane and do not intersect.
3. A (*solution, statement*) is a value of a variable that makes an equation true.
4. Figures that are the same size and shape are (*similar, congruent*).
5. (*Complementary, Supplementary*) angles are two angles whose sum is 90°.
6. A (*circle, sphere*) is the set of all points in space that are the same distance from a center point.
7. The perimeter of a circle is the (*circumference, circumcenter*).
8. The (*area, volume*) of a figure is the number of square units it encloses.
9. A(n) (*isosceles, scalene*) triangle has no congruent sides.
10. A (*rhombus, square*) is a parallelogram with four right angles and four congruent sides.
11. A number that is the square of an integer is a (*perfect square, square root*).
12. A (*pyramid, prism*) is a three-dimensional figure with triangular faces that meet at one point.
13. A speed limit of 65 mi/h is an example of a (*ratio, rate*).
14. A (*cone, cylinder*) has two congruent parallel bases that are circles.

Name ______________________ Class ______________ Date ____________

Puzzle 8-10

Volumes of Prisms and Cylinders

A bead company makes beads by pouring plaster into molds that have a hollow cylinder (1.0 cm diameter) in the middle. When the bead dries, the cylinder provides a hole so that the bead may be strung. The company is currently producing a necklace that includes three types of beads: rectangular prisms, triangular prisms, and cylinders. The beads are pictured below with their dimensions. The beads for each necklace require a total of 86.58 cubic centimeters of plaster to make. The necklace includes an equal number of each type of bead.

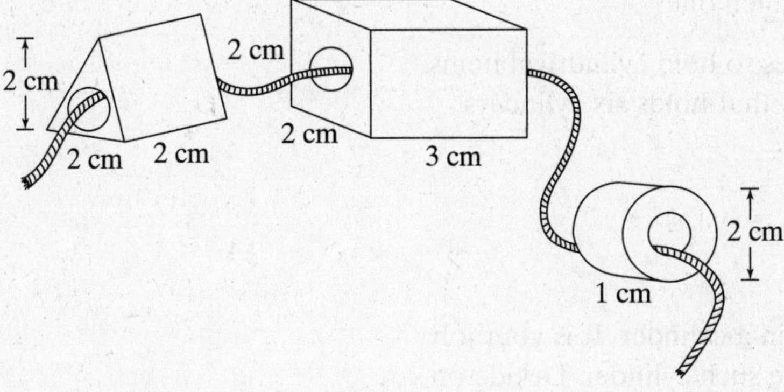

How many of each type of bead is used to make the necklace?

____

Name ______________________ Class ______________ Date ______________

Chapter 8 Project: Shape Up and Ship Out

Design Boxes for Shipping Cylinders

Beginning the Chapter Project

Space is money! So before cargo is prepared for shipment in large shipping containers, it is packaged in smaller containers, based on its size and shape.

Cans of tuna are examples of items you buy in cylindrical containers. Would you pack two cylinders side-by-side or one above the other? One arrangement wastes cardboard! But which one?

In this chapter project, you will design boxes to hold cylindrical items. Your final product will be a model of a box that holds six cylinders.

Activities

Activity 1: Analyzing

Choose an everyday item that is packaged in a cylinder. It is your job to design a rectangular box for shipping one such cylinder. Decide on the length, width, and height of the box. Remember, don't waste cardboard.

Activity 2: Drawing

Use the cylinders you chose in Activity 1. Sketch two ways that you could package two of the cylinders in rectangular boxes. Label the dimensions of both boxes. Estimate which box uses less cardboard.

Activity 3: Writing

Describe at least three different ways you can pack four of your cylinders in rectangular boxes. Which box has the least surface area? Calculate the surface area of the box.

Activity 4: Calculating

Give at least three ways you can pack six of your cylinders in rectangular boxes. Find the surface area and volume of each box. Build a model of the box that uses the least cardboard.

Chapter 8 Project: Shape Up and Ship Out (continued)

Finishing the Project

Your job calls for boxing shipments of cylinders. You don't want to waste cardboard, so design the boxes wisely! Remember, there can be lots of different ways to pack the cylinders, so pick the best arrangements for the six cylinders.

Reflect and Revise

Ask a classmate to review your project with you. See if your classmate agrees that you have thought of the best arrangement of six cylinders. If necessary, improve on your model.

Extending the Project

Research the average dimensions of a semi-truck. Determine how many of your boxes can fit in a semi-truck. How many cylinders can you deliver in one truck load?

Research a factory in your area that ships its product across the country or overseas. Generate a list of concerns that businesses have about the design of a package when it has to travel so far.

Visit PHSchool.com for information and links you might find helpful as you complete your project.

Name ______________________ Class ______________ Date ____________

Chapter Project Manager

Getting Started

Read about the project. As you work on it, you will need several sheets of paper. If available, a spreadsheet program also can be used. Keep all your work for the project in a folder, along with this Project Manager.

Checklist	Suggestions
❑ Activity 1: analyzing	❑ Look in your kitchen cupboard or in the newspaper advertisements to find objects that are packaged in cylinders.
❑ Activity 2: drawing	❑ Trying setting the cylinders next to one another or on top of each other.
❑ Activity 3: writing	❑ Use the box you created in Activity 2 and add on.
❑ Activity 4: calculating	❑ Try making three stacks of two, two stacks of three, six stacks of one, or one stack of 6.
❑ Recommendations	❑ Check all of your calculations to be sure you chose the box with the least surface area.

Scoring Rubric

3 You provide nine drawings of box designs: one for a single cylinder, two for two cylinders, and three each for four and six cylinders. For the two-four, and six-cylinder designs you methodically and accurately calculate the surface areas to determine which boxes require the least amount of cardboard. Your completed project includes explanations of your work and a model of your best six-cylinder design.

2 You provide at least seven of the required designs, and most of your surface area calculations are both easy to follow and accurate. You complete a model of your best six-cylinder design.

1 You only complete a few box designs with accompanying surface area calculations. Your work is either inaccurate or sloppy.

0 You do not complete a majority of the box designs or surface area calculations.

Your Evaluation of Project Evaluate your work, based on the Scoring Rubric.

Teacher's Evaluation of Project

Name ______________________ Class ______________ Date ______________

Chapter Project Teacher Notes

About the Project

Students will use their knowledge of geometry and measurement to design a box in which to ship cylindrical containers.

Introducing the Project

Ask students:

- *Name some products that are packaged in cylinders.*
- *How do you think cylinders would best fit in a box?*
- *How can you test the best designs for a package?*

Activity 1: Analyzing

Discuss with students why the width and height of the box must be at least equal to the diameter and height of the cylinder.

Activity 2: Drawing

Have students exchange their package sketches with a partner to estimate which box uses less cardboard.

Activity 3: Writing

This activity will help students see that a taller box does not necessarily have a greater surface area than a shorter box.

Activity 4: Calculating

Suggest students clearly label the measurements on each box. Have them organize the surface area and volume of each box in a table.

Finishing the Project

You may wish to plan a project day on which students share their completed projects. Encourage students to explain their process as well as their products. Have students review their methods for calculating the dimensions of the cylinder and the boxes, and for making the model of their box for the project.

Visit PHSchool.com for information and links you might find helpful as you complete your project.

Name ____________________ Class ____________ Date ____________

✔ Checkpoint Quiz 1

Use with Lessons 8-1 through 8-4.

Find the area of each figure.

1. 2.5 cm, 2.5 cm

2. 15 cm, 14 cm, 12 cm, 13 cm

3. 14 m, 11 m, 9 m, 20 m

____________ ____________ ____________

4. Choose the unit you would use to estimate the area of a baseball field: ft^2, mi, ft, yd^2, mi^2. ____________

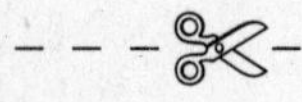

Name ____________________ Class ____________ Date ____________

✔ Checkpoint Quiz 2

Use with Lessons 8-5 through 8-9.

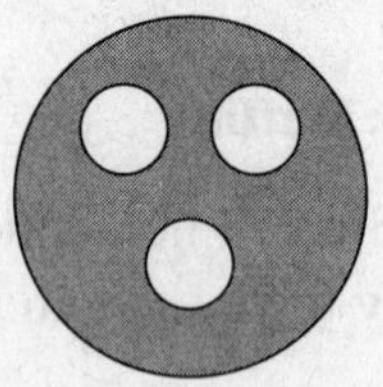

1. The diameter of the large circle at the right is 8 in. The diameter of each small circle is 2 in. What is the area of the shaded region? Use 3.14 for π. ____________

Find each missing length. Round your answer to the nearest tenth.

2. 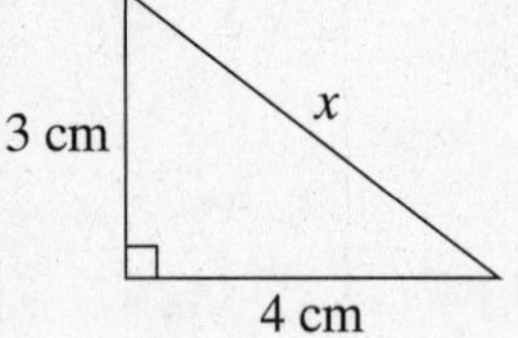

3. 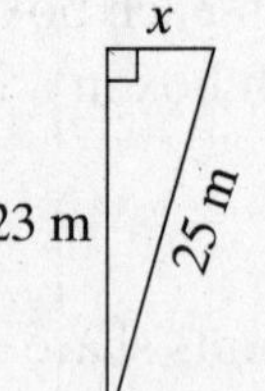

4. 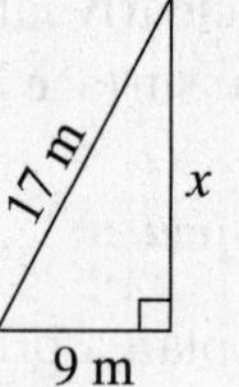

____________ ____________ ____________

Find the surface area of each rectangular prism.

5. length = 7 m
width = 4 m
height = 3 m

6. length = 9 cm
width = 3 cm
height = 2 cm

7. length = 6 m
width = 15 m
height = 4 m

____________ ____________ ____________

8. Find the surface area of a cylinder with a radius of 3.5 cm and a height of 7 cm. ____________

Name ________________ Class ________ Date ________

Chapter Test — Form A

Chapter 8

Estimate the area of each shaded region. Each square represents 25 in.^{2}

1. ________________

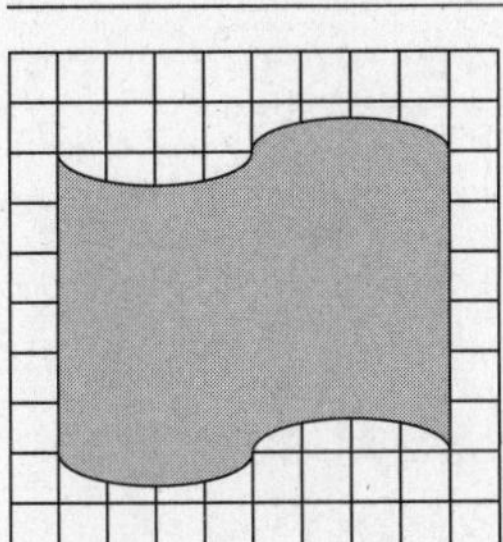

2. ________________

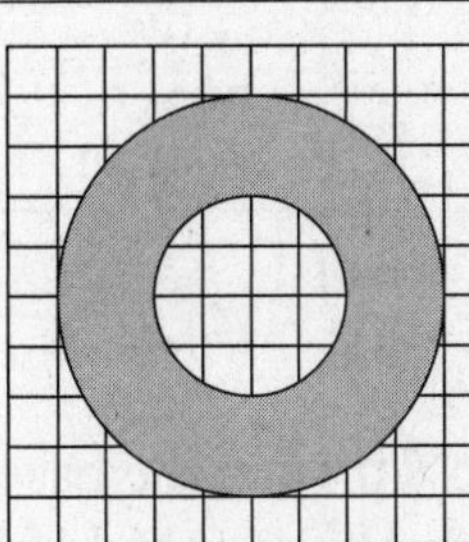

Find the area of each figure.

3. ________________

12 ft

36 ft

4. ________________

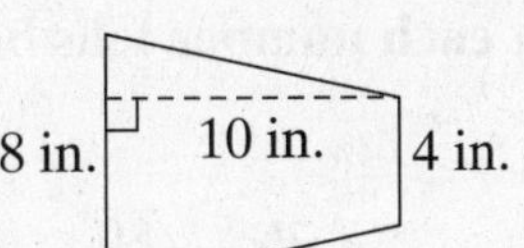

5. ________________

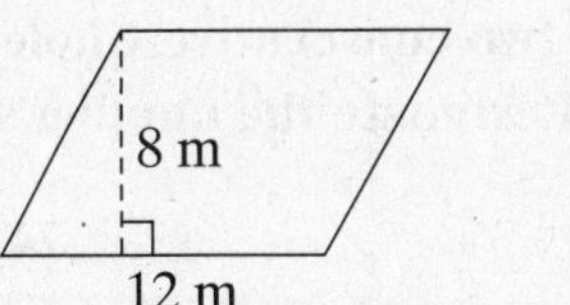

Find the circumference and area of each circle. Round to the nearest tenth.

6. ________________

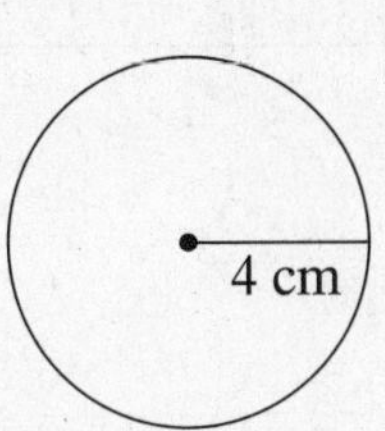

7. ________________

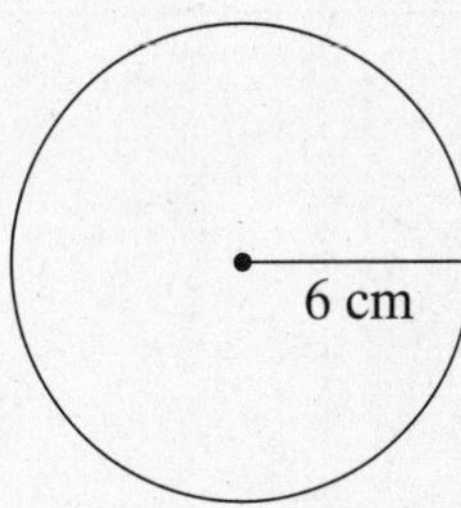

Simplify each square root.

8. $\sqrt{225}$ ________

9. $\sqrt{16}$ ________

10. $\sqrt{324}$ ________

11. $\sqrt{400}$ ________

12. $\sqrt{289}$ ________

13. $\sqrt{36}$ ________

14. A square indoor play space has an area of 121 ft^2. What is the perimeter of the play space? ________

Identify each number as *rational* or *irrational.*

15. $\sqrt{64}$ ________

16. $2\frac{5}{6}$ ________

17. $-1.\overline{2}$ ________

18. $\sqrt{50}$ ________

Chapter Test (continued) Form A

Chapter 8

Find each missing length to the nearest tenth of a unit.

19. ____________

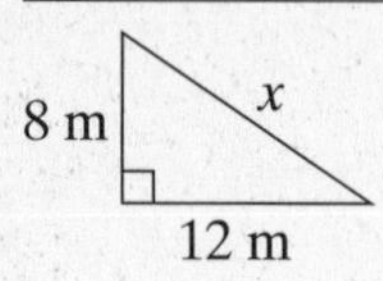

20. ____________

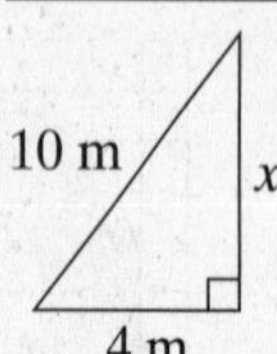

21. ____________

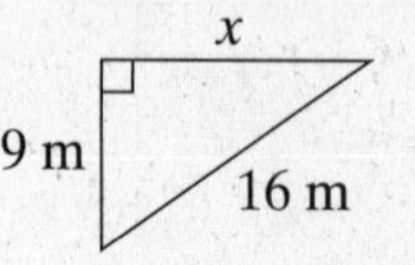

22. A 25-ft ladder is placed 8 ft from the base of the house. How high up the side of the house can the ladder reach? Round your answer to the nearest foot.

____

Find two consecutive whole numbers that each number falls between. Then estimate the number's value.

23. $\sqrt{31}$ ____________

24. $\sqrt{14}$ ____________

25. $\sqrt{80}$ ____________

26. $\sqrt{140}$ ____________

Find the surface area of each figure. If necessary, round to the nearest tenth.

27. ____________

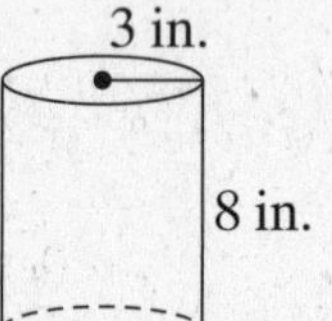

28. ____________

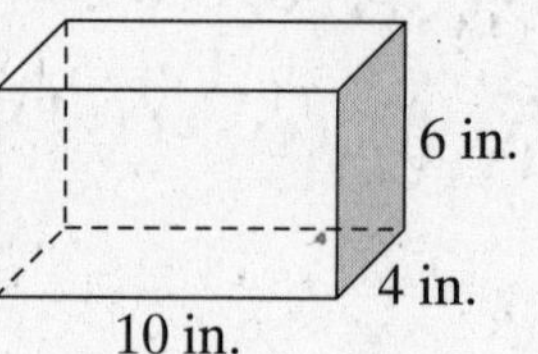

Find the volume of each figure. If necessary, round to the nearest tenth.

29. ____________

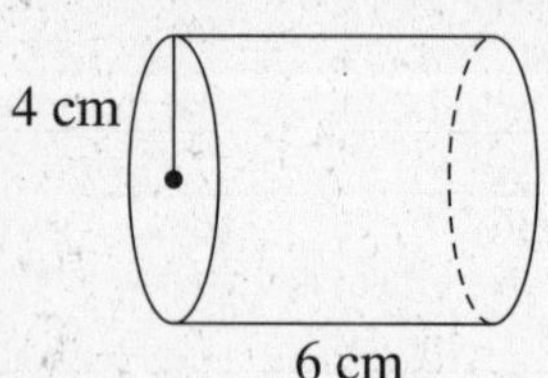

30. ____________

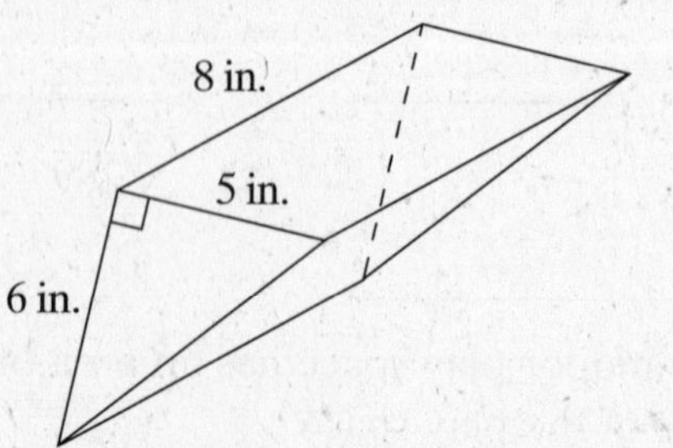

31. The area of a rectangular playground is 2,700 ft^2. The length is 3 times the width. What are the dimensions of the playground?

____

Name ______________________ Class ______________ Date ______________

Chapter Test **Form B**

Chapter 8

Estimate the area of each shaded region. Each square represents 25 in.^{2}.

1. ______________________

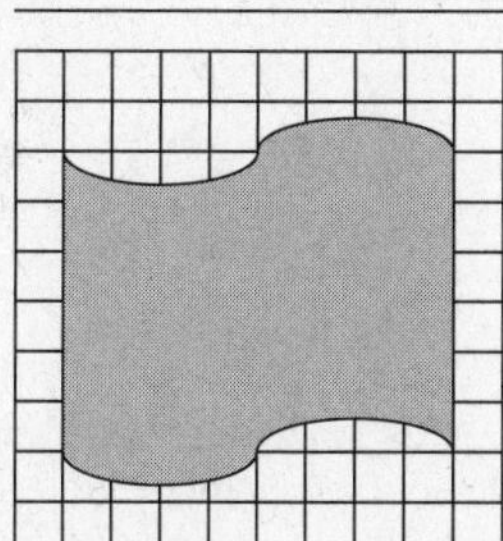

2. ______________________

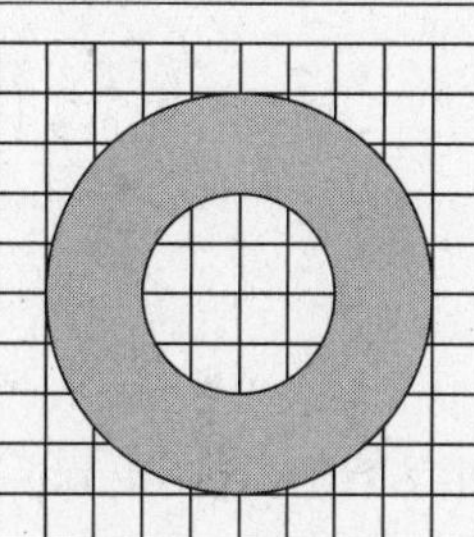

Find the area of each figure.

3. ______________________

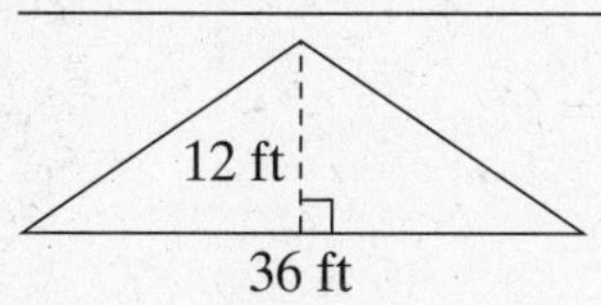

4. ______________________

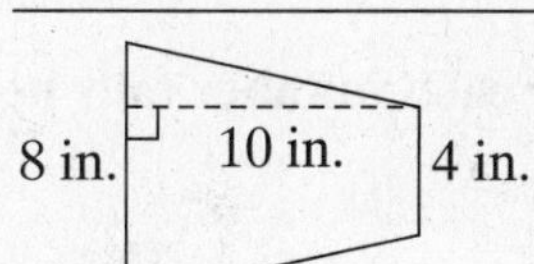

5. ______________________

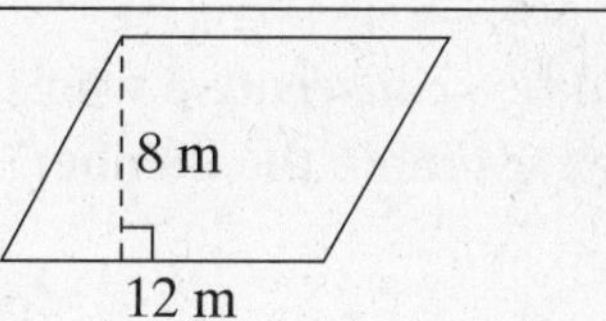

Find the circumference and area of each circle. Round to the nearest tenth.

6. ______________________

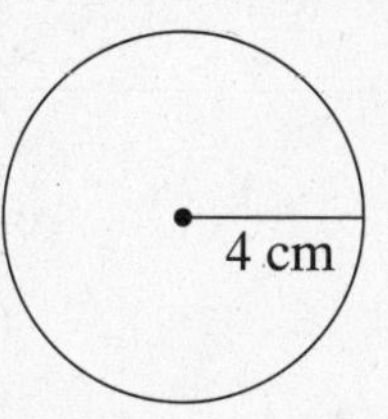

7. ______________________

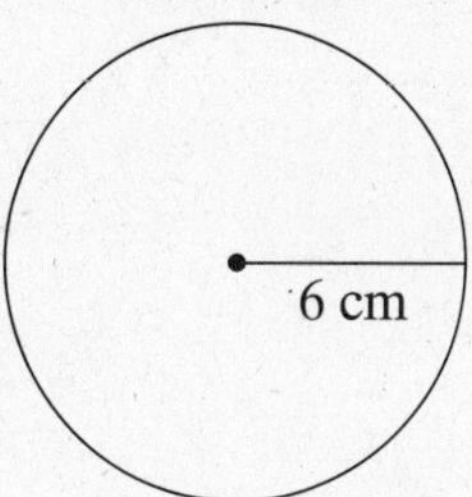

Simplify each square root.

8. $\sqrt{225}$

____

9. $\sqrt{16}$

____

10. $\sqrt{400}$

____

Identify each number as *rational* or *irrational.*

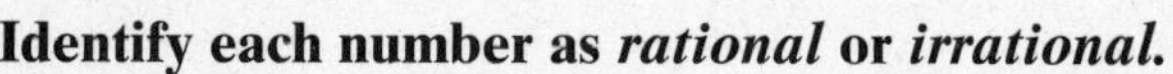

11. $\sqrt{64}$ ______________

12. $-1.\overline{2}$ ______________

13. $\sqrt{50}$ ______________

Name ____________________ Class ____________ Date ____________

Chapter Test (continued) Form B

Chapter 8

Find each missing length to the nearest tenth of a unit.

14. ____________________

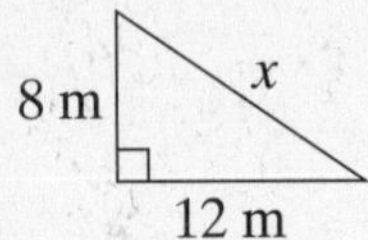

15. ____________________

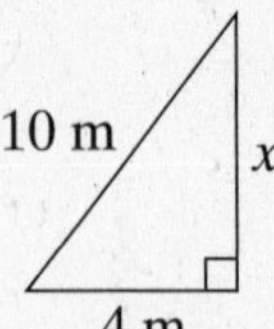

16. A 25-ft ladder is placed 8 ft from the base of the house. How high up the side of the house can the ladder reach? Round your answer to the nearest foot.

____

Find two consecutive whole numbers that each number falls between. Then estimate the number's value.

17. $\sqrt{31}$

18. $\sqrt{80}$

____________________ ____________________

Find the surface area of each figure. If necessary, round to the nearest tenth.

19. ____________________

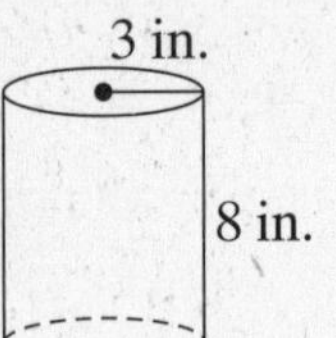

20. ____________________

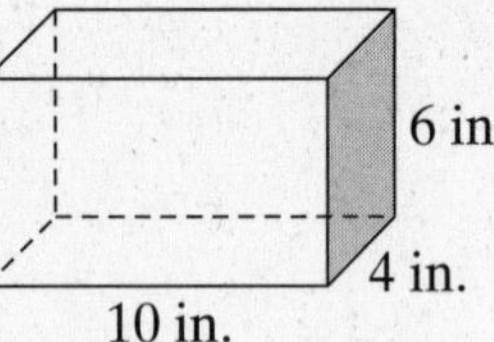

Find the volume of each figure. If necessary, round to the nearest tenth.

21. ____________________

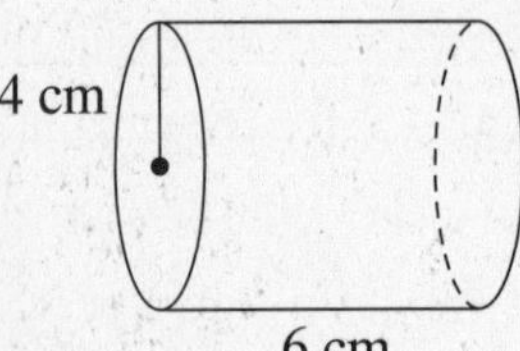

22. ____________________

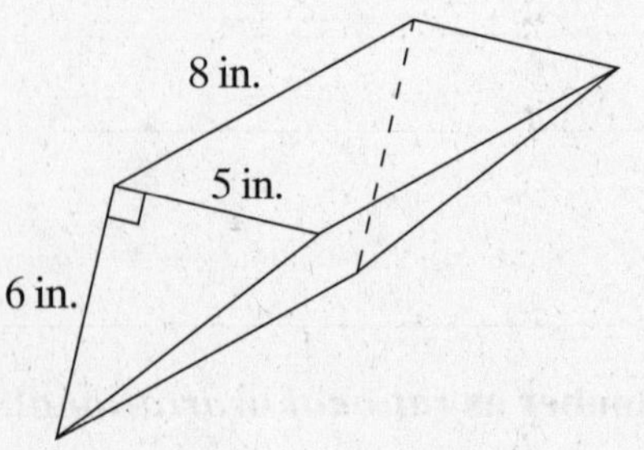

Name ______________________ Class ______________ Date ______________

Alternative Assessment — Form C

Chapter 8

ZIGZAG SAILING

Dwayne wants to sail his boat across a circular lake that has a diameter of 1,000 yards. He has one problem: The wind is blowing directly toward him. To solve the problem, Dwayne learned to zigzag, or "tack," his boat at a 45° angle to the wind, as shown in this picture.

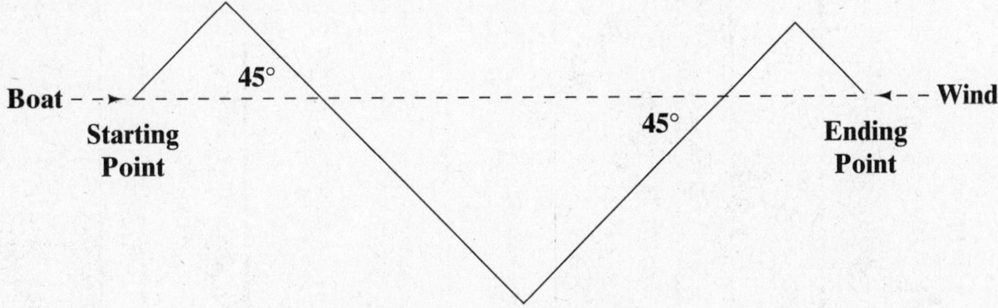

Show all of your work on a separate sheet of paper.

1. Make a scale drawing of a circular lake with a 1,000-yd diameter on grid paper. Then draw a path across the lake, using the zigzag method Dwayne was taught for tacking. Start on one side of the lake and go to the opposite side. Label the scale for your lake and the approximate length of each segment of your path. Use a ruler, a compass, and a protractor.

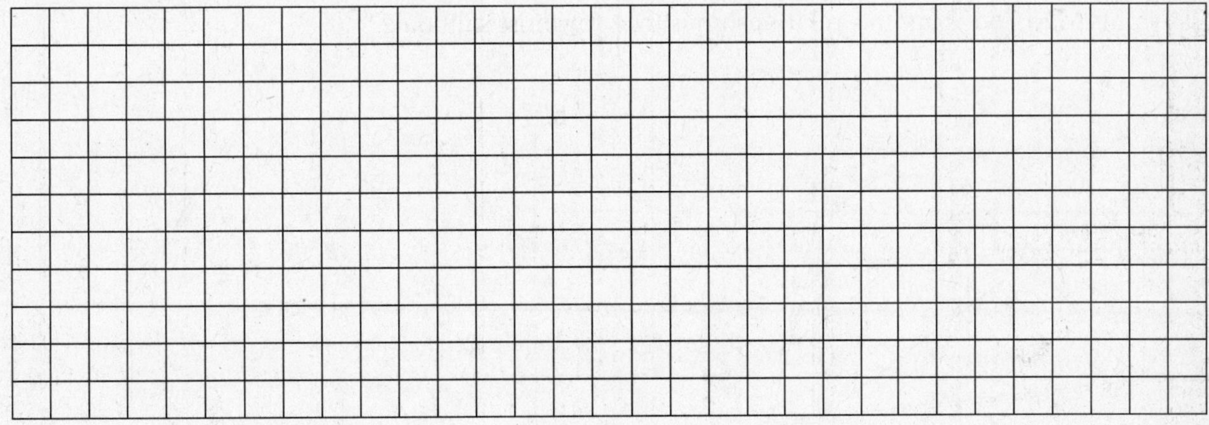

2. **a.** Using your path, how far would Dwayne travel in all?

   b. With 45° tacking, are there other paths shorter than this path?

   c. With 45° tacking, are there longer paths?

   d. Draw several more paths to confirm your decisions. What can you conclude? Explain.

Alternative Assessment (continued) Form C

Chapter 8

3. This is a drawing of Dwayne's sailboat. The area of the sail is very important to the speed of the boat. What is the approximate area of the sail on Dwayne's boat?

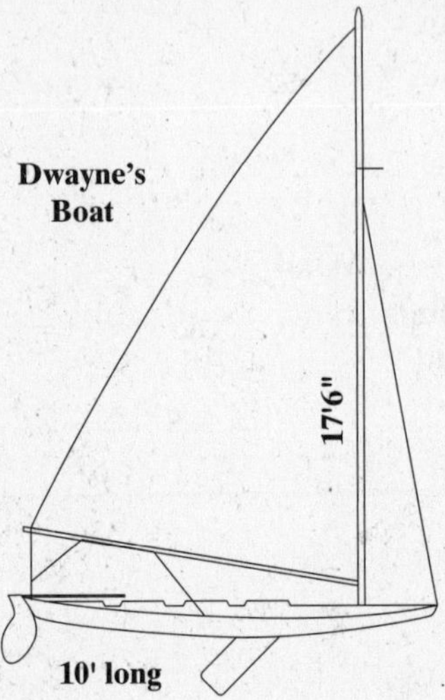

Excursion

Shown below are drawings of two other sailboats. The length (not including rudder) of each boat is labeled. Use a ruler to estimate the dimensions of each sail. Label the dimensions and find the area of each sail. How do the areas of the sails compare to the lengths of the boats? Do you think this relationship is true for most sailboats? Explain.

a.

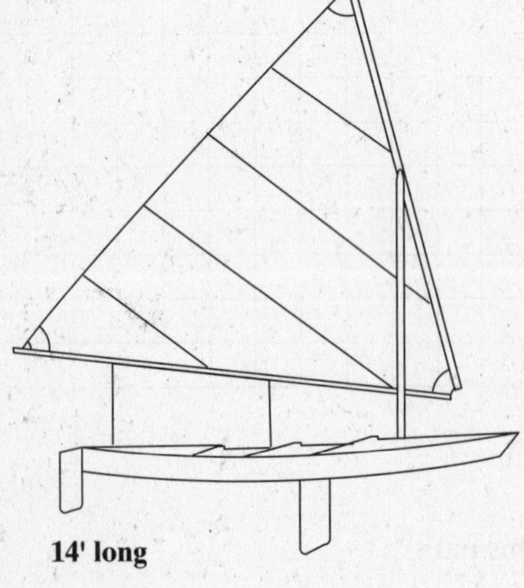

b.

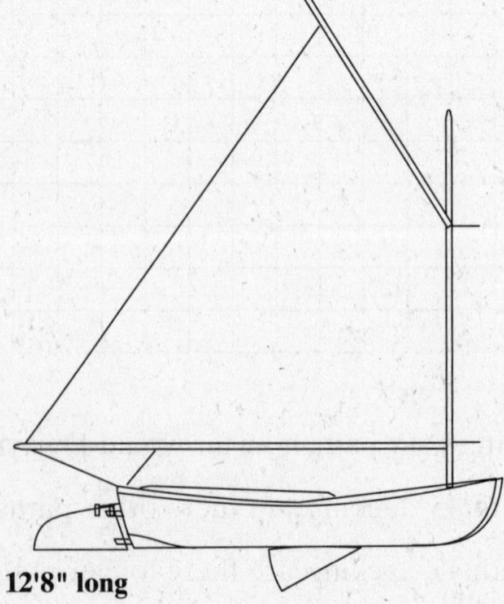

Name ______________________ Class ______________ Date ______________

Cumulative Review

Chapter 1–8

1. What is 3.9256 rounded to the nearest hundredth?

A. 3.9 **B.** 3.92

C. 3.93 **D.** 3.927

2. Find $3\frac{3}{4} \times 4$.

F. $7\frac{3}{4}$ **G.** 12

H. $12\frac{3}{4}$ **J.** 15

3. Find the sum mentally.
$5.4 + 4.3 + 0.7 + 1.6$

A. 10 **B.** 11

C. 11.5 **D.** 12

4. How many inches are there in 2 yd 2 ft 5 in.?

F. 53 in. **G.** 101 in.

H. 149 in. **J.** not here

5. Find the sum $2\frac{1}{3} + 1\frac{1}{4}$.

A. $1\frac{7}{12}$ **B.** $3\frac{1}{12}$

C. $3\frac{2}{7}$ **D.** $3\frac{7}{12}$

6. Which variable expression means "a number decreased by 7"?

F. $7n$ **G.** $7 - n$

H. $n - 7$ **J.** $\frac{n}{7}$

7. Which measure is that of an obtuse angle?

A. 14° **B.** 54°

C. 84° **D.** 94°

8. A floor plan has a scale 2 cm : 3 m. What is the actual length of a room measuring 30 cm on the floor plan?

F. 5 m **G.** 20 m

H. 45 m **J.** 90 m

9. Out of 240 marbles, 180 marbles are red. What percent of the marbles are red?

A. 18% **B.** 25%

C. 42% **D.** 75%

10. A photograph is 8 in. by 10 in. Sally must enlarge it so its sides are 125% of the original. What will the enlarged photograph measure?

F. 6.4 in. by 8 in.

G. 10 in. by 12.5 in.

H. 16 in. by 20 in.

J. 64 in. by 100 in.

11. What percent is $\frac{3}{5}$?

A. 30% **B.** 35%

C. 60% **D.** 75%

12. A triangle has two angles that measure 28°. What type of triangle is it?

F. isosceles **G.** right

H. acute **J.** equilateral

Cumulative Review (continued)

Chapter 1–8

13. Find the area of the triangle below.

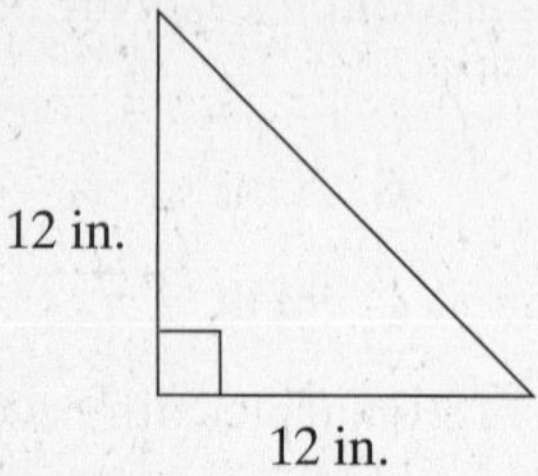

A. 144 in.^2 **B.** 96 in.^2

C. 72 in.^2 **D.** 24 in.^2

14. Find the area of the trapezoid below.

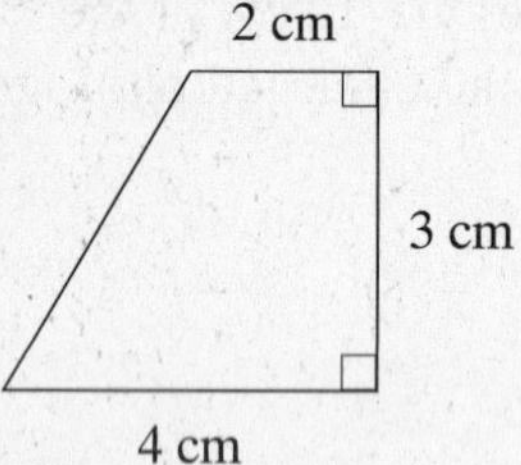

F. 9 cm^2 **G.** 12 cm^2

H. 18 cm^2 **J.** 24 cm^2

15. The volume of a cube is 216 cm^3. Find the value of x.

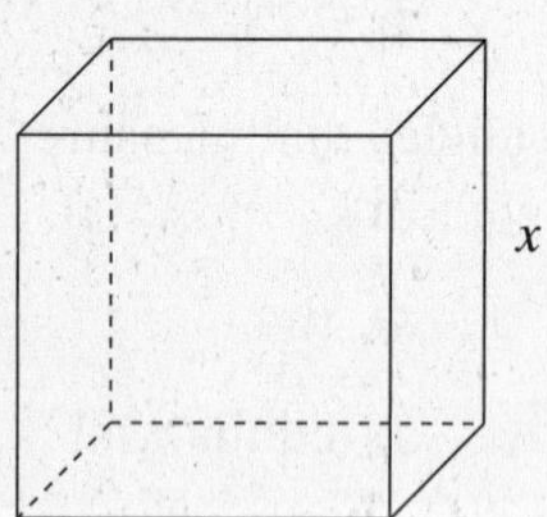

A. 3 cm **B.** 4 cm

C. 5 cm **D.** 6 cm

16. What are two integers whose product is -28 and whose sum is -3?

F. $-14, 2$ **G.** $14, -2$

H. $-7, 4$ **J.** $7, -4$

17. How many square yards of carpeting are needed to carpet a room 4 yd by 5.5 yd?

A. 9.5 yd^2 **B.** 11 yd^2

C. 19 yd^2 **D.** 22 yd^2

18. Solve $4y + 12 = 0$.

F. 0 **G.** -3

H. -8 **J.** -48

Short Response

19. In a trivia game, your team answered 32 out of 40 questions correctly. The opposing team answered 16 out of 20 questions correctly. Was the ratio of correctly answered questions to incorrectly answered questions the same or different for both teams? Explain.

____

____

20. Draw a diagram to represent the following problem. Two friends live 28 miles apart on a straight road. One can bicycle 3 miles per hour faster than the other. They start at the same time and meet after cycling for 2 hours. What rate did each cycle?

____

Name ______________________ Class ______________ Date ____________

Chapters 5–8 Answers

Chapter 5

Practice (regular) 5-1

1. 182 to 10; 182 : 10; $\frac{182}{10}$ **2.** 284 to 1,000; 284 : 1,000; $\frac{284}{1{,}000}$ **3.** 10 : 12; or 5 : 6 **4.** 39 : 34 **5.** $\frac{2}{3}$ **6.** $\frac{3}{1}$ **7.** $\frac{3}{14}$ **8.** Yes, they are equivalent. **9.** No, they are not equivalent. **10.** Yes, they are equivalent. **11.** 3 : 10

Guided Problem Solving 5-1

1. 2 cups of water; 3 cups of flour; 9 cups of flour **2.** Find the number of cups of water you will need with 9 cups of flour. **3.** You can use multiplication to find new numbers that share the same proportional relationship as the numbers in the original recipe. **4.** $\frac{2}{3}$ or 2 : 3 **5.** 9 cups **6.** $\frac{2}{3} = \frac{6}{9}$ **7.** 6 cups **8.** Since 9 cups is three times 3 cups, the number of cups of water needed is also tripled. **9.** 32 black tiles

Practice (adapted) 5-1

1. 182 to 10; 182 : 10; $\frac{182}{10}$ **2.** 284 to 1,000; 284 : 1,000; $\frac{284}{1{,}000}$ **3.** 39 : 34 **4.** $\frac{2}{3}$ **5.** $\frac{3}{1}$ **6.** $\frac{3}{14}$ **7.** Yes, they are equivalent. **8.** No, they are not equivalent. **9.** 3 : 10

Activity Lab 5-1

Check students' work.

Reteaching 5-1

1. 2 to 6; 2 : 6; $\frac{2}{6}$ **2.** 3 to 5; 3 : 5; $\frac{3}{5}$ **3.** 6 to 5; 6 : 5; $\frac{6}{5}$ **4.** 2 to 3; 2 : 3; $\frac{2}{3}$ **5.** 6 to 16; 6 : 16; $\frac{6}{16}$ **6.** 5 to 16; 5 : 16; $\frac{5}{16}$ **7.** 8 to 8; 8 : 8; $\frac{8}{8}$ **8.** 3 to 8; 3 : 8; $\frac{3}{8}$ **9.** 2 to 16; 2 : 16; $\frac{2}{16}$ **10.** 2 to 5; 2 : 5; $\frac{2}{5}$ **11.** Sample answers: 4 : 10; 6 : 15 **12.** Sample answers: 3 to 5; 36 to 60 **13.** 2 : 3 **14.** $\frac{2}{1}$ **15.** $\frac{3}{50}$ **16.** 4 : 9

Enrichment 5-1

1. 72; 45 **2.** $\frac{8}{5} = 1.6$ **3.** Check students' answers. **4a.** 4; 4; 1.3 **4b.** 4.8; 4.8; 1.6 **4c.** 6; 6; 2 **5.** Check student's drawings.

Puzzle 5-1

1. 3 to 4; 15 : 20; $\frac{6}{8}$ **2.** 10 to 4; 5 to 2; $\frac{100}{40}$ **3.** 1 to 3; 2 : 6; 3 to 9 **4.** 4 to 6; $\frac{2}{3}$; 10 : 15 **5.** 30 to 35; 12 to 14; $\frac{6}{7}$ **6.** 10 to 16; 5 : 8; $\frac{20}{32}$ **7.** 1 to 6; 20 to 120; 5 : 30 **8.** 25 to 30; 5 to 6; $\frac{10}{12}$

Practice (regular) 5-2

1. 50 mi/h **2.** \$9.40/h **3.** 40 pages/h **4.** 52 words/min or 3,120 words/h **5.** 311 parts/h **6.** 25 books/shelf **7.** \$.0099/sheet; \$.00858/sheet; 500 sheets **8.** \$1.29/lb; \$1.267 lb;12 oz **9.** \$.1193/oz; \$.1242/oz; 15 oz **10.** \$.63/lb; \$.498/lb; 5 lb **11.** \$.3125/pencil; \$.2276/pencil; 25 pencils **12.** \$.2225/bagel; \$.2317/bagel; 4 bagels **13a.** Yolanda; 1 yd **13b.** $11\frac{1}{9}$ yd, or 11 yd 4 in.

Guided Problem Solving 5-2

1. Population density is the number of people per unit of area. **2.** Find the population density for Alaska. **3.** that you are going to divide the number of people by the area **4.** 626,932 people **5.** 570,374 mi^2 **6.** $\frac{626{,}932 \text{ people}}{570{,}374 \text{ mi}^2}$ **7.** 1.099 people/mi^2 **8.** 1 person/mi^2 **9.** Because the number of people in Alaska isvery close to the number of square miles **10.** \$4.74/member

Practice (adapted) 5-2

1. 50 mi/h **2.** \$9.40/h **3.** 40 pages/h **4.** 52 words/min or 3,120 words/h **5.** \$.0099/sheet; \$.00858/sheet; 500 sheets **6.** \$1.29/lb; \$1.267 lb;12 oz **7.** \$.1193/oz; \$.1242/oz; 15 oz **8.** \$.63/lb; \$.498/lb; 5 lb **9.** \$.3125/pencil; \$.2276/pencil; 25 pencils **10.** \$.2225/bagel; \$.2317/bagel; 4 bagels **11.** Yolanda; 1 yd

Activity Lab 5-2

1a. \$6.00/class **1b.** \$7.50/class **1c.** \$6.50/class **2a.** 1 hour; \$6.00/hour **2b.** 15 hours; \$5.00/hour **2c.** 10 hours; \$5.20/hour **3.** Sample answers: Location of School, times of her other activities, how to get to the school **4.** Sample answer: Clodagh's Dance because the classes are shorter and she can pay by the class.

Reteaching 5-2

1. 25; 25; \$.10/copy **2.** 100; 100; \$.06/copy **3.** 50; 50; \$.09/copy **4.** 60 mi/hr **5.** 26 mi/gal **6.** 333 m/min **7.** \$1.50/ticket **8.** \$.07/oz; \$.0875/oz; 18 oz **9.** \$1.58/yd; \$1.30/yd; 6 yd **10.** \$1.75/pair; \$1.50/pair; 6 pairs **11.** \$.30/oz; \$.50/oz; 1 lb

Enrichment 5-2

1a. $\frac{10.77 \text{ pesos}}{1 \text{ dollar}}$; $\frac{107.7 \text{ pesos}}{10 \text{ dollars}}$ **1b.** $\frac{0.58 \text{ pound}}{1 \text{ dollar}}$; $\frac{2.9 \text{ pounds}}{5 \text{ dollars}}$ **1cu.** $\frac{0.84 \text{ euros}}{1 \text{ dollar}}$, $\frac{5.88 \text{ euros}}{7 \text{ dollars}}$ **1d.** $\frac{6.24 \text{ kunas}}{1 \text{ dollar}}$, $\frac{18.72 \text{ kunas}}{3 \text{ dollars}}$ **2a.** $\frac{10.77 \text{ pesos}}{1 \text{ dollar}}$; $\frac{2{,}692.5 \text{ pesos}}{250 \text{ dollars}}$ **2b.** $\frac{0.84 \text{ euros}}{1 \text{ dollar}}$, $\frac{210 \text{ euros}}{250 \text{ dollars}}$ **3a.** $\frac{0.84 \text{ euros}}{0.58 \text{ pound}}$; 1.45 euros per pound **3b.** $\frac{1.45 \text{ euros}}{1 \text{ pound}}$, $\frac{69.6 \text{ euros}}{48 \text{ pounds}}$

Puzzle 5-2

1. A **2.** C **3.** L **4.** E **5.** V **6.** R **7.** S **8.** H **9.** O **10.** P
A CLEVER SHOPPER

Practice (regular) 5-3

1. yes **2.** no **3.** no **4.** yes **5.** no **6.** yes **7.** no **8.** yes **9.** yes **10.** no **11.** no **12.** no **13.** not proportional **14.** proportional

Chapters 5–8 Answers (continued)

15. proportional **16.** not proportional **17.** proportional **18.** not proportional **19.** not proportional **20.** proportional **21.** proportional **22.** not proportional **23.** proportional **24.** proportional **25.** no **26.** yes

Guided Problem Solving 5-3

1. 4 parts blue; 5 parts yellow; 16 quarts of blue paint; 25 quarts of yellow paint **2.** Determine whether you will get the desired shade of green with 16 quarts of blue paint and 25 quarts of yellow paint. **3.** Yes; if the ratio of 16 to 25 is the same as the ratio of 4 to 5, you will get the desired shade of green. **4.** $\frac{4}{5}$ **5.** $\frac{16}{25}$ **6.** $4 \cdot 25 \stackrel{?}{=} 5 \cdot 16$; $100 \neq 80$ **7.** no **8.** No, the ratios are not the same. **9.** The cross products are not equal. **10.** No, it is not. The boy-to-girl ratio in your math class is $\frac{5}{4}$; the boy-to-girl ratio in your study group is $\frac{5}{3}$.

Practice (adapted) 5-3

1. yes **2.** no **3.** no **4.** yes **5.** no **6.** yes **7.** no **8.** yes **9.** yes **10.** not proportional **11.** proportional **12.** proportional **13.** not proportional **14.** proportional **15.** not proportional **16.** not proportional **17.** proportional **18.** no **19.** yes

Activity Lab 5-3

1. $\frac{1}{4}$ cup Italian dressing; $3\frac{3}{4}$ medium potatoes; $\frac{3}{4}$ cup chopped celery; 3 hard boiled eggs; $\frac{3}{4}$ teaspoon salt; $\frac{3}{8}$ cup salad dressing or mayo **2.** Sample answer: Each person can eat about 2 slices, so they need to buy 2 packages, which will cost $5.00. **3.** Four people row to the island, one or two row back to pick up the others. **4.** Check students' answers. **5.** Check students' answers.

Reteaching 5-3

1. 60; 60; yes **2.** 48; 2; 48; yes **3.** 8; 64; 16; 80; no **4.** yes **5.** yes **6.** yes **7.** yes **8.** yes **9.** yes **10.** no **11.** no **12.** yes

Enrichment 5-3

1.

3	6	9	12
5	**10**	**15**	**20**

Sample answer: $\frac{3}{5} = \frac{6}{10}, \frac{9}{15} = \frac{12}{20}, \frac{9}{15} = \frac{3}{5}, \frac{6}{10} = \frac{12}{20}$

2.

4	8	20	32
11	**22**	**55**	**88**

Sample answer: $\frac{4}{11} = \frac{8}{22}, \frac{20}{55} = \frac{8}{22}, \frac{4}{11} = \frac{32}{88}, \frac{32}{88} = \frac{20}{55}$

3. Sample answer:

11	22	33	44
15	30	45	60

$\frac{11}{15} = \frac{22}{30}, \frac{33}{45} = \frac{44}{60}, \frac{22}{30} = \frac{33}{45}, \frac{44}{60} = \frac{11}{15}$

4. Sample answer:

16	32	48	64
20	40	60	80

$\frac{16}{20} = \frac{32}{40}, \frac{32}{40} = \frac{48}{60}, \frac{16}{20} = \frac{48}{60}, \frac{16}{20} = \frac{64}{80}$ **5.** Sample answer: $\frac{8}{5} = \frac{24}{15}, \frac{5}{15} = \frac{8}{24}$ **6.** Sample answer: $\frac{27}{6} = \frac{18}{4}, \frac{4}{6} = \frac{18}{27}$ **7.** Sample answer: $\frac{\$6}{\$2} = \frac{\text{21 apples}}{\text{7 apples}}, \frac{\text{21 apples}}{\$6} = \frac{\text{7 apples}}{\$2}$ **8.** Sample answer: $\frac{\text{15 hr}}{\text{80 mi}} = \frac{\text{6 hr}}{\text{32 mi}}, \frac{\text{6 hr}}{\text{15 hr}} = \frac{\text{32 mi}}{\text{80 mi}}$ **9.** 21 resistors, 9 capacitors, 6 transistors; 28 resistors, 12 capacitors, 8 transistors

Puzzle 5-3

Pairs A, C, D, and F must form proportions.

Practice (regular) 5-4

1. 8 **2.** 14 **3.** 15 **4.** 7.5 **5.** 28 **6.** 6 **7.** 35 **8.** 20 **9.** 9 **10.** 6 **11.** 2 **12.** 18 **13.** $12,000 **14.** 1c **15.** 67.5 min **16.** 364 mi **17.** 60 days **18.** 18 eggs

Guided Problem Solving 5-4

1. Find how many students should attend school to keep the same student-to-teacher ratio. **2.** Yes, because you have two ratios that need to be equal. **3.** $\frac{450}{15}$ **4.** $\frac{x}{17}$ **5.** $\frac{450}{15} = \frac{x}{17}$ **6.** 510 students **7.** yes, $\frac{450}{15} = 30$ and $\frac{510}{17} = 30$ **8.** 6 black marbles

Practice (adapted) 5-4

1. 8 **2.** 14 **3.** 15 **4.** 7.5 **5.** 28 **6.** 6 **7.** 35 **8.** 9 **9.** 6 **10.** 2 **11.** $12,000 **12.** 1c **13.** 67.5 min **14.** 364 mi **15.** 60 days

Activity Lab 5-4

1. 15 ft : 10 ft **2.** 11 in.: $8\frac{1}{2}$ in. **3.** no **4.** Sample answer: 30 in. × 20 in., 3 ft × 2 ft **5.** Yes, because the length : width ratio is equivalent **6.** Sample answer: No, because the length : width ratio is not 3 : 2; the poster will be slightly narrower than $8\frac{1}{2}$ in. **7.** Yes, at the bottom or top of the flyer.

Reteaching 5-4

1. $10.85 **2.** 336 **3.** 6; n; 1 **4.** 30; $30n$; 1 **5.** 162; $9n$; 18 **6.** $n = 6$ **7.** $n = 2$ **8.** $n = 12$ **9.** $n = 66$ **10.** $n = 10$ **11.** $n = 5$

Enrichment 5-4

1.

	Best Supermarket	Top Value Supermarket
Chicken	$3.89/lb	$3.96/lb
Broccoli	$.99/package	$.96/package
Strawberries	$.99/pt	$.97/pt
Dinner rolls	$.15/roll	$.10/roll

Chapters 5–8 Answers (continued)

2. Best, \$36.88; Top Value, \$36.74 **3.** Top Value Supermarket **4.** Best, \$5.18; Top Value, \$1.30 **5.** Sample answer: Actual cost: Best—\$42.06, Top Value— \$38.04; buying at Top Value is less expensive and saves time.

Puzzle 5-4

Team A has errors in Exercises 4 and 6; Team B has an error in Exercise 1; Team A has more errors, so Team B wins.

Practice (regular) 5-5

1. $\angle J$ **2.** $\angle O$ **3.** $\overline{MO}$ **4.** $\overline{JK}$ **5.** 4 : 3 or 3 : 4 **6.** 4 **7.** 12 **8.** $8\frac{4}{7}$ **9.** $x = 12$; $y = 13\frac{1}{3}$ **10.** 2.5 **11.** 10 **12.** 288 ft **13.** 20 in.

Guided Problem Solving 5-5

1. Find the longer side of the rectangle. **2.** No, the ratio of the are as cannot be set equal to the ratio of the shorter sides because the area is in square units and the length of the shorter side is not. **3.** The length of the longer side of the rectangle whose area is 32 in^2 **4.** 8 in. **5.** $\frac{8}{4} = \frac{2}{1}$ **6.** $1 \times 288, 2 \times 144, 3 \times 96, 4 \times 72, 6 \times 48, 8 \times 36, 9 \times 32, 12 \times 24, 16 \times 18$ **7.** 12×24 **8.** 24 in. **9.** Since the rectangles are similar, the lengths of the corresponding sides must be in proportion. **10.** 15 in.

Practice (adapted) 5-5

1. $\angle J$ **2.** $\overline{MO}$ **3.** 4 : 3 or 3 : 4 **4.** 4 **5.** 12 **6.** $8\frac{4}{7}$ **7.** $x = 12$; $y = 13\frac{1}{3}$ **8.** 2.5 **9.** 10 **10.** 20 in.

Activity Lab 5-5

Check students' work.

Reteaching 5-5

1. $\overline{QR}$; $\overline{RS}$; $\overline{SQ}$ **2.** $\overline{BC}$; $\frac{12}{n}$; 30 **3.** 80 **4.** 7.5

Enrichment 5-5

1. 0.65; 1.54 **2.** 0.65; 1.54 **3.** 0.65; 1.54 **4.** 0.65; 1.54 **5.** 0.65; 1.54 **6.** The tangent ratio for the angles having the same measure is the same regardless of the length of the sides.

Puzzle 5-5

$x = 15$; $y = 5$; $z = 20$; $w = 20$
Since $x = 15$ and $w = 20$, the missing piece will fit.

Practice (regular) 5-6

1. 94.5 km **2.** 131.25 km **3.** 14.7 km **4.** 3,780 km **5.** 47.25 km **6.** 74.55 km **7.** $\frac{1}{6}$ in. **8.** $\frac{5}{8}$ in. **9.** $\frac{5}{16}$ in. **10.** $\frac{3}{8}$ in. **11.** $\frac{5}{12}$ in. **12.** $\frac{5}{6}$ in. **13.** 80 km **14.** 50 km **15.** 55 km **16.** 95 km **17.** 50 km **18.** 20 km **19a.** 1 in. : 12 ft

19b.

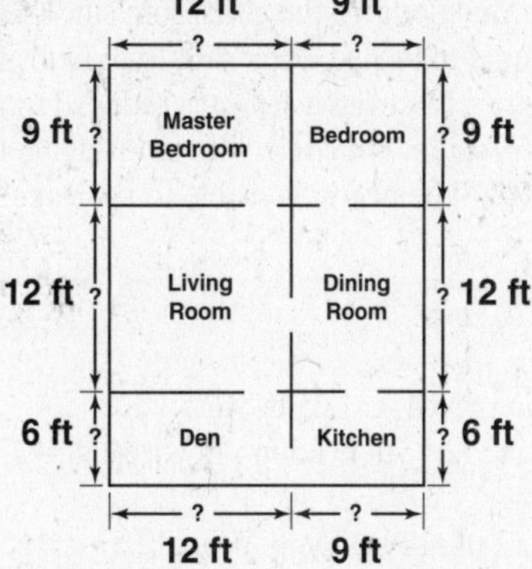

Guided Problem Solving 5-6

1. Explain how you find the length of the drawing of an object with an actual length of 51 ft. **2.** the scale, the actual length, a ratio or proportion, and the answer **3.** the ratio that compares a length in a drawing to the corresponding length in the actual object **4.** 2 in. = 17 ft **5.** 51 ft **6.** $\frac{2}{17} = \frac{x}{51}$ **7.** 6 in. **8.** Every 2 in. represents 17 ft. Fifty-one feet is 3 times 17 ft. Three times 2 in. is 6 in. Therefore, the object should be 6 in. long in a drawing. **9.** 75 ft

Practice (adapted) 5-6

1. 94.5 km **2.** 131.25 km **3.** 3,780 km **4.** 47.25 km **5.** $\frac{1}{6}$ in. **6.** $\frac{5}{8}$ in. **7.** $\frac{3}{8}$ in. **8.** $\frac{5}{12}$ in. **9.** 80 km **10.** 50 km **11.** 55 km **12.** 95 km **13a.** 1 in. : 12 ft

13b.

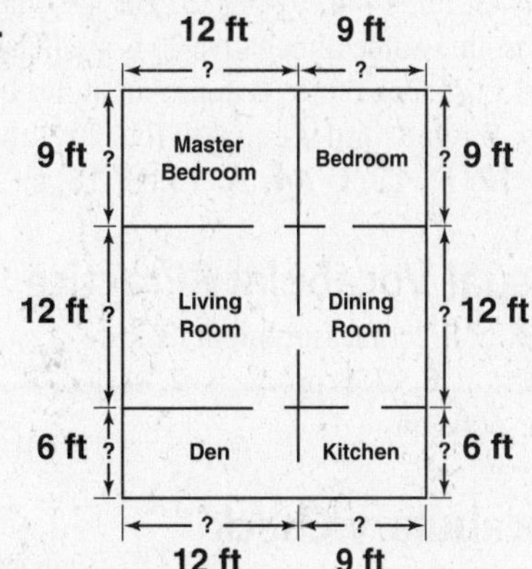

Activity Lab 5-6

Check students' work.

Reteaching 5-6

1. 2; 4; 200 m **2.** 2; 2; 100 m **3.** 2; 225; 4.5 cm **4.** 2; 150; 3 cm **5.** 3.5 cm

Name ______________________ Class ______________ Date ______________

Chapters 5–8 Answers (continued)

Enrichment 5-6

1a. 2,724 miles. **1b.** 290 in. **1c.** Sample answer: about 34,140 in. No, you can't place the model in the classroom since 43,140 in. is approximately equal to 948 yd, over 9 football fields in length. **2.** Sample answer: No, even if Earth is reduced to a speck of dust, the solar system is a circle with a 6-ft diameter. The sun and planets would be nearly invisible to the naked eye.

Puzzle 5-6

Sven's map:
a. 0.5 in.; 25 yd **b.** 1 in.; 50 yd **c.** 1.25 in.; 62.5 yd **d.** 1 in.; 50 yd **e.** 0.25 in.; 12.5 yd **f.** 1.5 in.; 75 yd; total = 275 yd
Rick's map:
w. 0.25 in.; 17.5 yd **x.** 2 in.; 140 yd **y.** 0.25 in.; 17.5 yd **z.** 1 in.; 70 yd; total = 245 yd
Rick's route is shorter.

Chapter 5A Graphic Organizer

1. Ratios, Rates, and Proportions **2.** 6 **3.** Using a Variable **4.** Check students' diagrams.

Chapter 5B Reading Comprehension

1. 74, 1994, 12.4 **2.** How fast were the winds of Hurricane Gordon? **3.** mi/h **4.** No, the winds need to be in excess of, or more than, 74 mi/h in order to be classified as a hurricane. Winds of 74 mi/h would not qualify as a hurricane. **5.** 1994 **6.** 12.4 mi/h **7.** $x - 12.4 = 74$ **8.** 86.4 mi/h **9.** a

Chapter 5C Reading/Writing Math Symbols

1. $\frac{a}{b}$, or $a : b$ **2.** $\frac{x}{4} < \frac{5}{2}$ **3.** $5n + 4$ **4.** $\frac{5}{24} \neq \frac{1}{5}$ **5.** x is less than or equal to 25. **6.** The absolute value of negative 20 is greater than the absolute value of 15. **7.** One ounce is approximately equal to twenty-eight grams. **8.** One third is equal to four twelfths. **9.** D **10.** G **11.** H **12.** F **13.** C **14.** A **15.** B **16.** E

Chapter 5D Visual Vocabulary Practice

1. equivalent ratios **2.** indirect measurement **3.** rate **4.** unit rate **5.** proportion **6.** cross products **7.** scale **8.** unit cost **9.** similar polygons

Chapter 5E Vocabulary Check

Check students' answers.

Chapter 5F Vocabulary Review Puzzle

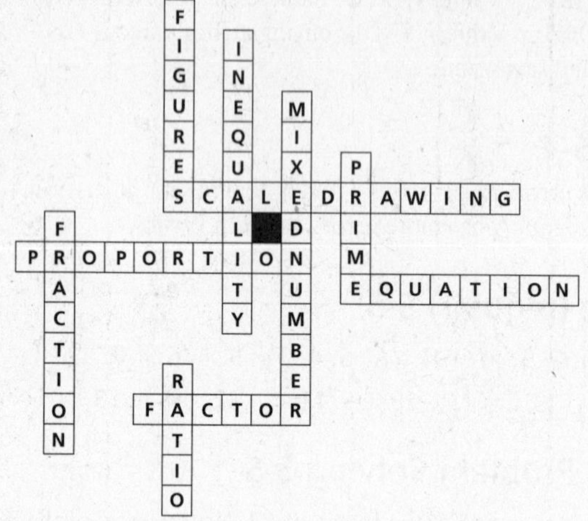

Chapter 5 Checkpoint Quiz 1

1. $\frac{4}{60}$; 4 to 60 **2.** $\frac{5}{2}$; 5 to 2 **3.** $\frac{3}{15}$; 3 to 15 **4.** 3 to 5 **5.** $\frac{5}{9}$ **6.** 1 : 4 **7.** \$0.21/oz; \$0.17/oz; \$0.125/oz; \$0.128/oz; 12 oz for \$1.50 is the better buy. **8.** \$144

Chapter 5 Checkpoint Quiz 2

1. yes **2.** no **3.** yes **4.** $x = 72$ **5.** $x = 9$ **6.** $x = 8$ **7.** 253 min **8.** $x = 10$ **9.** 30 ft

Chapter 5 Test (regular)

1. 7 : 8 **2.** no **3.** yes **4.** no **5.** 5 apples for \$1.20; the unit rate, \$.24 < \$.29 **6.** 0.42 km/min **7.** \$14.40/h or \$.24/min **8.** 0.6 curtain panels per day **9.** \$72; sample answer: work backwards **10.** 5 to 9; 5 : 9 **11.** 8 : 3, $\frac{8}{3}$ **12.** 12 to 15; $\frac{12}{15}$ **13.** $n = 5$ **14.** $x = 9.15$ **15.** $t = 16$ **16.** Yes; sample answer: The ratios form a proportion; $\frac{24 \text{ min}}{3 \text{ mi}} = \frac{16 \text{ min}}{2 \text{ mi}}$ **17.** about \$.10/oz **18.** $x = 26; y = 24$ **19.** 10 in. **20.** 240 km **21.** 64 km **22.** 336 km **23.** 10, 12, 14 **24.** Yes. Use 3 toothpicks to make one triangle. Use 6 toothpicks to make a second triangle with 2 toothpicks for each side.

Chapter 5 Test (below level)

1. 7 : 8 **2.** no **3.** yes **4.** 5 apples for \$1.20; the unit rate, \$.24 < \$.29 **5.** 0.42 km/min **6.** \$14.40/h or \$0.24/min **7.** 5 to 9; 5 : 9 **8.** 8 : 3, $\frac{8}{3}$ **9.** $n = 5$ **10.** $x = 9.15$ **11.** Yes; sample answer: The ratios form a proportion; $\frac{24 \text{ min}}{3 \text{ mi}} = \frac{16 \text{ min}}{2 \text{ mi}}$ **12.** about \$.10/oz **13.** $x = 26; y = 24$ **14.** 10 in. **15.** 240 km **16.** 64 km **17.** 10, 12, 14

Chapter 5 Alternative Assessment

Exercise	Points	Explanation
1.	2	About 1.6 mile; Martina judged in good shape

Chapters 5–8 Answers (continued)

	1	Answer outside of range or incorrect judgment
	0	No answer OR incorrect answer with no judgment
2.	2	Jeb is in poor shape. Response justified by proportional thinking.
	1	Answer is incorrect or poorly justified
	0	No answer OR incorrect answer without justification
3.	2	Both students are in about the same shape—fair to good; justified answer.
	1	Correct answer with justification given OR incorrect answer with justification
	0	No answer OR incorrect answer without justification
4.	2	Correct explanation of method; answer of 880 ft
	1	Correct method with incorrect answer OR correct answer without explanation
	0	No answer OR incorrect method with incorrect answer
5.	2	Correct graph of appropriate kind
	1	Graph incomplete, confusing, or incorrect
	0	No response OR inappropriate type of graph
Excursion	5	Plan includes goal and a conditioning schedule that increases distance or speed
	4	Plan includes goal and presents a conditioning schedule, but lacks concept of increasing difficulty
	3	Plan includes goal, but only provides a general idea of conditioning schedule
	2	Plan lacks goal, but includes conditioning schedule
	1	Plan lacks goal and conditioning schedule
	0	No response

Chapter 5 Cumulative Review

1. A **2.** J **3.** B **4.** J **5.** B **6.** G **7.** D **8.** J **9.** C **10.** J **11.** B **12.** F **13.** A **14.** J **15.** C **16.** H **17.** C **18.** H **19.** 120 **20.** If the cross products are not equal, the ratios do not form a proportion. Sample answer: change 39 to 38. **21.** $0.\overline{09}$; $0.\overline{18}$; $0.\overline{27}$; $0.\overline{36}$; prediction; $0.\overline{45}$; $0.\overline{54}$

Chapter 6

Practice (regular) 6-1

1. 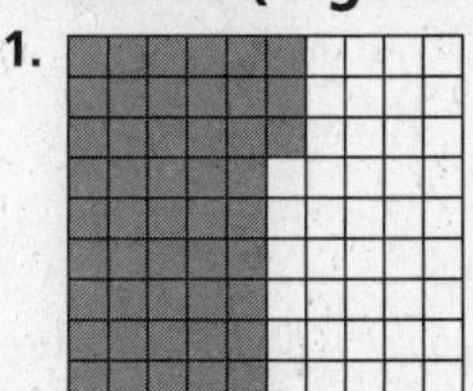 **2.** 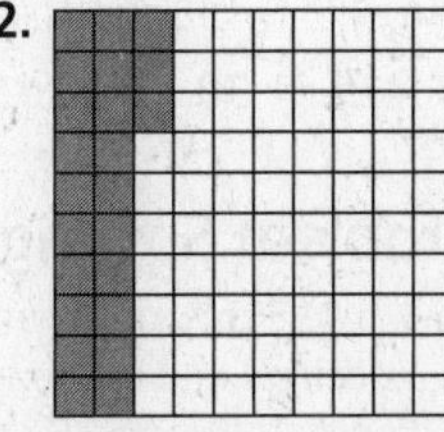

3. 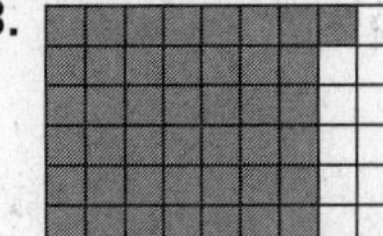

4. 80% **5.** 60% **6.** 90% **7.** 30% **8.** 24% **9.** 7% **10.** 18% **11.** 36% **12.** 40% **13.** 70% **14.** 16% **15.** 64% **16.** 55% **17.** 95% **18.** 54% **19.** 82% **20.** 36% **21.** 40% **22.** 75% **23.** $\frac{1}{2} + \frac{1}{4}$ **24.** $\frac{1}{2} + \frac{1}{8}$ **25.** Sample answer: $\frac{1}{2} + \frac{1}{3} + \frac{1}{15}$ **26.** $\frac{1}{2} + \frac{1}{12}$

Guided Problem Solving 6-1

1. Nineteen-twentieths of the troops had never before been in a battle. **2.** Find the percent of the troops that had previously been in a battle. **3.** $\frac{19}{20}$ **4.** $\frac{1}{20}$ **5.** 100 **6.** $\frac{5}{100}$ **7.** 5% **8.** 95%; 95% + 5% = 100%; yes **9.** 60%

Practice (adapted) 6-1

1. 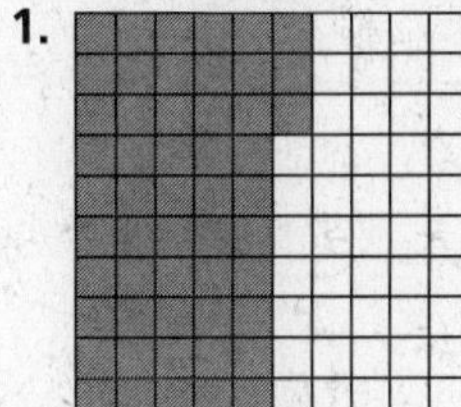 **2.** 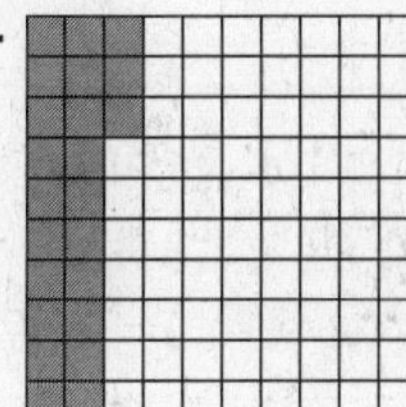

3. 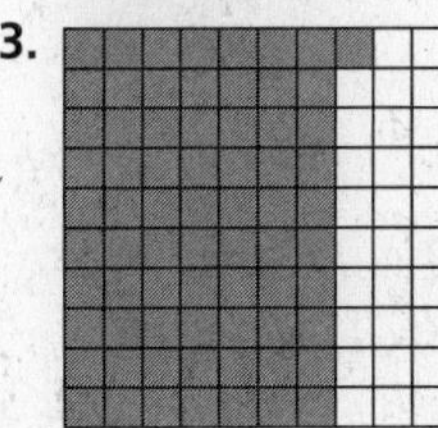

4. 80% **5.** 60% **6.** 90% **7.** 24% **8.** 7% **9.** 18% **10.** 40% **11.** 70% **12.** 16% **13.** 36% **14.** 40% **15.** 75% **16.** $\frac{1}{2} + \frac{1}{4}$ **17.** $\frac{1}{2} + \frac{1}{8}$ **18.** $\frac{1}{2} + \frac{1}{12}$

Activity Lab 6-1

1–2. Check students' work. **3b.** 20; 10; 4; 1 **3c.** $\frac{20}{100}$; $\frac{10}{50}$; $\frac{4}{20}$; $\frac{1}{5}$ **4.** Use the 100-counter model to see how many counters are $\frac{1}{5}$ of 100 counters; 20% **5.** It is the same, because 0.20 is equal to 20% and $\frac{1}{5}$. **6.** 60, 80, 40; 30, 40, 20; 12, 16, 8; 3, 4, 2 **7.** 60% = 0.60 = $\frac{3}{5}$; $\frac{4}{5}$ = 0.80 = 80%; 0.40 = 40% = $\frac{2}{5}$

Reteaching 6-1

1. 30% **2.** 40% **3.** 55% **4.** 40% **5.** 65% **6.** 45% **7.** 60% **8.** 17% **9.** 72% **10.** 80% **11.** 25% **12.** 4% **13.** 35%

Chapters 5–8 Answers (continued)

14. 84% **15.** 30% **16.** 40% **17.** 99% **18.** 55% **19.** 10% **20.** 78% **21.** 95%

Enrichment 6-1

1. a **2.** d **3.** c **4.** c **5.** d **6.** b
Explanations will vary.

Puzzle 6-1

1. P **2.** I **3.** N **4.** E **5.** A **6.** P **7.** P **8.** L **9.** E **10.** S
PINEAPPLES

Practice (regular) 6-2

1. $\frac{13}{20}$; 0.65 **2.** $\frac{3}{8}$; 0.375 **3.** $\frac{4}{5}$; 0.8 **4.** $\frac{1}{4}$; 0.25 **5.** $\frac{9}{50}$; 0.18 **6.** $\frac{23}{50}$; 0.46 **7.** $\frac{87}{100}$; 0.87 **8.** $\frac{2}{25}$; 0.08 **9.** $\frac{43}{100}$; 0.43 **10.** $\frac{11}{20}$; 0.55 **11.** $\frac{47}{50}$; 0.94 **12.** $\frac{9}{25}$; 0.36 **13.** 53.3% **14.** 14% **15.** 56% **16.** 4.1% **17.** 37.5% **18.** 58.3% **19.** 38.7% **20.** 28.3% **21.** 22.2%

22.

1. 1	2. 3	4		
	4		3. 5	4. 3
5. 5	6	6. 5		2
0		7. 1	8. 1	4
	9. 4	5	6	
10. 6	3		11. 5	12. 5
13. 5	8			4
14. 9	5	15. 5		3
		16. 6	0	5

Guided Problem Solving 6-2

1. Write your grades in order from least to greatest. **2.** Write the numbers as percents or as fractions with common denominators. **3.** the number of quizzes taken **4.** 85%, 90%, 80%, 92%, 84%, 79% **5.** 79%, 80%, 84%, 85%, 90%, 92% **6.** 510 **7.** 85% **8.** yes **9.** 60%, 65%, 75%, 80%, 81%, 89%; 75%

Practice (adapted) 6-2

1. $\frac{13}{20}$; 0.65 **2.** $\frac{3}{8}$; 0.375 **3.** $\frac{4}{5}$; 0.8 **4.** $\frac{9}{50}$; 0.18 **5.** $\frac{23}{50}$; 0.46 **6.** $\frac{87}{100}$; 0.87 **7.** $\frac{43}{100}$; 0.43 **8.** $\frac{11}{20}$; 0.55 **9.** $\frac{47}{50}$; 0.94 **10.** 53.3% **11.** 14% **12.** 4.1% **13.** 37.5% **14.** 38.7% **15.** 28.3%

16.

1. 1	2. 3	4		
	4		3. 5	4. 3
5. 5	6	6. 5		2
0		7. 1	8. 1	4
	9. 4	5	6	
10. 6	3		11. 5	5

Activity Lab 6-2

1. Stock 1: $3\frac{1}{8}$; Stock 2: $3\frac{3}{4}$ **2.** 24% increase **3.** 30% decrease **4.** On Friday, Stock 1 increased 41% from Thursday's price. **5.** \$3.50 **6.** \$4.35 **7.** about 14.2% **8.** Check students' work.

Reteaching 6-2

1. 75% **2.** 48% **3.** 80% **4.** 575% **5.** $\frac{9}{20}$ **6.** $\frac{3}{5}$ **7.** $\frac{4}{25}$ **8.** $\frac{1}{4}$ **9.** $\frac{3}{8}$ **10.** $\frac{99}{100}$ **11.** $\frac{2}{5}$ **12.** $\frac{43}{50}$ **13.** 0.35 **14.** 0.48 **15.** 0.08 **16.** 0.12 **17.** 0.055 **18.** 0.006 **19.** 39% **20.** 73.5% **21.** 34% **22.** 40% **23.** 60% **24.** 600%

Enrichment 6-2

1. 50% **2.** 45% **3.** 65% **4.** 15% **5.** 27% **6.** 24% **7.** 9% **8.** 21% **9.** 18% **10.** 6%

11.

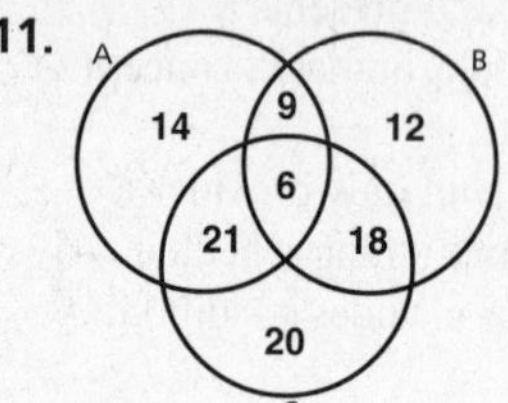

Puzzle 6-2

$50\% = 0.5 = \frac{1}{2}$; $75\% = 0.75 = \frac{3}{4}$; $62.5\% = 0.625 = \frac{5}{8}$; $80\% = 0.80 = \frac{20}{25}$; $87.5\% = 0.875 = \frac{7}{8}$; $25\% = 0.25 = \frac{3}{12}$

Practice (regular) 6-3

1. C **2.** B **3.** A **4.** C **5.** B **6.** A **7.** C **8.** A **9.** $>$ **10.** $<$ **11.** $<$ **12.** $>$ **13.** $=$ **14.** $>$ **15.** 140% **16.** 137% **17.** 0.8% **18.** 525% **19.** 170% **20.** 162.5% **21.** 185% **22.** 1.4% **23.** 112.5% **24.** 0.3% **25.** 180% **26.** 0.25% **27.** 530% **28.** 0.41% **29.** 8.3% **30.** 0.09% **31.** 83% **32.** 2,000% **33.** 1.75; $1\frac{3}{4}$ **34.** 1.2; $1\frac{1}{5}$ **35.** 0.004; $\frac{1}{250}$ **36.** 0.00625; $\frac{1}{160}$ **37.** 7.5; $7\frac{1}{2}$ **38.** 8.25; $\frac{33}{4}$ **39.** about 0.89% **40.** about 0.31%

Guided Problem Solving 6-3

1. The snow pack was 126% of the average snow pack. **2.** Write the percent as a decimal and as a fraction in simplest form.

Name ______________________ Class ______________ Date ______________

Chapters 5–8 Answers (continued)

3. Divide by 100. **4.** 126; 100 **5.** $1\frac{13}{50}$ **6.** 1.26 **7.** 126; yes **8.** $\frac{33}{50}$

Practice (adapted) 6-3

1. C **2.** B **3.** A **4.** B **5.** A **6.** C **7.** $>$ **8.** $<$ **9.** $<$ **10.** $>$ **11.** $=$ **12.** $>$ **13.** 140% **14.** 137% **15.** 525% **16.** 170% **17.** 185% **18.** 1.4% **19.** 0.3% **20.** 180% **21.** 530% **22.** 0.41% **23.** 0.09% **24.** 83% **25.** 1.75; $1\frac{3}{4}$ **26.** 1.2; $1\frac{1}{5}$ **27.** 0.004; $\frac{1}{250}$ **28.** about 0.89%

Activity Lab 6-3

1. 1.3, $1\frac{3}{10}$ **2.** 0.006; $\frac{3}{500}$ **3.** 4.21; $4\frac{21}{100}$ **4.** 61.72; $61\frac{18}{25}$ **5.** 125% **6.** 231% **7.** 859% **8.** 1,296%

Reteaching 6-3

1. $\frac{1}{10{,}000}$; 0.0001 **2.** $\frac{9}{2000}$; 0.0045 **3.** $\frac{1}{500}$; 0.002 **4.** $\frac{67}{10{,}000}$; 0.0067 **5.** $\frac{3}{2}$; $1\frac{1}{2}$; 1.5 **6.** $\frac{9}{4}$; $2\frac{1}{4}$; 2.25 **7.** $\frac{93}{50}$; $1\frac{43}{50}$; 1.86 **8.** $\frac{201}{100}$; $2\frac{1}{100}$; 2.01

Enrichment 6-3

1. about $\frac{1}{2}$% **2.** $\frac{0.5}{100}$ **3.** $\frac{5}{1000}$ **4.** Sample answer: About 5 bats in a group of 1000 bats have rabies. **5.** $\frac{1}{200}$ **6.** 200 bats **7.** Sample answer: Write $\frac{1}{2}$% as a fraction. Then find an equivalent fraction with a numerator of 1. **8.** Sample answer: No, it is only an average. Some groups will have more than one rabid bat and others will have none.

Puzzle 6-3

$\frac{67}{20} = 335\%$; $\frac{129}{50} = 258\%$; $\frac{19}{8} = 237.5\%$; $\frac{23}{200} = 11.5\%$; $\frac{75}{20} = 375\%$; $\frac{2}{329} \approx 0.61\%$; $\frac{6}{767} \approx 0.78\%$; $\frac{35}{80} = 43.75\%$; $\frac{45}{13} \approx 346\%$; $\frac{59}{33} = 178.8\%$

The state of Rhode Island is 0.24% of the size of Alaska.

Practice (regular) 6-4

1. 112 **2.** 84 **3.** 4.5 **4.** 28 **5.** 20 **6.** 40 **7.** 80 **8.** 4 **9.** 150 **10.** 16.8 **11.** 54 **12.** 15 **13.** 17 **14.** 60 **15.** 19.665 **16.** 67.2 **17.** 72 **18.** 50.4 **19a.** 19 lb **19b.** 1 lb **19c.** 10% **19d.** 10 lb **20.** $120

Guided Problem Solving 6-4

1. 17,000 forest fires; 40% **2.** Find 40% of 17,000. **3.** You can multiply 17,000 by the equivalent decimal to find the percentage. **4.** 40% **5.** 0.4 **6.** 17,000 **7.** $17{,}000 \cdot 0.4 = 6{,}800$ **8.** 6,800 **9.** $17{,}000 \cdot 0.5 = 8{,}500$; yes **10.** 24 shirts

Practice (adapted) 6-4

1. 112 **2.** 84 **3.** 4.5 **4.** 28 **5.** 20 **6.** 40 **7.** 16.8 **8.** 54 **9.** 17 **10.** 60 **11a.** 19 lb **11b.** 1 lb **11c.** 10% **12.** $120

Activity Lab 6-4

1. What is 35% of 47; 16.5 **2.** What is 75% of 4?; 3 **3.** What is 25% of 80?; 20 **4.** What is 24% of 40?; 9.6 **5.** What is 3% of 90?; 2.7 **6.** What is 20% of 55?; 11 **7.** What is 8% of 74?; 5.9 **8.** What is 10% of 15?; 1.5 **9.** What is 16% of 36?; 5.8 **10.** What is 1% of 100?; 1

Reteaching 6-4

1. 0.15; 0.15; 12 **2.** 0.04; 0.04; 2.8 **3.** 0.7; 0.7; 14 **4.** 8 **5.** 16 **6.** 40 **7.** 6.3 **8.** 1.32 **9.** 14 **10.** 5.6 **11.** 20.68 **12.** 16.5 **13.** 36 **14.** 77 **15.** 320 **16.** 113.1 **17.** 74.8 **18.** 574 **19.** $63 **20.** $1,468.50

Enrichment 6-4

1a. 15 **1b.** 12 **1c.** 6 **1d.** 9

2.

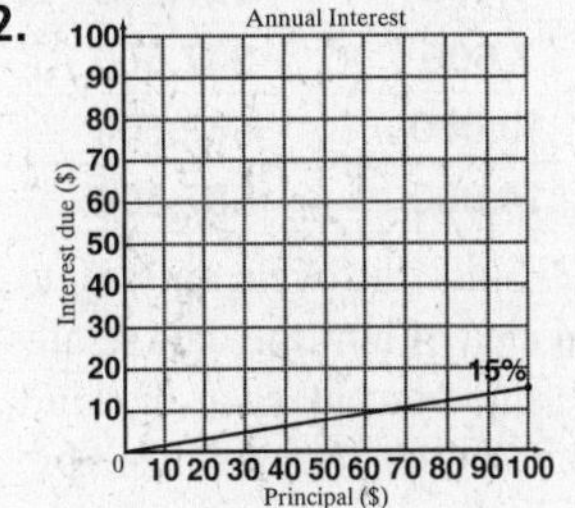

3. Sample answer: It is a line that has a positive slope. It does not have a steep slope. **4.** Sample answer: Find the point on the graph that is above 65.2. Interest is the corresponding value on the vertical axis. The interest is about $10.00. **5.** Sample answer: To help you decide if you can afford the interest on a specific loan. **6–7.** Check students' answers.

Puzzle 6-4

$\frac{1}{25}$; 0.2; $\frac{1}{50}$; $\frac{1}{4}$; $\frac{1}{10}$; 39%
OREGON

Practice (regular) 6-5

1. 80 **2.** 148.75 **3.** 55.6% **4.** 95 **5.** 21.44 **6.** 60 **7.** 300% **8.** 102 **9.** 9.6 **10.** $74\frac{2}{3}$ **11.** $160 **12.** 128 people **13.** 560 employees **14.** about 55%

Guided Problem Solving 6-5

1. 9 books; 55% **2.** Find how many books the library has on the topic. **3.** 45% **4.** Sample answer: b **5.** 9 books **6.** $\frac{9}{b} = \frac{45}{100}$ **7.** $b = 20$ **8.** 20 books **9.** $0.55(20) = 11$; $11 + 9 = 20$; yes **10.** 15,000 people

Practice (adapted) 6-5

1. 80 **2.** 148.75 **3.** 55.6% **4.** 95 **5.** 21.44 **6.** 60 **7.** 300% **8.** 102 **9.** $160 **10.** 128 people **11.** 560 employees **12.** 55.13%

Chapters 5–8 Answers (continued)

Activity Lab 6-5

1a. 18 **1b.** 4.5 **2a.** 11.25 **2b.** 4.5 **3a.** 10% **3b.** 4.5 **4.** Sample answer: Each method uses the same factors and same products. The order in which the factors are multiplied differs. However, regardless of the order in which each problem is done, the answer is the same. **5.** Sample answer: Since the order doesn't matter, first multiply the two factors that are easy to compute mentally, such as 50% of 200 (100). Then find 140% of 100 (140). **6.** 600 **7.** 900

Reteaching 6-5

1. n; 12; 16 **2.** n; n; 82; 410 **3.** 9; $5n$; $100 \cdot 9$; 180 **4.** 60; 60; 1,200 **5.** 100; 4.8; 100; 80 **6.** 170; 51; $170n$; $100 \cdot 51$; 30 **7.** $n = 75$ **8.** $n = 55$ **9.** $n = 150$ **10.** 92.4 **11.** 60 **12.** 80%

Enrichment 6-5

1.

Kind of Novel	Percent of Community	Number of People in Community	Budget
Fantasy	10%	4,000	$25,000
Historical	11%	4,400	$27,500
Science Fiction	19%	7,600	$47,500
Romance	25%	10,000	$62,500
Mystery	35%	14,000	$87,500

2–4. Sample answers are given. **2.** Since the circle represents 100% of the whole, it gives a visual idea of how the data relates to the whole. **3.** Would spend the same percentage as the kind of books preferred. **4.** Use children's books recommended by various national groups. Survey results probably are not valid for children, since adults are more likely to be surveyed.

Puzzle 6-5

H. 79.7% **G.** 83.3% **T.** 77.8% **E.** 96.0% **I.** 93.9%
EIGHT

Practice (regular) 6-6

1. 75% **2.** 20.8 **3.** 96 **4.** 66.7% **5.** 39.8 **6.** 340 **7.** 20.2% **8.** 475.8 **9.** 135.5 **10.** 59.5% **11.** 90.7 **12.** 875 **13a.** 85% **13b.** $7.61 **14.** 360,000 people

Guided Problem Solving 6-6

1. 72 cookies; 20% of the cookies **2.** Find how many cookies are at the bake sale. **3.** *is* **4.** Sample answer: c **5.** 72 **6.** $0.2c$ **7.** $0.2c = 72$ **8.** $c = 360$ **9.** 360 cookies **10.** $0.2(360) = 72$; yes **11.** 40 cards

Practice (adapted) 6-6

1. 75% **2.** 20.8 **3.** 96 **4.** 66.7% **5.** 39.8 **6.** 340 **7.** 20.2% **8.** 475.8 **9a.** 85% **9b.** $7.61 **10.** 360,000 people

Activity Lab 6-6

1a. 15 **1b.** 12 **1c.** 6 **1d.** 9 **2–3.** Check students' work. **4.** Sample answer: Locate 62 on the x-axis. Draw a vertical line up from this point until it intersects the graphed line. Then draw a horizontal line to the y-axis. The value on the y-axis is 15% of 62. **5–7.** Check students' work.

Reteaching 6-6

1. $0.09 \cdot 150 = n$ **2.** 13.5 **3.** 120 **4.** 61.5 **5.** 256 **6.** p% of 75 is 12 **7.** 16% **8.** 30% **9.** 70%

Enrichment 6-6

1. 120 ears **2.** 78 ears **3.** percent of yellow ears, white ears **4.** 100% **5.** $\frac{78}{120} = \frac{x}{100}$ **6.** subtraction **7.** 65% **8.** 35% **9.** $120p = 42$; $p = 0.35 = 35\%$ **10.** $\frac{120 - 78}{120 + x} = 0.28$; $x = 30$ ears

Puzzle 6-6

1. $0.35 \cdot 900 = x$; $x = 315$ **2.** $0.25x = 1{,}554$; $x = 6{,}216$ **3.** $0.20 \cdot 4{,}985 = x$; $x = 997$ **4.** $0.80x = 35{,}012$; $x = 43{,}765$ **5.** $0.02 \cdot 404{,}750 = x$; $x = 8{,}095$ **6.** $0.63x = 567$; $x = 900$

Practice (regular) 6-7

1. $18.73 **2.** $22.88 **3.** $56.43 **4.** $218.78 **5.** $92.44 **6.** Sample answer: $1.95 **7.** Sample answer: $2.70 **8.** Sample answer: $2.25 **9.** $30 **10.** $6,400 **11.** $30 **12.** $384 **13.** $1,120 **14.** $640 **15.** $1,490 **16.** $1,492.50 **17.** $111.82 **18.** You and your sister each earn $24.50.

Guided Problem Solving 6-7

1. 6%; the first $500; 8%; sales over $500; $800 sale **2.** a percent of the amount of a sale **3.** addition and multiplication **4.** $300 **5.** $30 **6.** $24 **7.** $54 **8.** $50 and $30; $25; $55; yes **9.** $170

Practice (adapted) 6-7

1. $18.73 **2.** $22.88 **3.** $56.43 **4.** $218.78 **5.** Sample answer: $2.70 **6.** Sample answer: $2.25 **7.** $30 **8.** $6,400 **9.** $30 **10.** $384 **11.** $1,120 **12.** $640 **13.** $111.82 **14.** $92.44

Activity Lab 6-7

Store	Price	Discount	Tax	Shipping	Total Cost
1	$199.99	15%	4%	5%	$185.63
2	$250.00	20%	10%	No Cost	$220.00
3	$229.00	10%	5%	2%	$220.73
4	$179.00	5%	7%	15%	$209.25
5	$150.00	None	12%	20%	$201.60

1. Sample answer: Daniela should purchase the bike from store #1, because store #1 has the lowest price after the discount, taxes, and shipping are calculated. **2.** Sample answer: Even

Name ______________ Class ______________ Date ______________

Chapters 5–8 Answers (continued)

though store #5 had the lowest price on the bicycle, it offered no discount, and the tax and shipping charges were much higher than at the other stores.

Reteaching 6-7

1. \$10.40 **2.** \$9.21 **3.** \$65.27 **4.** \$340.80 **5.** \$6.80 **6.** \$28.76 **7.** \$180 **8.** \$6,000 **9.** \$96 **10.** \$132

Enrichment 6-7

1. \$12,000 **2.** \$200 **3.** \$125,000 **4.** $\$5{,}000 \cdot 0.04 + \$495{,}000 \cdot 0.08 = \$39{,}800$ **5.** \$51,800 **6.** Sample answer: Income is set and not dependent upon the whims of the economy or how competitors react. **7.** Sample answer: Potential income is much less than the potential income at the Supply House. **8.** Sample answer: Office Stores, Inc. for steady income and to gain experience. Once experienced, you can change jobs.

Puzzle 6-7

1. 2	7	2. 8	.	4. 2	5				
0		.		1					
.		0		2			6. 5		
7		3. 4	7	2	.	5	0		
9				.			3		
				1			7. .	7	0
		5. 5	.	2	5		0		
							0		

Practice (regular) 6-8

1. 30% decrease **2.** 8.3% increase **3.** 22.9% decrease **4.** 773% increase **5.** 65% decrease **6.** 40% decrease

7. Enrollment in Center City Schools From 1995 to 2000

Year	Enrollment	Change from Last year (number of students)	Change from Last Year (%)	Increase or Decrease
1995	18,500	–	–	–
1996	19,300	800	4%	increase
1997	19,700	400	2%	increase
1998	19,500	200	1%	decrease
1999	19,870	370	2%	increase
2000	19,200	670	3%	decrease

Guided Problem Solving 6-8

1. 1,200 and 900 **2.** last season **3.** Find the percent of change. **4.** 300 yd **5.** $\frac{(1{,}200 - 900)}{1{,}200} = \frac{x}{100}$ **6.** $1{,}200x = 30{,}000$ **7.** 1,200 **8.** 25% **9.** decrease **10.** It is a decrease because the number of yards gained this season is less than the number of yards gained last season. **11.** 60%; an increase

Practice (adapted) 6-8

1. 30% decrease **2.** 8.3% increase **3.** 22.9% decrease **4.** 773% increase **5.** 65% decrease

6. Enrollment in Center City Schools From 1995 to 2000

Year	Enrollment	Change from Last year (number of students)	Change from Last Year (%)	Increase or Decrease
1995	18,500	–	–	–
1996	19,300	800	4%	increase
1997	19,700	400	2%	increase
1998	19,500	200	1%	decrease
1999	19,870	370	2%	increase
2000	19,200	670	3%	decrease

Activity Lab 6-8

1a. 0.58 cm **1b.** decrease **1c.** 29% **2.** 49% decrease **3.** 24% increase **4.** 28% decrease **5.** Tuesday and Wednesday; Friday and Saturday **6.** Check students' answers.

Reteaching 6-8

1. 20; 20; 20; 50; increase of 50% **2.** 6; 6; 6; 40; decrease of 40% **3.** 0.5; 0.5; 100; $0.5 \cdot 100$; 125; increase of 125% **4.** 150% **5.** 10% **6.** 100% **7.** 25% **8.** 40% **9.** 10% **10.** 25% **11.** 43% **12.** 50% **13.** 10% **14.** 4% **15.** 1%

Enrichment 6-8

1. percent increase **2.** 60 ft. by 60 ft. **3.** 50% longer **4.**

Baseball

Softball

5. a **6.** 90 ft. **7.** $A = s^2$ **8.** 3,600 ft^2 **9.** 8,100 ft^2 **10.** 4,500 ft^2 **11.** 125% **12.** Sample answer: Solve a simpler problem, make a table.

Puzzle 6-8

Sunday: 71°F; Monday: 85°F; Tuesday: 72°F; Wednesday: 68°F; Thursday: 80°F; Friday: 78°F; Saturday: 65°F

Chapter 6A Graphic Organizer

1. Percents **2.** 8 **3.** Working Backward **4.** Check students' diagrams.

Chapter 6B Reading Comprehension

1. The graphs show why people purchase insurance and who buys insurance when renting a car. **2.** wanted extra coverage **3.** 100% **4.** 18–24 **5.** 35–54 **6.** weren't sure existing policies provided enough **7.** a

Chapter 6C Reading/Writing Math Symbols

1. 3 ft : 1 yd **2.** 47.6% **3.** $37\% > \frac{1}{3}$ **4.** 1 m : 100 cm **5.** 106% **6.** $\frac{1}{4} < 26\%$ **7.** 8 qt : 2 gal **8.** 93.32% **9.** $|-16|$ **10.** $\frac{78}{100}$ **11.** The absolute value of negative 7.3 is 7.3. **12.** thirty and

Name ______________________ Class ______________ Date ______________

Chapters 5–8 Answers (continued)

8 hundredths percent **13.** 50 percent is greater than two fifths. **14.** 2 hours to 120 minutes **15.** 55 divided by 100 **16.** one tenth is less than 12 percent.

Chapter 6D Visual Vocabulary Practice

1. calculate **2.** graph **3.** represent **4.** solve **5.** explain **6.** verify **7.** pattern **8.** substitute **9.** model

Chapter 6E Vocabulary Check

Check students' answers.

Chapter 6F Vocabulary Review

1. F **2.** C **3.** A **4.** E **5.** B **6.** D **7.** K **8.** J **9.** L **10.** M **11.** H **12.** G

Chapter 6 Checkpoint Quiz 1

1. 0.6; $\frac{3}{5}$ **2.** 1.25; $1\frac{1}{4}$ **3.** 0.008; $\frac{1}{125}$ **4.** 90% **5.** 112.5% **6.** 0.8% **7.** 33%, 0.36, $\frac{2}{3}$, $1\frac{1}{3}$ **8.** 5%, 0.052, $\frac{1}{5}$, 0.5 **9.** 0.13, 0.13, 113%, $1\frac{2}{3}$ **10.** 0.00759, 0.075, $\frac{1}{2}$, 75%

Chapter 6 Checkpoint Quiz 2

1. 25% **2.** 60% **3.** 6 **4.** 12.5% **5.** 62.5% **6.** 160 **7.** 20% **8.** 40.5 **9.** \$20 **10.** \$158.61

Chapter 6 Test (regular)

1. 0.04 **2.** 60% **3.** 2.25 **4.** 0.32% **5.** 0.0072 **6.** 520% **7.** $\frac{17}{20}$ **8.** 60% **9.** $\frac{3}{50}$ **10.** 37.5% **11.** $3\frac{1}{2}$ **12.** 160%

13. 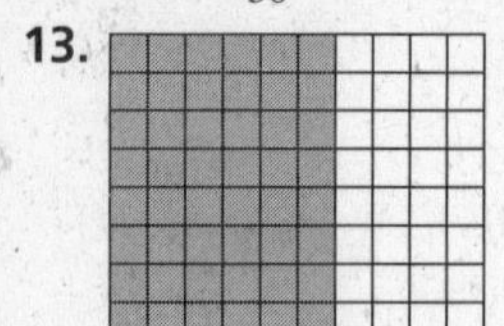 **14.** 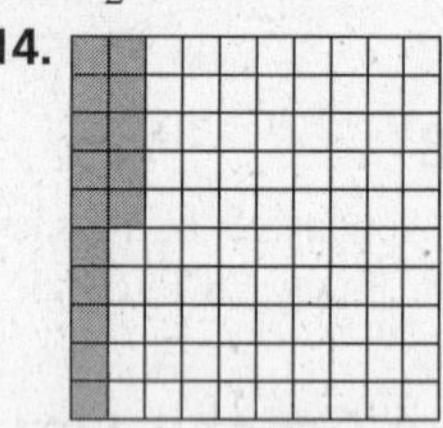

15. 52.5% **16.** 56 **17.** $63 = 0.25x; x = 252$ **18.** $0.2x = 80; x = 400$ **19.** $72x = 12; x = 16\frac{2}{3}\%$ **20.** $0.12 \cdot 600 = x; x = 72$ **21.** 20.3%; decrease **22.** 9.6%; increase **23.** 15% **24.** \$25,000 **25.** 980 employees **26.** about 15% **27.** 6% **28.** 492 tickets

Chapter 6 Test (below level)

1. 0.04 **2.** 60% **3.** 0.32% **4.** 0.0072 **5.** $\frac{17}{20}$ **6.** 60% **7.** 37.5% **8.** $3\frac{1}{2}$ **9.** 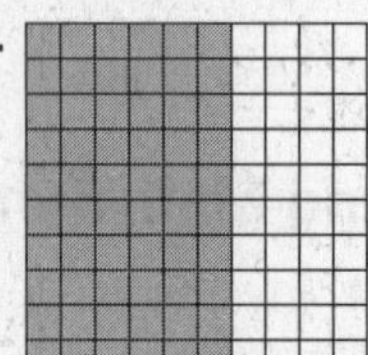 **10.** 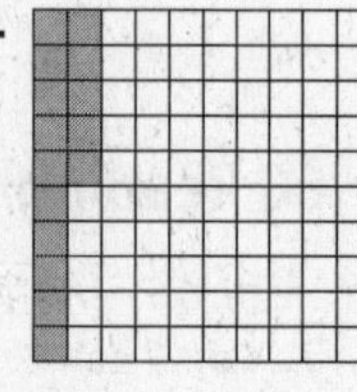

11. 52.5% **12.** 56 **13.** $63 = 0.25x; x = 252$ **14.** $0.2x = 80; x = 400$ **15.** $72x = 12; x = 16\frac{2}{3}\%$ **16.** 20.3%; decrease **17.** 9.6%; increase **18.** 15% **19.** 980 employees **20.** about 15% **21.** 492 tickets

Chapter 6 Alternative Assessment

	1%	2%	3%	4%	5%	6%	7%	8%	9%
\$1,000	\$1,010	\$1,020	\$1,030	\$1,040	\$1,050	\$1,060	\$1,070	\$1,080	\$1,090
\$2,000	\$2,020	\$2,040	\$2,060	\$2,080	\$2,100	\$2,120	\$2,140	\$2,160	\$2,180
\$3,000	\$3,030	\$3,060	\$3,090	\$3,120	\$3,150	\$3,180	\$3,210	\$3,240	\$3,270
\$4,000	\$4,040	\$4,080	\$4,120	\$4,160	\$4,200	\$4,240	\$4,280	\$4,320	\$4,360
\$5,000	\$5,050	\$5,100	\$5,150	\$5,200	\$5,250	\$5,300	\$5,350	\$5,400	\$5,450
\$6,000	\$6,060	\$6,120	\$6,180	\$6,240	\$6,300	\$6,360	\$6,420	\$6,480	\$6,540
\$7,000	\$7,070	\$7,140	\$7,210	\$7,280	\$7,350	\$7,420	\$7,490	\$7,560	\$7,630
\$8,000	\$8,080	\$8,160	\$8,240	\$8,320	\$8,400	\$8,480	\$8,560	\$8,640	\$8,720
\$9,000	\$9,090	\$9,180	\$9,270	\$9,360	\$9,450	\$9,540	\$9,630	\$9,720	\$9,810

Exercise	Points	Explanation
1.	2	All 75 parts of the table are correct. See table for answers.
	1	At least 37 of the 75 parts of the table are correct.
	0	No answer OR less than 37 of the 75 parts incorrect
2.	1	0.01, 0.02, 0.03, 0.04, 0.05, 0.06, 0.07, 0.08, 0.09
	0	No answer or some are incorrect
3.	2	Find the number midway between \$1,010 and \$1,020; find the number midway between \$5,400 and \$5,450.
	1	One answer is incorrect.
	0	No answer or both are incorrect
4.	2	Find the number midway between \$1,010 and \$2,020; find the number midway between \$6,360 and \$7,420.
	1	One answer is incorrect.
	0	No answer or both are incorrect
5.	2	Sample answer: In the \$1,000 row, add the amounts for 1% and 9%; In the \$5,000 row, multiply the amount for 6% by 2
	1	One answer is correct.
	0	No answer or both are incorrect
6.	1	$S = I + (I \times R)$
	0	No answer or answer is incorrect
Excursion		Sample answer: Jocelyn needs about \$15,000 for her first year at college. Use $S = I + (I \times R)$ to figure how much Jocelyn's grandparents need to give her. $\$15{,}000 = I + (I \times 0.2)$ $I = \$12{,}500$ $\$15{,}000 = I + (I \times 0.3)$ $I = \$11{,}538.46$ $\$15{,}000 = I + (I \times 0.4)$ $I = \$10{,}714.29$ $\$15{,}000 = I + (I \times 0.5)$ $I = \$10{,}000$ $\$15{,}000 = I + (I \times 0.6)$ $I = \$9{,}375$
	5	There is a well thought out estimate, a well-organized table and the connection is made between interest and amount of money saved total.

Chapters 5–8 Answers (continued)

4 There is a well thought out estimate, the table is organized, the connection is made between interest and amount of money saved total, but the answer is not quite organized.

3 There is a well thought out estimate, the table is organized, the connection is made between interest and amount of money saved total, but the answer is not quite organized and some of the calculations are incorrect.

2 The estimate is not realistic, the answer lacks organization, or there are quite a few calculation errors.

1 The estimate is not realistic, the answer lacks organization, and there are several calculation errors.

0 No response

Chapter 6 Cumulative Review

1. A **2.** G **3.** B **4.** H **5.** D **6.** F **7.** C **8.** H **9.** D **10.** J **11.** B **12.** F **13.** D **14.** J **15.** C **16.** H **17.** D **18.** J **19.** A **20.** J **21.** C **22.** H **23.** B **24.** H **25.** A **26.** 42% **27.** Since $\frac{8}{24}$, or $\frac{1}{3}$, relates to no precise decimal or percent, using a fraction would be the only exact measurement. **28.** Decimals and percents are most alike, because they are both fractions with denominators that are powers of ten.

Chapter 7

Practice (regular) 7-1

1. parallel **2.** parallel **3.** parallel **4.** intersecting **5.** parallel **6.** intersecting **7.** parallel **8.** $\overleftrightarrow{CD}$ and $\overleftrightarrow{EF}$ **9.** Sample answer: $\overrightarrow{HG}$ **10.** Sample answer: A, G, B **11.** Sample answer: $\overrightarrow{AB}$, $\overrightarrow{CD}$ **12.** Sample answer: $\overleftrightarrow{AB}$, $\overleftrightarrow{CD}$

13. Sample answer:

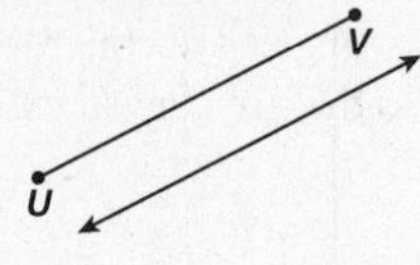

14. Sample answer:

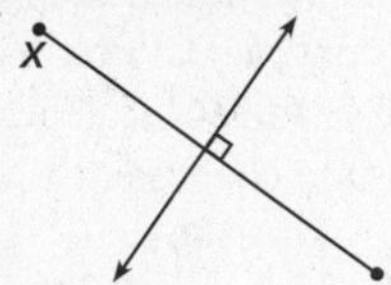

Guided Problem Solving 7-1

1. A ladder is a device that helps you reach things that are high off the ground. Check students' drawings. **2.** The rungs are the steps that you climb. Check students' drawings. **3.** Determine if the rungs are parallel, intersecting, or skew. **4.** no **5.** yes **6.** no **7.** no **8.** yes **9.** Parallel lines are lines in the same plane that do not intersect; yes **10.** Answers will vary.

Practice (adapted) 7-1

1. parallel **2.** parallel **3.** parallel **4.** intersecting **5.** $\overleftrightarrow{CD}$ and $\overleftrightarrow{EF}$ **6.** Sample answer: $\overline{HG}$ **7.** Sample answer: A, G, B

8. Sample answer: $\overrightarrow{AB}$, $\overrightarrow{CD}$

9.

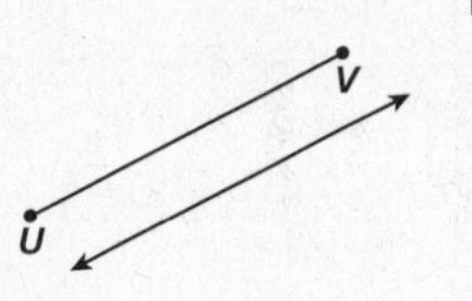

10.

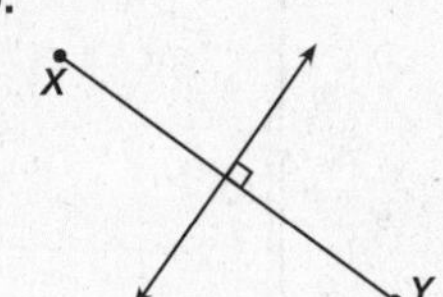

Activity Lab 7-1

1–3, 5.

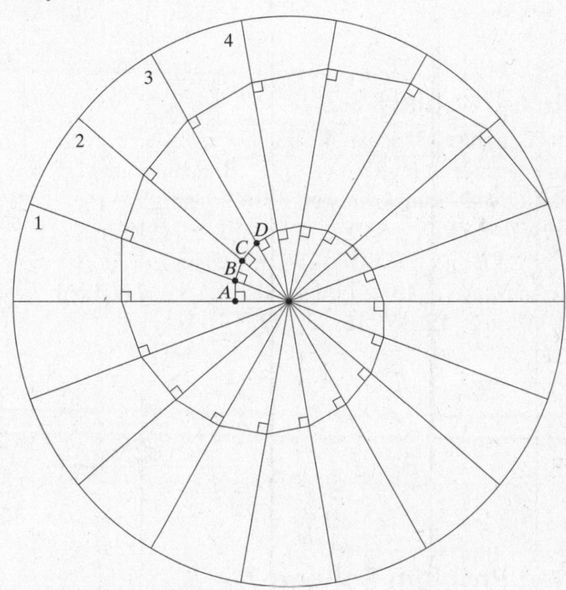

4. Check students' work.

Reteaching 7-1

1–3. Sample answers are given. **1.** $\overline{XZ}$, $\overline{WZ}$, $\overline{WX}$, $\overline{XY}$, $\overline{YZ}$, $\overline{ZM}$, or $\overline{MX}$ **2.** M, W, X, Y, or Z **3.** $\overleftrightarrow{WX}$ and $\overleftrightarrow{XY}$, $\overleftrightarrow{WZ}$ and $\overleftrightarrow{ZY}$ **4.** $\overleftrightarrow{WZ}$ and $\overleftrightarrow{XY}$, **5.**

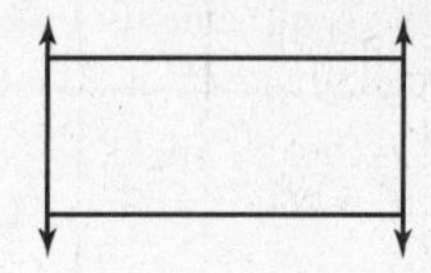

5a. parallel **5b.** intersecting

6. A B

7. B C

Enrichment 7-1

1. Sample answer:

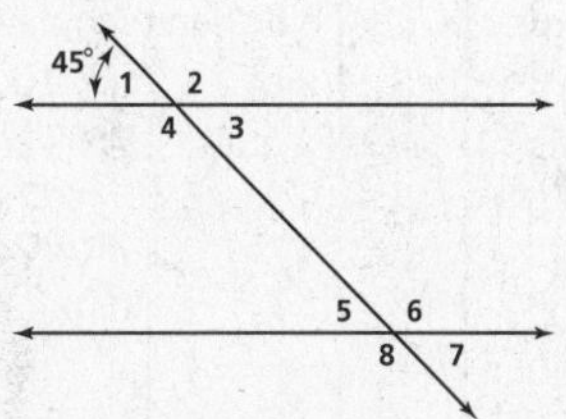

2. Check students' answers. **3.** They are equal. **4.** They are equal. **5.** 11 and 21; 19 and 14; 18 and 15; 36 and 35; 30 and 34; 17 and 36; 18 and 32; 2 and 9; 3 and 8.

Chapters 5–8 Answers (continued)

Puzzle 7-1

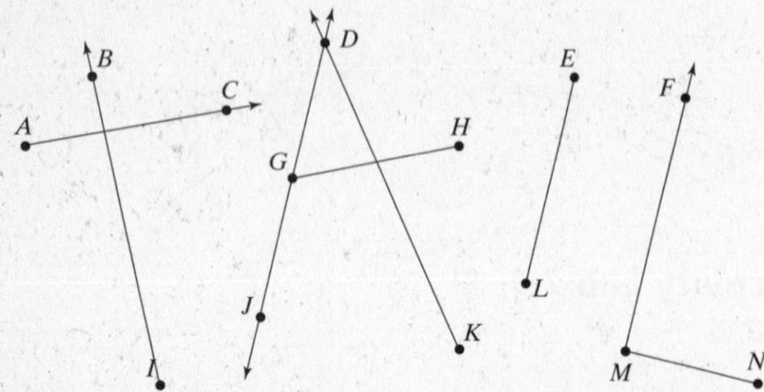

Practice (regular) 7-2

1. right **2.** obtuse **3.** acute **4.** straight **5.** acute **6.** right **7.** Sample answer: $\overleftrightarrow{XU}$, $\overleftrightarrow{ST}$, $\overleftrightarrow{XP}$, $\overleftrightarrow{QY}$ **8.** Sample answer: $\overline{XN}$, $\overline{XP}$, $\overline{QN}$ **9.** Sample answer: $\angle VXW$ and $\angle UXP$ **10.** $\angle QNT$, $\angle SNQ$, $\angle SNY$, $\angle YNT$ **11.** $\angle MSW$ and $\angle UST$, $\angle SXP$ and $\angle VXW$ **12.** $\angle MSX$ and $\angle MSU$, $\angle MSX$ and $\angle XST$ **13.** $\angle QNX$ and $\angle XNS$; $\angle TNP$ and $\angle PNY$ **14.** 67° **15.** 17° **16.** 23° **17.**

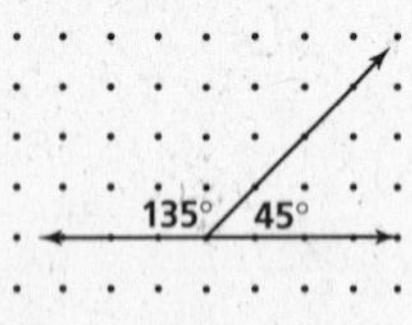

Guided Problem Solving 7-2

1. Determine whether an angle can ever have the same measure as its complement. **2.** If there is an angle that has the same measure as its complement, show that the sum of the angles is 90°. If there is not an angle that has the same measure as its complement, explain why. **3.** two angles whose sum measures 90° **4.** The angle is half of 90°. **5.** 45° **6.** yes **7.** Sample answer: The complement of a 45° angle is a 45° angle, and the sum of 45° and 45° is 90°. **8.** yes; Sample answer: The supplement of a 90° angle is a 90° angle, and the sum of the 90° and 90° is 180°.

Practice (adapted) 7-2

1. right **2.** obtuse **3.** acute **4.** straight **5.** acute **6.** right **7.** Sample answer: $\overleftrightarrow{XU}$, $\overleftrightarrow{ST}$ **8.** Sample answer: $\overline{XN}$, $\overline{XP}$, $\overline{QN}$ **9.** Sample answer: $\angle VXW$ and $\angle UXP$ **10.** $\angle QNT$, $\angle SNQ$, $\angle SNY$, $\angle YNT$ **11.** $\angle QNX$ and $\angle XNS$; $\angle TNP$ and $\angle PNY$ **12.** 67° **13.** 17° **14.**

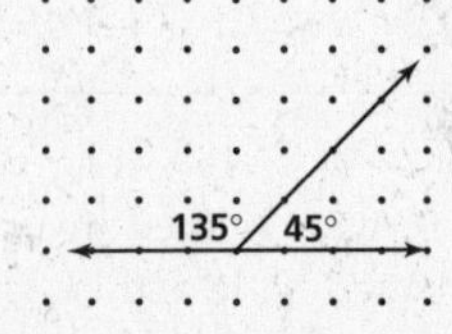

Activity Lab 7-2

1. 45° **2.** vertical angles; $m\angle AGH = m\angle FGB = 45°$ **3.** $m\angle AGF = m\angle FGB = 135°$ **4.** 45° **5.** $m\angle CHG = 135°$; $m\angle CHE = 45°$; $m\angle EHD = 135°$ **6.** Sample answer: Angles in the same positions relative to the parallel and intersecting lines have equal measures. **7.** 20° **8.** 160° **9.** 70° **10.** 90°

Reteaching 7-2

1. 146°; obtuse **2.** 34°; acute **3.** 50°; acute **4.** 90°; right

Enrichment 7-2

1. 360°

2a. 360°, **2b.** 360°,

2c. 360°,

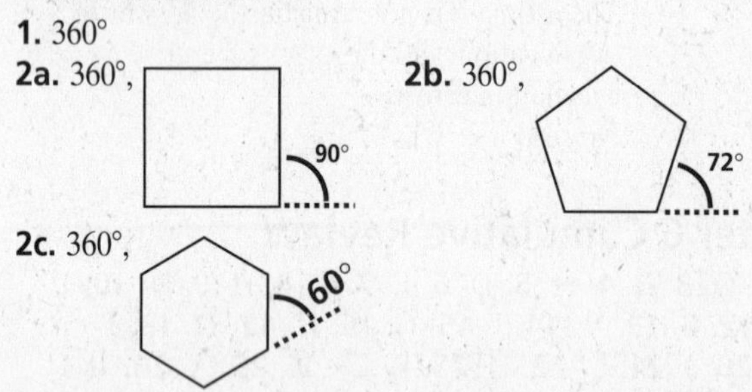

3. Sample answer: The sum of the exterior angles is always 360°. **4a.** 360° **4b.** 360° **4c.** 360° **4d.** 360° **5.** Sample answer: The same, since the sum of the exterior angle measures is the same for all polygons regardless of the number of sides.

Puzzle 7-2

1. $\overleftrightarrow{TH}$ **2.** $\overleftrightarrow{ER}$ **3.** $\angle IGH$ **4.** $\angle TAN$ **5.** $\angle GLE$
THE RIGHT ANGLE

Practice (regular) 7-3

1. 125° **2.** 67° **3.** 36° **4.** 53° **5.** 72° **6.** 50° **7.** scalene acute **8.** isosceles; angles cannot be determined **9.** right; sides cannot be determined **10.** equilateral, acute **11a.** right **11b.** No; sides are not congruent. **11c.** No; no two angles are congruent. **11d.** Yes, the triangle is scalene; no two sides are congruent if no two angles are congruent.

Guided Problem Solving 7-3

1. Determine the measure of $\angle E$. **2.** $m\angle A = 31°$; $m\angle B = 93°$; $m\angle D = 60°$ **3.** 180° **4.** 124° **5.** 56°; 56° **6.** 116° **7.** 64° **8.** The sum of the angles of a triangle is 180°. **9.** 32°

Practice (adapted) 7-3

1. 125° **2.** 67° **3.** 53° **4.** 72° **5.** scalene acute **6.** isosceles; angles cannot be determined **7.** equilateral, acute **8a.** right **8b.** No; sides are not congruent. **8c.** No; no two angles are congruent.

Name ______________________ Class ______________ Date ______________

Chapters 5–8 Answers (continued)

Activity Lab 7-3

1a. 100° **1b.** obtuse **1c.** scalene **2a.** 110° **2b.** obtuse **2c.** scalene **3a.** 70° **3b.** acute **3c.** acute **4a.** 90° **4b.** right **4c.** scalene **5a.** 60° **5b.** acute **5c.** equilateral

Reteaching 7-3

1. scalene; obtuse **2.** equilateral; acute **3.** isosceles; right **4.** scalene; obtuse **5.** scalene; acute **6.** isosceles; acute **7.** $x = 105°$ **8.** $x = 34°$

Enrichment 7-3

1–4. Sample answers are given.

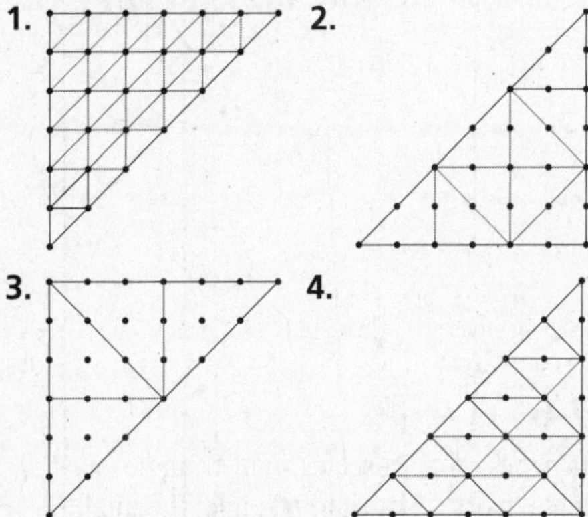

Puzzle 7-3

1. 12 **2.** 8 **3.** 3 **4.** 5 **5.** 2 **6.** 5 **7.** 1

Practice (regular) 7-4

1. rhombus; irregular **2.** octagon; irregular **3.** hexagon; regular **4.** parallelogram, rectangle; rectangle **5.** parallelogram, rhombus; rhombus **6.** trapezoid; trapezoid **7–9.** Sample answers are given:

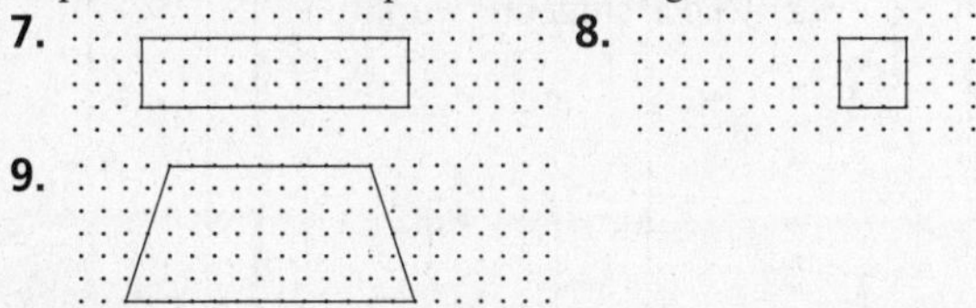

10. Check students' answers. Sample answer: $\angle P$ is a right angle.

Guided Problem Solving 7-4

1. Determine whether a quadrilateral can be both a rhombus and a rectangle. **2.** quadrilateral, rhombus, and rectangle **3.** A quadrilateral is a polygon that has 4 sides. **4.** A rhombus is a parallelogram with 4 congruent sides. **5.** A rectangle is a parallelogram with 4 right angles. **6.** yes **7.** A square is a rhombus because it has four congruent sides. It is a rectangle because it has four right angles. **8.** No. A figure can have four congruent sides without having four right angles.

Practice (adapted) 7-4

1. quadrilateral; irregular **2.** hexagon; regular **3.** parallelogram, rectangle; rectangle **4.** trapezoid; trapezoid **5–7.** Sample answers are given:

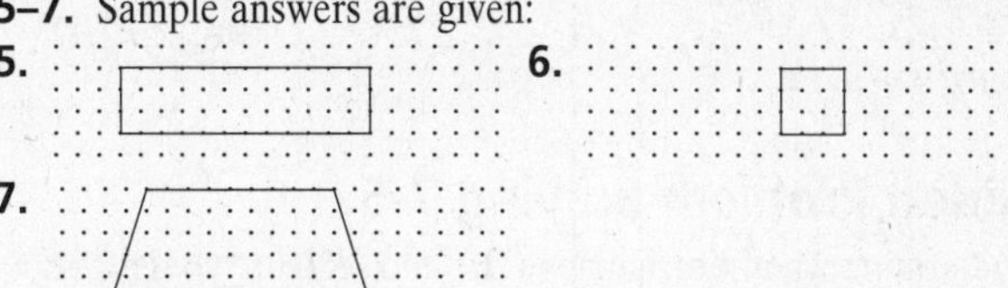

Activity Lab 7-4

1a. Check students' work. **1b.** 180° **2a.** Check students' work. **2b.** 360° **3a.** 540° **3b.** 720° **3c.** 1,080° **4a.** The measures of the angles of a triangle always total 180°. The measure of the angles of a quadrilateral always equal 360°. **4b.** The total of the measures of the angles increases as the number of sides increases. **5a.** Check students' work. **5b.** Sample answer: The measure of the third angle is 180° minus the sum of the measures of the other two angles; 100° **6a.** 1,440° **6b–c.** Check students' work.

Reteaching 7-4

1. rectangle **2.** rhombus **3.** trapezoid **4.** Check students' drawings. **5.** Check students' drawings. **6.** Check students' drawings.

Enrichment 7-4

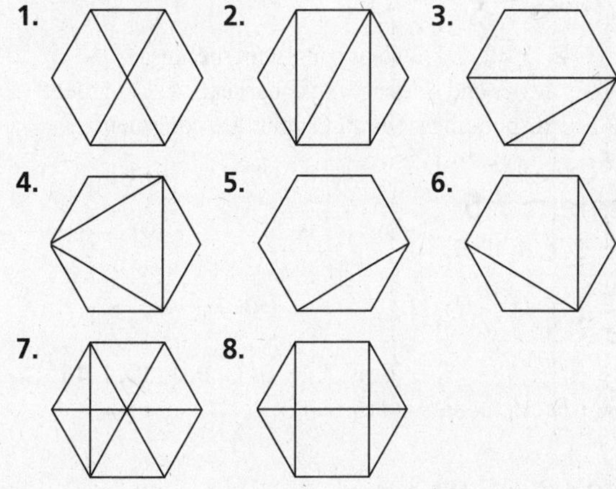

Puzzle 7-4

1. pentagon **2.** parallelogram **3.** regular hexagon **4.** rhombus **5.** trapezoid **6.** octagon
IRREGULAR

Practice (regular) 7-5

1. Congruent, because all corresponding angles and corresponding sides are congruent. **2.** Congruent, because all corresponding

Chapters 5–8 Answers (continued)

angles and corresponding sides are congruent. **3.** Not congruent, because corresponding sides are not congruent. **4.** $\triangle NLM$ **5.** $\triangle FED$ **6.** $\triangle RTS$ **7.** $\overline{AB} \cong \overline{DE}, \overline{BC} \cong \overline{EF}, \overline{AC} \cong \overline{DF}$, $\angle A \cong \angle D, \angle B \cong \angle E, \angle C \cong \angle F$ **8.** $\overline{JK} \cong \overline{MN}, \overline{KL} \cong \overline{NO}$, $\overline{JL} \cong \overline{MO}, \angle J \cong \angle M, \angle K \cong \angle N, \angle L \cong \angle O$ **9a.** $\angle FED$ **9b.** $\overline{FE}$ **9c.** $\angle A$

Guided Problem Solving 7-5

1. Determine whether triangles *GHI* and *JKL* are congruent. **2.** Corresponding parts have to be congruent. **3.** Corresponding angles are congruent. **4.** nothing **5.** no **6.** Since it is not known if the corresponding sides are congruent, it is unknown if the triangles are congruent. **7.** Yes, because all corresponding parts are congruent.

Practice (adapted) 7-5

1. Congruent, because all corresponding angles and corresponding sides are congruent. **2.** Not congruent, because corresponding sides are not congruent. **3.** $\triangle NLM$ **4.** $\triangle RTS$ **5.** $\overline{AB} \cong \overline{DE}$, $\overline{BC} \cong \overline{EF}, \overline{AC} \cong \overline{DF}, \angle A \cong \angle D, \angle B \cong \angle E, \angle C \cong \angle F$ **6a.** $\angle FED$ **6b.** $\overline{FE}$ **6c.** $\angle A$

Activity Lab 7-5

1. $\overline{AC} \approx 10.82$; $\angle A = 40°$; $\angle B = 90°$ **2–5.** Check students' work. **6.** Sample answer: Yes. If two figures are congruent, they have congruent angles and their measurements are in proportion, so they are similar.

Reteaching 7-5

1. $\overline{QR}$; $\angle R$ **2.** $\overline{YW}$; $\angle X$ **3.** Not congruent, because corresponding angles and sides are not congruent. **4.** Congruent, because all corresponding sides and angles are congruent.

Enrichment 7-5

1. d. **2.** c. **3.** e. **4.** d. **5.** a.

Puzzle 7-5

1. C **2.** O **3.** D **4.** K **5.** B **6.** F **7.** H **8.** G **9.** J **10.** I **11.** L **12.** A **13.** Check students' work.

Practice (regular) 7-6

1. $\overline{RN}, \overline{PQ}$ **2.** $\overline{OM}, \overline{OP}, \overline{OQ}$ **3.** $\overline{MN}$ **4.** $\angle MOP$ **5.** $\overset{\frown}{MRN}$ **6.** $\overset{\frown}{MR}, \overset{\frown}{NQ}$ **7.** $\overline{MN}$ **8.** $\overline{NQ}$ **9.** $\overset{\frown}{XY}, \overset{\frown}{ZY}, \overset{\frown}{XZ}$ **10.** $\overset{\frown}{XZY}$, $\overset{\frown}{XYZ}, \overset{\frown}{ZXY}$ **11.**

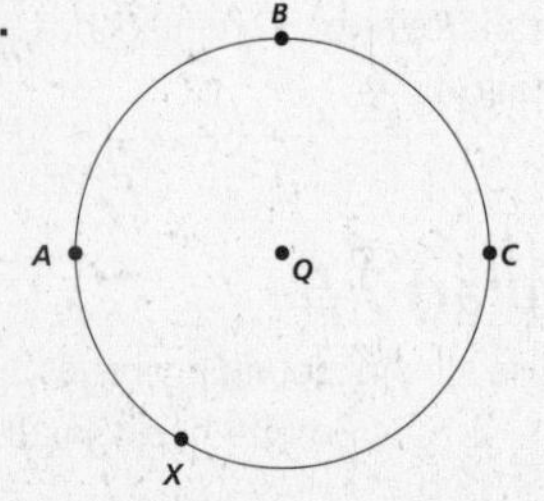

Guided Problem Solving 7-6

1. Determine whether a radius can also be a chord. **2.** radius, chord **3.** A radius is a segment that connects the center of a circle to the circle. **4.** One is on the circle and the other is on the center of the circle. **5.** A chord is a segment that has both endpoints on the circle. **6.** no **7.** A radius cannot be a chord because one of the endpoints of a radius is the center and is not on the circle. **8.** Yes, because both endpoints of the diameter are on the circle.

Practice (adapted) 7-6

1–6. Sample answers are given. **1.** $\overline{RN}, \overline{PQ}$ **2.** $\overline{OM}, \overline{OP}, \overline{OQ}$ **3.** $\overline{MN}$ **4.** $\angle MOP$ **5.** $\overset{\frown}{MRN}$ **6.** $\overset{\frown}{MR}, \overset{\frown}{NQ}$ **7** $\overset{\frown}{XY}, \overset{\frown}{ZY}, \overset{\frown}{XZ}$ **8.** $\overset{\frown}{XZY}, \overset{\frown}{XYZ}, \overset{\frown}{ZXY}$ **9.**

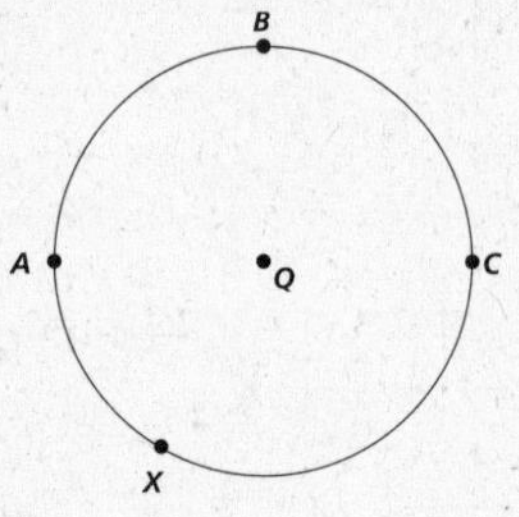

Activity Lab 7-6

1–3. Check students' work. **4a.** isosceles right triangle **4b–5a.** Check students' work. **5b.** right triangle; the angle opposite the diameter is a right angle.

Reteaching 7-6

1. $\overline{PR}, \overline{SP}, \overline{PT}$ **2.** $\overline{SQ}, \overline{ST}$ **3.** Sample answer: $\overset{\frown}{SQ}, \overset{\frown}{RT}, \overset{\frown}{SQT}$ **4.** $\overline{LK}, \overline{HG}$ **5.** Sample answer: $\angle HML, \angle HMK, \angle KMG$ **6.** $\overline{LK}, \overline{HG}$ **7.** Sample answer: $\overset{\frown}{KHL}, \overset{\frown}{KGL}$ **8.** Sample answer: $\overline{ML}, \overline{MK}$

Enrichment 7-6

1.

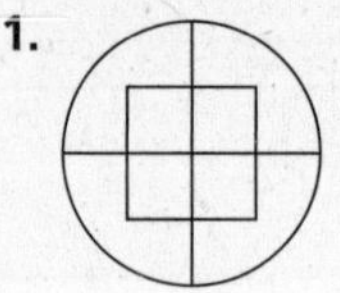

2. Check students' work.

Puzzle 7-6

1. I **2.** D **3.** A **4.** H **5.** O

Chapters 5–8 Answers (continued)

Practice (regular) 7-7

1. Successful United States Space Launches 1957–1995

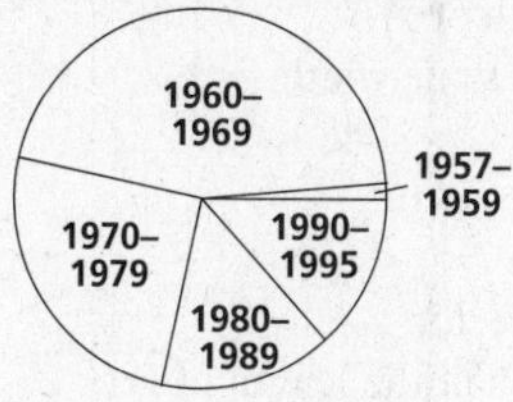

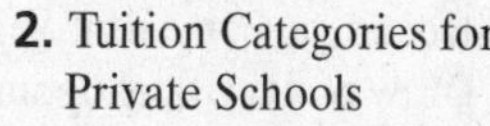

2. Tuition Categories for Private Schools

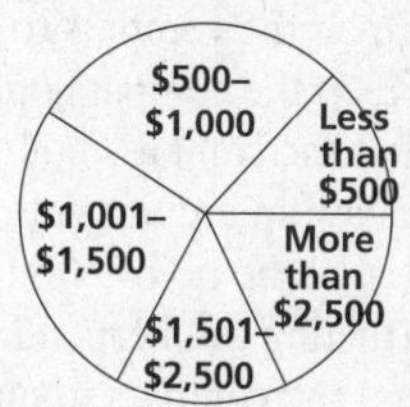

3. Car Color Preference of Seventh-Grade Class

Red
Green
White
Blue

3a. $33\frac{1}{3}\%$ **3b.** 3.7% **3c.** 85.2% **3d.** 88.9%

Guided Problem Solving 7-7

1. Use the table to make a circle graph. **2.** 25 **3.** $\frac{11}{25} = \frac{n}{360}$; $n = 158.4°$ **4.** $\frac{5}{25} = \frac{n}{360}$; $n = 72°$ **5.** $\frac{5}{25} = \frac{n}{360}$; $n = 72°$ **6.** $\frac{2}{25} = \frac{n}{360}$; $n = 28.8°$ **7.** $\frac{2}{25} = \frac{n}{360}$; $n = 28.8°$

8. Student Volunteers per Week

Day 5
Day 4
Day 1
Day 3
Day 2

9. Yes **10.** Students

10
3
5
28
15

Sports
Band
Student Council
Horticulture
Clubs

Practice (adapted) 7-7

1. Successful United States Space Launches 1957–1995

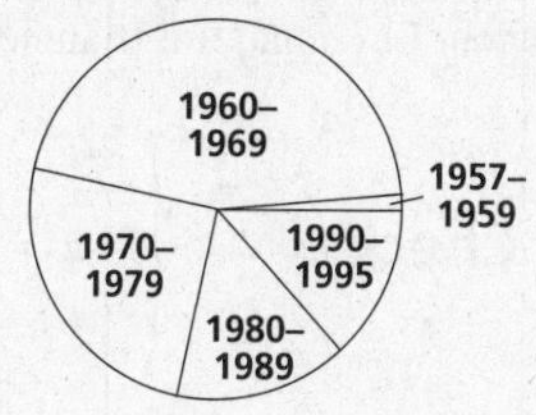

2. Tuition Categories for Private Schools

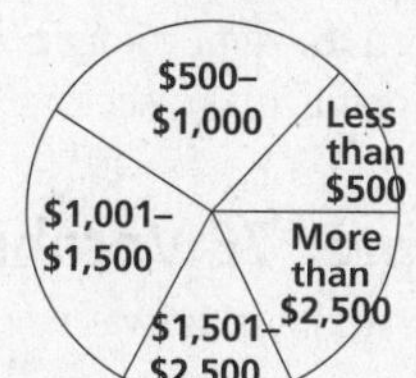

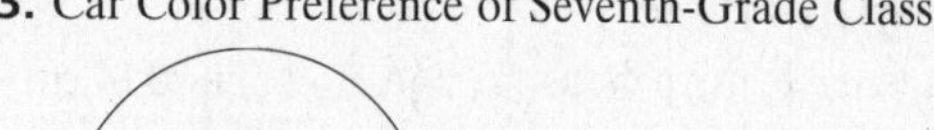

3. Car Color Preference of Seventh-Grade Class; $33\frac{1}{3}\%$

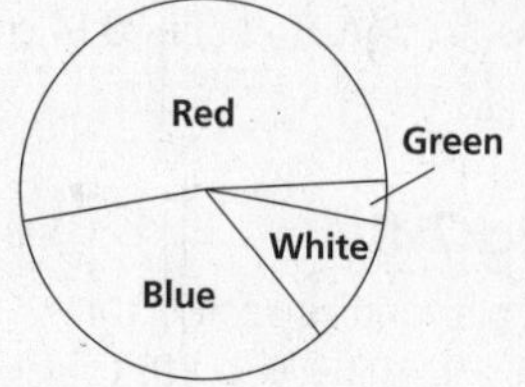

Activity Lab 7-7

1–4. Check students' work. **5a.** 100% **5b.** 360° **5c.** Check students' work.

Reteaching 7-7

1. Tuesday's Music CD Sales

Type of Music	Number of CDs Sold	Central Angle Measure
Country	10	**75°**
Rock	8	**60°**
Jazz	16	**120°**
Rap	14	**105°**
Total	**48**	**360°**

Check student's graphs.

Enrichment 7-7

1. It is one half the value of the preceding year. **2.** No, the value is $\frac{1}{2}$ the prior year's value. It can be zero only if prior value is zero. **3.** Yes, eventually there will be no market for the item. **4a.** 50% **4b.** 25% **4c.** 12.5% **4d.** 6.25% **4e.** 3.125% **4f.** 1.5625% **5.** No, they total 98.4375%. The remaining percent is the value for the remaining life of the component. **6.** 7 sectors

7.

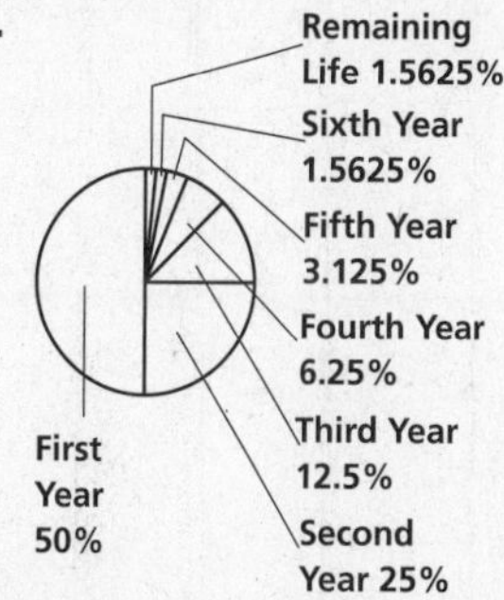

7a. 180° **7b.** 90° **7c.** 45° **7d.** 22.5° **7e.** 11.25° **7f.** 5.625°

Puzzle 7-7

Julian: $\frac{40}{160} = \frac{n}{360}$; $n = 90°$; section E.

Jim: $\frac{47}{160} = \frac{n}{100}$; $n = 29.375\%$; section G.

Wilson: $\frac{53}{160} = \frac{n}{360}$; $n = 119.25°$; section C.

Jorge: $\frac{20}{160} = \frac{n}{100}$; $n = 12.5\%$; section A.

Chapters 5–8 Answers (continued)

Practice (regular) 7-8

1–6. Check students' constructions. **7.** 5 in. **8.** 9 mm **9.** 4 cm **10.** 6 yd

Guided Problem Solving 7-8

1. $2\frac{1}{2}$ times **2.** congruent segment; perpendicular bisector **3–8.** Check students' constructions. **9.** 10 in.; yes **10.** Check students' constructions.

Practice (adapted) 7-8

1–3. Check students' constructions. **4.** 5 in. **5.** 9 mm **6.** 4 cm **7.** 6 yd

Activity Lab 7-8

1–3. Check students' work. **4.** yes **5.** 90° **6.** 1.25 in. **7.** $\overline{GH}$

Reteaching 7-8

1.

2.

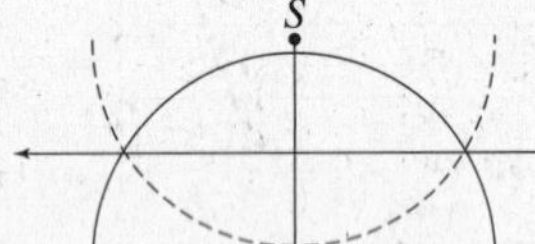

3.

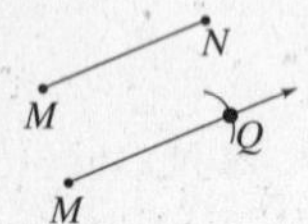

4.

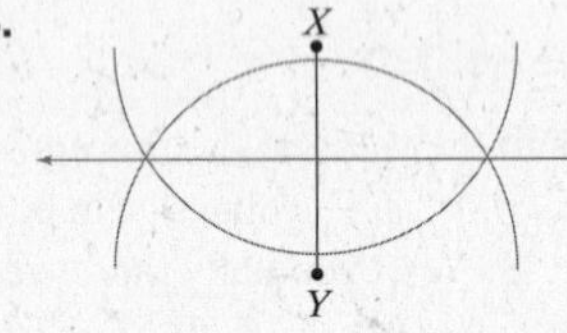

5.

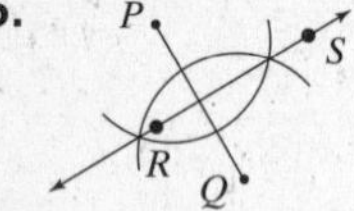

Enrichment 7-8

1–7.

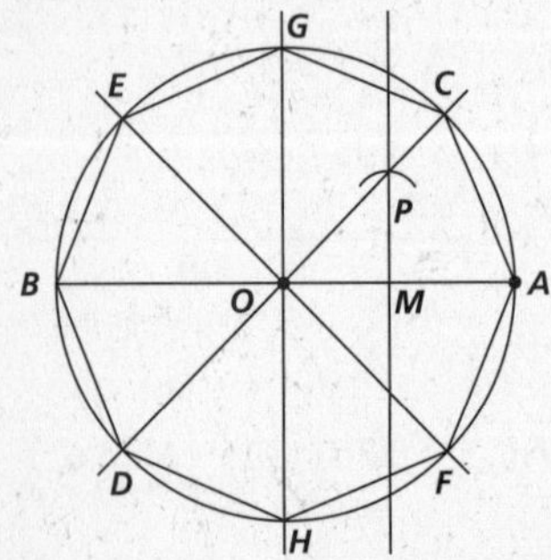

8. Sample answers: parallel lines, equilateral triangle, square, rectangle, trapezoid, parallelogram; check students' work.

Puzzle 7-8

Constructing a Congruent Segment:

- Draw a ray with endpoint C.
- Open the compass to the length of $\overline{AB}$.
- Keep the compass open to the same width.
- Put the compass point at C.
- Draw an arc that intersects the ray.
- Label the point of intersection D.

Constructing the Perpendicular Bisector

- Set the compass to more than half the length of $\overline{AB}$.
- Put the tip of the compass at A and draw an arc intersecting $\overline{AB}$.
- Keeping the compass set at the same width, put the tip at B and draw another arc intersecting $\overline{AB}$.
- Points C and D are where the arcs intersect.
- Draw $\overleftrightarrow{CD}$.
- The intersection of $\overline{AB}$ and $\overleftrightarrow{CD}$ is point M.

Chapter 7A Graphic Organizer

1. Geometry **2.** 8 **3.** Drawing a Picture **4.** Check students' diagrams.

Chapter 7B Reading Comprehension

1. housing **2.** medical **3.** Each of the three categories accounts for 5% of the income spent. **4.** 100% **5.** \$2,400 × 15% = \$360 **6.** \$1,900 × 3 5% = \$95 **7.** 7% of the monthly budget is \$60. The monthly income is \$857.14. **8.** b

Chapter 7C Reading/Writing Math Symbols

1. H **2.** D **3.** G **4.** B **5.** E **6.** A **7.** F **8.** C **9.** The measure of angle B is 80 degrees. **10.** Triangle ABC is congruent to triangle HIJ. **11.** Angle XYZ is congruent to angle MNP. **12.** The length of segment BC is 4. **13.** Segment DJ is congruent to segment KL. **14.** The length of segment DJ is equal to the length of segment KL. **15.** The measure of angle P is equal to the measure of angle R. **16.** The length of segment BC is one-half the length of segment TU.

Chapter 7D Visual Vocabulary Practice

1. midpoint **2.** obtuse angle **3.** hexagon **4.** adjacent angles **5.** chord **6.** right triangle **7.** pentagon **8.** equilateral triangle **9.** perpendicular bisector

Chapter 7E Vocabulary Check

Check students' answers.

Chapters 5–8 Answers (continued)

Chapter 7F Vocabulary Review Puzzle

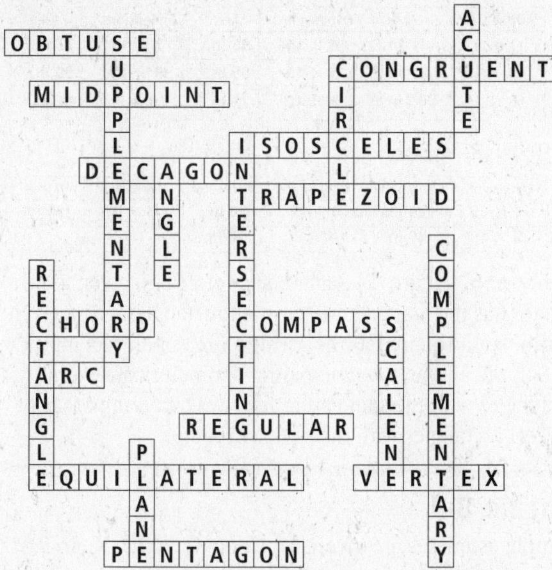

Chapter 7 Checkpoint Quiz 1

1. 60°; acute **2.** 130°; obtuse **3.** 180°; straight **4.** right triangle **5.** 48°; 138° **6.** 72°; 162° **7.** 16°; 106°
8–11. Sample answers are given.
8. **9.** **10.** **11.**

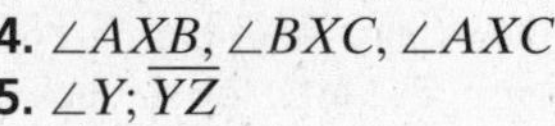

Chapter 7 Checkpoint Quiz 2

1. Automobile Colors

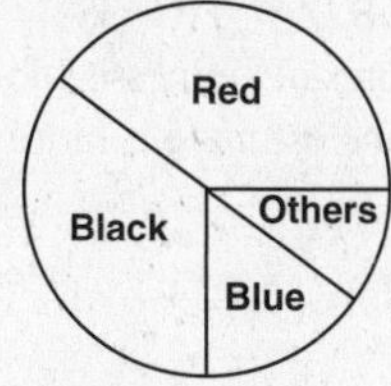

2. $\overline{AB}$ or $\overline{AC}$ **3.** $\overline{AC}$
4. $\angle AXB, \angle BXC, \angle AXC$
5. $\angle Y$; $\overline{YZ}$

Chapter 7 Test (regular)

1. $\overline{JK}, \overline{QR}, \overline{LM}$ **2.** $\overline{JK}, \overline{KM}, \overline{PR}, \overline{NP}$ **3.** $\overline{NJ}, \overline{PK}, \overline{JL}, \overline{KM}$ **4.** 133° **5.** 25° **6.** 52°; 142° **7.** 18°; 108° **8.** 78°; 168° **9.** 39°; 129° **10.** Check students' constructions. **11.** Check students' constructions. **12.** $x = 75°$; scalene; acute **13.** $x = 45°$; isosceles; right **14.** pentagon **15.** trapezoid **16.** hexagon **17.** $\overline{SU}$ **18.** $\overline{RQ}$ **19.** $\angle S$ **20.** $\overline{ST}, \overline{SU}$ **21.** $m\angle Q$, 40° **22.** $\overline{MS}$; $\overline{QS}$; $\overline{NS}$ **23.** $\overline{MP}, \overline{NQ}, \overline{QM}$ **24.** $\angle NSQ$; $\angle MSN$; $\angle MSQ$ **25.** $\overline{MQ}$
26. Budget

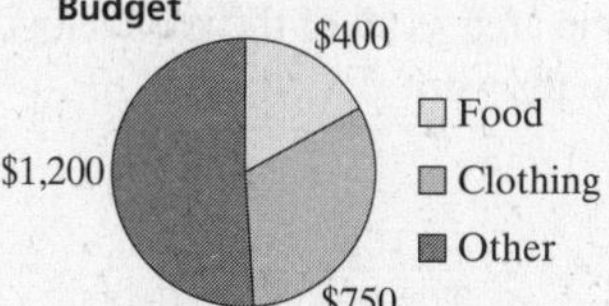

Chapter 7 Test (below level)

1. $\overline{JK}, \overline{QR}, \overline{LM}$ **2.** $\overline{NJ}, \overline{PK}, \overline{JL}, \overline{KM}$ **3.** 133° **4.** 25° **5.** 52°; 142° **6.** 18°; 108° **7.** Check students' constructions. **8.** $x = 75°$; scalene; acute **9.** $x = 45°$; isosceles; right **10.** pentagon **11.** trapezoid **12.** $\overline{SU}$ **13.** $\angle S$ **14.** $\overline{ST}, \overline{SU}$ **15.** $m\angle Q$, 40° **16.** $\overline{MS}$; $\overline{QS}$; $\overline{NS}$ **17.** $\angle NSQ$; $\angle MSN$; $\angle MSQ$ **18.** $\overline{MQ}$
19. Budget

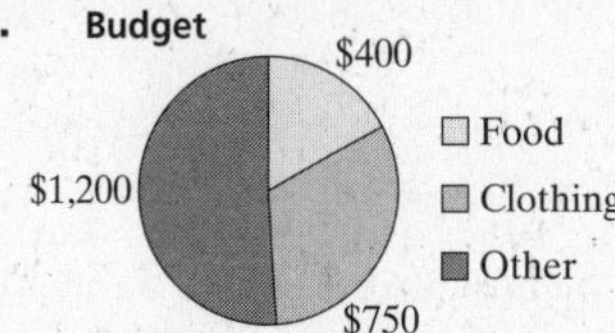

Chapter 7 Alternative Assessment

Exercise	Points	Explanation
1.	1	Design with squares rotated or shifted — Sample: 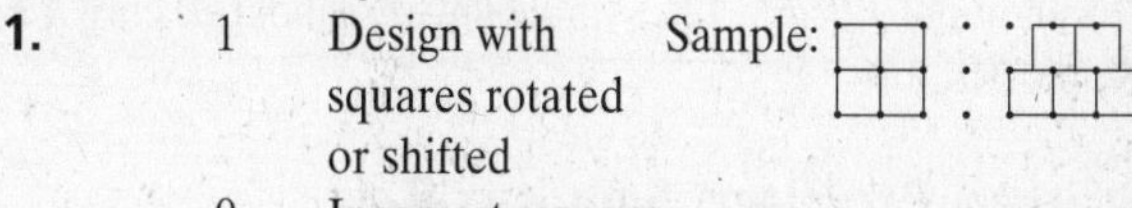
	0	Incorrect response
2.	1	No; the triangles are not equilateral (regular).
	0	Incorrect response OR no explanation
3.	1	Four equilateral triangles inside each of Ira's triangles — Sample: 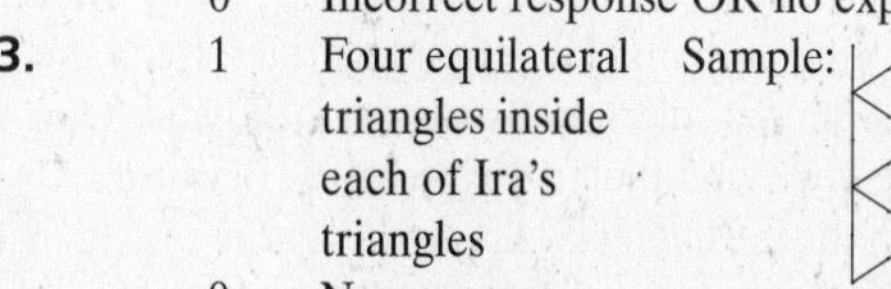
	0	No response
4.	1	No, or a reasonable incorrect effort
	0	No response
5.	1	Yes — Sample:
	0	Incorrect response
6. a–c.	1	360°
	0	Incorrect response
7.	2	The sum of the measures of the angles at any vertex in these patterns is 360°.
	1	Incorrect conclusions due to computational error
	0	Completely incorrect response OR no response
Excursion	5	Two designs following guidelines
	4	Same as above, except with one nonregular polygon
	3	Same as above, except without all areas covered
	2	One correct design
	1	Polygons shown in an effort to find design
	0	No response

Sample of first design:

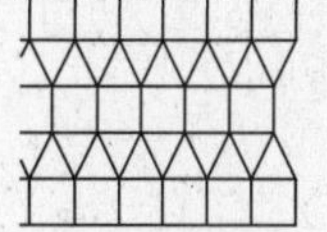

Samples of second design:

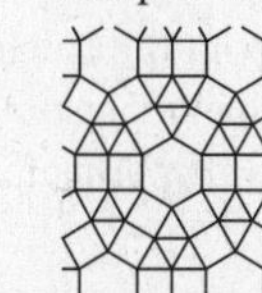

Name ______ Class ______ Date ______

Chapters 5–8 Answers (continued)

Chapter 7 Cumulative Review

1. A **2.** G **3.** D **4.** G **5.** A **6.** J **7.** B **8.** J **9.** B **10.** F **11.** C **12.** G **13.** C **14.** G **15.** B **16.** J **17.** A **18.** F **19.** $\overline{FC}, \overline{FB}, \overline{FD}$ **20a.** Sample answer: $\angle ABE$ and $\angle EBD$ **20b.** Sample answers: $\angle ABD$ and $\angle DBC$, $\angle EBC$ and $\angle ABE$

Chapter 8

Practice (regular) 8-1

1. Sample answer: 10 yd **2.** Sample answer: 10 yd **3.** Sample answer: 15 yd **4.** Sample answer: 13 yd **5.** 12 ft; a truck cab is quite tall **6.** 8 in.; a book is not very wide **7.** 8 in.; a pizza is not very big **8.** 2 ft; a bathtub is not very deep **9.** Sample answer: about 9 cm^2 **10.** Sample answer: about 19 cm^2 **11.** Sample answer: about 12 cm^2 **12.** Sample answer: about 20 cm^2 **13.** ft **14.** in. **15.** mi^2

Guided Problem Solving 8-1

1. Explain how to use a piece of string to estimate the perimeter of the puzzle piece. **2.** The perimeter of an object is the distance around the object. **3.** Wrap it around the puzzle piece. **4.** Take the length of string used and lay it beside a ruler. Read the measurement from the ruler. **5.** Because it is difficult to lay the string out exactly around the puzzle piece. **6.** Because it is difficult to find the perimeter of the curves of the puzzle piece with a ruler. **7.** Sample answer: Estimate the length and width of the rectangular center. Calculate the area of the rectangle. The puzzle piece's area will be more than the area of the rectangle.

Practice (adapted) 8-1

1. 10 yd **2.** 10 yd **3.** 15 yd **4.** 13 yd **5.** 12 ft; a truck cab is quite tall **6.** 2 ft; a bathtub is not very deep **7.** Sample answer: about 9 cm^2 **8.** Sample answer: about 19 cm^2 **9.** Sample answer: about 12 cm^2 **10.** ft **11.** mi^2

Activity Lab 8-1

1–3. Check students' answers.

4.

Figure	Length (cm)	Width (cm)	Area	Perimeter (cm)
1	7.5	3	22.5	21
2	11	2	22	26
3	5.5	3.5	19.25	18

greatest area: Figure 1; greatest perimeter: Figure 2; least area: Figure 3; least perimeter: Figure 3 **5.** Check students' answers

Reteaching 8-1

1. 6 ft; a refrigerator is about the height of a person **2.** 8 ft; a stop sign is a little taller than a person **3.** Area ≈ 17; perimeter ≈ 20 **4.** Area ≈ 10; perimeter ≈ 14

Enrichment 8-1

1.

Dimensions	Area	Dimensions	Area	Dimensions	Area
1 × 17	17 $in.^2$	4 × 14	56 $in.^2$	7 × 11	77 $in.^2$
2 × 16	32 $in.^2$	5 × 13	65 $in.^2$	8 × 10	80 $in.^2$
3 × 15	45 $in.^2$	6 × 12	72 $in.^2$	9 × 9	81 $in.^2$

2. 9 × 9 **3.** square

4.

Dimensions	Perimeter	Dimensions	Perimeter	Dimensions	Perimeter
1 × 36	74 in.	3 × 12	30 in.	6 × 6	24 in.
2 × 18	40 in.	4 × 9	26 in.		

5. 6 × 6 **6.** square **7.** Sample answers: For a given area, a square has the least perimeter of all rectangles. For a given perimeter, a square has the greatest area of all rectangles. **8.** Sample answers: by comparing perimeters of several rectangles with the same area; also, by comparing areas of several rectangles with the same perimeter

Puzzle 8-1

Sample estimates are given. **U.** 32 ft^2 **C.** 20 ft^2 **K.** 16 ft^2 **L.** 51 ft^2 **Y.** 9.5 ft^2
LUCKY

Practice (regular) 8-2

1. 16 m^2 **2.** 115 cm^2 **3.** 32 $in.^2$ **4.** 80 mm^2 **5.** 192 mm^2 **6.** 322 km^2 **7.** 3,120 mi^2 **8.** 285 $in.^2$ **9.** 1, 6; 2, 3 **10.** 320 m^2 **11.** 1,152 yd^2; 136 yd **12.** 17 ft^2, 32 ft^2, 45 ft^2, 56 ft^2, 65 ft^2, 72 ft^2, 77 ft^2, 80 ft^2, 81 ft^2

Guided Problem Solving 8-2

1. Estimate the area of Tennessee from the map shown. **2.** a parallelogram **3.** Use the formula $A = bh$ where b is the base and h is the height. **4.** 110 mi **5.** 380 mi **6.** $A = 110 \cdot 380$ **7.** 41,800 mi^2 **8.** More; the southeast corner of Tennessee does not fill the parallelogram completely, so the estimate is more than the actual area. **9.** 21,875 ft^2

Practice (adapted) 8-2

1. 16 m^2 **2.** 115 cm^2 **3.** 32 $in.^2$ **4.** 80 mm^2 **5.** 192 mm^2 **6.** 322 km^2 **7.** 1, 6; 2, 3 **8.** 320 m^2 **9.** 1,152 yd^2; 136 yd

Activity Lab 8-2

1. Check students' sketches. Measures of parallelograms: $b = 1, h = 12; b = 2, h = 6; b = 3, h = 4; b = 12, h = 1; b = 6, h = 2; b = 4, h = 3$ **2.** Check students' work. **3.** Sample answer: The parallelograms that have one measure equal to 12 look larger because they are so long, but these parallelograms have the same area as all of the parallelograms on the page. **4.** Check students' work.

Reteaching 8-2

1. 30 cm^2 **2.** 32 ft^2 **3.** 35 m^2 **4.** 9.03 $in.^2$ **5.** 0.63 ft^2 **6.** 25.92 $in.^2$ **7.** 28 $in.^2$ **8.** 13.5 m^2 **9.** 2.5 cm^2

Name ______________________ Class ______________ Date ______________

Chapters 5–8 Answers (continued)

Enrichment 8-2

6 cm^2; 12 cm^2; 24 cm^2 **1.** The area doubles. **2a.** $4 \cdot 6 = 24$ **2b.** $8 \cdot 6 = 48$ **2c.** $16 \cdot 6 = 96$ **3.** The area quadruples. **4a.** $6 \cdot 9 = 54$ **4b.** $12 \cdot 9 = 108$ **4c.** $24 \cdot 9 = 216$ **5.** The area increases by nine times. **6.** The area increases by an amount equal to the square of the scale factor.

Puzzle 8-2

1. 4,838 **2.** 40 **3.** 320 **4.** 800 **5.** 60 **6.** 3,840 **7.** 128 **8.** 340

Practice (regular) 8-3

1. 8.2 ft **2.** 23.9 in. **3.** 34.6 cm **4.** 416 ft **5.** 299 cm^2 **6.** 59.22 mi^2 **7.** 26.8 km^2 **8.** 1,325 yd^2 **9.** 4, 4, 4; 5, 5, 2; 3, 3, 6; 2, 2, 8; 1, 1, 10 **10.** Area: 12.7 m^2; perimeter: 16.2 m

Guided Problem Solving 8-3

1. Find the perimeter of the rhombus. **2.** Measure the length of each side and add the lengths together. **3.** An equilateral triangle is a triangle whose sides are all equal lengths. **4.** Check students' answers. **5.** Check students' answers. **6.** Check students' answers. **7.** 24 in. **8.** 4×6 in. = 24 in.; yes **9.** 20 in.

Practice (adapted) 8-3

1. 8.2 ft **2.** 23.9 in. **3.** 34.6 cm **4.** 416 ft **5.** 299 cm^2 **6.** 59.22 mi^2 **7.** 26.8 km^2 **8.** 1,325 yd^2 **9.** 4, 4, 4; 5, 5, 2

Activity Lab 8-3

1. 1×150; 2×75; 3×50; 5×30; 6×25; 10×15; 150×1; 75×2; 50×3; 30×5; 25×6; 15×10 **2.** 1×300; 2×150; 3×100; 4×75; 5×60; 6×50; 10×30; 12×25; 15×20; 300×1; 150×2; 100×3; 75×4; 60×5; 30×10; 25×12; 20×15 **3–4.** Check students' work.

Reteaching 8-3

1. 17 yd **2.** 14.5 m **3.** 7.6 ft **4.** 30 cm^2 **5.** 8 m^2 **6.** 35.1 cm^2 **7a.** 37.4 in. **7b.** 89.61 in^2

Enrichment 8-3

1. 1, 2, 4, 8, 16, 32, 64; The sum of each horizontal row is double the sum of the row above it. **2.** Sample answer: The numbers in the rows that go diagonally to the right are the same as the numbers in the rows that go diagonally to the left. **3.** Each number is the sum of the two numbers above it. **4.** 1, 7, 21, 35, 35, 21, 7, 1

Puzzle 8-3

1. C **2.** A **3.** C **4.** T **5.** U **6.** S
CACTUS

Practice (regular) 8-4

1. 135 ft^2 **2.** 199.82 mm^2 **3.** 240 $in.^2$ **4.** 96.25 mi^2 **5.** 88 m^2 **6.** 144 $in.^2$ **7.** 1,001 ft^2 **8.** 86 cm^2 **9.** 2,848 m^2 **10a.** 1,125 cm^2 **10b.** 2,475 cm^2 **11.** 1, 7; 2, 6; 3, 5; 4, 4

Guided Problem Solving 8-4

1. 17 in. long; 39 in. long; 16 in. **2.** Find the area of the dulcimer. **3.** Use the formula $A = \frac{1}{2}h(b_1 + b_2)$. **4.** 16 in. **5.** 17 in. and 39 in. **6.** $A = \frac{1}{2}(16)(39 + 17)$ **7.** 448 $in.^2$ **8.** The bases are the parallel sides. **9.** $A = \frac{1}{2}(16)(20 + 36) = 448$ $in.^2$; they are equal because $17 + 39 = 20 + 36 = 56$.

Practice (adapted) 8-4

1. 135 ft^2 **2.** 199.82 mm^2 **3.** 96.25 mi^2 **4.** 88 m^2 **5.** 1,001 ft^2 **6.** 86 cm^2 **7a.** 1,125 cm^2 **7b.** 2,475 cm^2 **8.** 1, 7; 2, 6; 3, 5; 4, 4

Activity Lab 8-4

1. $\frac{11}{48}$ yd^2 **2.** $\frac{1}{16}$ $in.^2$ **3.** $\frac{1}{6}$ ft^2 **4.** $\frac{3}{32}$ mi^2 **5.** Check students' answers.

Reteaching 8-4

1. 33 ft^2 **2.** 748 ft^2 **3.** $33\frac{1}{4}$ $in.^2$ **4.** 98 m^2 **5.** 838 km^2 **6.** 2,586 yd^2

Enrichment 8-4

1. 144 $in.^2$

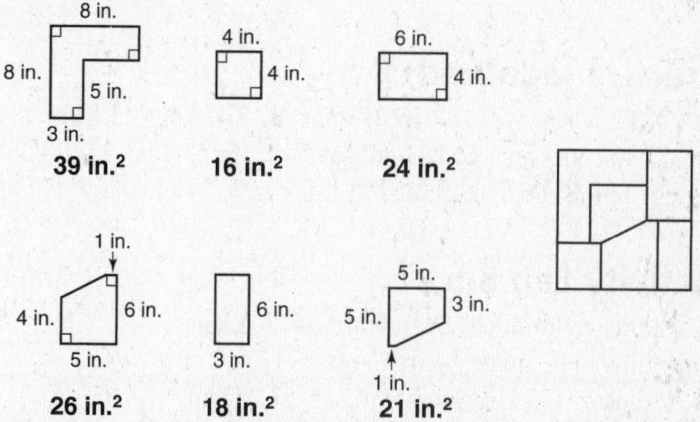

2.

Type of Wood	Cost per board foot	Board feet per section	Cost per section	Puzzles per section
Cherry	\$5.50	4	**\$22**	**4**
Maple	\$3.80	8	**\$30.40**	**8**
Red Oak	\$4.00	8	**\$32**	**8**
White Oak	\$3.50	4	**\$14**	**4**

3. Sample answers: time to make, uniqueness of product, price of similar products, profit desired **4.** Sample answers: cherry \$16.50, maple \$11.50, red oak \$12, white oak \$11; to allow for profit, price set at three times cost of wood **5.** Sample answers: 12 cherry, 16 maple, 16 red oak, 8 white oak

Chapters 5–8 Answers (continued)

Puzzle 8-4

1. area of shape I = 96 in.^{2}; area of shape II = 84 in.^{2} area of shape III = 64 in.^{2} area of shape IV = 104 in.^{2} area of shape V = 72 in.^{2} area of shape VI = 156 in.^{2} **2.** 576 in.^{2}

3.

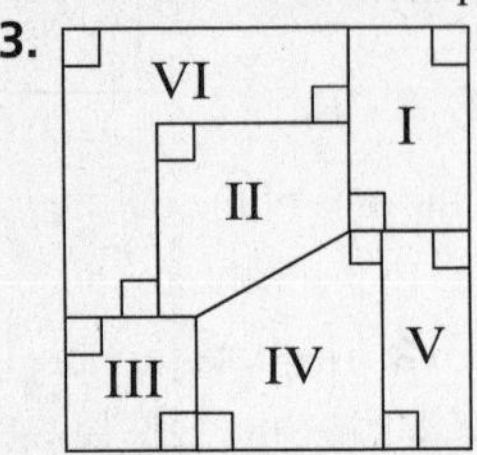

4. 576 in.^{2} **5.** The area of the square is the sum of the areas of the pieces.

Practice (regular) 8-5

1. 9.4 in.; 7.1 in.^{2} **2.** 12.6 m; 12.6 m^2 **3.** 22.0 ft; 38.5 ft^2 **4.** 37.7 km; 113.1 km^2 **5.** 25.1 mi; 50.3 mi^2 **6.** 94.2 in.; 706.9 in.^{2} **7.** 98.0 m; 764.5 m^2 **8.** 53.4 yd; 227.0 yd^2 **9.** 52.8 m; 221.7 m^2 **10.** 12.7 km **11.** 14.6 ft **12.** 66.8 in. **13.** 192 in.^{2}

Guided Problem Solving 8-5

1. 60 in.; circumference; area **2.**

3. Find the circumference and area of the front wheel of a high-wheel bicycle. **4.** 60 in. **5.** 30 in. **6.** Use the formula $C = 2\pi r$. **7.** 188.5 in. **8.** Use the formula $A = \pi r^2$. **9.** 2,827.4 in.^{2} **10.** Divide the area by π and find the square root; divide the circumference by 2π. **11.** C = 75.4 in.; A = 452.4 in.^{2}

Practice (adapted) 8-5

1. 9.4 in.; 7.1 in.^{2} **2.** 12.6 m; 12.6 m^2 **3.** 37.7 km; 113.1 km^2 **4.** 25.1 mi; 50.3 mi^2 **5.** 98.0 m; 764.5 m^2 **6.** 53.4 yd; 227.0 yd^2 **7.** 12.7 km **8.** 66.8 in. **9.** 192 in.^{2}

Activity Lab 8-5

1. Radius = 15 miles ; Search area = 706.5 mi^2
2. Radius = 63 miles; Search area = 12,463 mi^2
3. Radius = 135 km; Search area = 57,227 km^2
4. Radius = 300 miles; Search area = 282,600 mi^2

Reteaching 8-5

1. 154 cm^2 **2.** 13 in.^{2} **3.** 79 m^2 **4.** 3 cm^2 **5.** 28 ft^2 **6.** 201 yd^2

Enrichment 8-5

1. 21.5 ft^2 **2.** 13.76 in.^{2} **3.** 60.75 cm^2 **4.** 70.14 yd^2 **5.** 30.5 m^2 **6.** 28.065 in.^{2} **7.** 100.48 ft^2 **8.** 81.5 cm^2

Puzzle 8-5

9.72 cm^2; 7.74 cm^2; 7.74 cm^2; 7.625 cm^2; 36.56 cm^2; 80.415 cm^2; 18.84 cm^2; 11.44 cm^2

Practice (regular) 8-6

1. 8 **2.** 9 **3.** 10 **4.** 11 **5.** 1 **6.** 6 **7.** 5 **8.** 4 **9.** 16 **10.** 14 **11.** 7 **12.** 15 **13.** rational **14.** irrational **15.** rational **16.** rational **17.** rational, integer, whole **18.** irrational **19.** 8 km **20.** 9 m **21.** 11 ft **22.** 15 in. **23.** 14 yd **24.** 13 cm **25.** 0 or 3 **26.** 56 yd **27.** 8, 9 **28.** 7, 8 **29.** 11, 12 **30.** 8, 9 **31.** 13, 14 **32.** 14, 15

Guided Problem Solving 8-6

1. Write three irrational numbers between 4 and 5. **2.** An irrational number is a number that cannot be written as a ratio of two integers. As decimals, irrational numbers neither terminate nor repeat. **3.** 16; 25; Sample answer: $\sqrt{17}$ **4.** Sample answer: 4.12112111211112… **5.** Sample answers: $\sqrt{19}$, 4.71771777177771… **6.** infinitely many **7.** yes; no; no **8.** Sample answers: $\sqrt{5}$, 2.30330333033330…, 2.52552555255552…

Practice (adapted) 8-6

1. 8 **2.** 9 **3.** 10 **4.** 11 **5.** 1 **6.** 6 **7.** 5 **8.** 4 **9.** 16 **10.** rational **11.** irrational **12.** rational **13.** rational **14.** rational, integer, whole **15.** 8 km **16.** 9 m **17.** 11 ft **18.** 56 yd **19.** 8, 9 **20.** 7, 8 **21.** 11, 12

Activity Lab 8-6

Fourth column of table: 3.464; 3.606; 3.742; 3.873; 4.000; 4.123; 4.243; 4.359; 4.472; 4.583
Sixth column of table: 4.690; 4.796; 4.899; 5.000; 5.099; 5.196; 5.292; 5.385; 5.477; 5.568
1a. 2.449 **1b.** 2.828 **1c.** 3.162 **1d.** 3.464 **1e.** 3.873 **1f.** 5.099 **2.** The product of the square roots equals the square root of the product. **3.** Check students' answers.

Reteaching 8-6

1. 12 **2.** 6 **3.** 10 **4.** 50 **5.** 18 **6.** 20 **7.** 7 cm **8.** 9 in. **9.** 12 cm **10.** 25 in. **11.** 26 ft **12.** 60 yd **13.** rational **14.** irrational **15.** rational **16.** rational

Enrichment 8-6

1. 192 cm **2.** square **3.** $P = 4s$ **4.** Divide the perimeter by 4. **5.** Multiply the length of the side by itself. **6.** 48 cm **7.** 2,304 cm^2 **8.** Multiply the square root of the area by 4. **9.** 1,600 cm^2 **10.** 2 cm

Puzzle 8-6

Y. rational **N.** irrational **G.** rational **E.** rational **B.** irrational **I.** irrational **N.** irrational **U.** irrational **I.** rational **M.** irrational

Name ______________________ Class ______________ Date ______________

Chapters 5–8 Answers (continued)

R. irrational **A.** rational **M.** rational **R.** irrational **A.** rational IMAGINARY NUMBER

Practice (regular) 8-7

1. 13 ft **2.** 15.8 cm **3.** 12.1 m **4.** $x = 22$ cm **5.** $x = 51$ in. **6.** $x = 16$ ft **7.** $x = 25$ m **8.** $x = 111$ yd **9.** $x = 18$ mi **10.** $x = 23.0$ m **11.** $x = 39.8$ ft **12.** $x = 12.6$ mi **13.** 70.7 yd **14.** 67.4 ft

Guided Problem Solving 8-7

1. 26 ft; 24 ft; height **2.** Find the height of the pole.

3.

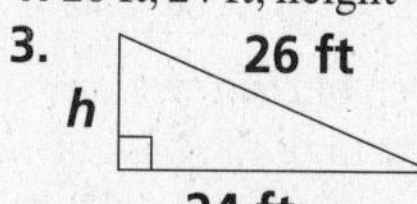

4. $a^2 + b^2 = c^2$ **5.** c **6.** a or b **7.** 10 ft **8.** $10^2 + 24^2 = 26^2$; yes **9.** 8 in.

Practice (adapted) 8-7

1. 13 ft **2.** 12.1 m **3.** $x = 22$ cm **4.** $x = 51$ in. **5.** $x = 25$ m **6.** $x = 111$ yd **7.** $x = 23.0$ m **8.** $x = 39.8$ ft **9.** 70.7 yd **10.** 67.4 ft

Activity Lab 8-7

1. 1.7; 4; 3; 6.9; 10; 6 **2.** steady increase of measures in each column **3.** Sample answer: measures in Column 2 are about 1.7 times those in Column 1; measures in Column 3 are 2 times those in Column 1 **4.** $\frac{y}{2}$ **5.** $\frac{\sqrt{3}y}{2}$ **6.** Check students' work.

Reteaching 8-7

1. $a = 18$ ft **2.** $c = 26$ in. **3.** $x = 9.4$ m **4.** $x = 4.2$ cm **5.** 6.7 ft **6.** 24.1 cm

Enrichment 8-7

1. 5.0 cm **2.** 12.0 cm **3.** Sample answer: The side opposite the 30° angle is one half the length of the hypotenuse. **4.** 2.0 cm **5.** 3.0 cm **6.** 4 cm **7.** 7 cm **8.** Sample answer: The hypotenuse is the length of one side times $\sqrt{2}$.

Puzzle 8-7

Pennsylvania

Practice (regular) 8-8

1. triangle; triangular prism **2.** circle; cylinder **3.** hexagon; hexagonal pyramid **4.** circle; cone **5.** rectangle or square; rectangular or square pyramid **6.** rectangle; rectangular prism

7.

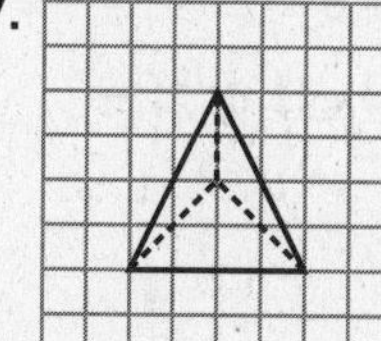

8.

9.

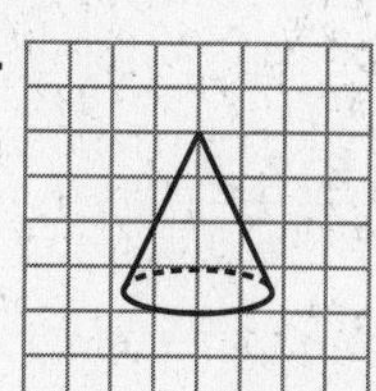

10.

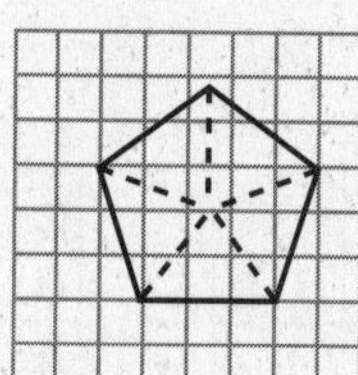

Guided Problem Solving 8-8

1. Find the total area of all the faces of the figure. **2.** 3 **3.** 2 **4.** $A = lw$ **5.** $A = \frac{1}{2}bh$ **6.** $b = 2$ m; $h = 3.5$ m **7.** 3.5 m^2 **8.** 7 m^2 **9.** 2 m × 6 m; 6 m × 4 m; 6 m × 3.5 m **10.** 12 m^2; 24 m^2; 21 m^2 **11.** 64 m^2 **12.** yes; 5 **13.** 642 $in.^2$

Practice (adapted) 8-8

1. triangle; triangular prism **2.** circle; cylinder **3.** hexagon; hexagonal pyramid **4.** circle; cone

5.

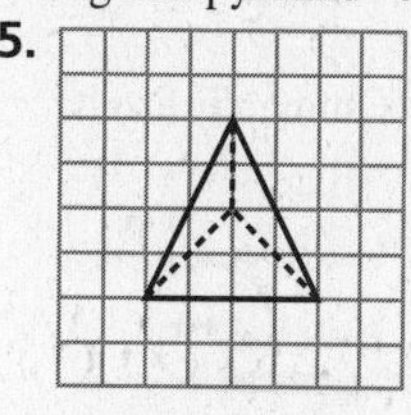

6.

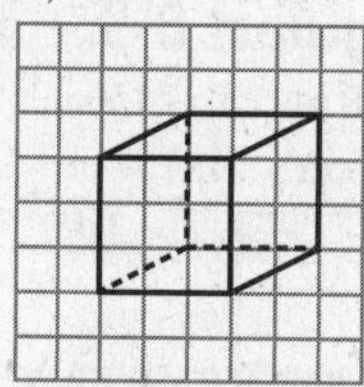

7.

8.

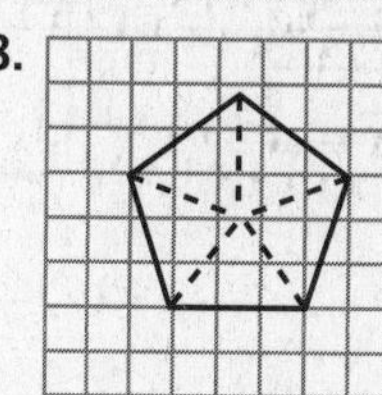

Activity Lab 8-8

1. square pyramid; 8; 5 **2.** pentagonal prism; 15; 7 **3.** triangular prism; 9; 5 **4.** Check students' work; shapes in locomotive are: square pyramid, square prism, triangular prism, truncated cone, 4 cylinders.

Reteaching 8-8

1. rectangular prism **2.** cylinder **3.** square pyramid **4.** cone **5.** triangular prism **6.** hexagonal prism **7.** cylinder **8.** rectangular prism **9.** sphere

Enrichment 8-8

1. a **2.** d **3.** c **4.** **5.** **6.**

Chapters 5–8 Answers (continued)

Puzzle 8-8

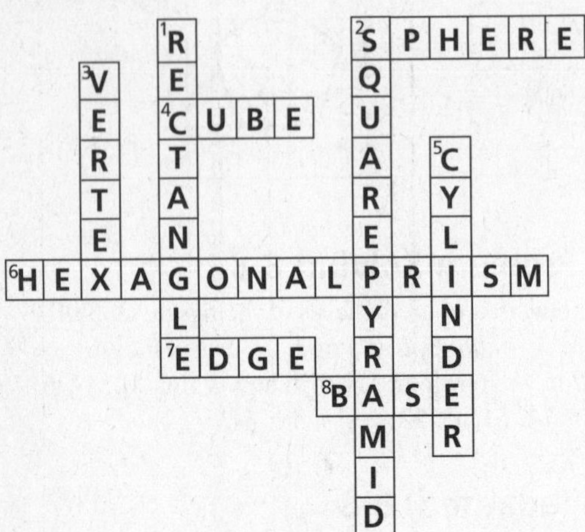

Practice (regular) 8-9

1. 594 cm^2 **2.** 418 m^2 **3.** 3,150 $in.^2$ **4.** 157 mm^2 **5.** 628 ft^2 **6.** 730 cm^2 **7.** 108 $in.^2$ **8.** 138 m^2

9. 5 7 5 5 9 7 5 **10.** 3 in. 8

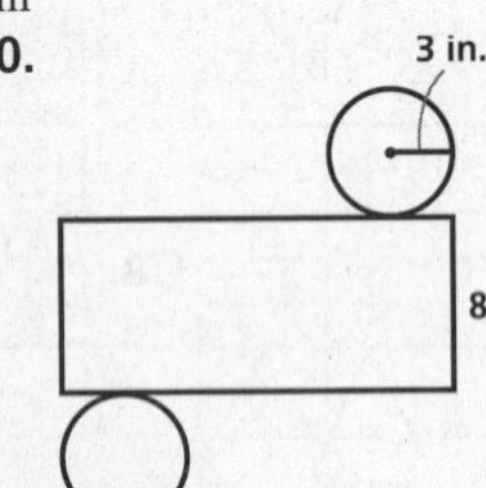

Guided Problem Solving 8-9

1. Find the surface area of the bar of soap. **2.** Round it to the nearest tenth of a centimeter. **3.** Add the areas of the two circular faces to the area of the rectangular face. **4.** $A = \pi r^2$ **5.** 39.3 cm^2 **6.** $A = 2\pi rh$ **7.** 31.4 cm^2 **8.** 70.7 cm^2 **9.** yes; yes **10.** 207.3 $in.^2$

Practice (adapted) 8-9

1. 594 cm^2 **2.** 418 m^2 **3.** 3,150 $in.^2$ **4.** 157 mm^2 **5.** 108 $in.^2$ **6.** 138 m^2

7.

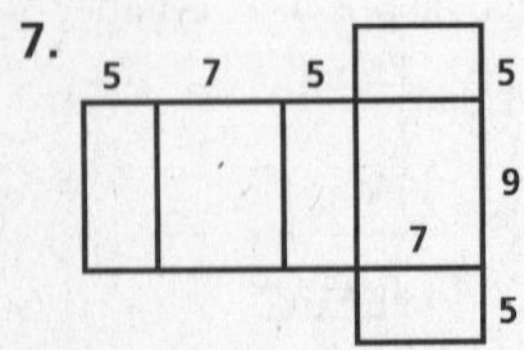

8.

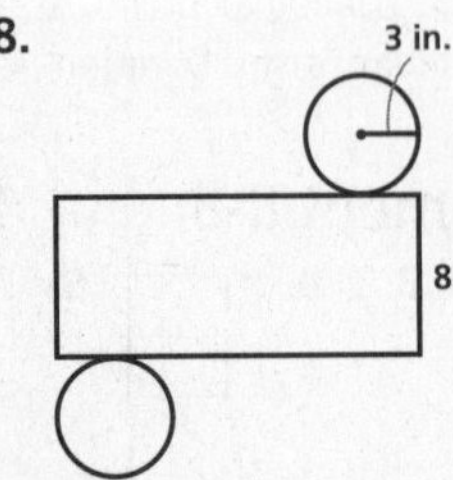

Activity Lab 8-9

1. 228 cm^2; 276 cm^2; second prism 2. 1,256 cm^2; 628 cm^2; first cylinder **3–7.** Check students' answers.

Reteaching 8-9

1. 10 ft^2 **2.** 103 cm^2 **3.** 1,570 yd^2; Check students' drawings. **4.** 124 m^2; Check students' drawings.

Enrichment 8-9

1a. 1 cm^2 **1b.** 1 cm^2 **1c.** 1 cm^2 **1d.** 1 cm^2 **1e.** 1 cm^2 **1f.** 1 cm^2 **1g.** 6 cm^2 **2.** The area of each face is the same. **3.** $1 + 1 + 1 + 1 + 1 + 1 = 6 \times 1 = 6$ **4.** Sample answer: $A = 6F$

5.

Number of painted faces	6	5	4	3	2	1	0
Number of cubes	0	1	0	8	40	56	48

6. 165 square units **7.** Find the surface area of each section and add them together. Then subtract the area of the base of the bottom sections and two times the areas of the bases of the middle and top sections.

Puzzle 8-9

1. V **2.** A **3.** R **4.** G **5.** O **6.** D
AVOGADRO's Number

Practice (regular) 8-10

1. 1,120 $in.^3$ **2.** 640 ft^3 **3.** 144 cm^3 **4.** 42 $in.^3$ **5.** 1,512 m^3 **6.** 49,260 m^3 **7.** 31 ft^3 **8.** 1,680 mm^3 **9.** 2,036 $in.^3$ **10.** 70 cm **11.** 1.5 ft **12.** 15 m

Guided Problem Solving 8-10

1. diameter is 203 ft; height is 25 ft; 1 gal ≈ 231 $in.^3$ **2.** Find how many million gallons of water the tank holds. **3.** Convert cubic inches to gallons. **4.** $V = \pi r^2 h$ **5.** 809,136.8 ft^3 **6.** 1,398,188,390 $in.^3$ **7.** 6,052,763.6 gal **8.** about 6 million gallons **9.** 5,634,782 gallons; yes **10.** about 31 L

Practice (adapted) 8-10

1. 1,120 $in.^3$ **2.** 640 ft^3 **3.** 42 $in.^3$ **4.** 1,512 m^3 **5.** 49,260 m^3 **6.** 2,036 $in.^3$ **7.** 70 cm **8.** 1.5 ft **9.** 15 m

Activity Lab 8-10

1. 216, 516; 216, 312; 216, 252; 216, 228; 216, 216 **2.** The dimensions of the base change, but the base has a constant area of 36 $units^2$. The height stays the same. **3.** As the dimensions become closer to the dimensions of a cube, the surface area becomes less for the same volume. **4.** Check students' work; the outcome is the same.

Reteaching 8-10

1. 6; 2; 3; 36 $in.^3$ **2.** 8; 8; 4; 803.8 cm^3 **3.** 79 cm^3 **4.** 24 m^3 **5.** 7 m^3

Chapters 5–8 Answers (continued)

Enrichment 8-10

1. 216 cm^3; 276 cm^2 **2.** 216 cm^3; 228 cm^2 **3.** 216 cm^3; 252 cm^2 **4.** 216 cm^3; 312 cm^2 **5.** 216 cm^3; 492 cm^2 **6.** 216 cm^3; 246 cm^2 **7.** 216 cm^3; 340 cm^2 **8.** 216 cm^3; 216 cm^2 **9.** the cube
10. For rectangular prisms with equal volume, the cube has the smallest surface area. In rectangles with equal area, the square has the smallest perimeter.

Puzzle 8-10

volume of triangular prism bead $= 4 - 0.5\pi \approx 2.43$ cm^3
volume of rectangular prism bead $= 12 - 0.75\pi \approx 9.645$ cm^3
volume of cylindrical bead $= \pi - 0.25\pi \approx 2.355$
volume of the three beads ≈ 14.43
The necklace will include six of each type of bead.

Chapter 8A Graphic Organizer

1. Measurement **2.** 10 **3.** Measuring to Solve **4.** Check students' diagrams.

Chapter 8B Reading Comprehension

1. the size of the Grand Canyon **2.** about 10 million years **3.** 277 miles long by 18 miles wide by one mile deep **4.** 277 miles × 18 miles = 4,986 square miles **5.** 4,986 square miles ÷ 113,000 square miles is approximately 4%. **6.** The Grand Canyon is 18 miles wide at its widest point. Therefore, using 18 miles as its width gives a maximum area. **7.** 1 mile × 4,986 square miles = 4,986 cubic miles **8.** a

Chapter 8C Reading/Writing Math Symbols

1. area **2.** volume **3.** length **4.** area **5.** length **6.** volume **7.** area of a triangle **8.** volume of a rectangular prism **9.** area of a parallelogram, area of a rectangle **10.** circumference of a circle (length) **11.** area of a circle **12.** area of a square **13.** length of the hypotenuse of a right triangle **14.** area of a trapezoid **15.** volume of a cylinder **16.** circumference of a circle (length)

Chapter 8D Visual Vocabulary Practice

1. Pythagorean Theorem **2.** prism **3.** base **4.** edges **5.** cone **6.** vertices **7.** pyramid **8.** perfect square **9.** circumference

Chapter 8E Vocabulary Check

Check students' answers.

Chapter 8F Vocabulary Review

1. hypotenuse **2.** parallel **3.** solution **4.** congruent **5.** complementary **6.** sphere **7.** circumference **8.** area **9.** scalene **10.** square **11.** perfect square **12.** pyramid **13.** rate **14.** cylinder

Chapter 8 Checkpoint Quiz 1

1. 6.25 cm^2 **2.** 84 cm^2 **3.** 153 m^2 **4.** yd^2

Chapter 8 Checkpoint Quiz 2

1. 40.82 $in.^2$ **2.** 5 cm **3.** 9.8 m **4.** 14.4 m **5.** 122 m^2; 84 m^3 **6.** 102 cm^2; 54 cm^3 **7.** 348 m^2; 360 m^3 **8.** 230.8 cm^2

Chapter 8 Test (regular)

1. about 1,200 $in.^2$ **2.** about 900 $in.^2$ **3.** 216 ft^2 **4.** 60 $in.^2$ **5.** 96 m^2 **6.** 25.1 cm; 50.3 cm^2 **7.** 37.7 cm; 113.1 cm^2 **8.** 15 **9.** 4 **10.** 18 **11.** 20 **12.** 17 **13.** 6 **14.** 44 ft **15.** rational **16.** rational **17.** rational **18.** irrational **19.** 14.4 m **20.** 9.2 m **21.** 13.2 m **22.** 24 ft **23.** 5 and 6; 5.5 **24.** 3 and 4; 3.7 **25.** 8 and 9; 8.9 **26.** 11 and 12; 11.8 **27.** 207.3 $in.^2$ **28.** 248 $in.^2$ **29.** 301.6 $in.^3$ **30.** 120 $in.^3$ **31.** 30 ft and 90 ft

Chapter 8 Test (below level)

1. about 1,200 $in.^2$ **2.** about 900 $in.^2$ **3.** 216 ft^2 **4.** 60 $in.^2$ **5.** 96 m^2 **6.** 25.1 cm; 50.3 cm^2 **7.** 37.7 cm; 113.1 cm^2 **8.** 15 **9.** 4 **10.** 20 **11.** rational **12.** rational **13.** irrational **14.** 14.4 m **15.** 9.2 m **16.** 24 ft **17.** 5 and 6; 5.5 **18.** 8 and 9; 8.9 **19.** 209.3 $in.^2$ **20.** 248 $in.^2$ **21.** 301.6 $in.^3$ **22.** 120 $in.^3$

Chapter 8 Alternative Assessment

Exercise	Points	Explanation
1.	4	Circle with a given scale; zigzag path drawn at 45° angle to wind; segments of the path correctly labeled
	3	Circle with a given scale; zigzag path drawn at 45° angle to wind; segments incorrectly labeled
	2	Circle with given scale; part of path drawn at 45° angle to wind
	1	Circle with incorrect scale; all of path incorrectly drawn
	0	No response
2. a.	1	Estimate about 1,400 yd
	0	Incorrect or no response
b–c.	1	No
	0	Incorrect or no response
d.	1	All paths would be the same total length, and all paths would be equal to the extreme path of tacking 45° to the left for half the trip and then tacking 45° to the right for the second half of the trip, a total of about 1,400 yd.
	0	No response
3.	2	About 87.5 ft^2 (0.5 × 17.5 ft × 10 ft)
	1	Incorrect answer due to computational error
	0	Incorrect process and response

Name ______________________ Class ______________ Date ______________

Chapters 5–8 Answers (continued)

Excursion

5 Dimensions labeled; sailboat *a.* approximately 88 ft^2; sailboat *b.* approximately 95 ft^2; longer boat has smaller sail; no, longer boat would likely need a larger sail

4 Same as above, except one incorrect area

3 Same as above, except one incorrect dimension

2 Correct *process* for finding dimensions and areas

1 Partially correct attempt at finding dimensions and areas

0 Other incorrect response OR no response

Chapter 8 Cumulative Review

1. C **2.** J **3.** D **4.** G **5.** D **6.** H **7.** D **8.** H **9.** D **10.** G
11. C **12.** F **13.** C **14.** F **15.** D **16.** H **17.** D **18.** G
19. the same; both ratios, $\frac{32}{40}$ and $\frac{16}{20}$, simplify to $\frac{4}{5}$.
20. 5.5 mi/hr and 8.5 mi/hr;

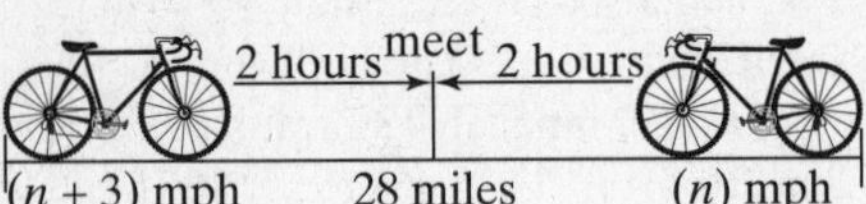